Learning on the Job

Steven F. Wilson

Learning on the Job

WHEN

BUSINESS

TAKES

ON

PUBLIC

SCHOOLS

Harvard University Press

Cambridge, Massachusetts

London, England

2006

Wilson, Steven F., 1959–
    Learning on the job: when business takes on public schools / Steven F. Wilson.
        p.   cm.
    Includes bibliographical references and index.
    ISBN 0-674-01946-6
        1. Privatization in education—United States. 2. Public schools—United States—
Administration. I. Title.

LB2806.36.W56 2005
379.1'0973—dc22   2005045986

Contents

Preface

Was it moxie—or arrogance? The business plan for Advantage Schools, the for-profit school management company my colleagues and I started in 1996, promised investors we would "create a new generation of outstanding public schools that would enable students—regardless of their socioeconomic background—to reach the heights of academic achievement."

I admit I'm uneasy reading these words today. But at the time, we thrilled to the company's plan. Charter school legislation was sweeping the states, and with it the opportunity to build a network of new schools that would serve students from the most troubled urban neighborhoods. Open to all students, publicly funded and tuition-free, and accountable for meeting new state education standards, our charter schools would truly be public institutions. Yet Advantage, the company that ran them, would be fueled by not only private capital but also the entrepreneurial drive to succeed.

Outside the sclerotic bureaucracies of big-city school systems, we could make good on our promise. Children would learn faster in schools where only instructional programs proven effective were employed, where the culture was centered on student achievement, and where staff at all levels were held accountable for results. Teachers, parents, and investors signed on to the plan. In time, some of the best-known names in venture capital backed the company, including Credit Suisse, Chase Capital, and the Silicon Valley firm Kleiner, Perkins, Caufield and Byers, whose influential partner John Doerr believed in the marriage of entrepreneurship and school reform.

From our office in Boston, we prepared to launch in the fall of 1997 our first two elementary schools—one in Rocky Mount, North Carolina, a small, racially mixed city an hour's drive from Raleigh, and the other in a low-income Latino neighborhood of Phoenix, Arizona. With only months between the award of the charters and opening day, we rushed to find and renovate buildings that could each house hundreds of students. Both schools staggered through difficult openings in the fall. Our parents hung on.

By the spring, we felt we were at last on track. Teachers once skeptical of the company's curriculum announced they were converts. Parents told moving stories of their children's progress. A boy who had hated school told his mother one day that he wanted to spend his allowance on books. A girl delayed in reading suddenly took to calling out street signs from the car. A child whose parents spoke only Spanish and were intimidated coming to the school, now acted as their interpreter at parent-teacher meetings. And when the first test scores came back, we learned that at most grade levels, our students had substantially outpaced their peers across the nation. Our kindergartners in Rocky Mount, for example, who were beginning their education with us, rose thirty-five percentile rank points over the year, from the 47th to the 82nd percentile.

Making just these two schools into all that we had promised would have been challenge enough. But our goal had never been merely to let a few hundred students slip the knot of failed schools: it was to prove that our plan could work at scale. Over the next years, Advantage staff worked feverishly to open additional urban schools wherever charters were available, including Massachusetts, Texas, Illinois, Michigan, New Jersey, Pennsylvania, and the District of Columbia.

By the fall of 2000, we were educating nearly ten thousand children. For all the company's problems—and they were legion—I was proud of what our students and their teachers had achieved. During the previous school year, students had on average gained more than nine percentile rank points on nationally normed tests; in our strongest schools, scores climbed nineteen percentile rank points. Even if our most ambitious goal—that by the time our students completed high school, many would obtain the prestigious international baccalaureate diploma—was still but a distant dream, we knew we were already changing lives.

All the while, the company continued to lose money. Turning a profit running schools had proven much more difficult than any of us had expected. To cover our costs, we needed to open still more schools. When the dot-com bubble burst, however, further growth was the last thing our long-patient investors were willing to fund. I lost my job, the investors sold the company, and the adventure was over.

Advantage was the most exciting project I've ever undertaken. My colleagues were bright, skilled, and committed, and we were engaged in one of the most challenging missions in American society, the drive to improve urban education. In theory, the rigors of private management would create both better schools and a return for our investors. We discovered just how difficult that was. We had been arrogant, and we were humbled.

The project over, my enthusiasm remained. I wanted to know how other private organizations that ran public schools were faring. What were their stories? Where had they succeeded where we had failed? This book is my attempt to find out.

In writing it, my purpose was not to tell the story of Advantage (as lively a tale as it could be, in the right hands), but to examine objectively seven diverse private organizations that had set out to run public schools. Of course, I make no claim to an equal understanding of the seven, and inevitably they receive unequal attention: my knowledge began with Advantage, and far more has been written about Edison (the largest education management organization, or EMO, and the only to have been subject to the disclosure requirements of a publicly traded corporation) than all the others combined. While executives were nearly always eager to share their experiences and candid observations, it should be remembered that all of the organizations are currently privately held companies with no obligation and little business interest in disclosing sensitive information or proprietary plans.

Some would say that as a founder of one organization and, since finishing the book, a consultant to another—Edison Schools—I am hardly qualified to write objectively about the industry. But throughout the project, that has been my aim. I am not a social scientist, yet much of my career has been spent researching and developing public policy. If the data suggest that private management of public schools is failed policy, I am prepared to reach this conclusion. If, however, the early results are positive, the experiences of the organizations may offer lessons for the improvement of American public education.

Learning on the Job

Introduction

Can a unique American strength, private-sector entrepreneurship, aid a troubled institution, the public schools? Or is private management of public schools an ill-fated experiment, a distraction from the hard work of improving district schools from within?

For most of the last century, America's public schools enjoyed an exclusive franchise: public funds in each community were granted to just one provider of educational services, the local school district. For better or worse, the market forces that animate private industry—entrepreneurial innovation and competition, private investment, and the potential for personal gain—played no part in primary and secondary public education.

But in the last decade, all that began to change. With charter school legislation came a wave of for-profit education management companies (EMOs) that proposed to manage the new schools under contract to their community boards. Other companies signed on to the job of turning around school districts' poorest performing schools. Still others sought to open cyber charter schools, which would deliver curricula via the Internet to home-schooled students. Company founders promised superior academic results to families—and profits to their investors.

Grasping the immensity of the potential new market, Wall Street and Silicon Valley investors lavished hundreds of millions of dollars in private capital on the start-up firms. Thousands of charter school students began to receive an education planned and managed not by local school officials, but by private companies. Still more students saw their district schools turned over to education management firms.

The number of students attending schools—charter or traditional— managed by for-profit companies remains relatively small. As of 2005, some 240,000 students attended 535 schools run by education management organizations; in comparison, more than 1 million students are estimated to be home-schooled.[1] Yet private management of public schools is a front-page debate in many communities, and it is not too soon to ask what we have learned to date from this controversial experiment in American education. Are students learning faster in privately managed schools? Can money be made in running public schools? And what role—if any—can business and entrepreneurship play in improving educational opportunities for children, especially those from disadvantaged families?

To put private management in context, it is useful first to consider briefly the history and structure of public education in the United States, trends in educational investment and student outcomes, constraints on public school management, the movement for educational standards and accountability, and the origin of charter schools.

The Structure of Public Education

The prevailing institutional structure of public schooling in the United States is taken for granted by most Americans. So consistent is the particular arrangement from one part of the country to the next, and so long has it been in place, that it is today synonymous with public education itself.

Laws in every state authorize local education agencies to establish and operate public schools at taxpayer expense. Primary and secondary education have been the responsibility of state and local governments; the federal government has traditionally played only a secondary role. In the nation's more than fifteen thousand school districts, there is typically a school board or committee, a superintendent, and a district office. The school board is the district's legislative body and the superintendent its executive, and the school board's policies and programs are fulfilled by the district office and school staff. Most states also have a board of education or the like, a state education officer (variously titled), and an education bureaucracy, all of which enjoy specific powers to regulate the local school districts. Under state compulsory attendance laws, all children must attend school. Government not only finances but also owns and operates the public schools, whose services are provided free of charge to parents.[2]

The present system of public schools in this country was not inevitable; it was the legislative result of long-forgotten political battles waged in the second half of the nineteenth century and the first half of the twentieth. As historian Diane Ravitch has noted, when the story of these battles is told, it is generally in the form of a morality tale: from the common school movement of the mid-nineteenth century to the Progressive era reforms of the early twentieth, "public-spirited reformers" fought for universal education and against parochialism, graft, and patronage. State by state, a system of public education was created. It declared itself democratic, enlightened, and beyond the reach of politics. Impartial experts and professional educators would ensure that the public school system served only the public interest of universal education.[3]

Of course, the true story of the rise of public schooling in America is more complex, its ending more ambiguous. While the common school movement is celebrated without reservation in nearly every historical account, the common school movement, led by Horace Mann, Massachusetts state legislator and first secretary of the state's board of education (1837–1848), was not without a dark side.

Many are surprised to learn that before the mid-nineteenth century, a great variety of schools received public funds. As Ravitch recounts, parents in cities and towns had many options for their children's schooling. Beyond what instruction they could themselves offer their children, parents could choose from Latin grammar schools, "dame schools" (which offered instruction by individual women, usually from their homes), boarding schools, sectarian schools, schools operated by private benevolent associations, private venture schools, private academies, and subscription schools, where parents collaborated to establish a school or a schoolmaster recruited students. Many schools were publicly funded; some both charged tuition and received public subsidies.[4]

Prior to the advent of public high schools, the states chartered academies (much as they did colleges) that offered secondary education; by 1850, there were by one count more than six thousand academies across the country.[5] Some academies were organized as stock companies, with each shareholder contributing funds to the schools and entitled to vote for the trustees. Like the charter schools of today, academies were founded by entrepreneurs and overseen by an independent board of trustees.[6] Academy founders petitioned the state for a charter and were organized as "private" corporations; public funds often represented a crucial component of their financing. In New York State, for example, the board of regents evaluated proposals for new academies and the receipt of public funds, much as it today reviews and approves applications for charter schools. The regents inspected the quasi-public schools and required periodic reports.[7] They neither founded the schools themselves nor mandated their establishment by cities and towns, but rather relied on private initiative for their proliferation.

By mid-century, the academies were a long-established component of state education policy. A 1859 report of the Massachusetts legislature's Joint Standing Committee on Education declared that academies "were to be regarded as in many respects, and to a considerable extent, public schools; as a part of an organized system of public and universal education; as opening the way, for all the people, to a higher order of instruction than the common schools can supply."[8] But the schools came under increasing attack by common school proponents. Theodore Sizer reports that in 1873, one critic, addressing a convention of the National Education Association (NEA), charged, "They tend to destroy the high school."[9]

In the early 1800s, the urban poor were educated in either charity schools sponsored by churches or public schools that enrolled primarily children from disadvantaged families. Over time, these schools became the basis of urban public school systems and monopolized public funding. These early common schools were hardly secular, however; moral education was for the movement's leaders of far greater importance than instruction in academic skills.[10] Children often recited prayers, read from the Bible, and sang hymns. In 1848, Mann boldly claimed that "if all the children in the community, from the age of four years to that of sixteen, could be brought within the reformatory and elevating influences of good schools, the dark host of private vices and public crimes which now embitter domestic peace and stain the civilization of the age might, in ninety-nine cases in every hundred, be banished from the world."[11]

The leaders of the common school movement, many of whom were evangelical Protestants, were often vehement anti-Romanists.[12] Nativists in both the anti-Catholic Native American Party and the Know-Nothing Party were determined to deny state funding to Catholic schools following the wave of immigrants from Europe in the 1840s. In campaigns in state after state during the 1850s, Protestant groups and state education officials succeeded in passing legislation that prohibited funding to "nonpublic" schools. Despite Mann's own wishes, explicit Protestant instruction and practice in public schools declined as well throughout the second half of the nineteenth century. But it was not until 1963, with the Supreme Court's decision prohibiting school prayer, that the public schools became by law nonreligious.

John Chubb and Terry Moe observe in *Politics, Markets, and America's Schools* that as the public school system developed, powerful interests battled over the structure of democratic institutions that would organize and govern the public schools. The structure that prevailed gradually became embedded in the very fabric—political and social—of American life. Many battles have since been waged in public education—over forced busing to promote racial desegregation, the education of the disabled, and most recently, state education standards and high-stakes testing. Yet as Chubb and Moe note, no matter how heated the struggles over policy and resources, no matter how vehement the criticism of the schools' failings, the system "stood above it all."[13] The institutional framework was never seriously challenged. Indeed, it served to express and often to resolve these bitter conflicts. The charter school laws passed in the 1990s marked the first successful challenge to the institutional structure itself.

Rather than existing apart from politics, the American public education system carries considerable political clout, often exercised on its own behalf. Organized education interests, including the unions, have vilified charter schools for taking funds away from the "public schools"; in response, charter school advocates insist that their schools are in fact public, open to all, and publicly funded. It is in this context that the EMO industry entered the education market.

Alternative Models for Public Education

In the United States, government ownership and operation are in the public mind defining characteristics of public education. In many other industrialized nations, however, including France, the Netherlands, Belgium, and Australia, government funds schools it neither owns nor operates. Independent bodies, including Catholic dioceses and even secular organizations, run schools that receive public funds.[14]

The institutional structure of the American higher education system, too, widely considered the finest in the world, stands in sharp contrast to that of our elementary and secondary education system. Public community colleges, state colleges, and universities compete for students with an extraordinarily diverse array of private institutions of higher education. Most private colleges and universities are organized as nonprofit institutions, although large, for-profit providers of postsecondary education, like the publicly traded University of Phoenix and DeVry, are rapidly gaining ground (and are highly profitable).

Postsecondary education is not the only sphere of cooperation between the public and private sectors in pursuit of educational goals. After-school programs and tutoring programs are often provided by for-profit and nonprofit private providers at public expense. Private organizations operate publicly funded Head Start centers. Adult education and skills training are delivered through a wide range of private organizations, funded in whole or in part by state and federal funds. The contrast between these educational sectors and our monolithic public system of K–12 education could not be greater.

Education Spending and Results

In the late 1950s, Americans were shocked when Sputnik raised the possibility that the Soviet Union might be overtaking us in math and science. The sense of urgency was short-lived, however, and education reformers soon turned away from academic performance. Over the next twenty years, the school wars centered on radical pedagogical innovations, the distribution of resources, and "equity"—equal access to educational services—not on the quality of education. By the mid-1970s, there were signs of trouble. SAT scores were declining steadily. Several prominent commissions subsequently decried the lowering of academic standards, the rise of nonacademic electives, and students' incompetence in foreign languages. Yet it was not until the thunderbolt of the 1983 report *A Nation at Risk* that the country was awakened to the pervasive weaknesses of the public school system.

The report, the most influential school reform document of the twentieth century, warned that the country's education system was "being eroded by a rising tide of mediocrity that threatens our very future as a Nation and a people." Still more memorably, it admonished, "If an unfriendly foreign power had attempted to impose on America the mediocre educational performance that exists today, we might well have viewed it as an act of war. As it stands, we have allowed this to happen to ourselves . . . We have, in effect, been committing an act of unthinking, unilateral educational disarmament."[15] *Risk* was a resounding call to arms, and it provoked a vast mobilization of resources—financial, intellectual, and political—over two decades to improve the performance of the public school system.

The growth in education spending in recent decades has continued a century-long climb. Real spending per student rose from $164 in 1890 to $4,622 in 1990, an increase of 2,718 percent in real (inflation-adjusted) terms.[16] Economist Caroline Hoxby calculated the rise in real, inflation-adjusted per-pupil spending between 1982 and 2000 at $5,930 to $9,230, an increase of 56 percent.[17] What drove the increase in spending? Researcher Eric A. Hanushek of Stanford University has identified three critical factors: declining ratios of pupils to teachers (the result of smaller class sizes and other changes in staff deployment, including the use of specialist teachers, small-group pull-out instruction, and lighter teaching schedules for single-subject teachers); the escalating costs of instructional staff; and increases in "noninstructional" expenses, including support staff (clerical staff, counselors, administrators, and so on), pensions, and health insurance. In 1950, there was one staff member—whether teacher, administrator, clerical staff, or other school employee—for every nineteen students; by 1997, there was one for every nine.[18] The largest share of the increase in spending went to decreasing the student-teacher ratio, which declined from 18.6:1 in 1982 to 15:1 in 1999.[19] And while teacher salaries have not kept pace with wages in other sectors, they have risen, without the offsetting productivity gains from technological innovation seen in other industries; teacher salaries climbed on average (in real terms) 12 percent between 1982 and 2000.[20]

Those who banked on dramatic academic gains from this investment were disappointed. For thirty years, reading scores have remained essentially flat across all three age levels of students tested by the National Assessment of Educational Progress (NAEP).[21] While both nine- and thirteen-year-olds gained slightly more than four points (on a scale from 0 to 500) from 1971 to 1999, the oldest students tested, seventeen-year-olds, increased their scores by only 2.6 points; after peaking in 1990, their scores declined slightly through the 1990s.[22] Math gains were somewhat greater; from 1973 to 1999, nine-year-olds advanced thirteen points, and thirteen-year-olds ten points. But as in reading, most of the gains evaporated for the oldest students: seventeen-year-olds gained only four points, representing only a few months of math learning.[23] On the SAT, math scores rose modestly through the 1980s and 1990s (by less than 20 percent of a standard deviation), while verbal scores remained largely unchanged.[24] The most recent long-term NAEP data, from 2003 and 2004, show marked progress among nine-year-olds in reading and math since 1999, but little or no improvement among thirteen-year-olds or seventeen-year-olds.

Academic underperformance is cause for concern in communities rich and poor, but it is an outright crisis in our cities. Between 1965 and 2001, the federal government directed more than $125 billion of supplemental resources to schools that serve children from low-income families; Title I allocations in fiscal year 2002 totaled $10.4 billion.[25] The Title I program now reaches more than 15 million children annually. Two-thirds of elementary schools nationwide participate.[26] But this investment seems to have done little to close the gap in academic performance between students in low- and high-poverty schools, as Herbert Walberg and others have noted. Consider, for instance, the gap in NAEP math performance between two classes of nine-year-old students, the first enrolled in schools with 76 to 100 percent of students eligible for free or reduced-price lunch, and the second with fewer than 25 percent. In 1988, average scores of the first, high-poverty group lagged behind those of students in the second by twenty points; in 1996, the gap remained at twenty-one points.[27] NAEP data for 2000 show the gap had increased further, to more than twenty-seven points.[28]

Mirroring the difference in performance by economic circumstance is the equally stubborn gap in performance between white students and their black and Hispanic peers. From 1971 to 1980, the difference in NAEP reading scores between black and white nine-year-olds narrowed considerably, from forty-four points to thirty-two points; it declined further to twenty-nine points by 1988. But that success was not sustained; by 1996, the performance of black students had begun to fall, and by 1999 the gap had widened to thirty-five points.[29] The most recent long-term NAEP data show the gap again narrowing to twenty-six points, but only time will tell if this improvement is sustained.[30]

Since the early 1980s, the variation in per-pupil spending across schools diminished. In 1982, as Hoxby reports, per-pupil expenditure at schools at the tenth percentile was 0.67 that of median spending. By 1999, that ratio had increased to 0.80. Similarly, spending at the ninetieth percentile had declined from 1.6 to 1.47 times the median.[31] In sum, while spending grew throughout the system, it increased disproportionately at the schools with the fewest resources. According to a 2004 Council of Great City Schools report, per-pupil spending for 2001–2002 was higher than the state average in 68 percent of cities studied, up from 62 percent in 1995–1996.[32] A wave of school funding litigation and the standards movement have led state legislatures to couple accountability systems with funding formulas that create more egalitarian distribution of school funds across districts. Poor districts remain vulnerable to economic downturns, however, because wealthy districts can compensate for slowdowns in state education spending by raising property taxes. And parity in absolute levels of resources may not be enough to close gaps in achievement. Advocates for urban school districts make a strong case that these schools need substantially greater resources to remediate the social and educational disadvantages of the population they serve. Others, including many founders of education management organizations, argue that results will depend as much on how the money is spent as on the amount of resources provided.

In international comparisons of student achievement, American public education as a whole fares poorly. Our system of primary and secondary education is among the least efficient in the developed world. According to an analysis of twenty-seven countries by the highly respected Organization for Economic Cooperation and Development (OECD), per-student expenditures in the United States in 2000 were second highest for primary education, exceeded only by Denmark, and also second highest for secondary education, exceeded only by Switzerland.[33] Despite this investment, American students perform relatively poorly in math and science. In mathematical literacy, American fifteen-year-olds performed worse than students in seventeen of the twenty-seven nations, and in science worse than students in thirteen countries; students in France, the United Kingdom, and Canada outperformed students in both subjects, with the highest performers being from Korea and Japan.[34] Another respected international point of comparison for student achievement is the Trends in International Mathematics and Science Study (TIMSS).[35] In 1995, the last year for which high school data are available, among students in the last year of secondary school education, students ranked nineteenth of twenty-one tested nations in mathematical literacy. Coming in ahead of only South Africa and Cyprus, the United States trailed behind less economically and technically advanced nations such as Slovenia and Lithuania.[36]

Constraints on Public School Management

Decades of increasing investments in the public education system have generated few returns in academic achievement. Why has public education proven so difficult to improve? Among proposed explanations are systemic constraints on how resources are allocated; the burdens of regulatory compliance; court-ordered desegregation; new mandates for special populations, including the disabled and non-English speakers; the constant flux of students in and out of schools, which fractures their education and disrupts the progress of their peers; ever greater competition for skilled labor, raising the cost of teaching staff; more children arriving at school with social and educational deficits; and a student population with increasingly diverse ethnic and cultural backgrounds. Yet none of these begin to account for either the cost increases or the stagnant outcomes. Growth in special education students, among the most proffered explanations, accounted for less than 20 percent of expenditure growth between 1980 and 1990.[37] And even this factor cannot be considered purely exogenous. In recent decades, many urban districts have placed vast numbers of students (particularly minority boys) in expensive special education programs after branding them "learning disabled" or "emotionally disturbed," often merely because they failed to progress in regular education classes. In turn, these costly placements have sapped resources from regular education, exacerbating its instructional failings. Rising costs for special education result at least as much from the policy choices of public managers (both district administrators and the state officials who write the intricate rules with which districts must comply) as from changes in the student population or new external mandates.

Those who have suggested that the underlying problem might be the system itself—the institutional structure of public education—have encountered fierce opposition. Organized interests have successfully resisted calls for radical change in the organization and delivery of public education, none more than the two national teachers unions, the NEA and the American Federation of Teachers (AFT). Today, the majority of K–12 public school teachers belong to a local union, nearly all of which are NEA and AFT affiliates. Together, the two unions count 3.5 million public school teachers, support staff, preschool teachers, and college faculty among their members.[38]

Unlike private-sector unions, teachers unions face limited opposition in securing their objectives. Private employers face the loss of business if costs rise, so they resist unionization in the first place and aggressively bargain for their interests when they must. But public schools face, for all practical purposes, no competition. Whatever happens, school boards and unions alike know that the children and the money will be there. Unions have little to lose from pressing their demands, and management little cause to resist them.

In the first half of the last century, routine exploitation of teachers prompted the formation of unions. Back then, marriage was a basis for a woman's dismissal, men were paid more than women for the same work, and pregnant women could not teach. Beginning in 1959 in Wisconsin, the states enacted collective bargaining laws for public employees, and today bargaining is the norm in much of the country. Generally, one union represents all the teachers throughout the district, whether or not they are union members: the contract it negotiates binds everyone. Union dues are deducted automatically from paychecks, and in some states, "agency fees" are charged to nonunion members in lieu of dues.

One might expect that the scope of collective bargaining in school districts would be limited to teacher compensation, fringe benefits, and basic working conditions. In actuality, nearly every aspect of schooling—including policy matters once considered the prerogative of management—is now encompassed in bargaining. The result is that the most prescriptive teacher contracts, which may run three hundred pages or more, dictate virtually every detail of what may and may not happen in schools. And the teachers' contract is only one rule book governing the school. Where teachers are unionized, often every other employee group is unionized as well, including the lunchroom aides, the custodians, and the teaching assistants. Each arrives with a hefty union contract of its own.

At least as much blame for the present rules should be ascribed to public school managers: the elected and appointed school boards. The underlying assumption in bargaining is that both sides will protect and lobby for their interests. Unions have done so. But over decades of collective bargaining negotiations, school boards have failed to protect management's rights; with their powers so severely eroded, district executives find their authority to deliver a quality education hopelessly compromised.[39]

Collective bargaining and union rules also powerfully affect school culture. Central features of successful schools—a powerful instructional leader at the helm; an environment of collaboration, trust, and informality; passionate commitment among staff to the school mission—are difficult to nurture in many public schools. Not only does collective bargaining promote bureaucracy, its adversarial premise—that, unless protected, staff will be exploited by management—also creates a culture in which staff feel suspicious and chronically beleaguered.

Accountability and the Standards Movement

In the early 1980s, many governors turned to business leaders for help in making the public schools more cost-effective. Education was the states' largest budget item, representing on average 40 percent of total spending.[40] States regulated inputs, like educational spending, class size, and teacher certification, but were often silent on what students had to learn or be able to do on graduation. Massachusetts, for example, required of high school students only physical education and one year of American history.

Governors were concerned that any further investment pay off in a well-educated workforce. Business leaders attributed the strength of the private sector to accountability for performance and to incentives that drive improvement—both absent, in their view, in the public school system. They encouraged governors to establish standards for educational quality and devise rewards for meeting these standards and sanctions for falling short.

The notion that all children should be held to the same elevated standards was entirely new in American education; it represented not an evolution of past practices but a revolution in public policy. Before, discussion of school reform centered on what went into education: spending levels, student demographics, class sizes, and teacher preparation. Now the focus was almost entirely on end results: the performance of students and schools. Standards changed the national conversation on school improvement.

States began to impose academic standards on districts, defining in detail what students should know and be able to do at each grade level. They also devised ambitious testing regimens to hold students and schools accountable to these standards. By 1996, fourteen states had adopted academic standards; by 2002, forty-nine states had standards in English, math, science, and history or social studies, amounting to a de facto national strategy for school reform.[41] Under these systems of external accountability, school results (in the form of aggregate test scores and sometimes letter grades) were publicly reported.

By the late 1990s, state tests had entirely displaced national standardized tests in many states as the principal measure of school quality. Schools that chronically failed to meet expectations were branded "underperforming" and ultimately could be "restructured" or taken over by the state. The bar was set and in some states sanctions imposed for individual students; high school students who failed the new tests could be denied a diploma. Passage of the federal No Child Left Behind Act of 2001 (NCLB) in effect mandated standards-based reform in every state, by requiring annual testing and demonstration of "adequate yearly progress" in every district and school.

Even with state standards in place, the absence of internal incentives broke the chain of accountability and insulated school staff, at least in the short term, from consequences for poor performance. The second, and no less important, component of the business leaders' vision was an accountability structure within the schools' walls through which teachers would be rewarded or sanctioned for their effectiveness. Such systems of internal accountability were only rarely implemented. The incentives and reforms that business leaders advocated, including merit pay and career ladders, were bitterly opposed by unions, and the reform of tenure, let alone its abolishment, was simply off the table.

At the state level, the NEA or AFT affiliates are generally the most powerful force in the legislature. In the statehouses, their professional lobbyists are a constant presence as they move from one legislator's office to the next, pressing their case. Few senators and representatives will cross teachers on an important vote, regardless of its merits; to defy the union often invites defeat at the next election.[42] The result is that what many consider enduring obstacles to school improvement, like tenure, are in effect untouchable.

Charter Schools

And so it is an abiding irony that Albert Shanker, then president of the American Federation of Teachers, was the first to champion charter schools, perhaps the most radical school reform enacted in the past century.[43] In a 1988 address to the National Press Club and a later article, he envisioned a "fundamentally different model of schooling" where "we rethink age-old assumptions." The new structure would "enable any school or any group of teachers . . . within a school to develop a proposal for how they could better educate youngsters and then give them a 'charter' to implement that proposal." At the end of the charter period, "the school could be evaluated to see the extent to which it met its goals, and the charter could be extended or revoked."[44]

In 1991, Minnesota became the first state to enact charter school legislation, and California followed suit a year later. Six more states passed charter laws in 1993. By the middle of the decade, nineteen states allowed the new schools.[45] The idea had struck a deep chord with educators, school reform activists, and politicians long frustrated with the public education system and skeptical that it could ever be reformed from within.

In an improbable alliance, the right and the left came together in many states in support of the new schools. Conservatives saw in charter laws the infusion of "competition" and "market forces" into the monopolistic system of public education. Many liberals embraced the idea no less passionately: charters afforded a kind of radical decentralization, where teachers and parents were empowered to devise innovative educational programs and build vibrant new learning communities. For some school reform advocates, the appeal of charter schools was the opportunity to create a collection of diverse, often experimental programs, while others saw them as a vehicle for creating an array of high-quality schools that all deployed practices known to be effective. State by state, the charter movement gained a colorful following of religious conservatives, progressive teachers, home-schooling parents, minority activists, corporate leaders—and education entrepreneurs.

Charter schools resist a simple definition. Former assistant secretary of education Chester Finn describes them best, as "independent public schools of choice, freed from rules, but accountable for results."[46] While the legal framework of charters varies from state to state, the underlying mechanism is the same. Typically, nearly anyone—teachers, businesspeople, activists, or parents—with a cogent idea for a new public school may propose to found one and serve on its governing board. Generally, local school districts may grant charters. Most states' statutes also authorize at least one state body—the state board of education, a newly formed charter authority at the state level, or, in some cases, any public university—to review charter proposals and approve new schools. If approved, the governing board of the new school enters into an agreement with the authorizer for a period, typically five years, under which the school is eligible to receive public funds in proportion to the number of enrolled students. The schools generally enjoy a high level of autonomy; they are set free from district school board policies and many state and local education regulations (though not special education laws or safety codes), although they must adhere to state education standards and participate in state testing regimens. Parents choose the new school for their children; students are not assigned to the school on the basis of geography, as in most districts. While details vary, charter laws require that the schools be open to all students within the district or a specific region, and if there are more applicants than seats, that the school conduct a lottery for admission.[47] Teachers, too, work in the school by choice and generally are not governed by the union contracts of the district in which the school is located but are free to unionize if they so choose. If at any time the school fails to meet the terms of its charter, the authorizing agency may revoke it. At the end of the agreement's term, if the academic results have been unsatisfactory, the authorizer may decline to renew the charter. In either instance, the school closes.

Charter schools proposed a new definition of "public school": Charter schools are public schools open to, paid for by, and held accountable to the public. No longer need schools be governed by a district school board, overseen by a superintendent and central office bureaucracy, and staffed with government employees.

As the movement gained steam, long-frustrated school reformers exulted. Fundamental changes in the public schools may have been next to impossible, but charter schools—however few—provided a beachhead for reform. In states like Massachusetts, Michigan, and New York that passed strong laws, charter principals could lead and manage their schools. They could write job descriptions and hire and fire the staff they deemed right for their program. They could choose the curricula and pedagogy they believed would be most effective for their students. They could control the entirety of their budgets, rather than merely the annual "instructional supplies" account of some $100 a student typically entrusted to district principals. Free of the district's union contracts, charter principals could forge new organizational structures.

By early 1997, twenty-five states and the District of Columbia had passed charter legislation. Since then, many additional states, including two of the most populous, have adopted strong laws or strengthened weak ones. New York passed exemplary legislation in 1998, and California corrected the defects of its early law in the same year. By January 2003, thirty-nine states and the District of Columbia had passed charter laws. A charter advocacy organization, the Center for Education Reform, has developed criteria for the strength of states' charter laws; ideally, charter laws grant schools legal and operational autonomy and equitable per-pupil funding, exempt them from districts' collective bargaining agreements, waive key provisions of state education code, impose no limits on the number of schools that can be launched, and do not require district consent. In a 2003 analysis, the center awarded an A or B grade to the laws of twenty states—these states' strong laws "foster the development of numerous, genuinely independent charter schools"— and a C, D, or F to twenty others, whose weak laws "provide little chance for the growth of charters outside existing educational structures."[48] Charter schools today enroll some 580,000 students, little more than 1 percent of all public school students nationally.

Yet not all jurisdictions created favorable settings for private education management organizations. While in a few states private companies could hold a charter directly, in many they could enter into a contract with a charter school governing board to manage the educational program and day-to-day operations of an independent charter school. When the industry was getting under way in 1997, only eight states— Arizona, Delaware, Illinois, Massachusetts, Michigan, New Jersey, North

Carolina, Texas—and the District of Columbia had strong charter statutes that created conditions favorable to private education management.[49] Still today, charter laws in Hawaii, Iowa, Mississippi, and Tennessee prohibit charter schools altogether from contracting with for-profit private managers.[50] Almost every state's charter law has some provisions that present challenges to EMOs seeking to establish and operate new schools.

The Education Management Industry

In the new bargain that charters extended—authority and autonomy in exchange for accountability—education entrepreneurs saw an opportunity. Private organizations could help start and run public schools, free of many of the debilitating constraints of the district system. In K–12 education, EMO founders saw a market where revenues continually increased (through public appropriations); where there was an absence of competition (in each community, the district schools enjoyed an exclusive franchise); and where existing management (education officials at all levels, from state officials to principals) rarely subjected spending decisions to productivity analysis. A carefully chosen school design, EMO founders believed, could accelerate student learning. They concluded that there must be an opportunity to operate better schools at lower cost—and thereby make a profit.

Their convictions were bolstered by the school choice movement. Choice advocates advance several theories for why choice improves school quality. In a competitive marketplace, providers vie for consumers by offering higher quality and lower prices. If schools are obliged to compete for students, the quality of the education service they provide will increase and costs will decline. Parents, as consumers of education, will sort themselves among service providers, who will adapt their offerings to meet the needs and preferences of their customers. Finally, providers may more readily engage consumers in the production of services, enhancing quality.[51]

Over the course of the 1990s, an industry emerged: private management of public schools. Industry pioneers varied widely in background. There were experienced educators frustrated with the constraints of school districts, policy activists who had helped draft charter legislation, and businessmen who had wrangled with their local schools. All aimed to apply business practices to the public schools. Education Alternatives, the first for-profit EMO, made national news in 1990 when it assumed responsibility for the South Pointe Elementary School in Miami Beach, Florida. And the Edison Project, originally conceived in 1991 as a for-profit manager of affordable private schools, changed course and opened its first four public schools in 1995.

Some companies, like Education Alternatives, entered into contracts with district school boards to operate one or more schools. Others, including National Heritage Academies, operated only charter schools under contract to the schools' boards of trustees. Still others operated both district and charter schools. The scope of services the organizations provided varied considerably as well. Some offered only administrative services to their client schools, like purchasing, payroll, and accounting. Others managed schools comprehensively, implementing their own curriculum, hiring the school staff, overseeing all day-to-day school operations, and assuming responsibility for academic outcomes.

By the 2004–2005 school year, there were some fifty-nine for-profit EMOs running one or more schools, for a total of 535 schools serving nearly 240,000 students in twenty-four states and the District of Columbia.[52] Of these organizations, thirty-five operated fewer than four schools. Eight organizations were of medium size, operating between four and nine schools, and sixteen companies were large, operating ten or more schools. In addition to Edison, which educated more than 68,000 students, major EMOs include National Heritage Academies (roughly 26,000 students), Chancellor Beacon Academies (now Imagine Schools, more than 18,000 students), The Leona Group, k12, Mosaica Education (about 10,000 students), Charter Schools USA, and White Hat Management. The school network KIPP (which stands for Knowledge Is Power Program) was founded in 2000 as a nonprofit organization and in 2004–2005 operated thirty-eight schools, educating 6,000 students in fifteen states and the District of Columbia.[53]

The Seven Organizations

By necessity, this book focuses on just seven organizations: Advantage Schools, Chancellor Beacon Academies, Edison Schools, KIPP, Mosaica Education, National Heritage Academies, and SABIS Educational Systems. All but one (Advantage) continue to manage schools. Each is or was among the largest private managers of public schools, as measured by the number of students in their schools. Six of the seven organized as for-profit corporations; KIPP is the sole nonprofit. All aimed to produce superior academic outcomes, and most have managed schools comprehensively, rather than providing specific services such as payroll, accounting, or staff development.

Chapter 1 introduces the organizations that are the subject of *Learning on the Job*. Who were their founders, and what drove each to try his hand at running public schools? What visions did they hold for their schools and their students? Chapter 1 tells their stories.

Chapter 2 examines education management as a business and the seven organizations' varied business designs. Each organization confronted key strategic choices: Would it operate locally or nationally? Would it run charter schools exclusively, or contract to manage district schools? Would it replicate a single instructional approach in all its schools, or would its principals be free to shape their own schools?

Chapter 3 turns to the educational programs of the seven organizations. From the choice of curricula and instructional methods to the use of technology, how did each plan to operate superior schools? Before anything else, the organizations would have to establish a safe and orderly environment. But as Chapter 4 examines, the greater challenge was to establish a culture of achievement at every school that transformed students' conceptions of themselves and their futures.

Chapter 5 catalogues the seven organizations' challenges and missteps as they attempted to realize their business models, outperform district-run schools, and make good on promises to their families—and their investors. Which strategies have worked and which have not?

Few challenges proved more vexing than finding capable school leaders. What qualifications did private managers look for in school leaders? How did they find candidates, and how did those whom they hired fare? Principals are the subject of Chapter 6.

Private management of public schools—especially for-profit management—has aroused intense political resistance. Chapter 7 explores the roots of this resistance and recounts two of the EMOs' bitterest fights—in Albany and San Francisco.

The next two chapters examine the student achievement and financial records of the seven organizations. While conclusions are necessarily preliminary, Chapter 8 evaluates the organizations' claims to accelerating student learning in their client schools. How robust are these claims? What conclusions have other evaluators drawn regarding the organizations' academic results? Chapter 9 assesses their financial performance. Of the for-profits, which is making a profit today? And can nonprofit school networks like KIPP become self-sustaining? Can money be made in running public schools? What will come of business's involvement in public education, and in what niche of this theoretically enormous market will it find a profitable place?

The Conclusion distills what we have learned from the first decade of private management. What hard-won lessons can be passed on to future school entrepreneurs? If entrepreneurial initiative has a role in public education, what actions, public and private, would clear the path to more successful involvement of the private sector in public schools?

1

The Organizations

While the founders of the six education management organizations and KIPP shared a belief in the promise of private management for improving public education, it would be a mistake to assume that they agreed on what made for good schools. Certainly there were shared convictions—for example, the need for higher expectations of students and for better discipline in schools—but their disparate educational beliefs and prescriptions inevitably reflected the enduring lack of consensus among educators. Each organization reflected the particular passions, convictions, and skills of its founder. The story of private management of public schools begins with the story of these individuals and the organizations they created: Edison Schools, Chancellor Beacon Academies, SABIS, National Heritage Academies, Mosaica Education, KIPP, and Advantage Schools.

The First Wave of Private Management

In the early 1990s, two initiatives in private management of public schools drew the attention of the national media for their novelty and ambition. Boston University took on the management of the troubled Chelsea, Massachusetts, school district, and the first for-profit EMO, Education Alternatives, Inc., won contracts to manage schools in Miami,

Baltimore, and Hartford. Their stories presaged, often in uncanny detail, what the seven organizations would experience later in the decade.

BOSTON UNIVERSITY'S CHELSEA PROJECT

Boston University's outspoken president, John Silber, made national headlines on May 3, 1989, when he signed a historic ten-year agreement between the university and the school committee of Chelsea, Massachusetts.[1] Never before had a school district surrendered its management to a private university.

The city of Chelsea, which sits just north of Boston across the Mystic River, was in disarray. Once a thriving suburb with fine schools, Chelsea was by the 1980s wracked by poverty and crime, and its schools were among the worst in the state.[2] Some 3,700 students attended the city's five schools; the newest building dated to 1909. Immigrants from Latin America and Southeast Asia had streamed into the two-square-mile city, and per capita income was the lowest of those for any city in the state.[3] Teen pregnancy rates consistently ranked among the highest in Massachusetts. During the late 1980s, the city spent only 17 percent of its municipal budget on schools, the lowest in the state. By 1989, more than 50 percent of students who began high school in Chelsea did not graduate, the highest drop-out rate in Massachusetts.[4]

Silber's proposal drew little support from the education establishment. The state education commissioner, Harold Raynolds, criticized members of the school committee for abdicating their elected responsibilities. "We are deeply distressed that a person would run for public office and then hand it off to someone else," he said. Charles V. Willie, professor of education at Harvard University, told the *New York Times* that the arrangement "has serious implications for the concept of self-determination and accountability which go to the heart of the development of public education in this country. Boston University as a private institution with a self-perpetuating board of trustees is simply not accountable to the citizens of Chelsea as a school board would be." Silber retorted, "Some of the old guard in the educational establishment are desperately concerned that we'll succeed. I think those representatives of the educational establishment who've sat on the sidelines and watched the destruction of the public schools ought to wait and see what we can do."[5] Another Harvard education professor, the eminent Harold Howe, who had served as U.S. commissioner of education, said no university should be running a school. Apprised of Harvard's stance, Silber quoted *Henry V:* "If they will fight with us, bid them come down, Or void the field; they do offend our sight."[6]

Many hoped the university's engagement would mark a new era for the city's schools. Chelsea's mayor, John Brennan, urged the school committee to accept the takeover. "I implore you," he said. "We're stagnated, burned out . . . We're looking for the brainpower of a Boston University to come in." Under the contract, the school committee delegated its authority to the university, which would "manage and operate" the school system and appoint the district's chief executive.[7] Others turned to the courts to try and block the project. The Massachusetts Federation of Teachers sought a preliminary injunction to prevent the agreement's implementation. At the signing ceremony, the Chelsea Commission on Hispanic Affairs issued a statement calling the event "a day of shame."[8] The day the governor signed special enabling legislation into law, fifty-one Hispanic residents also went to court. It was nearly seven years before the litigation was resolved by the state's Supreme Judicial Court. The school committee's delegation of authority to the university did not violate, as the plaintiffs had alleged, the "anti-aid" provision of the Massachusetts Constitution barring the grant of public monies to schools not under the control of "public agents."[9] The court noted the extensive supervisory controls the committee had over the university's actions. Not only could it freely terminate the agreement at any time and over-rule by two-thirds vote any actions by the university, but also the university was obligated to make final decisions in open meetings with documents deemed to be public records, to furnish regular reports to the committee, and to submit the use of public funds for audit.

Boston University set out to rebuild the system from the ground up, identifying seventeen ambitious goals for the "partnership," including a revitalized curriculum, improved test scores, and a decreased dropout rate.[10] The relationship was termed a "partnership," yet so long as the contract remained in effect, it was clear who was in charge. Peter Greer, who oversaw the project as the dean of Boston University's School of Education, remarked, "Our management contract is set up to allow us to really lead, not to be arrogant dictators, but to avoid what Boston goes through, dealing with every group, every faction, and then nothing gets done. We seek their ideas, but this is not a 50–50 partnership. We're putting our reputation and money on the line and the kids can't wait." A year into the project, a longtime Chelsea teacher and union official, Michael Heichman, said he agreed with many of the university's actions but resented its attitude: "This is a colonial kind of relationship," he remarked. "If they had come in a cooperative way, involved teachers and the community more, I think they would be further ahead."[11]

Were Silber the CEO of a private corporation, his confrontational language and top-down style would be unexceptional. But it was dynamite to the culture of school systems. Silber did nothing to conceal his impatience with the statutory requirements of open meetings, public records, and financial audits. Even though the school committee could override decisions of the university, its delegation to a private corporation seemed to many undemocratic; it defied an essential tradition of local control over the schools. More recent elements of the education culture were also violated. "School-based management," a bottom-up model where the district delegates authority to a school council of the principal, teachers, and parents, was the vogue in school reform circles, but Silber's staff was perceived as calling the shots from on high. Educators, lest they offend anyone, spoke in polite euphemisms, while Silber's "shockers" (as dubbed by the media) made headlines by giving voice to what many felt but dared not say.

The project's early results were mixed. By 1995, the district's annual high school dropout rate had fallen from 20 percent to 8 percent, but the next year Chelsea's SAT scores were the lowest in the state.[12] Student performance on standardized tests, while improved, remained unexceptional. In reading, third-graders scored at the 25th percentile, and tenth-graders, the highest grade tested, at the 24th. On state tests, Chelsea's scores were similar to those of other urban districts, which as a whole performed poorly.[13] Even by 1998, after nearly a decade of stewardship, Chelsea was among the poorest performing districts in the first administration of the Massachusetts Comprehensive Assessment System (MCAS). It placed 204th out of 208 districts ranked.[14]

Today, after two renewals of the contract, Boston University continues to run the Chelsea schools, which now enroll 5,600 students. Much has been accomplished. The university drove the construction of four elementary schools, two middle schools, and a new high school, with the state picking up 100 percent of the $133 million in costs.[15] Per-pupil spending is up dramatically, and the university has increased teacher salaries every year of the partnership. It brought technology, equipment, and up-to-date books to the district. A coherent curriculum has been implemented across the grades, accompanied by sustained investment in professional development programs for faculty.[16] Silber's prized early learning program serves four hundred three- and four-year-olds, and an "intergenerational literacy project" that teaches parents the skills they need to help their children and to find work has reached two thousand parents over the last fifteen years. To date, Boston University has raised more than $10 million for the project and donated another $12 million, including in-kind contributions.[17]

These increased "inputs" are beginning to pay off, at least by intermediate outcome measures. Attendance rose from 85 percent before Boston University's involvement to more than 94 percent in 2001–2002. The high school dropout rate has continued to decline; in 1997–1998 it was 16.3 percent annually, whereas by 2002–2003 it had fallen to 8.2 percent. Since the university instituted an advanced placement (AP) program at the high school, the number of AP exams taken by high school students has climbed from 13 in 1996 to 122 in 2003. In 1989, barely more than half of the graduating high school class went on to postsecondary education; by the class of 2002, 70 percent did.[18]

The true test of the partnership, of course, is student achievement. In the early grades, progress has been impressive. Even though for more than two-thirds of students English is a second language, on the 2003 Iowa Literacy tests, Chelsea third-graders made substantial increases in their national percentile rank over their 1997 scores. Percentile rank climbed from 29th to 44th in vocabulary, 33rd to 56th in reading comprehension, and 41st to 74th in spelling.[19] The university is moving third-graders to national norms in reading.

The challenge of sustaining this performance in the later grades is exacerbated by Chelsea's unusually high rate of attrition. More than one-quarter of all students leave the system each year, and new students, who have not benefited from the university's instruction, take their place. Yet there is progress in the upper grades. On the SAT, the average total score of Chelsea high school students rose from 727 in 1994–1995 to 888 in 2002–2003, while the percentage of students taking the test increased slightly. Still, overall scores on the MCAS remain among the lowest in the state; achievement gains over the last several years have been modest. The *Boston Globe* ranked Chelsea's MCAS scores at 204th out of 210 districts for 2003, up from 207th in 2001.[20]

Silber asserts that the university is meeting its contractual goal of providing a "national model of urban education," although fifteen years into the partnership, the university is far from achieving its stated academic objectives. Still, Chelsea was among just three urban school districts in 2003 that made adequate yearly progress under NCLB.[21] According to studies conducted at the Donahue Institute of the University of Massachusetts and at the Beacon Hill Institute of Suffolk University, the district performs better than its demographic makeup would predict. Considering family income and other demographic characteristics, the Donahue Institute's study found the city's schools the fourth most "effective" in the state. And the Beacon Hill Institute's study judged Chelsea's tenth-graders first in Massachusetts for performing beyond predictions based on their socioeconomic characteristics.[22] While the superintendent wrote in her annual report to the legislature that she took "passing comfort" in these findings, the project never accepted demographics as destiny, and the university remains committed to its original objective of elevating academic performance to the state average.[23] The university continues its long march toward that elusive goal. Many educators privately consider it virtually unattainable, despite their public obeisance to the credo that "all children can learn."

Throughout its tenure, the university has been both welcomed and resented. Silber's criticism of the schools aroused indignation and fueled his detractors. To mollify opponents, he appointed a Latina, Diana Lam, as the project's first superintendent. "We thought she'd be a great success because it was sort of useful with that predominant Hispanic population to put in somebody that's Hispanic," Silber reflected. But Lam's progressive vision of education and mayoral ambitions irked Silber. Lam resigned after two years. Today, he says, "She's a bad person." Doug Sears, who has also held the position of Chelsea superintendent and is now dean of Boston University's School of Education, had a more nuanced appraisal. "I would indict her for taking off on us, for getting stars in her eyes and running for mayor. She figured out politically early on that Silber was unpopular . . . She did some pretty unpleasant things, in my view, to create some distance from the university. She used the immediate notoriety we gave her to get out in the press and build her name."[24]

Leadership problems continued to plague the project. By 1992 the district was on its fourth superintendent, John Gawrys Jr. When he left in May 1995, Chelsea's schools still faced many of the same problems as before. Relations between activists for Spanish-speaking residents and Silber remained chilly; a state-appointed Chelsea Oversight Panel found in each of the first four years that the university was not involving parents enough.[25]

It also took years for the university to clarify its educational vision for Chelsea. At the heart of Boston University's plan was an ambitious expansion of the role of schools. Chelsea's schools would not only provide an academic education to the community's school-age children, but also serve as health providers and family education centers for preschoolers and parents. The agenda was an eclectic mix of elements—from instruction in phonics and classes in moral education to fight teenage pregnancy, to "individual learning plans" for each student. The choice of Lam as the project's first leader, at a time when Silber was distracted by a run for governor, exacerbated this programmatic incoherence. In the early years, the project became a laboratory for ideas emanating from schools of education. Professors from Boston University's own education school arranged seminars on educational theories and techniques like cooperative learning and how to teach children from different cultures. There were conflicting views on early childhood education as well. Some educators counseling the schools were committed to a developmental rather than an instructional focus. Others denied that the literacy programs they promoted were based on whole language, rather than phonics. "Our lack of clarity was exploited," says Sears.[26]

The university inherited the culture of the Chelsea school system, with its history of academic failure. The district's faculty, most of whom were tenured, did not share Silber's iconoclastic pedagogical convictions: "Part of that delay that we suffered first was that we had all those teachers who'd been indoctrinated in the look-say method and who'd been told by schools of education the stupid notion that learning to read is as instinctive as learning to speak . . . We had to put up with that obstacle to phonics."[27]

It was only with the appointment of Sears as superintendent in 1995 that instruction became a central focus. Faculty recruiting, instruction, and professional development were at last aligned. The university implemented the structured Open Court reading program, which is today driving gains. "We certainly should have used Open Court sooner," says Sears.[28]

Still another regulatory constraint, until a 2002 popular referendum overturned it, was the state's bilingual education law. Says Silber,

Seventy-six percent of the students were Hispanic, and they were struggling with English. We fought tooth and nail to get immersion instead of bilingual. We finally got that, and I think that is going to improve things a lot. But up until this last year, we had to contend with [the state's mandated] bilingual education program, which trapped these kids in Spanish instead of encouraging their immersion in English. By the way, it is interesting that the Chinese wanted no part, and most of the Asians wanted no part, of bilingual education—they knew what they had to do to succeed.[29]

Years were also spent wrangling with the constraints of unionization. Silber's first fight was with the principals. The university knew that its ability to manage would be severely constrained if principals remained unionized. "We told them, take a strike, and we're going to replace every damn one of you," Silber recalls threatening the principals shortly before Massachusetts legislated principals out of unions as part of its education reform plan.[30] Silber also took on the Chelsea Teachers Union. Boston University won authority over all staff appointments and promotions, while constructing stable and productive relationships with the unions. Even so, the university's authority is today not substantially greater than that of a superintendent in a conventional district. The university lacks the power to make the kinds of personnel decisions that corporate CEOs (and heads of private schools) take for granted, including the right to assign and remove staff unconstrained by restrictive credentialing requirements, seniority rules, and state tenure laws.

Silber imagines what it would be like to build an exceptional urban system free of these inherited constraints:

Now when you come into a school district de novo, where there are no teachers, any mistake that you've made you can't blame on the teachers union, because they wouldn't have been in the union unless you'd hired them . . . When you inherit a school district like Chelsea . . . you inherit a group of teachers who are very hard to deal with and it takes time to change them, either by increasing their education on the one hand or by letting them retire or letting them go someplace else and picking up new people . . . Let's suppose that Chelsea voted to have a charter school district where all of a sudden all your union contracts are null and void. They give you the buildings . . . If you had a charter school district, where all the buildings are empty [of staff], and they are turned over to a charter superintendent, who has charter principals, and all of these principals start hiring from scratch with no commitments from any union, that would be wonderful.[31]

So why wouldn't Dr. Silber walk up to the Massachusetts Statehouse and say, "I want to make Chelsea a charter district," and propose such legislation?

I'll tell you why: because I am not a goddamn fool. There are political realities out there . . . You don't have a chance of getting it. All you get is a huge outcry from the teachers union, which owns the Legislature of Massachusetts in fee simple. They don't rent the legislature like they do in some states—they own the legislature. That's just the way it is. All that would do is jeopardize all that we were trying to do, and it wouldn't get us anything, and that is why we don't go for it. But is it a good idea? Yes . . . If I were governor, I would push legislation like that.[32]

The next wave of private managers would in many cases benefit from the clean slate that Silber covets. Would building a network of high-performing schools, each from the ground up, prove easier than transforming a low-performing school system?

EDUCATION ALTERNATIVES

In Madeleine L'Engle's beloved children's tale *A Wrinkle in Time*, an imaginary corridor—a tesseract—takes children to faraway worlds. USA Schools, a company established by Control Data Corporation to examine the role of business in school reform, gave the name the Tesseract Way to its progressive school design. In 1986, John Golle, a former Xerox salesman and founder of Golle and Holmes, a provider of corporate training programs, acquired the rights to the Tesseract teaching system for less than $100,000 and founded an education management company, Education Alternatives, Inc. (EAI). Golle established his first experimental school in Eagan, Minnesota, a middle-class community outside of Minneapolis. The private elementary school opened in 1987 to 220 students.[33]

Golle was frustrated by the limitations of conventional schooling. His son, who suffered from learning disabilities, "was stripped of his self-esteem and finally gave up on learning altogether," he said.[34] In the Tesseract school, there would be no grades, few textbooks, and little testing. Lines of desks would give way to flexible, carpeted spaces with all furniture on wheels. Computers would be abundant, and class sizes small. Children would work at their own pace, alone or in small groups, toward educational and emotional goals set out in their "personal education plans." Teachers would be guides, not lecturers, and children, whenever possible, would learn by doing. Learning-disabled children and the academically gifted would work together. There would be no physical education or art teachers, but more money would be made available to classroom teachers for purchasing "manipulatives" and instructional materials of their choice.

A year later, Education Alternatives opened a second private academy in Paradise Valley, Arizona, outside of Phoenix. With tuitions of $3,000 to $6,000, both schools sought to occupy a niche between parochial schools and elite private schools that charged $8,000 or more. Soon after, Golle raised $5 million from forty-two investors. He estimated that, five years out, he would operate twenty schools with annual revenues of $30 million, and his investors would realize annual returns of 30 percent. "Private schools are usually single-plant operations with no economies of scale," Golle later explained. "We'd gain the efficiencies of buying pencils, desks, and computers in bulk."[35]

Golle reported that students were performing better than their peers nationally, but expenses were running 20 percent higher than he had planned. To compensate, EAI raised tuition. Enrollment declined. Golle was discouraged. "It looked as if it were time to fold up the tent," Golle recalled.[36]

Then Dade County, Florida, one of the largest districts in the country, announced that it was inviting proposals to run some of its schools. As the only bidder currently running schools, Education Alternatives was well positioned, and the company was awarded a five-year, $1.2 million contract in 1990 to manage the new South Pointe Elementary School. The bright, pastel-hued building was set in one of Miami Beach's poorest neighborhoods, just blocks behind but worlds apart from South Beach's streets of trendy restaurants. More than 85 percent of the children qualified for free or reduced-price lunch; many were from newly arrived immigrant families for whom English was a second language.[37]

To achieve Golle's goal of a student-teacher ratio of fifteen to one in the 550-student school, the union agreed to EAI's plan to pair each classroom's "master" teacher with an education graduate student from the University of Miami on a part-time basis. To supplement the funds received from the district, Golle committed to raising $440,000 annually in private monies from foundations and corporations, part of which would pay EAI's fee of $200,000 to $275,000 a year.

Much like at the company's private schools, there would be no grades and few lesson plans. Low-income families would be able to tap at no cost the same progressive education from which middle-class children benefited. Golle was exuberant. "I'm not ashamed to admit that if our system works, the world is going to beat a path to our door," he said in 1990. In his recast business plan, privately managed public schools would constitute 60 percent of the company's revenues; the balance would come from consulting and the licensing of proprietary Tesseract components, like its "Whole Math" curriculum. "Out of 16,000 districts in the United States, we're betting 100 will try us," he offered in 1991.[38]

South Pointe was EAI's showcase, and journalists and educators flocked to see the school. EAI's president, David Bennett, attributed the school's apparent success to its educational design and its power to rid the school of teachers who did not perform. "Rarely is that authority vested in principals," he explained. But Keith Geiger, then president of the National Education Association, saw it differently. "South Pointe works because EAI is putting $1.2 million of its own into that school," he told *Business Week*. "Let's do that in every school in the U.S. and then see if they're successful."[39]

Golle pressed ahead. In April 1991, he took EAI public, raising $7.5 million for debt retirement and operating capital. Golle said he welcomed the scrutiny to which a publicly traded company would be subject. "For this company to be able to grow and sustain itself, there must be public disclosure detailing how we contract, how we operate. When you're dealing with people's children, you have to be honest, open, and above suspicion."[40]

In 1992, Baltimore announced that EAI would manage eight elementary schools and one middle school in a five-year deal. With the district's test scores ranked nineteenth among twenty-three Maryland districts, the board saw EAI as an agent of change, and Golle promised the company would bring a "breath of fresh air." EAI teamed up with KPMG Peat Marwick and Johnson Controls World Services to form a consortium known as the "Alliance for Schools that Work." KPMG would bring expertise in accounting, financial management, and systems, and Johnson would provide facility management. The alliance, Golle claimed, would "dramatically improve student performance without spending additional dollars." He would sharply reduce administrative spending, return most of the savings to the classroom, and retain 5 percent of revenues as profit.[41]

But the company encountered intense resistance. Angry parents picketed at one school, protesting the company's plans to place special education students in regular classrooms. At another, teachers refused to attend EAI's training sessions. Others complained about the replacement of paraprofessionals with young interns as teachers' aides, the elimination of school counselors and specialists, and the loss of teacher planning periods.

Bringing private-sector efficiencies to the Baltimore schools proved more difficult than expected. EAI had pledged to cut costs on support services and redirect the savings to the classroom. But its Alliance partners found that the district's transportation and food service programs were cost-effective and that custodial staff had already been cut by half. To improve decrepit physical plants—stairwells in one school stank of urine from broken plumbing—EAI spent heavily on facilities. Still more investment went to computers, as technology was a cornerstone of the company's school design.[42]

At the end of its first year in Baltimore, EAI issued a press release claiming dramatic test score gains. Its 4,800 Baltimore students had progressed 0.88 grade levels on average in three months during the spring. The company's stock rose on the news. But the accompanying report by its contractor, Computer Curriculum Corporation, showed that fewer than a thousand students had made such gains, and that a more representative group had made only one-third as much progress. The company also claimed that school attendance had increased dramatically under its management, while its critics claimed the reverse was true. Golle said the press release was an inadvertent mistake.[43]

By 1994, the teachers union was in full attack. "EAI has lied about test results, shifted money from classroom instruction to overhead and profit, and denied services to special education and disadvantaged youngsters," charged Albert Shanker. Yet that summer, EAI landed a still larger commitment. It signed a five-year contract to manage the entire district of Hartford, Connecticut, with 23,500 students and a $200 million budget.[44] Promising to slash the district's bureaucracy, it offered to be paid entirely out of savings. The victory was short-lived. Eight months into the contract, the company had not yet put in place new purchasing and payroll systems. Local officials and district staff balked at the company's involvement, and teachers and parents protested plans for staff reductions and larger classes. "As long as God gives me breath, I will fight EAI," vowed one parent at a contentious meeting of the school board.[45] So powerful was the resistance to EAI's work that the company's role was scaled back to the management of just five of the district's thirty-two schools.

Then began the company's collapse. In May 1995, the Baltimore city council began a review of the company's finances, lobbying activities, and legal fees, and its president made the contract a central issue in her campaign to unseat Mayor Kurt Schmoke.[46] Schmoke won handily but criticized EAI and sought to renegotiate its contract, claiming that it was simply too expensive in a period of fiscal crisis. When EAI balked at a $7 million reduction in its expected $44 million payment for the year, Baltimore ended its partnership.[47] At about the same time, EAI's contract with Dade County came up for renewal, and district superintendent Octavio Visiedo let it lapse. EAI's stock price, which had risen as high as $48.75, plummeted to $4.75. By late 1995, the president, chief operating officer, and chief financial officer had all resigned. And in January 1996, Hartford, mired in a dispute with EAI over monies owed the company, voted to end its contract. Although Golle tried gamely to enable the company to make the transition to being an operator of individual charter and private schools, the company filed for bankruptcy in 2000.[48]

The spectacular fall of Education Alternatives had many causes. The ambiguous relationships it accepted with its client public authorities, beginning in Dade County, were an important contributor. In Baltimore, the company assumed it would control finances and have the authority to replace staff at failing schools. But as education researchers Paul Hill, Lawrence Pierce, and James Guthrie have noted, the contract permitted the district school board to step in and reassert its authority over the schools, before ending the contract altogether. EAI agreed to be evaluated on the basis of student test scores, attendance, parental support, and other criteria. Yet the contract was silent on how these factors would be measured or interpreted. The teachers union filled the void with its own influential evaluation, which was harshly critical of the company, and EAI lacked the quality of data to respond effectively. An evaluation performed after the company was terminated found that students in EAI schools had learned at a faster rate than students in comparable Baltimore schools.[49]

EAI's many problems—overwhelming political resistance, faddish school design, grandiose promises, excessive expansion, and ambiguous and unenforceable contracts—anticipated those of the next wave of management companies.

The Second Wave

By the mid-1990s, when the Edison Project had completed its period of research and development and was preparing to open its first schools, and when charter school management companies were shopping their business plans to venture capitalists, the most important lesson of the early initiatives had been learned: Simply taking over the central office of existing school districts and ousting traditional superintendents in favor of private-sector managers—whether businesspeople, as in the case of Education Alternatives, or university administrators, as at Boston University—was not enough to effect decisive improvement in schools. Corporations might have "private-sector expertise" to bring to bear on the school district, and universities might wield intellectual capital. But the most enterprising private managers could not easily overcome the institutional resistance and entrenched interests of a dysfunctional school system.

When the second wave of education management organizations began, the focus was on transforming individual schools rather than the school district as a whole. Beacon Education Management, founded as Alternative Public Schools in 1992, started with just one school in 1995. Edison, despite its grand ambitions, launched just four schools that same year, its first year of operations.

EDISON SCHOOLS

No education management company has had a more dramatic history than Edison Schools. From the announcement of its audacious plans to transform American education to the dramatic crash in its stock price, Edison's is a riveting story in both American education and business.

As an undergraduate at the University of Tennessee in 1969, H. Christopher Whittle and three classmates produced a guide for students called *Knoxville in a Nutshell.* When the venture started turning a profit a few years later, it had become a youth publishing company called 13–30 that promised advertisers an efficient means of reaching young readers through free, targeted publications.[50]

In 1979, 13–30 acquired the floundering *Esquire,* which was losing a half million dollars a month. As Phillip Moffitt, Whittle's business partner and college classmate, ably managed a stable of young writers, Whittle deployed his soon-to-be legendary sales skills to sell advertisers on the "new" *Esquire,* the bible for "the new American man." In these presentations, Whittle's remarkable fusion of charm, bravado, and business acumen first triumphed. As he later told the *New Yorker,* "If I had a forty-five-minute sales meeting, I'd spend thirty or forty hours preparing . . . Most of this time, I'd be thinking. I'd try to structure a transaction that worked for buyer and seller, and maybe I'd come up with twenty iterations. Once I settled on an approach, I'd figure out how to present it. That's an art. There are crescendos, drumrolls, and cymbal crashes. A well-crafted presentation is almost musical. You have to startle the audience. There's a little bit of Broadway."[51]

The takeover was "the business equivalent of open heart surgery," according to *Inc.,* and to some "like turning over your beloved grandmother to a couple of kids with rusty penknives"; but in any case 13–30's gambit was soon a financial and editorial success.[52] In 1986, Whittle and Moffitt parted company, and *Esquire* was sold to the Hearst Corporation for a lucrative profit.

Whittle inherited 13–30's other ventures, which became the foundation of a still more ambitious media company, Whittle Communications. One high-profile Whittle project, the enormously controversial Channel One, provided schools with television equipment in exchange for a guaranteed audience of middle and high school students for its news and current events programming and commercials. Channel One, Whittle pledged, would bolster the cultural literacy of students; many kids think "Chernobyl is Cher's full name," he quipped. Whittle induced Time, Inc. (later Time Warner) to pay $185 million for a 50 percent interest in Whittle Communications; of this, Whittle personally received $40 million. Soon construction began in Knoxville of the company's $55 million Georgian-style headquarters, dubbed "Whittlesburg," capable of housing a thousand employees.[53] By 1992, its third season, Channel One claimed that it was reaching 6.8 million students in over ten thousand schools—some 40 percent of teenagers in school.[54] The channel would go on to win more than 150 programming honors, including the prestigious Peabody award for outstanding achievement in electronic media.

Appalled by the prospect of television commercials in the classroom, the education establishment rose up in opposition. California and New York State both sought to prohibit commercial television in public schools. Whittle persevered, tirelessly pitching Channel One to school districts. It was during these visits to schools that Whittle conceived of his still more ambitious plan, a for-profit schooling company for the technological age: "That's when I thought of Edison," he later recounted. "This would be better than public life: A mission and free enterprise. A blend of capitalism and mission. This goes to the heart of the debate: Should capitalism be in the public sector? I felt this as a real calling." Albert Shanker told the *Wall Street Journal* that the venture could "change the whole ballgame" because Edison "would have the freedom to try things that the public educational bureaucracy can't do."[55]

When Whittle in 1992 announced that he had recruited the president of Yale, Benno C. Schmidt Jr., to run the project, the *New York Times* ran the story on the front page. Edison's original business plan was to open a thousand private schools nationwide that, at about $5,500 in annual tuition, were affordable to middle-class parents. "The reason this hasn't been done before is that this thing is a matter of D-Day dimensions," Schmidt told the *Times*. "At first, frankly, I thought the notion that I would leave the presidency of a 300-year-old institution for something so new and risky was outlandish, like leaping into the abyss. But if this venture succeeds, there's nothing, there's nothing that could be done, aside from changing human nature, that would be more constructive for our society." And were the project to fail? "It will have been a noble effort," he said. "And I will no longer have tenure."[56]

Whittle Communications planned to invest $60 million and expected total costs for an initial two hundred schools to approach $2.5 billion. In addition to Schmidt, Whittle recruited an A-list team of education reform experts and leading superintendents. John Chubb joined Edison and became the company's chief education officer. Chester Finn was also a member of the original "design team," along with Nancy Hechinger from Apple Computer, and Dominique Browning, a senior editor at *Newsweek*. The early Edison blueprint was extraordinarily ambitious: all students would study algebra by the eighth grade and calculus in the twelfth. Foreign language instruction would begin in prekindergarten, and students would be bilingual by the fifth grade. Latin would be taught in grades six through eight. Every child would play a musical instrument and participate in weekly ethics seminars. "We are admittedly shooting for the stars," Schmidt said in 1993.[57]

In these early days, Edison spent lavishly. Top executives earned salaries in the high six figures and traveled in private jets. The company leased space on Fifth Avenue, where teams of developers forged the Edison school design. Yet Whittle Communications was beginning to unravel. The company's expansion into electronic media, begun in the late 1980s with the simultaneous launch of Channel One and Special Reports TV, followed later by the test of Medical News Network, had required considerable capital. When revenue for the new media fell short of projections, cash flow problems began to mount. By 1994, the company's investors, which included Time Warner, Philips Electronics, and Associated Newspapers, lost confidence in Whittle and installed as president an executive from Philips. Channel One's assets were sold in the fall of 1994 for about $250 million to a media entity backed by leveraged-buy-out billionaire Henry Kravis.[58]

Meanwhile, Edison had abandoned its original business plan of building brand new schools, owing to the difficulty of raising the required billions of dollars in capital. Instead, it looked to operating public schools under contract to school boards. The design team, led by Schmidt, which originally had focused on a grand vision of "reinventing" the school, had turned—quite sensibly—to selecting from among commercially available instructional programs, while extending the school day and year, aggressively introducing computer technology into the schools, and emphasizing teacher preparation and development.

For a time, many doubted that Edison would successfully raise the money it needed to open its first four schools. Eventually Edison announced that the Sprout Group, a New York venture capital firm, had invested $12 million in the company. In the fall of 1995, the first four schools opened: Washington Edison Elementary in Sherman, Texas; Dodge-Edison Partnership Elementary in Wichita, Kansas; Dr. Martin Luther King Jr. Academy in Mount Clemens, Michigan; and the Boston Renaissance Charter School in Boston, Massachusetts.[59] The following year, Edison opened schools in four more cities; by Edison's measure (where the expansion into the middle or high school grades was considered an additional school, even if in the same facility), in fall 1997, the company counted some two dozen schools scattered about the country. By a conventional count, Edison operated twenty-one schools.

On November 12, 1999, with fifty-one schools educating 24,000 students around the country, Edison went public, raising $122 million in new capital.[60] By August of 2000, the share price had soared to $32; it hit a high of $36.75 in February 2001.

But the good times were not to last. In a protracted and brutal fight, splashed across newspapers nationwide, Edison sought to win its largest contract ever—to take over forty-five schools in Philadelphia and to manage the district office as well.[61] At a two-day public hearing, the city council, politicians, community leaders, union leaders, and parents grilled Edison officials. "Privatization would be devastating for our children," said J. Whyatt Mondesire, president of the Philadelphia chapter of the NAACP. "It would lead to profit-making on the backs of our 210,000, mostly black students." He called politicians and local businessmen who would partner with private managers to run schools "vultures," intent on "feeding off the so-called carcass of the public schools." But Whittle, joined by ten members of his management team, asserted that "learning," not "earnings," was his company's concern.[62]

The teachers union launched its assault. Sandra Feldman, AFT president, said, "The governor's proposal to seize control of Philadelphia schools and then hand that control to outsiders is an untested pie-in-the-sky scheme that is educationally and fiscally unsound. Instead of dealing with the problems in Philadelphia, Gov. Schweiker is shirking his responsibility. The unfortunate result for Philadelphia's citizens is the worst case scenario—a hostile takeover of the schools, a flawed plan that has failed elsewhere, and a brash attempt to circumvent the will of the people." Hundreds of high school students walked out of class and formed a human chain around district headquarters chanting anti-Edison slogans. "We're not guinea pigs, and that's what Edison wants to do to us. If they fail us, we're done," said one sixteen-year-old.[63]

In the end, Edison took control of just twenty schools—a contract of unprecedented scale, but to Wall Street an instance of Edison falling short of its promises. By mid-2002, its stock had plummeted, driven down by the highly publicized clash in Philadelphia, a Securities and Exchange Commission inquiry into Edison's accounting practices, the defection of some of its schools, lifelong unprofitability, and the back-to-basics mood of the stock market. The NASDAQ threatened to delist Edison, which was trading at less than $.15 a share. "For most companies, it would have been the perfect storm," Schmidt later observed.[64]

With the start of the 2002–2003 school year, Edison embarked on a turnaround plan that stressed profitability over growth. The company promised its first quarter of positive net income in the quarter ending June 30, 2003. Board member Charles J. Delaney, a former hedge fund manager and former president of UBS Capital, assumed the role of vice chairman and imposed new financial controls. Edison closed out unprofitable contracts, trimmed corporate staff by about 10 percent, and expanded its lucrative summer school business. It sold the land in Harlem where it had planned to build its headquarters.

After a raucous start to the year in Philadelphia, Edison managed to stabilize its schools there and win begrudging respect from the school district's CEO. Test scores released in June of 2003 showed modest increases for Edison students after their first months in Edison's program, but other schools that the district had "restructured" showed greater gains. "Our first year in a district is always our stormiest," said Edison spokesman Adam Tucker. "We're very pleased, and we're moving ahead."[65]

But Wall Street had lost faith. As Edison reported its financial progress throughout the year, its share price failed to recover. Stockholders gave the company no credit for its improvement. In May 2003, the company announced that Whittle was leading a team to take the company private once again, by buying all outstanding shares. Withdrawing from the public market would benefit the company, Whittle said. "For one thing, it gets rid of all the noise that can swirl around us and be manipulated by our critics." A prominent early investor, Jeffrey T. Leeds, agreed: "When you're public, you're more visible. You're the one in the red suit."[66]

When Whittle announced in September 2003 that Edison had in fact completed its first profitable quarter—reporting $10.2 million of net income compared to a loss of $48.9 million the year before—it warranted only a brief bulletin in the *New York Times*. Yet Whittle remained irrepressible. Looking ahead for Edison, he envisioned aggressive development of the company's proprietary "Benchmarks" software for monitoring student performance. Could he see the company once again going public? "There is a high probability of that," he enthused.[67]

Test scores at the end of Edison's second year in Philadelphia showed major gains on the Pennsylvania System of School Assessment (PSSA). While Edison ran fewer than one-third of the schools targeted by the district for extensive reform (twenty of sixty-four), it was responsible for half of the schools in the district that had made "adequate yearly progress" for the first time (eleven of twenty-one). Paul Vallas, chief executive officer for the school district of Philadelphia, had only praise for the company: "They have clearly demonstrated their ability to take on this challenge and make a critical contribution throughout a period of transformation. They've operated as a true partner."[68] And in the third year of the company's assignment, interim assessments forecast another year of strong gains—an increase of ten percentage points in the number of students passing the PSSA test. In April 2005, the district awarded Edison two additional elementary schools.

Edison, unmatched in both scale and ambition, dominated the emerging education industry. As it lurched from triumph to crisis and back, Edison overshadowed six smaller organizations that also set out to create new and high-quality public schools. But their stories were often no less interesting.

CHANCELLOR BEACON ACADEMIES

Chancellor Beacon Academies resulted from the 2002 merger of Chancellor Academies and Beacon Education Management, both for-profit, privately held education management companies.

William R. DeLoache and John C. Eason, two investment managers who had tried unsuccessfully to reform the Nashville school district through school choice, attended a 1992 meeting of the Association of Educators in Private Practice, a group of entrepreneurial educators. "Bill and I came away thinking," Eason later recounted, "we needed to consider starting a firm whose mission was helping create autonomous public schools operated outside the standard school districts."[69] The company they founded, Alternative Public Schools (APS), did not win its first bids to manage schools, but DeLoache and Eason persevered. In March of 1995, the school board of Wilkinsburg, Pennsylvania, just outside of Pittsburgh, hired APS to run the Turner Elementary School beginning in September of that year. APS promised it would lengthen the school year, provide before- and after-school programs, write individual learning plans, and boost student achievement. The local teachers union filed suit against the school board. After a legal battle that lasted more than two years, a judge determined that the district did not have the authority to turn over the school's management to a private contractor, and the contract ended prematurely.[70]

From the outset, Eason and DeLoache envisioned the business differently than did other education management companies. They believed in the charter movement's promise of grassroots reform and local board control. The APS model was not to impose its own educational plan on its client schools, but rather to assist in implementing the board's chosen curriculum and pedagogy, whatever they were. APS would provide an array of services to meet the needs of the particular school client, including payroll, accounting, human resources, professional development, and curriculum support. DeLoache and Eason placed their faith in autonomy and authority: capable principals, empowered to make decisions, would run good schools.

The strategy had obvious benefits. It would enable APS to appeal to a wide range of prospective charter school clients, rather than only those that subscribed to a particular educational philosophy. APS could provide a menu of services, and the client could choose to obtain only a few from APS, or elect to have APS run the school comprehensively. And it would help to build a harmonious relationship with customers—charter school founders and boards who often had strong (sometimes idiosyncratic) views on how to educate their charges. APS could remain simply a service provider to its school customer, rather than an educational authority determined to have things done its way.

Unlike its predecessor in school management, Education Alternatives, which operated in Baltimore and Hartford under the constraints of union agreements, APS insisted on the power to hire and fire all the school's teachers and administrators. "If you want maximum improvement in a school," DeLoache contended, "it is essential that the management entity control the personnel." Yet the company also stressed that the venture was "a cooperative effort with teachers, rather than just some company using their skills without making them effective partners."[71] To link teachers with the long-term success of APS, the company planned to award them stock options in the company.

By early 1997, Alternative Public Schools had hired an experienced educator, Michael Ronan, who soon became chief operating officer, and later president and CEO.[72] At the time of his hire, Ronan was superintendent of schools in Uxbridge, Massachusetts, a working-class mill town of ten thousand located forty miles from Boston. Ronan had been one of the few superintendents to embrace market-oriented reform proposals. Under his management, Uxbridge was the first district to admit out-of-district students under the state's controversial interdistrict school choice plan. The move brought new students to seats that would otherwise have gone unfilled—and additional revenues to support the district's initiatives to improve services. Most school districts bitterly opposed the new choice law, but Ronan embraced it: "Districts that are losing students need to make a list of who is leaving and find out what school these children would normally have attended. That list has to find its way to the appropriate principal's desk with a very simple directive: 'Contact all these families and find out why they have chosen to go elsewhere.' After we have collected the information, we need to develop an action plan to improve our programs and compete more effectively." A rarity among superintendents, Ronan was a charter school enthusiast. The new schools, he said in 1996, "are taking the poorest and neediest children and doing things with them that the public schools have said they can't do."[73]

William Hambrecht, the legendary investment banker whose firm, Hambrecht and Quist, had helped take Apple Computer public, personally invested $6 million in the company. Hambrecht saw still other benefits in APS's strategy. Small schools would minimize political resistance and could be accommodated in available real estate. With a third party providing the school building, APS's capital requirements could be minimized.[74]

APS continued to grow, changing its name to Beacon Education Management in 1997. Two years later, it completed the acquisition of a Michigan operator of charter schools, JCR and Associates. In 2000, Kindercare invested in Beacon, and the company's CEO joined the Beacon board. By the summer of 2001, Beacon was managing twenty-five schools with 7,500 students in five states and Washington, D.C. The company needed to raise more capital to fuel growth, and it was difficult to attract private equity investors. It either had to raise money on the public market or secure a strategic partner. Advantage Schools and Beacon discussed a merger, while Beacon moved ahead with plans for an initial public offering in August in hopes of raising as much as $33 million. But Beacon was not yet turning a profit—$19.2 million in revenue had yielded a $4.6 million net loss in the nine-month period ending March 31, 2001. As underwriter, the company engaged Hambrecht's firm, W. R. Hambrecht and Company.[75]

Edison's stock had continued to fall during the summer of 2001, and many investors approached for the Beacon initial public offering (IPO) already had money in Edison and said "we have enough in this industry already."[76] Days before the offering, the company pulled it, citing poor market conditions, and the company searched instead for a merger partner. Meanwhile, Beacon continued to expand; by the fall of 2001 the company claimed thirty-six client schools. In January 2002, Beacon announced its merger with Chancellor Academies under the new name Chancellor Beacon Academies.

Chancellor Academies had begun as Cambridge Academies and was founded by Octavio Visiedo, Alan Olkes, Kevin Hall, and John J-H Kim in 1999. Visiedo's six years as superintendent of schools for Miami-Dade County, the fourth largest school system in the country, capped a thirty-year career in the public schools. "I figured that somebody who understood public policy and education could develop a good charter school business and take off with it," he explained. John Kim had worked for McKinsey and Company, a leading management consulting firm, and cofounded Crimson and Brown Associates, a recruiting firm for minority college and professional school graduates, which he later sold to Kaplan. He had also served as president of Kaplan Learning Services, where he developed and marketed education services for the K–12, higher education, and corporate markets.[77]

As Visiedo employed his intimate knowledge of public schools to garner contracts, Kim raised more than $60 million in private equity capital for the company. The first investment was from E. M. Warburg Pincus and Company of New York, a prestigious venture capital firm. In later rounds of financing, Warburg was joined by Goldman Sachs and Zesiger Capital Group, also of New York. At the time of the merger with Beacon, Warburg led a round of $26 million.[78]

Florida law offered a hospitable policy environment to for-profit management companies, and in some communities there was even the possibility of public capital for new school construction. In the language of business, Chancellor Academy's "value proposition" was small classes. In many rapidly growing communities in Chancellor's home state, school districts were struggling with overcrowding and large class sizes. "Your child won't get lost here," Visiedo promised parents. Today's pitch is the same: "That's what every Chancellor Beacon representative says to parents. That's what the parent I met with this morning said resonated with her." Families drawn to Chancellor Beacon's new schools, Visiedo said, were "looking for safety and superior academic performance."[79]

Chancellor Academy's first two charter schools opened in August 2000; within one year the company was operating more than a dozen schools in Washington, D.C.; Florida; and Arizona, another state with burgeoning school enrollments. Chancellor's merger with Beacon created one of the largest education management companies. "Chancellor Beacon Academies helps students across the nation achieve their personal best," the company's website proclaims.[80]

One pressure that Visiedo claims not to have felt was impatience from its primary backer, Warburg Pincus. The investors took a long-term perspective, and with the stock market collapsing, didn't push for an immediate initial public offering. Warburg's partners were interested in the quality of Chancellor's educational product, wanting to see schools and asking questions about the classroom climate. "How is your product better?" investors asked Visiedo.[81] Remarkably, many EMO institutional investors had remarkably little interest in the companies' educational products and focused entirely on financial statements, projections, and student enrollment levels. For example, most of Advantage Schools' investors, after joining the company's board, never visited an Advantage school, and the board meetings almost never touched on teaching and learning.

Mergers are notoriously challenging, and Chancellor's integration with Beacon was no exception. "When we did the Beacon merger," Visiedo reflected, "they said it would be difficult. But in my wildest dreams it was never this difficult." According to Wade Dyke, who became Chancellor Beacon's chief executive officer, Beacon brought neither the strong "operational systems" nor the "established board relationships" they had expected.[82] Kim and Ronan left soon after the merger, both returning to Massachusetts, and Visiedo consolidated his control of Chancellor Beacon as chairman and CEO. Within a year, Chancellor Beacon had managed to smooth over many of the merger's difficulties.

Visiedo, who remains as chairman, and many of his senior executives hold one advantage over nearly every other education management company: they are educators. His chief operating officer, Alan Olkes, had also been superintendent of the Dade County schools as well as a teacher and principal. To their client school boards and regulators, they're "one of us"—not businessmen who have never run a school or taught in a classroom, but colleagues who understand their problems. "We have scar tissue, too," he confides, invoking the team's years in school administration.[83] His sales pitch—"we want to be one of the tools in your tool box"—strikes a chord with many districts looking for a way out of overcrowding and underperformance, but avoids the conflict that arises when EMOs are seen as business-focused interlopers.

Those who get in the way of Visiedo's corporate vision may soon find themselves out of work. He "rewards internal dissent" but at the same time claims that he has "fired a lot of people . . . I know what happens, and how a school moves on." When the principal of one of the company's schools blamed the corporation for not giving promised raises, Visiedo fired the "renegade."[84]

Chancellor Beacon claimed in 2003 that, unlike the competition, its financial performance comes close to what was projected in its original business plan. Student enrollment and EBITDA—earnings before interest, taxes, depreciation and amortization, a widely used measure of operating profitability—were similar to what it had projected, and the company anticipated that it would become profitable in the 2004–2005 school year. By early 2004, Chancellor Beacon claimed to be the second largest EMO in the United States, serving 18,000 students from pre-K to the twelfth grade, in sixty-seven public schools.[85]

In June of 2004, Chancellor Beacon announced that it was merging with an Arlington, Virginia, seed-stage organization, Imagine Schools, the name by which the company would now be known. Imagine is the creation of Dennis Bakke, the former CEO of AES, a highly successful energy company, and his wife, Eileen Bakke, an educator. Dennis Bakke would take the company's reins as president and chief executive officer, and Visiedo would stay on as chairman.

Bakke has committed up to $100 million to the merged company, an enormous sum by EMO standards. He can afford the investment. AES, the company he cofounded in 1981, supplies power to 11 million people in twenty-seven countries and has revenues of over $8 billion.

From AES's inception, Bakke has pursued an iconoclastic philosophy of radical decentralization. Employees would make decisions at the ground level, and he would function as an evangelist, ensuring that "our leaders would be first and foremost the keepers of, the interpreters of, the teachers of our principles and values." Beyond this, he would serve as "chief advisor . . . chief celebrator, cheerleader." In a 1999 interview, Bakke explained: "It's fun to make decisions. But I tend to limit myself to one decision a year. It's hard." In Bakke's formulation, the purpose of business is "to serve the world and not to make money." At a press conference in Brazil, Bakke brought a picture of Mother Theresa to illustrate "what I meant by serving." He claimed to be delighted when, in a newspaper story about him the next day, the headline asked, "Christian or Communist?"[86] Today Bakke is spreading his gospel in the best-seller *Joy at Work: A Revolutionary Approach to Fun on the Job.*

Senior managers at Chancellor report that Bakke intends to apply the philosophy that proved successful at AES to the business of running schools. The company would shift decision-making to the school level, "allowing each local school to develop a unique focus and personality that is appropriate to its communities." As Eileen Bakke explains, "One-size-fits-all is not the best solution to the educational challenges at the K–12 level." As at AES, "fun" will be a core value of the corporation, along with "integrity" and "justice."[87]

SABIS

Nearly every organization that proposed to manage public schools in the 1990s was a start-up. Established companies in the "education industry"—textbook publishers, teacher training providers, and food-service companies—that had for years profited from contracts with school districts stayed away from managing public schools outright, deterred by the controversy. Almost no organization could say it had run schools before, let alone point to academic results from a time-tested school design. Each would have to develop everything on the fly, from curriculum to infrastructure, policies to accounting systems.

SABIS was the exception. An established, for-profit education company based in Beirut, Lebanon, SABIS operated private, tuitioned schools in many countries before it opened its first public charter school in the United States. While other EMOs assembled a school design only months before opening their first school's doors, SABIS had refined its college-preparatory curriculum over several decades and thousands of students.

The first school in what is now the SABIS School Network was founded in 1886 by Louisa Procter and Tanios Saad as a school for girls in the village of Choueifat, near Beirut. A century ago, most girls in that region could not read and write, and society frowned on educating them. Saad, a teacher, believed that women were central to the transmission of a society's values and was determined to provide them with basic education. Despite regional turmoil, two world wars, and the death of Tanios Saad in 1953, the school continued to develop and expand. When Charles Saad passed away in 1981, daughter-in-law Leila Saad and educator Ralph Bistany worked to expand the reach of the school's program throughout the Middle East.[88] The name SABIS is a conflation of their names.

Bistany, trained as a mathematician and physicist, spent his career working in education. Now director-general of the SABIS School Network, he also developed the SABIS curriculum and proprietary academic monitoring system. In the early 1980s, SABIS branched out further, with a school in England. In 1985, it opened a private school in Minneapolis, its first site in the United States.[89]

When states began to enact charter school laws in the early 1990s, Bistany saw an opportunity to expand the business beyond tuitioned schools by running publicly funded charter schools. "We have developed a system based on efficiency," Bistany proclaimed to the *Boston Globe,* with characteristic bluntness. "I can make a lot of profit. We had to do very well to attract students and make them pay."[90]

William Edgerly, a prominent business leader who had spearheaded the business community's engagement with the Boston Public Schools, met Bistany and was impressed. Edgerly introduced Bistany to Peter Negroni, the superintendent of schools for Springfield, Massachusetts, who in turn arranged for SABIS to take over one of the city's worst performing schools, Glickman Elementary.[91] After hiring an entirely new staff, SABIS in the fall of 1995 reopened the school as the SABIS International Charter School to 450 students in kindergarten through seventh grade.

SABIS's first charter school was a triumph. When the doors opened, there were already a thousand students on the waiting list. As planned, SABIS expanded the school by one grade per year until it served 1,250 students in grades K–12. In 2001, its first high school class graduated, with every student receiving admission to a college or university.[92] The school was the highest scoring in Springfield at the middle and high school grade levels on the Massachusetts state test, MCAS, and the second highest at the elementary school level, and its scores on the Iowa Test of Basic Skills exceeded those of the district at all levels. Remarkably, even though 52 percent of the school's students qualified for free or reduced-price lunch, its high school students (tested at the tenth grade) outperformed the statewide average on the MCAS in English, math, and science. By 2003, the school was serving 1,313 students in an imposing building that SABIS constructed on a wooded lot on the outskirts of the city. More than 2,800 students are on the waiting list.[93]

SABIS had bold plans for expanding its international network of schools in the states. After Springfield's successful first year, the company's vice president for business development announced, "We are a business, and we want to be risk takers and stand a chance of losing money as well as making it. We have 14 schools world-wide with a little more than 10,000 students. We hope to have 100 in short order and that depends on charter school development."[94] The company invested heavily in expanding to states with supportive charter laws.

But the company's efforts to duplicate Springfield's striking results have been marked by bitter setbacks and public failures. In 1996, SABIS opened a second school in Massachusetts. A group of parents in Somerville, a community just outside Boston, had invited SABIS to open an alternative public school.[95] Although the school was received enthusiastically, within a few years relations between the board and SABIS had soured. Problems surfaced over finances and management control, and in 2001 the Somerville school ended its contract with SABIS. The chairman of the board said of SABIS's program, "One of the advantages is you get a base of support to get the school going, to get it open. One of the disadvantages is that, in some respects, it is a relatively standardized package."[96]

In the fall of 1997, the company opened an ambitious charter school in Chicago enrolling 1,600 students at two different locations. Many students arrived performing far below grade level and required extensive remediation. Textbooks for some students did not arrive until the spring, and at the end of the year, parts of SABIS's school design were not yet implemented. Despite these difficulties, Chicago International Charter School reported impressive gains on national standardized tests that first year, and the two campuses posted the highest percentage of any Chicago charter school of students at national norms.[97] SABIS had run the strongest charter school in the city.

But SABIS struggled to find the right leaders for the two campuses; the south campus was on its second principal and the north was on its third in mid-1998.[98] In the middle of the second school year, the Chicago school announced that it would end its partnership with SABIS. James Murphy, the chairman of the school's board, told the *Chicago Sun-Times* that "although they were operating the best charter school, our expectations were very, very high. Because of that, we decided to go in a different direction." Murphy contracted with Edison, and SABIS sued for breach of contract. Publicly, the board offered several explanations, including complaints by staff to the Equal Opportunity Commission and poor communication between SABIS and parents.[99] SABIS says the board wanted the company to invest more of its own funds in improving the school buildings, former parochial schools. In truth, SABIS and Murphy, an options trader and strong-minded school reformer, had clashed over control of the school—foreshadowing the bitter disputes with customer boards that would afflict SABIS in future charter school projects.

SABIS continued to open schools at the pace of one or two per year. By the fall of 2003, the company was operating charter schools in Springfield, Massachusetts; Flint, Michigan; Cincinnati, Ohio; Greensboro, North Carolina; Phoenix, Arizona; Schenectady, New York; and New Orleans, Louisiana. SABIS withdrew from its third Massachusetts school, in Foxborough, in June 2003 after years of discord with its board.

SABIS pledges that its schools "will prepare all students for success in college, equip them with the ability and desire for life-long learning, and strengthen their civic, ethical and moral values."[100] The company's approach defies the status quo of American progressive education. Instruction, led by the teacher, is not "student-centered" as urged by schools of education, and SABIS's teachers must follow the company's detailed directives, which violates the American tradition of teacher autonomy.

For better or worse, the American education culture celebrates teacher invention in the classroom. Generations of American teachers have been schooled in an ideology in which prestige is often accorded to those who exercise creativity rather than to those who obtain academic results for their students. In the SABIS approach, each teacher is provided with a "pacing chart" meticulously outlining the material to be covered each week. Each lesson covers three or four "points"—specific skills or "essential concepts" to be mastered by every child, such as identifying the subject and verb in a sentence, using "who" and "whom" correctly, and dividing monomials and polynomials. Frequent testing of students to determine whether they have mastered the material is at the core of SABIS's system of student and teacher accountability. But it is anathema to those educators who decry even the level of testing found in traditional American schools.

SABIS's leaders believe they know what works in educating children. They see no virtue in compromise, when to do so would degrade educational quality. They are unwilling to humor their clients or bow to political correctness in education, if the price is intellectual honesty. But in the tradition of local control of schooling, charter laws grant broad authority for shaping schools to local charter school boards. At the end of the day, SABIS works at their pleasure. Given its propensity to clash with its clients, can the company expand the reach of its program and build its business?

NATIONAL HERITAGE ACADEMIES

When the idea of the charter school was first introduced, many opponents argued that legislation permitting charter schools could pave the way for state-sponsored religious academies. In fact, the issue has arisen only rarely. Critics of one of the fastest growing school management companies, National Heritage Academies (NHA), based in Grand Rapids,

Michigan, contend that the company has flirted with Christian teachings in publicly funded schools. In response to such complaints, NHA has issued detailed guidelines that show its willingness to push up hard against the wall between church and state. Parent groups, the company advised, could pray at its schools and churches could hold services so long as they paid rent.[101]

When a group of parents, joined by the ACLU, sued the company and its Vanguard Charter Academy, they alleged that the company promoted religion, in violation of the Constitution. The school, they claimed, "allowed the distribution of religious materials during class, allowed a nearby church to use its facilities rent-free to conduct worship, conducted a mandatory staff retreat with distinct religious overtones and taught creationism as an accepted scientific theory." In September 2000, the judge dismissed the charges, ruling that the plaintiffs "provided no more than a scintilla of evidence to support a finding that any constitutionally impermissible conduct occurred." Nonetheless, the ACLU declared victory in October 2000: "Due to corrective action taken by Vanguard, the lawsuit has been rendered moot on most points and plaintiffs do not intend to appeal last month's dismissal of the case."[102]

Opened in 1996, Vanguard was among National Heritage's first charter schools in western Michigan. By 1999, the company had expanded to twenty-two schools with 8,600 students in Michigan and North Carolina. The schools appeal strongly to conservative Christian parents, many of whom might otherwise choose to send their children to private Christian schools or educate them at home. In 1999, nearly 20 percent of NHA students came from private schools. According to the *Wall Street Journal,* 44 percent of its teachers came from Bible colleges.[103]

National Heritage Academies was founded in 1995 as Educational Development Corporation by John Charles ("J. C.") Huizenga, a wealthy Michigan businessman, conservative Christian, and Republican activist. Huizenga's father, a high school dropout, established what would become Waste Management, Inc. Under the leadership of J. C.'s more famous cousin, Wayne Huizenga, Waste Management became the world's largest waste disposal company. Wayne also developed Blockbuster Video into a movie rental behemoth and billion-dollar enterprise.[104] J. C. skillfully and quietly invested his own inheritance in manufacturing concerns, including an offset printing plates company and a producer of automation equipment.

Huizenga's interest in education reform dates back to his undergraduate years at Hope College, where he was excited by the writings of economist Milton Friedman, an early advocate of school vouchers and market competition in education. In the early 1990s, Paul DeWeese, a physician who ran TEACH Michigan, an organization lobbying for school choice, engaged Huizenga in his drive to enact charter school legislation in Michigan. At about the same time, Huizenga's son was born, deepening his interest in education. To understand school reform, he learned, "we have to look at it from the parent's perspective."[105] He and his wife, a former teacher at a Christian school, looked ahead at their choices for their own child's education, including home-schooling, private school, or the public schools. "I said, wouldn't it be neat if we could come up with the best of all worlds? And out of that came the thought of, 'Gee, we'll apply for a charter and see what happens.'"[106]

Huizenga called on Mark DeHaan, later National Heritage's senior vice president for business development, who at the time was working for a social services agency, to help with the project. DeHaan assembled a volunteer curriculum committee, and their charter application, for the Excel Charter Academy in Grand Rapids, was awarded one of the first three charters from Grand Valley State University. Huizenga's new company, Educational Development Corporation (EDC), had only three months to open the school. After recruiting 174 children in three weeks and preparing the school's facility in five, the team opened the school's doors in the fall of 1995.[107] The following year, EDC opened three more schools in western Michigan, and in the third year, 1997, another four schools, also in Michigan.

Huizenga invested a sizeable amount of his own wealth in EDC; by 1997, he had sunk $8 million into the venture, and by 2000 more than $50 million. While the company as yet operated only regionally, Huizenga's vision was always on a larger scale. Early on, he wrote, "Our future is national in scope."[108]

In 1997, Huizenga recruited Peter Ruppert to oversee day-to-day operations as president, freeing Huizenga, who remained as chairman, to work on long-term planning for the company. Ruppert, a former marketing consultant who began his career at Procter and Gamble and holds a master's degree from Harvard Business School, saw an opportunity to "get on the ground with a high-growth business opportunity" and "take part in a chance to impact society in a positive way."[109]

When he joined the company, Ruppert committed to building the company to the national level, but in a prudent way, stating that "one thing we don't want to do is spread ourselves too thin."[110] Under his management, enrollment climbed, waiting lists swelled, and demand intensified for Huizenga's charter schools in other communities. By 1998, with thirteen schools in Michigan, EDC was ready to expand to other states. To coincide with its pending growth, the company changed its name to National Heritage Academies, which Ruppert said would reflect "academic excellence combined with character education and a moral focus."[111] In 1999, NHA opened its first two schools in North Carolina.

By the 2002–2003 school year, NHA was operating thirty-two schools across the country—twenty-four in Michigan and eight in New York, North Carolina, and Ohio. Huizenga hopes to expand to as many as two hundred schools.[112] While as a privately held company it does not disclose its finances, NHA says it broke even in 2000–2001 and turned a profit in 2001–2002. The company's frugal culture—the corporate office is lean, parents transport their children to school, students eat lunch at their desks—had paid off. Ruppert called the company's profit "a milestone not just for the company, but for the industry." *Inc.* ranked NHA among its fastest-growing companies for 2002. By the 2002–2003 year, NHA was claiming that its revenues had grown to $125 million and the company was continuing to operate at a profit.[113]

"The bottom line is, we see a huge market here," Huizenga said. "We see a certain amount of dissatisfaction with some ways education has been delivered. And that translates into a high probability of success." DeHaan has been blunter: "He's building a company that's going to have incredible value one day. These things are going to be very profitable. Ultimately, if we're successful, we're going to drive down the cost of education." But unlike many of its competitors, NHA rarely calls attention to itself. Neither does Huizenga. Unfailingly polite, his soft-spoken demeanor conceals the scope of his ambition. His brother Peter Huizenga, a Chicago venture capitalist, explained: "He's unassuming, he's slow talking, but if the competition underestimates him, that's a very serious flaw in their strategy."[114]

Proponents of charter schools have argued that the schools, propelled by a distinctive educational philosophy and chosen by both parents and staff, would foster the sense of community that research has found is characteristic of effective schools. National Heritage seems to be creating communities of shared values. "People used to pour their lives into their students, and I think to a certain degree, when the government gets involved in things, they get more impersonal and institutionalized," Huizenga explained in 1999. "Our desire was to bring back that intimacy of education. Not only do teachers care, the parents care, and the students start to care."[115]

"Our shared vision," the National Heritage website says, "is to build a national organization of over 200 charter schools that become the finest K–8 schools in the country. Using a partnership with parents as our foundation, we will achieve this by combining rigorous, 'back-to-basics' academics, strong moral development, and a universal commitment to all children." Certainly NHA's school design, with its strong emphasis on discipline and values education, is immensely popular with its parents. The reading curriculum is highly structured and rooted in phonics. Each month, the school teaches a different virtue, and all children wear uniforms. Every school has a "parents' room" where families can speak with teachers, meet over a cup of coffee, or plan school fundraisers. At some schools, parents and staff use the room for weekly prayer groups.[116]

Huizenga says that there is an ideological bond between the company and the founders of many of his client schools: a belief in the "free market." He denies that his schools teach religion, or even that his client board members chose National Heritage because of shared religious convictions. But Huizenga's own beliefs, and those of many of his executives, powerfully shape the company's culture. "My faith informs my actions," he said. "It's important to deliver on your actions. To respect people."[117]

Huizenga's business philosophy appears to be working. Unlike its competitors, NHA has not been troubled by poor relationships with customer boards. Despite its very rapid growth, it has not yet lost a management contract. DeHaan attributes this exceptional stability to "being open, being humble, being a real person, and allowing [the boards] to be real, to be humble, as well."[118]

The emphasis on humility is, in the end, persuasive. NHA, Ruppert believes, "runs good schools, but not great schools. Parents are excited about what we're doing, but the next mountain is to create great schools." As the company moved into urban, minority markets, Ruppert sketched a new school design modeled after exceptional inner-city schools. With a team of colleagues, he visited some of the most strikingly successful urban schools around the country. "What are these great schools doing in these broken down neighborhoods?" he asked. "And why are these successes not scalable?" Ruppert's team concluded that the best urban schools "help students create a powerful vision for their own future," know that "the cornerstone of a model academic program is early reading instruction," "set quantitative goals that are tied to objective external standards," and understand that "achievement is the key to effective discipline." He distilled ten such insights in a document called "Secrets to Unbelievable Success."[119] Rather than mandate the new design systemwide, he asked his principals if they wanted to test it in their schools. Seven new schools and eight existing ones signed on to implement it in the fall of 2003.

To sustain its growth, NHA is expanding in urban locations. Will NHA's new school design succeed in this challenging market?

MOSAICA EDUCATION

With its acquisition in September 2001 of competitor Advantage Schools, Mosaica Education became one of the largest K–12 companies. By the fall of 2003, Mosaica operated twenty-four schools, enrolling ten thousand students in seven states.[120] Mosaica was founded by the husband and wife team of Gene and Dawn Eidelman and is today run by the lawyer and venture capitalist they recruited as CEO, Michael Connelly.

Mosaica was not the Eidelmans' first for-profit education venture. While living in Atlanta, Dawn Eidelman, a specialist in nineteenth-century French and Russian literature and adjunct professor at Oglethorpe University, founded Prodigy Consulting, an operator of child care centers for corporations. Her husband, Gene, a Russian émigré with a background in real estate development, served as Prodigy's chief executive officer. From its launch in 1988, Prodigy grew to seventeen centers in seven states and annual revenues of more than $6 million. Corporate clients included General Motors, IBM, and Amoco. In 1995, the Eidelmans sold the company to the much larger Children's Discovery Centers of America.[121]

Dawn Eidelman returned to academia, taking up an assistant professorship at the University of Texas at Arlington. Teaching literature at the college level, she found that her students not only wrote poorly; they also didn't seem to care. That apathy, she believed, was seeded early in their education. She envisioned a new breed of schools where students learned differently, gaining both strong skills and an enthusiasm for learning.[122] Gene Eidelman thought "charters seemed simple" in contrast to child care. At Prodigy, a site took three years to enroll enough children to break even financially, and problems collecting revenues plagued the business. Neither problem would apply to the charter school business, he anticipated. Moreover, he was experienced in developing facilities and, because each Prodigy site had its own nonprofit board, Eidelman felt prepared to manage relationships with charter school boards.[123]

In 1997, with seed financing from the proceeds of Prodigy, the Eidelmans launched Mosaica with Dawn Eidelman as president. As her husband explained at the time, "Dawn sold the company Prodigy. She has some money to invest. We don't expect any profits for the first five years. We'll only make money if we're successful." The company would provide schools with a management blueprint and a set curriculum, and the students with a "world-class education." "Mosaica Education's purpose," according to the company's website, "is to open portals of opportunity for children and adults through excellence in education. A Mosaica school serves as a community pillar for life-long learning, pride and self-actualization." Mosaica pitched the curriculum as covering the three R's of reading, writing, and arithmetic, and a "fourth R," denoting, confusingly, "art or reasoning."[124]

The morning program teaches reading, math, and science as discrete subjects. Dawn Eidelman developed the Mosaica afternoon program, Paragon. The Paragon curriculum, which the company considers its "heart and soul," aims to teach "social science, literature, philosophy, drama, music, art, science, history, math, geography and character development through the hands-on study of 'great ideas' in world culture" in ten segments over the school year, each representing a period of time from prehistoric times to the present.[125] "The content-rich Paragon Curriculum converges [sic] high tech with the humanities," the Michigan Association of Public School Academies' website explained, "combining the rigors of a classical education with the relevance required by contemporary culture. The interdisciplinary program instills in students a captivating conceptual understanding and chronological picture of history, as well as awareness of the interrelationships between different domains of knowledge."[126] With its emphasis on hands-on learning, relevance to students' lives, interdisciplinary teaching, and multiple learning styles, it could serve as a catalog of American educational progressivism.

Mosaica wooed parents and charter boards with promises of abundant technology (one computer for every three children), limited class size (no more than twenty-five students), an extended day and year

(7.5 hours of instruction a day for two hundred days), and a personalized learning plan for each child. The company boasts of intensive parental involvement in its schools, with parents asked to donate time to the school each month.[127]

While implementing a relatively standard design across school sites, Mosaica promised flexibility to its client schools. Gene Eidelman said in 1997, "Our program is not a cookie cutter where it's the same program everywhere." Each school would respond to the demands of local districts and parents. To one Pennsylvania community, which sought the International Baccalaureate program and more foreign language, he said, "Dawn's Ph.D. is in comparative literature. We can enrich the . . . program with a total foreign language immersion if that's what the parents will want." Mosaica, he added, would adopt the district's math and phonics program. "Our program will work in any district," he said.[128]

Mosaica's first school opened in Saginaw, Michigan, in the fall of 1997. The school district, west of Detroit, was the seventh poorest in the country.[129] In its first year, the school enrolled four hundred children in kindergarten through sixth grade. Mosaica described plans to open forty-five schools across the states in five years, with thirty elementary and secondary schools and fifteen adult and vocational programs.

Mosaica hastened to submit charter proposals for schools in Michigan, Pennsylvania, and other states with charter laws. In 1997, the company had submitted forty-five proposals, of which only a few would be accepted.[130] In some instances, the company failed to find a location for the school. But there were other problems. Sidney Faucette, who had promoted Mosaica to school districts as the company's director of partnership development, resigned when his record as school superintendent of Virginia Beach, Virginia, was exposed in late 1997. A grand jury had found that he had transferred money around the district school budget in a multimillion dollar "shell game," made poor financial decisions, and spent recklessly. The revelation of Faucette's past gave some school boards pause. Before coming to Mosaica, he had accepted the superintendency of a school district in Georgia but had resigned after newspapers reported his past. Gene Eidelman attempted to reassure potential customers by explaining that Faucette had never handled money for Mosaica. "The position we hired him for was not financial," he said. "It was purely marketing."[131]

The following year, the Eidelmans opened a second school, the Mosaica Academy Charter School in Bensalem, Pennsylvania, just outside Philadelphia. Things did not go well. Though a number of neighboring districts bused students to the school, in accordance with Pennsylvania's charter school statute, the Philadelphia school district questioned the validity of the Mosaica charter and refused to provide transportation to the some 250 children who crossed into the Bensalem district to attend the school. A state judge ordered the Philadelphia school district to provide transportation as required by the charter statute, and the state education secretary withheld funds from the district that were due the charter school.[132]

Meanwhile, the company's first school in Saginaw was earning mixed reviews from parents. Mosaica reported gains in test scores from the fall to the spring of the first year, but parents complained that the school was unruly and the program unchallenging. Some returned their children to the local schools. Nonetheless, Mosaica sought capital to fund its growth plans. In October 1998, Mosaica announced that the New York investment firm Lepercq Capital Management had acquired a majority stake in the privately held Mosaica and that Michael Connelly, the president of Lepercq, would become Mosaica's chief executive officer. "Smart entrepreneurs know that when you start growing too fast," Gene Eidelman said, "you need to bring in more help."[133] Murphy and Partners, another New York investment firm, bought into Mosaica in April 1999, providing the company with an additional $10 million.

The Eidelmans knew Connelly well. He was on the board of Children's Discovery Centers when it purchased Prodigy, and he and Gene Eidelman had become friends. A former litigator in New York and Washington, D.C., Connelly had made the jump to venture funding in the early 1980s with leveraged buyouts and investments in cable television and radio stations. Later, he invested in education companies and other concerns, including a manufacturer of swimming pool enclosures.[134]

With Connelly on board, Mosaica opened five more schools in the fall of 1999, with four schools in Michigan and one in New Jersey. By the fall of 2000, Mosaica was running twelve schools in five states. The company reported that enrollment had doubled during the previous year, as it had each year since its inception.[135]

In the spring of 2001, the Bensalem, Pennsylvania, school's board of trustees decided to break away from Mosaica, claiming that the EMO had failed to uphold the terms of its contract and citing a "constant lack of attention to detail" by Mosaica.[136] "As a public agency entrusted with the responsibility of spending public funds wisely, we did not think we were receiving any value from our relationship with [Mosaica Education]," Board of Trustees President Kathleen Harr said. Mosaica filed suit, seeking thousands of dollars it claimed it was owed by the school.[137]

That summer, Mosaica acquired Advantage Schools in a transaction in which Advantage's principal investors provided substantial new capital for the combined company. Advantage was larger, operating fifteen schools with 9,000 students in the 2000–2001 school year, compared to Mosaica's 5,000 students.[138] Several Advantage schools did not stay on for the next school year, however, which reduced total enrollment for the combined company by the time the transaction closed and client schools reopened for the 2001–2002 school year.

Mosaica and two Advantage schools ended their relationships in 2002; a Mosaica school in Jersey City was also lost that year. In the summer of 2003, two large and profitable Mosaica schools in Detroit, including one acquired from Advantage, announced that they would end their relationships, a major setback for the company. The following year, a school in Wilmington, Delaware, also discontinued its relationship, and the Renaissance Advantage Charter School in Philadelphia dropped Mosaica for Edison. An Advantage-model school in Benton Harbor, Michigan, also ended its relationship with the company in 2004. All the while, Mosaica continued to open new schools; in 2003, one in Gary, Indiana, three small schools in Michigan, and one in Dover, Delaware, opened their doors.

Mosaica continues to seek new charters. The success of the company will ultimately hinge on its ability to demonstrate that its school design, including Paragon, accelerates student learning.

KIPP

KIPP, which stands for the Knowledge Is Power Program, is unique among the seven organizations in two essential regards. First, only KIPP is operated as a nonprofit. Second, and at least as significantly, KIPP was conceived not as a national initiative, but as two small schools; only many years later came the plan for a nationwide network of upper elementary and middle schools for disadvantaged and minority students. The schools would attempt to replicate the success of the first two sites by adhering to their central principles.

Founders Michael Feinberg and David Levin met in the summer of 1992 when they both enlisted with Teach for America (TFA), the teacher-training program that places recent college graduates in urban and rural schools serving disadvantaged students. Levin had just graduated from Yale and Feinberg a year earlier from the University of Pennsylvania. On a long drive together from their TFA initiation, they talked about their notions of good teaching: "We had big ideas and big plans. We talked the whole drive about the perfect school and the perfect system and what it would take to create them. Even then, before we had taught, we had the right instincts, I think, about the nature of good teaching, the need for hard work, and the effect on kids of high expectations."[139]

But their first year in the classroom was even harder than they expected. Feinberg said, "To be honest, I got my ass kicked." Levin said that his initial experience was "complete chaos" and the "kids were out of control." In an experienced educator, Harriett Ball, Feinberg and Levin found a mentor with whom they credit teaching them everything they know about teaching children. "We adopted her use of chants and rhymes, her ways of relating to kids, and her views of discipline and community accountability." From Rafe Esquith, the celebrated middle school teacher in Los Angeles, they adopted the credo of "there are no shortcuts." Extraordinary results required a total commitment by both teachers and students, demanding expectations, and a very long school day.[140]

Despite their difficult first year, Ball motivated the team to stay in education and "do everything possible to ensure that their students were achieving at the highest possible levels in the classroom."[141] After a long battle with the Houston school district, Feinberg and Levin obtained permission to open the first KIPP classroom in 1994 and coteach fifty fifth-graders, nearly all poor, Hispanic, and with limited English skills. "We worked until we dropped," Levin recalled. "After the KIPPsters went home, we spent nights figuring out what we could do better. I remember one entire evening spent arguing with Mike over how best to write an equation on the board . . . We had asked these kids and their parents to believe, to make a commitment, and to join the KIPP family. We had painted them a picture of the mountaintop. We had to deliver."[142]

The results at the end of the first year were astonishing. Half of the students in the KIPP classroom began the year with failing scores in math and English on the Texas state standardized tests; by the end of the year 98 percent of students had passed both tests. The following year, Feinberg opened the KIPP Academy in Houston; Levin opened a second KIPP Academy in New York City's South Bronx. Admission was by lottery. Both schools began with fifth grade and over time expanded to serve students through the eighth grade.

As Mike Feinberg tells the story,

If we're going to try to make a large impact, there is no quick, easy, magical solution. We had our fifth graders come to us from 7:30 in the morning to 5:00 in the afternoon, plus four hours on Saturdays, for a month during the summer. And we gave them two hours of homework every night. It wound up being very successful, but we still felt that one year was not enough. So we convinced both the Houston district, as well as the New York Board of Education, to let us open up KIPP *as schools,* still starting in fifth grade but now keeping the kids throughout the turbulent middle school years, bridging the gap between elementary and high school.[143]

At both schools, staff and students had to commit in writing to the nearly fanatical demands of the program. Teachers, who often began at seven in the morning and worked into the evening, carried cell phones and pagers to field questions from students about homework. Parents had to check homework every night, or they would see their child expelled from school. In Houston, students who misbehaved were "porched"—required to wear their uniforms inside out for days or even weeks, to not speak with other students, and to study in separate areas under a banner that read, "If you can't run with the big dogs, stay on the porch."

The two schools sustained the remarkable results of the first KIPP classroom. In Houston, on tests of grade-level proficiency, the school's first fifth-grade class progressed over four years on average 7.3 grade levels in each subject area; in math, they gained ten grade levels and left eighth grade performing better in math than the average American high school graduate. In New York, 95 percent of students in Levin's first graduating class were admitted to the city's top magnet and parochial high schools.[144]

The national media, from the *New York Times* to the *Washington Post,* flocked to the new schools. When *60 Minutes* aired its story in September 1999, KIPP was deluged with calls from politicians, reporters, and educators. Feinberg recalls one California superintendent who phoned to say, "Mr. Feinberg, please, I want to order 15 KIPP schools for next year."[145]

When Scott Hamilton, then managing director of the Pisces Foundation, an education philanthropy, visited KIPP in both Houston and Dallas in 1999, he was impressed: "These schools are remarkable," he thought. "They are built on simple and powerful insights about hard

work and the capacity of all students to succeed in rigorous yet supportive academic environments. They confront convincingly the myth of
social determinism, this false and cruel idea that race and class bind the
academic and intellectual prospects of children."[146] Hamilton would
later join KIPP National as cofounder and president.

The Pisces Foundation was funded by Donald and Doris Fisher,
founders of the Gap retail chain. Prior to joining Pisces, Hamilton had
overseen the launch of charter schools in Massachusetts as associate
commissioner of education and had worked for two U.S. secretaries of
education. At Pisces, Hamilton was interested in creating national school
networks that would move beyond the reach of one-off charter schools,
which were, in his experience, often educationally ill-conceived.[147]

Feinberg, Levin, and Hamilton developed a plan to roll out hundreds
of KIPP schools and have a national impact on school reform. The Fishers donated $15 million to create a new entity, based in San Francisco, to
"replicate the success of the new schools" on the conviction that "great
schools need great leaders." The new organization would select, train,
and support educators who would plan, open, and lead their own
"KIPP-like" schools.[148] In addition to selecting and training as many as
150 KIPP "fellows" each year, the national office would provide the fellows with curricular and operational support both before and after their
schools opened.

KIPP styles itself a school network and denies that it is, in fact, an education management organization. The program's purpose is not to
duplicate the Houston and New York City schools, but "rather to create a
group of schools unified by their fundamental adherence to The Five Pillars," the principles evolved from Feinberg and Levin's analysis of their
first two schools. These are stated as "High Expectations," "Choice and
Commitment," "More Time," "Power to Lead," and "Focus on Results."
As Feinberg put it, "Given that a big part of KIPP is culture, it cannot be
bottled . . . It is not simply buying specific software or a specific curriculum and implementing that; the success of KIPP goes a lot deeper." The
Bronx and the Houston schools, he noted, "do not use the same curricu-

lum, they do not follow the same teaching practices. So we took a long hard look at what makes both schools successful. What kept them the same after seven years of evolution. What kept them the same are the five pillars."[149]

By "High Expectations," KIPP means clearly defined and observable standards for academic achievement and conduct. "Choice and Commitment" refers to the fact that neither staff nor students are assigned to a KIPP school; children and adults alike have chosen to participate in the program and committed "to put in the time and effort required to achieve success." The third element, "More Time," underscores a strongly held tenet of the KIPP culture—that in school, as in life, there are no "shortcuts" to success—and translates into a longer school day and year. The "Power to Lead" refers to the centrality of the school leader to the KIPP formula, and the authority the leader has—unlike conventional schools—over school budget and personnel. Finally, "Focus on Results" captures KIPP's "no excuses" culture and its explicit aim to prepare all students for success in competitive high schools and colleges. High student performance is the unrelenting focus, and KIPP embraces standardized tests without apology as an objective measure of student attainment.[150] As words on a page, the pillars may seem platitudinous. But they accurately summarize the differences between KIPP schools and the typical public middle school.

KIPP licenses its schools under an agreement similar to that used by national retail and restaurant chains with their independently owned franchises. So serious is KIPP about the pillars that schools that fail to adhere to them can lose their licenses and the right to call themselves KIPP schools.

In its first three years, KIPP culled forty Fisher Fellows from among eight hundred applicants to run KIPP schools. Once enrolled in the KIPP School Leadership Program, candidates must complete a yearlong fellowship that includes six weeks at the University of California, Berkeley's Haas School of Business, and residencies at existing KIPP schools.[151] Fellows are immersed in a curriculum that covers organizational leadership and culture, academic leadership, operations management, and community development, and learn through lectures, case studies, discussions, and role-playing. During "Start-Up Boot Camp," they prepare a detailed school implementation plan for turning their "original vision" into a "viable, thriving school." In the final seven months of the fellowship, the fellows return to their communities to execute their plans, including hiring school staff, recruiting students, building a board of directors, fundraising, and developing the school's curriculum. The fellows reconvene twice during the period and receive assistance and guidance from KIPP staff and their peers. KIPP bears the full costs of the program and pays a $50,000 annual stipend for each fellow.[152]

The first KIPP fellows were selected in the summer of 2000 and began the yearlong training period. In the fall of 2001, three KIPP schools opened, followed by ten schools the following year (one of these lost its KIPP license soon after). In 2003, seventeen schools were successfully launched. KIPP's plan called for launching twenty-five schools a year from 2004 on, resulting in 235 schools by 2011–2012, the eleventh year of replication. Even though the expansion plan had been scaled back, the schedule would require raising over $100 million in philanthropic support over the period.

The first three replication schools posted strong gains on spring 2002 tests, and the KIPP brand remains strong. But the organization faces challenges. The extraordinary commitment KIPP demands of its school leaders and staff may not be sustainable. To sustain quality and preserve its brand, KIPP National may be forced to parachute in to rescue struggling schools. Can enough high-quality fellows be identified to meet KIPP's ambitious agenda for expansion? If launching and supporting many small schools proves more costly than anticipated, will KIPP's backers be willing to foot the bill?

ADVANTAGE SCHOOLS

The seventh organization is Advantage Schools, the company I founded in 1996 with two partners, Theodor Rebarber and John Dolan.[153]

At the beginning of my career, I launched two technology ventures. In the era of Apple Computer, I had seen how upstart companies could shake up established giants and reinvent industries. In the early 1990s, I spent five years working on urban education policy in a Boston think tank and, later, in Massachusetts state government. It's hard to imagine a greater contrast in organizational cultures than those of an entrepreneurial start-up and a big city school system. Could the drive and commitment of start-up companies reinvigorate public education?

In 1992, I wrote a book that offered an analysis of the Boston public school district—its programs, personnel systems, and how it spends its money.[154] I attributed the chronically poor performance of Boston and other big-city public school districts to a bureaucratic culture focused not on student results but on compliance with rules. Over the decades, I argued, the state legislatures, unions, central office administrators, and the courts had each imposed countless rules and regulations on the schools. Most were well-intentioned, meant to prevent the recurrence of some past failing or injustice. But principals and administrators had become so consumed with adhering—often unsuccessfully—to thousands of dictates that they paid little attention to the academic performance of their schools. In Boston alone, no fewer than four hundred court orders governed not only student assignment and mandatory busing but also details like the number of basketballs in each school. Union work rules prohibited a principal from entering his or her school on the weekend without paying a custodian four hours of wages to unlock the door. Urban principals, the chief executive officers of their schools, controlled neither their product (the curriculum and pedagogy), nor their staff, nor their budget. How could they manage and lead their schools? How could they succeed at educating economically disadvantaged children?

To transform the culture of big-city school systems, I proposed launching a number of schools, one at a time, that would operate by entirely different rules. The leaders of these "entrepreneurial schools" would be afforded real authority—in turn for unprecedented accountability for the academic results their students attained. If students were learning, principals would continue to enjoy authority and autonomy. If the schools fell short of their academic promises, they would be closed, and the building turned over to a new "management team" with a credible plan for educating students. Private-sector principles would be applied to public schools. In his introduction to the book, Harvard sociologist Nathan Glazer observed, "The private, profit-making sector is very different from the public schools, and no direct transfer from one to the other is possible, yet the private sector draws strength from a dynamic crucially important for the betterment of public schools: success is rewarded, failure brings an automatic judgment and conclusion and the release of resources for something that might work better."[155]

As the book's recommendations were being debated, I learned that its proposals were very similar to those embodied in the country's first charter school law, enacted in 1991 in Minnesota. Both offered school leaders a new bargain: authority and autonomy in exchange for accountability. Boston business leader William Edgerly championed the book's proposals with the city. When Boston's superintendent balked at implementing the book's recommendations, Edgerly and I turned to the state and drafted charter school legislation based on the book's prescriptions.[156] In the Massachusetts legislature, we found scant support among the rank-and-file. But Mark Roosevelt, cochair of the Joint Education Committee, had included a form of charter schools in the school reform legislation he introduced in the House of Representatives. Both the powerful president of the senate, Democrat William Bulger, and the Republican governor, William Weld, backed our tough bill.

As the law made its way through the legislature, I joined the administration of Governor William Weld as special assistant and director of strategic planning. I was able to devote only limited time to education issues, however, and soon itched to return to school reform. In 1996, I left the statehouse and founded Advantage Schools. Edgerly served as chairman of the board, and I as president. Rebarber, whom I had met at the U.S. Department of Education when he worked for Diane Ravitch, then assistant secretary for educational research and improvement, came on as chief education officer. Rebarber had also worked at Edison Schools and helped draft the charter law for the District of Columbia.

Advantage would focus exclusively on educating disadvantaged children, primarily in urban centers. There schools were most abjectly failing their clients, and parents would be the most eager for something that worked better. By only managing new charter schools, Advantage could create organizational cultures characterized by high expectations for students, staff accountability for academic results, and freedom from work rules and excess regulation. By deploying research-proven methods, the company could be certain of accelerating student learning, not just in one setting, but across our network of client schools.

The Advantage vision was to provide a classical education to urban students—at no charge to families. A powerful but little used reading program, Direct Instruction, would reliably get students reading in kindergarten. Every student would learn a foreign language from kindergarten and study Latin in middle school. In the last year of high school, many students would attain International Baccalaureate status. Newly built schools would be bright, attractive, and orderly. Students would be in uniform. Parents and staff would have chosen the school and committed to its cause. The intent was to demonstrate, as the 1997 business plan proclaimed, "the heights of academic achievement that inner-city students can routinely attain when the advantages of charter school governance are coupled with ambitious new academic standards."[157]

It was a thrilling mission, and it attracted both talented staff and deep-pocketed investors. While many venture capitalists wanted nothing to do with the thick politics of public schools, others saw an enormous potential market opening up to private innovation. Advantage attracted Fidelity Capital and Bessemer Venture Partners, two prominent venture capital firms, to invest, and in turn they attracted prestigious investors who brought the company credibility—including Kleiner, Perkins, Caufield and Byers, probably the country's best-known venture capital firm.

After opening its first two schools in 1997, Advantage grew at a dizzying pace. Six schools opened the following year, and the next year another eight. Each year, the company would learn in February, or later still, that charters had been awarded, leaving only months to build or renovate a school building large enough to house hundreds of students from kindergarten through the fifth grade. In the same short period, Advantage had to recruit the school's leader and staff and reach out to the community to attract families willing to take a chance on a school that was as yet nothing more than a signpost on the road. Staff delighted in doing what others would say was impossible—that was the company's culture.

By late 1999, the company had opened sixteen schools in nine states and the District of Columbia, employed nearly a thousand staff members, and posted $60 million in revenues. Every day, there were nearly ten thousand school meals served. Millions of dollars in construction projects were under way at any point. Obtaining debt financing to build schools was proving to be extraordinarily difficult, which meant that still more cash had to be raised from venture capitalists until real estate financing could be obtained. In turn, competing in the overheated capital markets for new equity investors—when dot-coms were promising spectacular returns—required, at the least, sustaining the company's history of rapid growth. There was a second imperative for growth. Only by reaching a critical mass of sites could the company become profitable, staunch the hemorrhaging of cash, and end its dependency on venture capital.

Beneath all the frenetic activity, problems were brewing. The operational infrastructure of the company—accounting, operations management, and regulatory reporting—had failed to keep pace with the company's growth. As a result, vendors in the schools' communities sometimes went unpaid, embarrassing school board members. Errors in paychecks angered teachers. State regulators disciplined the company for late or missing reports. Lunch monies and federal reimbursements at times went uncollected. Financial reports contained errors. Client school boards were frustrated by construction delays. The time of the senior management team was spent almost entirely on managing the chaotic cycle of school openings, raising capital, and building support systems like transportation and payroll; little time remained to hone teaching and learning.

To tackle the operational failings, I recruited a chief operating officer in 1999 who had run a large, multisite health care company but had no experience in education. He recruited corporate staff with operations experience in such industries as health care and technology; almost none had worked in schools. A rift quickly developed between the new and the old guard; each regarded the other with suspicion. New staff proved overconfident; lacking an understanding of school operations, including student transportation, federally subsidized meals programs, and public sector accounting, and failing to consult with veteran staff who had years of experience in schools, they only exacerbated the operational problems. Meanwhile, late financial reports and noncompliance with nuances of state regulations were quickly undermining the company's reputation.

Yet, for 1999–2000, the company reported its strongest year ever of academic gains. The nearly six thousand students tested in Advantage schools had on average, across all grades and subjects, moved up 9.1 rank points on norm-referenced standardized tests. Had we implemented our design more consistently, the gains would have been still stronger.[158]

But the company's investors had lost patience. The capital markets had turned sour, and the company lost its brief window to go public and provide liquidity to its investors. Attracted to the benefits of scale, the investors sold the company to competitor Mosaica Education in September 2001 and invested in the combined company.

It is unlikely that any of the seven organizations, in shaping their own plans, closely examined the experiences of their precursors, Boston University and Education Alternatives. Yet there was much to learn from them. "We were the guinea pigs who showed what wouldn't work," remarked Golle.[159] The two organizations wrestled with the very problems the seven were soon to confront. Both the university and EAI encountered powerful and sustained political resistance. Silber and Golle were both given to brash public statements and sweeping promises. Much time was lost to issues that were on the periphery of teaching and learning, delaying engagement in the improvement of instruction. Both organizations were ill-served by faddish educational programs that had scant record of accelerating student learning. Boston University's progress, too, was slowed by poorly chosen administrators. And Golle was undermined by ambiguous and unenforceable management contracts.

Would the second generation of organizations fare better? What business models and school designs would they deploy in their quest to run superior schools?

2

Business Models

Every business venture has a plan for how it will make money and create financial value for its stockholders. This business model is the commercial proposition of the company—it describes the operations and components of the business, what will be sold and to whom, and how the company will turn a profit.

In their concision, business models highlight the critical differences between companies in the same business, spelling out why some thrive and others struggle. Consider, for example, the personal computer business, where profit margins are thin and products are nearly identical. Dell's business model stands out. While its competitors continue to rely on traditional distribution channels, including mass-market retailers like Circuit City, Dell sells directly to the customer through its website, catalogs, and the telephone. By shipping directly from the factory, the company eliminates the expensive middlemen of distributors and retailers, slices inventory costs, and manufactures only what its customers want to buy. That means stronger profit margins and increasing market share for Dell, whose revenues nearly tripled from 1999 to today, from $18 billion to $51 billion.[1]

Business models are just as useful for understanding nonprofit organizations, for they too must compete in the marketplace and meet their financial goals. Consider health management organizations (HMOs), many of which are nonprofits. "Staff model" HMOs employ doctors directly, and they often own their facilities; "group model" or "network model" HMOs pay fees to independent physician groups and do not own physicians' offices. The choice of model can have major implications for financial performance, quality of care, and customer satisfaction.

Of course, in any industry, a good business model is no assurance of success. Luck aside, success depends as much on management's skill in executing the business plan and bringing the model to life.

Business Models in the Education Industry

The business of education management organizations is to assist school boards in starting and running public schools. At first glance, most EMOs appear to deploy essentially the same business model. Each enters into term agreements with the boards of either individual charter schools or school districts, under which it assumes responsibility for providing educational and operational services to one or more schools. For these services, it is either paid a fixed fee (generally a percentage of the school's revenues) or retains the surplus of each school's revenues over its costs. With enough schools under contract, the individual fees in aggregate will exceed the costs of running the corporate office, and the education management organization will realize a profit. (Nonprofit KIPP's "trademark license agreements" differ from EMO contracts in important respects, but, just as with EMOs, fees calculated as a percentage of revenue flow from member schools to the KIPP organization.)

Imagine that a hypothetical charter school run by an EMO enrolls five hundred students. The school receives $7,000 per student from federal, state, and local sources, for a total of $3.5 million in annual revenues. If the EMO were entitled to retain 12 percent of this total in management fees for the services it provides the school, it would receive $420,000 a year. Imagine further that it operates twenty such schools, which together generate $8.4 million in fees. If the EMO's central office costs $8 million a year to operate, the company would realize an annual surplus of $400,000. If it was a for-profit enterprise, the EMO would post $400,000 in pretax earnings.

Within this broad model, there are many and important variants. One EMO may offer at varying fees a menu of individual services from which school clients can choose, from accounting to teacher training. Another may implement its proprietary curriculum and manage schools comprehensively, for an all-inclusive fee.

From an investor's perspective, the ideal business is highly profitable, requires minimal capital, sustains rapid growth, and faces little risk in execution. Were all four criteria met, investors would be assured a high return on their investment.

Of course, few businesses can meet all these criteria. In actuality, entrepreneurs regularly secure capital investment for ventures that offer an attractive tradeoff among these attributes. A biotechnology start-up might tantalize investors with large future profits, but require substantial capital and pose product development and regulatory approval risks. A retail business might project modest profits at the store level, but plan to expand rapidly in leased locations, yielding strong profitability with minimal capital investment.

Can K–12 education be good business? Consider the basic model in light of these criteria: profitability, capital intensity (the business's requirement for capital, before its investors have an opportunity to liquidate their investment and realize a return), growth, and risk.

PROFITABILITY

EMO founders took it on faith that public-sector institutions, and large school districts in particular, deployed resources poorly—or worse, were riddled with waste and abuse. They assured investors that their own schools would be of high quality, efficient, and therefore profitable. But for many, the notion that primary and secondary public education can be profitable understandably arouses confusion and skepticism. Americans have long been told that the problem with their schools is insufficient funding. If our public schools lack the resources to educate children to an acceptable standard—as most Americans believe—then how could privately run schools, with the same funding, both perform better and operate at a surplus? Skepticism quickly turns to moral condemnation: managing schools for profit is not only a bad idea; it is wrong. Financial resources would be taken away from already under-resourced schools to enrich business owners and their investors.

It is far from clear, however, that insufficient resources are the cause of our schools' undistinguished performance. As described earlier, the United States consistently ranks among the highest-spending nations on education, yet it fares poorly in comparisons of international academic achievement. Among social scientists the debate continues over the relationship between school spending and student achievement. Eric Hanushek, who for three decades has studied the question, concluded in 1997, "The close to 400 studies of student achievement demonstrate that there is not a strong or consistent relationship between student performance and school resources, at least after variations in family inputs are taken into account."[2] "Resource support for schools," he writes, "has been high, and the problems of performance—which are real—result from other forces."[3] Still, the matter is far from resolved. One dissenter is Alan B. Krueger of Princeton University, who faults Hanushek's meta-analysis for weighting some studies more heavily than others and argues that alternative weighting schemes lead to opposite conclusions.[4] Indeed, Rob Greenwald, Larry Hedges, and Richard Laine at the University of Chicago performed a meta-analysis of studies of school inputs and achievement and found that "a broad range of resources were positively related to student outcomes, with effect sizes large enough to suggest that moderate increases in spending may be associated with significant increases in achievement."[5]

If the statistical relationship between spending and student outcomes is inconsistent, it confirms our own observations: some schools do poorly with abundant resources, while others do very well with relatively few. There is a wealth of anecdotal evidence that some schools and districts are unusually effective, while spending much less than poorer performing schools and school systems. The existence of these tantalizing outliers attests to the proposition that, at moderate spending levels, schools could both achieve at a high level and generate a surplus.

The fact is that some schools are much more efficient in their use of financial resources than others. Consider the original KIPP school in the South Bronx. The school operates at the same per-student spending level as other public middle schools, but for the seventh consecutive year, it is the highest performing in the Bronx.[6] A KIPP eighth-grade boy interviewed for this book had recently been admitted to a private high school on scholarship. When asked how KIPP had changed him, he said, "I learn faster now."[7] For SABIS, too, efficiency means learning faster. "Reducing 'wasted effort' and taking maximum advantage of each teaching situation increases learning efficiency. This does not require overworking students; efficiency simply enables students to learn essential skills with the least effort and time. Children can use saved time to learn and play more."[8] If efficiency is understood as better outcomes with a given level of resources, then KIPP's efficiency stems in part from the combination of relatively large classes, with fewer (and highly educated) teachers paid more to work longer days; at SABIS, it stems from relatively large classes and the company's proprietary instructional system.

Unfortunately, any discussion of "efficiency" has long been viewed with hostility in public education circles, including schools of education. As Hanushek writes,

Too often in the education debate, the meaning of efficiency has been twisted into something unpleasant and counterproductive. Efficiency does not mean a relentless, single-minded drive to cut costs. Nor does it mean reducing education to an assembly-line routine based on procedures certified as 'efficient.' What it does mean is that educators should measure both the costs and benefits of various approaches to education—and choose the approach that maximizes the excess of benefits over the costs in their particular circumstances. Today, by contrast, the benefits of new plans are often assumed rather than systematically measured.[9]

To produce strong academic outcomes and make a profit, EMOs would have to collect as much public and private revenues as possible, minimize school-level spending, and keep central office costs down.

PUBLIC AND PRIVATE REVENUES

Profit depends just as much on maximizing revenues as on minimizing costs. An EMO's revenues are a function of enrollment and how effectively it harvests the state, local, and federal funds for which its schools are eligible.

The great majority of school funding comes from municipal and state sources. Charter schools are funded on a "capitated" basis; for each enrolled student, a charter school is eligible to receive an annual amount equal to (or somewhat less than, depending on the state statute) what the school district spends annually from state and local sources per student. Under some states' charter laws, this capitation payment depends on student characteristics, such as grade level and whether the child is enrolled in special education or is recognized as limited in English language proficiency.

In predicting revenues for the schools they would manage, the EMOs and KIPP were aware that spending on K–12 education varies dramatically from state to state, district to district, and even from school to school within a district. Some markets would thus be more attractive than others. Arizona adopted in 1994 one of the country's most market-oriented charter laws but spent just $5,964 on average per student in 2001–2002, 49 percent less than New Jersey, a very high spending state, which spent $11,793 per student.[10] Personnel costs in Arizona were lower as well, but not enough to make up for low spending. The average teacher salary in Arizona was $36,966, only 32 percent less than New Jersey, which with one of the strongest teachers unions in the country, paid an average of $54,575.[11]

While federal dollars make up only a small portion of total K–12 public education funds (accounting for just 7.3 percent in 2000), successfully collecting all the federal funds to which schools are entitled is critical to financial performance. Schools are entitled to seek aid under the Elementary and Secondary Education Act (ESEA) of 1965 through federal entitlement streams such as Title I (which supports disadvantaged children). Additionally, schools have the opportunity to collect numerous smaller federal and state grants, for which they must apply specifically and, in some cases, compete for awards.

There is yet another source of revenue for public schools: private gifts. Each year, large school districts receive grants from community foundations, local corporations, and individual donors. In Boston, so-called external funds—federal and state entitlement and competitive grants, and private grants—make up more than 15 percent of the total revenues of the district.[12]

Drawn by favorable regulatory environments and strong demand, many organizations entered markets like Arizona, North Carolina, and Texas that were low in spending relative to other states. Some even chose to focus nearly exclusively on their low-spending home states, like Chancellor Academies and Charter Schools USA in Florida, a state which in 2000–2001 spent on average just $6,170 per student.[13]

SCHOOL-LEVEL SPENDING

Revenues are finite, and turning a profit would require spending less at the school level, where costs are concentrated. Teacher salaries and benefits account for well over half of school-level spending; in some districts they make up as much as 85 percent of total spending. Several EMOs' business models reflected an explicit change to the site's cost structure. Along with its high student-teacher ratio (thirty to one in later grades), SABIS's staffing model includes student "prefects," who assist in the classroom with tasks like distributing materials and checking other students' work—labor performed by paraprofessionals in conventional schools.[14] Further reducing costs for adult staff in some schools, SABIS pays students to work during nonschool hours—providing child care to working parents, tutoring other students on Saturdays, and assisting technology staff—instead of taking part-time jobs outside. Advantage Schools too had relatively large classes with as many as thirty children, but teachers delivered the largely scripted lessons of Direct Instruction to small instructional groups. To teach some of the groups, Advantage hired inexpensive "instructional assistants." Surprisingly, several private managers, including Chancellor Beacon Academies, have specifically promoted small class sizes, even though fewer students in each class mean more teachers and higher staffing costs.

Especially in urban schools, special education, with its specialized staffing, mandate of very small classes, and extraordinary compliance burden, saps resources from regular education. EMOs hoped that greatly strengthening basic instruction in the early grades—particularly reading instruction—would free their schools from the vicious cycle of excessive referral of students to costly special education programs. Bilingual education represented a similar opportunity. EMOs were aware that most parents wanted their child to learn English, yet many districts assigned students by default to "transitional" bilingual education classes, which often mandated low student-teacher ratios. Assigning fewer students to these costly categorical programs had the promise of greatly reducing school-level spending.

CENTRAL OFFICE SPENDING

The other opportunity for reducing costs concerns the central office. In the 1990s, it was nearly gospel that spending on administrative bureaucracy was out of control. New York City schools' central office at Livingston Street in Brooklyn was said to be larger then the entire governments of some European nations. A less sensational depiction of bureaucratic waste was to compare the number of administrators in the New York schools to the staff overseeing the city's parochial schools. While Livingston Street was estimated to employ between six thousand and seven thousand people to oversee the education of a million children, the archdiocese employed only a dozen or two to oversee a system that educated just over 100,000 students.[15] Of course the two are not strictly comparable; the Catholic schools are not subject to the same set of federal and state mandates.

The New York City schools' bureaucracy experienced a series of substantial cuts and reforms throughout the 1990s.[16] Yet even as late as 1997, historian Diane Ravitch mythologized the district bureaucracy: "Like a huge dinosaur, it is not particularly smart, has an insatiable appetite, moves awkwardly, yet exudes great power. Like wisteria, it is impossible to control; clip it back and it grows more vigorously than before."[17] The waste and abuse in the largest school system received enormous publicity.[18] So completely did the story inform public perception, it became axiomatic that bureaucratic excess typified public school administration.

Conservative think tanks and policy analysts popularized the idea that less and less money was reaching the classroom. While secretary of education, for example, William Bennett reported to the President, "Too much money has been diverted from the classroom; a smaller share of the school dollar is now being spent on student classroom instruction than at any time in recent history. It should be a basic goal of the education reform movement to reverse this trend toward administrative bloat and to reduce the scale of the bureaucratic 'blob' draining our school resources."[19]

Underlying these assertions was the facile equation of administrative spending with unnecessary spending, with only instructional expenses cast as legitimate. Districts categorized spending as "instructional" or "administrative," but drew the line in different places. Although such items as employee benefits, pensions, instructional materials, and clerical services may not have been considered "instructional" costs, they were necessary to school operations. Therefore common claims like "40 percent of school dollars never make it to the school, let alone the classroom" were at best highly misleading.

In any case, the thicket of education statutes, regulations, and federal court orders that had grown up around the public schools in the second half of the century mandated costly programs as well as monitoring and reporting. These burdens remain. In New York City, a 2004 study found that schools must comply with more than sixty sources of laws and regulations, including state education law (846 pages), state regulations (720 pages), 15,062 state commissioner of education decisions contained in forty-three volumes, the federal NCLB Act (690 pages), the Individuals with Disabilities Education Act, the Bilingual Education Act, the Children's Internet Protection Act, the Educational Opportunities Act, the Gun Free Schools Act, food safety regulations, and bias and sensitivity guidelines. To terminate an inept teacher requires as many as eighty-three steps (thirty-two alone to place a note in the teacher's file); to conduct an athletic event takes up to ninety-nine steps and legal considerations. Each set of rules arose from legitimate concerns, but together they impose a staggering compliance burden on the public schools.[20]

The laws and regulations of the 1970s that guaranteed services for the disabled prescribed in extraordinary detail the procedures districts must follow. Some districts, such as Boston, had special education enrollment grow to nearly one-quarter of total enrollment. Another cost, busing for desegregation, was often mandated by federal court order. Affirmative action requirements in hiring, bilingual education, and collective bargaining contracts (a dozen in Boston alone) also drove up administrative spending as new staff were hired to monitor and report compliance.

Some founders of management companies were seemingly unaware of the many legitimate (or at least unavoidable) functions performed by public school administrators, who were also assumed to be unmotivated and unproductive. High spending was seen as "fat": the product of (unidentified) waste, corruption, and abuse. In 1992, CEO of Education

Alternatives John Golle remarked to *Forbes*, "There is so much fat in the schools that even a blind man without his cane could find the way."[21] EMO business models rarely analyzed the workload of the district to determine which tasks were mandated from the outside (and would apply equally to them), and which could be avoided. Individual inefficiencies were not itemized and, when they were, their origin in regulation was often overlooked.

CAPITAL INTENSITY

The second characteristic of the ideal business model is minimum capital intensity. Running public schools should not inherently require significant capital. Individual schools can generate an operating surplus (retained by the organization, or captured in part as management fees) from their first year of operation, and the costs of the central office, while appreciable, can be quickly covered by the sum of such surpluses or fees. Capital is required primarily to cover operating losses until the point that total fees exceed the cost of the central office.

Yet one aspect of the charter school regulatory regime gave rise to an extraordinarily high demand for capital: under most charter laws, charter schools are not provided with facilities and lack access to public or private funds for the construction or renovation of school buildings. In the absence of public capital, EMOs substituted their own, driving up the capital intensity of their business models. Costs could be minimized by leasing and refitting commercial space for use as a school; Advantage renovated an office building in Phoenix at a cost of $850,000 to house more than five hundred students. At the other end of the spectrum, Edison, under pressure from city officials, spent more than $13 million to construct a charter school building in Albany, New York, that accommodates more than eight hundred students.

In nearly all states, charter schools lack taxing and direct bonding authority. They also have no credit history with which to borrow from commercial sources the funds needed for construction and renovations.

State and local governments will rarely loan them sufficient funds or provide them with critical credit enhancements that would make them an acceptable credit risk to commercial lenders.

By contrast, district school facilities are paid for by states and municipalities out of appropriations entirely outside of school operating budgets. The city or town issues bonds for their construction, and the debt service on this borrowing is paid out of annual municipal appropriations. Often this debt service is largely reimbursed by the state. For example, in Massachusetts, half or more of the cost of school building construction is typically reimbursed by the state; the state has committed to reimburse as much as 90 percent if the district adheres to a voluntary desegregation plan. Massachusetts spent just under $400 million in fiscal year 2002 alone on school construction through its reimbursement program.

If charter schools can access bond financing at all, they use revenue bonds (backed by the revenues of the school and not the full faith and credit of a governmental entity) at high interest rates. Transaction fees for charter bond issues are also much higher than they would be for a district, since many up-front costs, like fees for lawyers and advisors, are proportionately higher for one small transaction than for a district's typical issue, which supports several schools.[22] More commonly, charter schools have resorted to the private market for facilities-related debt at high rates.

Investors favor companies where growth will not require raising substantial additional capital, which would dilute their ownership positions. Unfortunately, given the funds required for school facilities, many EMO business models suffered from high capital intensity. A few were fortunate: National Heritage benefited from a founding investor driven by the company's social mission—an "angel"—willing to invest heavily in school construction. SABIS was an established business with millions of dollars on its balance sheet to help it penetrate the American charter school market. Others, including Edison, Advantage, and Chancellor, had nowhere to turn but to venture capitalists. By taking on these investors, they committed themselves to a dramatic buildup in schools and revenues. KIPP's schools, by contrast, started small enough that the need for facilities financing was postponed at each site by several years.

GROWTH

Even under optimistic assumptions, managing schools was going to be a low-margin and often capital-intensive business. To provide their stock-holders with an attractive return on investment, EMOs sought to compensate with rapid growth. Consider Edison. "In 20 years," Whittle predicted in 2000, "20% to 30% of public schools will be run by for-profits." Michael T. Moe, an analyst at Merrill Lynch who helped take Edison public, was no less bullish on the company's growth: by 2005, the company would manage 423 schools with over a quarter million students, for revenues of $1.8 billion. In less than a decade, he projected, for-profit companies could capture as much as 10 percent of the total spending on K–12 education.[23]

Venture capitalists only invest in companies that have a realistic plan for growing very large—and very quickly. Because most venture investments fail, each success has to make up for all those that end up as write-offs. To attract investment, entrepreneurs must convince the venture capitalist that a return of ten times the investment in five years is achievable. A public stock offering provides investors a market for their shares and the opportunity for liquidity. As a practical matter, only companies of $100 million or more in annual revenues can generally complete a successful initial public offering. The more capital that is required early on, the more the company has to grow in five years to produce an acceptable return.

The business plans of for-profit EMOs had to support these kinds of returns—and the projected value of the promise five years out was a function of the number of schools then operating and their profitability. Committing to returns on a scale that would appeal to venture capitalists wedded the company to an intensive growth plan, one that the founders had to balance with considerations of how many schools the team could realistically open and run.

Consider the implications of an EMO reaching $100 million in total revenues. Our hypothetical school has annual revenues of $3.5 million and pays its management company 12 percent of these revenues. (EMOs' actual fees have ranged from 10 to 22 percent.) Assuming that the management company can count 100 percent of the schools' revenues as its own (an issue discussed later), the growth plan would call for twenty-nine client schools by the end of five years: no small challenge.

The business models of nonprofit organizations also rely on a rapid buildup of schools. If KIPP aims to become self-sustaining, it will face the same challenge of bringing on enough member schools that the sum of the license fees paid by the schools covers the costs of the corporate office. Each school pays KIPP a percentage of its state and local revenues—1 percent in the first year, and 3 percent thereafter, not to exceed the average cost of one full-time teacher. With very small schools paying very low management fees, rapid growth is imperative if KIPP is to lessen its dependence on philanthropy.

RISK

Lastly, the ideal business model presents few risks to its realization. To assess the level of risk in a new venture, investors attempt to identify and evaluate sources of risk. In the schools business, the greatest risks are of three types: academic performance risks, financial model risks, and the problem of continuing value.

ACADEMIC PERFORMANCE RISKS

Every school management organization relies on its unique school design to do more with less: to raise student performance faster than surrounding traditional public schools can, while spending less, so that the school operates at a surplus and can afford to pay a management fee.

To secure contracts with school districts and charter boards, EMOs often promise to raise student achievement. Though specific commitments vary from organization to organization, companies have generally pledged in presentations, and later in the charter applications they have prepared on behalf of their client boards, to elevate student achievement significantly on nationally standardized tests, such as the Iowa Test of Basic Skills or the Stanford Achievement Test, over the term of the charter (typically five years). Frequently, companies promised substantial performance gains on new state tests, such as the Texas Assessment of Academic Skills (TAAS) or the Massachusetts Comprehensive Assessment System (MCAS). In its IPO prospectus, Edison acknowledged the critical nature of such promises to the business, describing management agreements as arrangements that "give us substantial control over a school . . . in return for meeting specified academic results."[24] Given that many traditional public schools had long struggled to elevate student achievement, bold predictions of achievement gains reflected the high confidence—some would call it blind faith—that founders had in their plans.

An EMO was at the greatest risk when it delineated academic performance commitments in the management contract itself. In Rocky Mount, North Carolina, one of Advantage's first schools, the company's contract promised that student performance in the Advantage school would surpass that in the district on standardized tests by the end of the contract term. SABIS's contracts, too, specifically stated that "expected" student progress was, on average, at least ten months of gain on a nationally recognized standardized test between the beginning of the school year and April.[25]

Even when academic commitments were not specified in the contract, the organization remained at risk, because a disaffected board could assert that the company was in breach of the agreement if the aspirations referenced in the charter application were not realized. Though academic goals outlined in charter applications might have been offered in the spirit of sales pitches, charter authorizers rightly committed boards, and by extension their management companies, to their achievement by referencing the entire charter application in the charter.

In principle, then, the failure to meet stated targets could expose EMOs to the risk of contract termination or nonrenewal, and in the case of charter schools, the decision by the state not to renew the school's charter. Moreover, such a failure would undermine the company's brand reputation and make it difficult to obtain additional contracts from charter schools and districts.

FINANCIAL MODEL RISKS

The basic financial model discussed earlier in the chapter was vulnerable to risks at both the site and corporate levels. At the site level, the school could suffer from lower-than-expected revenues and higher-than-expected spending, while at the corporate level, the task of supporting schools could prove more costly than projected.

The "site model" articulates a financial plan for the typical client school. The model sets out the number of students the school will educate, their distribution across grades and classrooms, and the number of teachers and other staff. A budget is drawn up that describes the school's projected total revenues (from state and local, federal, and private sources) and expenses (including staff compensation costs and all non-staff costs, such as transportation, rent, and instructional materials). By subtracting budgeted costs from revenues, the site model anticipates the surplus the school will generate, as well as how much of this will be paid out in management fees to the EMO (or in a license fee to KIPP) and how much will be retained at the site level as a year-end surplus. Of course, each actual school will depart from the model to some degree. But the organization's executives commit to investors or funders that the portfolio of schools will, on average, adhere to the site model.

On the revenue side, the greatest risk is that a school will open with fewer students than planned or will fail to retain them through the year. Because charter schools are funded on a per-student basis, even a small difference in enrollment can have a dramatic effect on the school's financial performance. Consider our hypothetical charter school with expected revenues of $3.5 million. If the school succeeds in enrolling on average only 425 instead of 500 students through the year, it will fall short of planned revenues by over half a million dollars, wiping out the school's site contribution entirely and requiring the EMO to fund its losses.

In some states, such as California and Texas, charter schools are paid not on the basis of their enrollment, but rather on students' actual attendance. The site model therefore reflects an assumption for average daily attendance as a percentage of total enrollment. In urban schools, where attendance is often poor, this assumption is critical. If the site model assumes 98 percent average daily attendance for planned revenues of $3.43 million, and only 90 percent of students come to school, the school will fall short of plan by $280,000 in revenues annually.

The budget presents several other revenue risks. In charter school settings, the capitation is typically by law a function of the average per-student spending of the district in which the school is located. Charter schools may anticipate a certain capitation level, but be unpleasantly surprised when the state or local district adopts questionable policies for computing the capitation and pays out a substantially smaller amount for each student attending charter schools within the district. Schools also run into trouble when they fail to harvest federal monies from federal and state grant programs, such as subsidies for breakfast and lunch, perhaps by failing to comply with these programs' complex regulatory or reporting requirements.

On the expense side, at the core of the model are classroom staffing assumptions: How many students will be in each classroom, and how many teachers and aides are needed to deliver the school's program. The financial models are highly sensitive to the addition of just a small number of staff members. If our school plans to pay a management fee of 12 percent, or $420,000 annually, the addition of just three staff members at $50,000 each can reduce by more than a third the monies available to pay the fee.

The greater problem for expense control is occupancy costs—the expense in rent or debt service on the school facility. There are often no firm plans for where a charter school will be sited at the time the charter is awarded and the management agreement is signed. The school's budget, filed as part of the charter application, only estimates occupancy cost. The actual siting of each school depends on what proves available in the area and can be made ready in the short time before the school is scheduled to open.

When it came to predicting corporate expenses, the EMOs and KIPP were flying blind. What would be the initial level of corporate expense necessary to support the first sites? What additional expense would be needed for each new school? For an organization to reach breakeven, the growth in total fees received has to outpace growth in the corporate expense of supporting an increasing number of schools. If not, the organization will fail to become self-sustaining or turn a profit.

Consider corporate spending as a percentage of total revenues. In an EMO, if fees are predicted to average 12 percent of revenues, corporate expenses, while still growing each year in absolute terms, will have to diminish to less than 12 percent of revenues for the organization to break even, let alone make a profit. If corporate spending grows faster than expected, it can dramatically increase the number of schools necessary to reach breakeven on a profit-and-loss basis—and the capital needed to fund the business until then.

THE PROBLEM OF CONTINUING VALUE

Another risk in the business model is the relatively short term of the contract: Will client schools elect to renew their agreements at the end of the term, typically five years, or will they be tempted to go it on their own and "self-manage"? There is ample reason to be worried. A client school board might exploit an EMO for its capital, know-how, and political connections to get a school built and opened. Once the school is stable and a credit to community board members, how essential will they consider the management organization?

Strategic Differences among the Models

While the industry shares a basic business model, the individual models of the six EMOs and KIPP contain critical differences that reflect strategic choices. These include whether the organization is for-profit or non-profit, manages primarily charter or contract schools, is national or regional in scope, targets urban or suburban markets, and has a small or expansive initial school size, and whether the model entails a high or low degree of academic prescription.

FOR-PROFIT OR NONPROFIT

The very first decision to be confronted by founders is whether to organize as a for-profit or a nonprofit corporation. The choice is philosophical and personal, as well as practical. Should the founders realize financial gains through stock ownership if the company proves successful? A for-profit structure would permit the founders—and potentially the company's employees, including schoolteachers—to own a piece of the company and take part in its financial success. It might also permit the company to raise large amounts of equity capital, by selling stock in the company to individual investors or venture capitalists.

Against these potential benefits, founders have to weigh the intense controversy that the idea of making money from schools provokes. Opponents can be expected to draw attention to the EMOs' for-profit structure and impugn their motives in every community they enter. Whatever pat responses the founders might devise for their critics, they have to wrestle privately with the underlying question: Is it right to make a profit managing public schools?

If they choose to be nonprofit, entrepreneurs avoid the political controversy that profit-making arouses, but it may be very difficult to raise the capital that the organization requires. Most large, established philanthropic foundations have been hostile to charter schools and market-based reforms and have stuck to funding initiatives within the public school system. In 1993, Walter Annenberg made headlines with his $500 million grant for public education, but the money was absorbed almost entirely by large school districts and organizations that sought to improve them.[26] A few conservative charities, including the Walton

Family Foundation, have generously supported the charter school movement, but nearly always in the form of individual grants to charter schools. The tens of millions of dollars required to launch a major EMO can be difficult to raise from philanthropic sources.

Since the year 2000, a small number of foundations have made very large commitments to education ventures. KIPP National was established with a gift from the Fisher Foundation, and the Fishers are expected to provide much of the $100 million in donations that KIPP is projected to require over its first ten years.[27] In 2003, the Gates Foundation committed $22 million to the NewSchools Venture Fund, a venture philanthropy based in San Francisco and spun off from fabled venture capital firm Kleiner, Perkins, Caufield, and Byers, to fund five new "charter management organizations," or CMOs.[28] The CMOs are a new variant of EMOs and depart from EMOs in five key ways: they are organized as nonprofit corporations to soften political resistance, manage only charter schools, limit or eliminate independent client school boards, operate initially in one state or region rather than nationally, and hew to a philosophy of cautious growth. NewSchools and Gates support the first and largest CMO, Aspire Public Schools, which opened its first schools in 1999 and now operates ten schools in five northern California counties, for a total enrollment of 3,100 students in grades K–11.[29] Aspire is planning a major expansion to Los Angeles.[30] Another CMO, Green Dot Public Schools, operates three small charter high schools in the Los Angeles area and aims to open one hundred schools.[31]

The NewSchools Venture Fund considers the nonprofit structure a decisive advantage in the current political environment. KIPP's director of "trailblazing," John Alford, would agree. Alford described discussions with potential school board members and community partners: "When Edison was in the news, that was the first question. 'Are you for-profit?'" When he assured them KIPP was not, "Oh good," was their reply. "Now I can talk to you."[32] A practical benefit of the nonprofit structure is the opportunity to hold charters directly, avoiding the perils of independent client boards.

CONTRACT SCHOOLS OR CHARTER SCHOOLS

To operate publicly funded schools, the six EMOs and KIPP could contract with a school district to manage one or more existing schools—known as contract schools. Or they could contract with the board of a charter school, either by working with individuals in a community who wished to open a charter school, or by contracting with the board of trustees of an existing charter school. In a third structure, contract charters, a variant of contract schools, the organization contracted with a school district to manage a charter school sponsored by the district. In this model, the district school board either uses its legal authority to charter a new school and contract with an organization to run it, or more commonly, converts an existing district school to charter status. Each vehicle offered distinct advantages.

Contracts with school districts brought two principal benefits: school facilities and the prospect of economies of scale.

Facilities. Because the schools that districts contracted out were already operating, the new school could occupy the existing building, usually at no cost. Even if the organization made minor improvements to the site—such as installing and wiring computers and replacing furniture—the cost and execution risks of such enhancements were negligible compared to those of siting and building a new charter school facility. With little investment required in the facility, contract schools promised lower capital intensity and higher operating margins than charter schools.

Economies of Scale. An EMO could benefit from certain economies of scale at the corporate level if it were awarded a contract for several schools in one district. Contracting out schools was controversial; months and sometimes years were invested rallying support from school board members, community leaders, and the media. Marketing expenses could be more easily absorbed if they resulted in an award to run several schools.

More importantly, a cluster of contract schools permitted the hiring of local support staff. Rather than repeatedly flying in personnel from the home office, the organization could employ local staff for operations, information technology, and curriculum support.

Central Office and Union Rules. But contract schools were not without disadvantages. When running a contract school, private managers had to comply with most or all of the rules that burdened the district's own schools, including state education laws, collective bargaining agreements, and many of the district's own policies and procedures. Of these, the most significant constraint was union contracts. Across the negotiating table, school boards long ago capitulated to the unions' insistence that principals have minimal authority over their staff. In most cases, principals have little say in who fills a staff vacancy; the principal can only choose from a pool of the most senior teachers in the district, whether or not they have relevant experience and are philosophically aligned with the school's program. Underperforming or obstructionist teachers cannot readily be reassigned or fired. Any attempt to particularize a job description—to make one teacher's role different from another—will be grieved by the union: one math position (and salary) has to be identical to the next. Paying more to attract teachers in high demand (for instance, science teachers) or awarding bonuses for exceptional achievement are prohibited; salaries are set by the union agreements and are generally strictly a function of the number of years spent teaching and the highest degree earned. District-wide seniority-based "bumping" procedures make it difficult to build a stable, cohesive faculty committed to the school's mission and ways and trained in the school design, because each year junior teachers can be summarily bumped out of their jobs by more senior faculty transferring into the school. By leaving principals with little discretion, union rules sap them of the power to manage and lead their schools. Unless they negotiated specific privileges with their client school districts, organizations that contracted to run schools would face the same debilitating constraints as district principals.

Charter schools, by contrast, are generally not constrained by the district's collective bargaining agreements or central office policies; charter school principals have the authority and autonomy to hire and deploy faculty in accordance with the school's design.

Culture and Choice. In his study of public bureaucracies, James Q. Wilson observed, "Every organization has a culture, that is, a persistent, patterned way of thinking about the central tasks of and human relationships within an organization . . . Like human culture generally, it is passed from one generation to the next. It changes slowly if at all."[33] When a private organization takes on a district school, it risks inheriting the school's and district's culture, which in many large systems is characterized by a burdensome bureaucracy and low expectations for academic achievement.

There was good reason to be concerned about the constraints the district school culture might impose. Rather than pursue an overarching mission, district schools often implement an array of diffuse programs, as Paul Hill and his colleagues have noted. An accretion of separate initiatives, often the result of external mandates or funding streams, substitutes for a coherent school design. School faculty subscribe to diverse teaching philosophies and values. Administrators spend most of their time neither leading the school nor honing instruction, but rather maintaining discipline or gathering and reporting evidence of compliance with the requirements of the state, the central office, the courts, and foundations.[34]

By contrast, charter schools offered the opportunity to build an entirely new organizational culture fueled by a crisp and compelling mission of academic achievement. Ideally, because both parents and staff have chosen the school, they subscribe to its vision and share its values. The school's leader can proclaim the school's cause without hesitation and has the authority to make and carry out bold decisions. The school does not hesitate to shape student's attitudes and values and persuades students to follow its rules and excel academically. A community is formed.

Funding. When it comes to securing operating funds, neither contracts nor charters presented a clear advantage. In contract schools, funding levels are the result of negotiations between the management organization and the district. Some charter school boards negotiate to hold back a small portion of revenues, to be spent at the board's discretion or for certain identified costs, such as legal expenses. But when it came to capital funding, contracts were decisively more attractive than charters. Charter schools have to pay occupancy costs out of operating revenues, reducing funds available for site costs, such as staff, management, and license fees.

GEOGRAPHIC ROLLOUT

A third difference across models is the strategic approach to growth. While the market for public school management is theoretically enormous—the United States spent $400 billion in fiscal year 2001 on K–12 education—the actual market has been limited to the small number of districts with school boards willing to contract out to private managers and to states that have robust charter laws and are actively issuing charters.[35]

Even states with laws favorable to private management often have statutory caps on the total number of charter schools, or on the number of new charters that can be issued each year. When Massachusetts enacted its charter law in 1993, it authorized only twenty-five autonomous charter schools statewide. Today, the total is capped at seventy-two. Further limiting the availability of charters is the tendency of authorizers to issue only a limited number to schools associated with management companies, and to avoid appearing to favor one company by spreading awards across organizations.

This smattering of actual opportunities for charter schools and for contracts with school districts compelled some companies to take a national approach to growth, especially in light of the intense pressure some EMOs felt to grow rapidly and reach the financial breakeven point. Edison and Advantage set out to create a national network of schools, opening schools in multiple states from the start, and continuing to expand opportunistically into additional states where statutory and contractual terms were favorable and they could win business. Another argument for geographic diversity is the political fragility of the underlying charter laws: each year, teachers unions and other foes of charters file legislation in states with strong charter laws to repeal or weaken the legislation (such as imposing a moratorium on new charters, or requiring charter schools to obtain approval from district school boards). If an election were to change overnight the power structure of a state—replacing, for example, a pro-charter governor with a successor indebted to the teachers unions—not only would the company's growth be arrested, but existing schools could be threatened as well. Indeed, if all schools were in that one state, the company's entire business would be imperiled. Geographic diversity shelters the company from this regulatory risk.

But there were strong advantages to staying local as well. Each state had its own education laws and regulations; mandated reporting formats; central computerized data collection system; special and bilingual education policies; discipline policies governing suspension and expulsion; and emerging academic standards and criterion-referenced testing regimens. Simply knowing the requirements of compliance in each state was a challenge. A local model would avoid the shuttling of corporate personnel to and from far-flung schools to develop real estate, hire and train staff, attend board meetings, and oversee implementation of the school design. More importantly, organizations operating locally can more effectively develop vital relationships with customers—not only school boards, but also authorizers and regulators. As Chapter 5 details, these relationships would prove to be of great consequence. Given the difficulties of operating nationally, CMOs are pursuing a regional approach to growth.

TARGET MARKET

The student populations targeted by the organizations varied widely. KIPP and Advantage saw it as their mission to open schools that would serve children in poor urban neighborhoods. In the 1999–2000 school year, 71 percent of Advantage students and 80 percent of KIPP's were from economically disadvantaged families. Schools were located in the most challenged minority neighborhoods, including the South Bronx; the impoverished Washington, D.C., neighborhood of Anacostia; and the Arbor Hill community of Albany, New York. Most National Heritage students, by contrast, were white, and only about one-quarter were poor, prior to the company's expansion outside of Michigan.

Chancellor Beacon operates schools in a great variety of settings. Chancellor's charter school in North Lauderdale, Florida, has a student body that is predominately poor; many students' families hail from Caribbean islands. Only a few miles away, Chancellor Charter School at Weston educates an affluent population from the surrounding gated communities, where the mean household income tops $100,000 and only 5 percent of students are considered poor. Edison aspired to operate schools in a wide variety of communities, but over time the mix of its students has become increasingly minority and low-income. Edison romanced school districts of all kinds, but the takers were primarily troubled urban schools with low test scores. "They were the ones most willing to take the chance, who felt they had nothing to lose," Adam Tucker explained.[36] In the 2003–2004 school year, African Americans made up 66 percent of Edison students, Hispanic students 19 percent, and Caucasian students only 13 percent. The percentage of students from low-income families grew from 57 percent in 1998–1999 to 78 percent in 2003–2004.[37] SABIS, for its part, has frequently operated schools that serve a demographically mixed population with moderate levels of poverty.

SCHOOL SIZE AND GRADE LEVEL CHOICES

Most EMOs' business plans determined initially that at least five hundred students would be needed for a school to be financially viable, as measured by the school's return on investment. Much smaller, and the school would not be able to afford to pay management fees, or the fees would be so small that it would take years to recoup the organization's initial investment—too many schools would have to be opened and be supported by the corporate office for the EMO to break even. Much larger, and the school's founding board and the charter authorizer would be likely to object, as most adhere to the popular view that smaller schools are more socially and educationally effective.

The six EMOs most often opened schools with grades K–5. Most models called for a school to add, facilities permitting, one grade each year, so that the school would grow with the children. For example, a school that begins with 540 children, or 90 in each grade K–5, would enroll 810 students as a K–8 school three years later.

Advantage typically opened with grades K–5 and then expanded each year by one grade; at only one school did it offer eighth grade prior to its sale to Mosaica. Mosaica followed a similar model, and National Heritage opened primarily schools serving K–4 or K–5 students, growing many to the seventh or eighth grade. Edison also routinely managed middle schools.

Most EMOs judged high schools to be too expensive and risky to operate, at least initially. SABIS is an exception. With a rigorous and proven high school model, SABIS routinely operates schools that educate students from kindergarten through twelfth grade. Edison occasionally serves high school students. During the 2002–2003 school year, twelve Edison schools operated through ninth grade or higher, with five of these serving students in all four high school grades.[38] Chancellor Beacon often offers a pre-K program, and five schools in 2003–2004 included one or more high school grades.[39]

KIPP has followed an entirely different model. Schools typically begin with the fifth grade and then add a grade each year through eighth grade, with eighty to ninety students at each grade level. KIPP is expanding into high schools; its first, in Houston, opened in 2004.

ACADEMIC PRESCRIPTION

The organizations differ greatly in the degree to which they prescribe a specific school design and curriculum at each of their schools.

Beacon Education Management began by offering a "variety of con-tracted services to develop school-based learning solutions" to "help educators improve the quality of education."[40] The company was edu-cationally agnostic and managed schools across the pedagogic spec-trum, from traditional to progressive. Beacon's school in Chelmsford, Massachusetts, implemented a progressive, interdisciplinary, "student-centered" school model. A few towns away, the Mystic Valley Regional Charter School in Malden offered subject-based, teacher-led Direct Instruction. In still other schools, the company provided only specific services, including administrative, financial, human resource, and ac-counting services.[41] In the founders' view, Beacon should not be hitched to a particular set of curriculum products, because they might not work with diverse state and local standards. Instead, the standards should drive the choice of curricula.

But Beacon's model of tailored services to individual charter schools proved unprofitable and difficult to bring to scale. The company also found that its model could not ensure strong academic outcomes. In 1999, Beacon's management changed course. New capital sources were beginning to come on line for school buildings, and Beacon decided that larger schools, making use of a consistent Beacon curriculum, would be a better business to be in. New schools would all follow the Beacon "Lightpoints" curriculum, with 70 percent of the curriculum prescribed by Beacon and 30 percent tailored by the individual school.[42] Light-points would be based in part on E. D. Hirsch's Core Knowledge se-quence. However sensible, the strategy was not sustained after the merger with Chancellor. The combined company's philosophy was to provide standards by subject and grade, but not to prescribe instruc-tional programs.

At the other end of the spectrum of academic prescription was Advantage. The company believed that leaving teachers to develop their own lesson plans in critical elementary subjects, as did most schools in the United States, made for a kind of institutionalized chaos. Teacher autonomy came at great cost to learning and was of particular harm to urban students from disadvantaged families. In the core subjects of elementary reading and math, all Advantage teachers used the largely scripted lessons of the Direct Instruction curriculum. When children fail to learn, contended Siegfried Engelmann, developer of Direct Instruction, it is because instruction is unclear or poorly organized; Direct Instruction offers meticulously crafted and field-tested lessons that Engelmann claims will succeed with virtually every early learner. To maximize academic outcomes, every Advantage school deployed essentially the same carefully chosen behavior systems, administrative structures, information systems, and even interior color schemes.

SABIS's program occupies a middle position on the spectrum. The company's "point system" prescribes in detail what is taught in each classroom each week, as well as the level of mastery of the concepts and skills that students must exhibit. SABIS believes this approach ensures that concepts are ranked in importance, placed in logical order, and taught appropriately. According to SABIS, the point system seeks "to maximize subject content coverage by pacing students through the set curriculum as rapidly as possible without sacrificing the expected level of mastery. Efficiency in teaching is the key—what and how much to teach in the allocated time."[43] Teachers, though, retain the freedom to develop and adjust their lesson plans.

Management Contracts

The EMO's management contract creates the framework in which the company operates. When the EMOs' founders and their corporate attorneys drafted the client contracts that would serve as templates, they were charting new territory. While by the mid-1990s there were a few model contracts to crib from—Edison's, most notably—the weaknesses within these agreements had not yet been revealed. Only later would their implications become clear: for the flow of school funds, for the treatment of employment and retirement benefits for teachers, and for the accounting treatment of revenues and profits.

Among the most important implications of contract structure are whether the EMO's interests will be protected if a client board moves to terminate the relationship and whether the school can obtain the tax-exempt determination from the IRS necessary to participate in tax-exempt bond financings.

Most contracts give the management organization broad responsibility for the education process at the school, including the design of the educational program, the selection and acquisition of instructional materials, the hiring and termination of personnel, and the training and oversight of teachers. The organization is also responsible for day-to-day operations, including business administration, contracting, payroll, and maintenance of the school's facilities.

Contract terms are generally five years, in rare cases ten years or longer. Most of National Heritage's contracts continue until expiration of the charter, unless terminated. Many contracts provide for automatic renewal unless either party gives advance notice of a desire to terminate. Advantage's contracts often gave the client the right to not renew only if students failed to achieve specified levels of academic performance or the company otherwise breached a provision of the contract.

In contract schools, the EMO is generally paid a fixed, negotiated amount either for the school as a whole or per enrolled student. Edison has frequently negotiated an amount equal to the district's average per-student revenues, less certain district expenses such as food service, transportation (if provided by the district), and insurance.[44] From this amount, the EMO pays out all school costs and is entitled to keep the balance as compensation for its services. In some contracts, incentive provisions permit Edison to receive additional revenues.

In charter schools, EMOs are compensated in one of two ways. In the surplus model, the EMO disburses from the school's revenues the school's expenses, in accordance with a budget negotiated between the EMO and the school's board. Edison generally has been paid on this basis, along with National Heritage in all locations.[45] Whatever is left over is retained by the EMO as compensation for its services, from which it in turn has to cover corporate expenses, including the cost of all services provided to the school. Under the fee model, the management company is entitled to receive a fixed percentage of the total revenues of the school; generally such fees may be paid only after all school expenses are satisfied. Advantage, Beacon, and Mosaica generally were or are compensated by this model. Beacon's fees were the lowest: 7 percent of revenues in its early contracts, and later 10 percent, as at its Central New York Charter School for Math and Science. Chancellor's fees were similar, at 10 to 12 percent of revenues. Fees of 12.5 percent at Mosaica's Our World Neighborhood Charter School were typical for the company. SABIS charged 15 percent at the Schenectady International Charter School. Advantage charged 22 percent at its Rocky Mount Charter School, although far less was in fact earned. In actuality, the negotiated percentage is often irrelevant: after all school-level expenses are paid (for salaries, rent, and other costs), the amount left over determines what the company can take in. The negotiated percentage represents an upper limit on the fee; often what is collected is much less, because the funds simply are not available. If the contractual percentage fee is set high enough, the fee model contract is largely equivalent to the surplus model contract.

Charter school board clients and their attorneys often balk at the surplus model. State departments and charter authorizers, who usually have approval rights over management contracts, also sometimes insist on the fee model. While acknowledging that the surplus model is appropriate on its merits, they are wary of defending it publicly. The less the management company spends on the school ("on children"), it would be said, the more money the management company makes.

In some contracts, all school staff are employees of the school; in others, they are employees of the EMO. In most, the EMO has the sole authority to hire and fire school staff other than the principal. Some state regulators have questioned whether the state charter law permits this delegation of responsibility to the EMO and insisted the contract require that such authority be subject to school board "oversight."

Edison's contracts have often subjected hiring and firing decisions to board approval, "not to be unreasonably held." Contracts nearly always provide for the EMO's selection of the school principal to be approved by the school's board. To ensure that the principal, the chief executive of the school, is accountable to the management company, EMOs have negotiated for the authority to fire the principal, but this has usually been successfully resisted by the board. Generally, contracts provide that termination of the principal is subject to the board's approval, seeding a power struggle between the board and EMO when the two disagree on the executive's performance. Several companies, among them Edison, Advantage, National Heritage Academies, and Chancellor Beacon, have also offered stock options to employees, including teachers.

The contract specifies the EMO's responsibility, if any, to raise student achievement. While many agreements allude to the parties' aspirations for student achievement, only Advantage and SABIS routinely committed to specific gains.

The management agreement also stipulates the EMO's obligations for building, opening, and running the school. In contract schools, the district agrees to provide a suitable facility, while in charter schools a facility must be found. Charter school boards often sought out for-profit EMOs to aid in securing a facility, and how EMOs structured their involvement in real estate had important consequences for the business. Some EMOs' contracts were careful to stipulate that the facility was explicitly the board's responsibility; others committed the EMO to securing a school facility through lease or purchase. Edison, in some charter management contracts, agreed to provide millions of dollars in loans and credit enhancements to assist the board in securing a facility. But many EMO contracts were unclear on who had precisely what responsibility for the school building, and the contract's silence on the largest issue facing the board and the EMO could result in later disagreements. If the facility proved more expensive to secure or develop than anticipated, the board could take the position that these overages should be absorbed by the EMO and not be borne by the school in higher rent costs.

Some EMOs, like Advantage, SABIS, and in some cases Edison, have agreed to fund any deficits the school might incur, up to a specified cap. This feature has been a valuable selling point to clients and aids in revenue recognition, but it creates considerable exposure to the EMO and impairs the school's ability to obtain tax-exempt standing from the IRS. Contracts frequently stipulate the EMO's right to recoup funded deficits in future years from the school.

To protect their investments in schools, EMOs have tried to place strict limits on the client board's right to terminate the contract during its term. Under all contracts, clients can terminate in the event of a material and uncorrected contract violation by the EMO (such as its failure to pay bills). The client's right to terminate for poor academic achievement during the contract's term (before, as the EMOs argued, they could reasonably be expected to post strong results) has varied, however. In some cases, Edison's and Beacon's clients could terminate for the company's failure to make "reasonable progress" toward goals for student achievement as measured by standardized test scores.[46] Clients of SABIS and National Heritage could also terminate for academic performance reasons during the term under certain conditions, but Advantage's generally could not. Edison's largest contract, for its Philadelphia cluster of schools, can be terminated at the district's discretion at any time.[47]

EMOs generally gave themselves an out if the school unexpectedly became a drag on the company's finances. Typically, this took the form of the right to terminate if the per-pupil revenues of the client school materially declined during the term of the contract. Edison could also terminate if the school's board failed to adopt Edison's recommendations "necessary for the implementation of the Edison school design."[48]

KIPP's Contracts

KIPP's trademark license agreements are for one year, but they renew automatically. KIPP agrees to provide services in the areas of community development, operations management, organizational leadership and culture, and academic leadership. It also agrees to "provide the school with access to assistance" in "fundraising, teacher recruitment, public relations, teacher training conferences and KIPP retreats" and assistance with real estate.[49]

The school agrees to adhere to the five pillars; KIPP has the right to undertake periodic formal evaluations of the schools and other actions to assess the quality of the school's academic program and determine if the school is indeed adhering to the pillars. If in KIPP's judgment the school's quality of education is unsatisfactory, KIPP may direct the school to take any actions it deems necessary, including changes to the school's academic program. Ultimately, KIPP may terminate the agreement, and the school forfeits the KIPP brand name. KIPP may also terminate the agreement if the school changes the principal. The school may terminate the agreement at the end of its term, but it is obligated to pay KIPP over time a "termination fee" of $200,000 to cover its costs in training the school's leader and opening the school.[50]

Each of the six EMOs and KIPP committed to parents to provide their children with a superior education. To what educational designs did the organizations turn to make good on their promises? Chapter 3 takes up the question.

3

School Designs

When it came to academic quality, private managers of public schools were quick to offer extravagant promises. Edison's schools would deliver a "world-class education" to their students, at public school spending levels. KIPP's schools would equip students with the "knowledge, skills and character needed to succeed in top-quality high schools, colleges, and the competitive world beyond." Advantage would enable students "to reach the heights of academic achievement."[1]

The audacity of these commitments is all the more striking when we consider that education management organizations opened schools primarily in urban centers, where students arrived performing far below their suburban peers. Test scores show 47 percent of fourth-graders in "central city" schools reading at the "below basic" level, and only 6 percent reading at the "advanced" level.[2] Moreover, the organizations found that charter schools often attract students with a history of academic failure. There is now mounting evidence that children entering charter schools perform, on average, academically below their district school peers—the reverse of the predictions of charter opponents, who warned that charters would "cream" the most able students, concentrating the least capable students in district schools.[3] Contract schools posed similar challenges, as districts were most likely to turn over to private managers schools with a long history of abject academic failure.

At each school, the organizations' executives promised parents, client boards, and regulators that students would outperform their peers in surrounding public schools. What gave education entrepreneurs confidence that they could achieve a level of academic performance that eluded traditional public schools? In short, what would they do differently?

Requirements of the School Design

Each of the education management organizations sought to open a large and potentially unlimited number of schools that would be funded at levels comparable to district schools yet produce superior results. That would require a school design that was efficient, scalable, and sustainable.

The primary requirement of the school design is that it deliver better academic outcomes for no more (and often less) money than district schools would spend. Developing a blueprint for high-efficiency schools seemed at once achievable and daunting. On the one hand, the United States appears to be an inefficient provider of elementary and secondary education—it spends more than nearly every other country, yet student performance is at best mediocre. On the other hand, successive waves of public school reforms and continually increased spending have done little to raise student achievement, and the chasm in performance between white and black teenagers remains.[4]

In the early 1990s, charter school founders set out to create a single high-quality school, frequently in an urban community where the surrounding public schools were the most inadequate. This was a laudable and very difficult undertaking. The challenge for the EMOs was starkly different: proliferation was both integral to their mission and essential to financial survival. Their students would have to learn at an accelerated rate not just at a few locations, but consistently across sites. In the language of venture capitalists, the school design had to be scalable. A single school might benefit from unique ingredients: an extraordinary founder, prodigious fundraising, or fanatically devoted teachers with elite educations. But the six EMOs had to rely on widely available ingredients to achieve success at every site. Typical, if well-chosen, teachers and ordinary levels of financial resources would have to be leveraged by tools, practices, and training that would permit staff, at every location, to perform at a higher level. For this, the EMOs would be accused of opening "cookie-cutter" schools. Some EMO founders not only saw nothing wrong with this, they believed it was their very mission—to make quality broadly available: "If you're going to do something, it has to be replicable," said National Heritage's J. C. Huizenga.[5]

Last, the educational design had to be sustainable. For example, more learning time might boost achievement, but require teachers to work exceptionally long hours. Could an organization induce that level of staff commitment indefinitely?

Levers of Change

At one level, it was axiomatic that parental choice, high expectations of students, and what founders perceived to be the rigor of private management would lead to improved student results. But each organization also placed faith in specific practices—whether their own innovations or established methods—to accelerate learning in each of its locations. Many organizations lengthened the school day and year, as the traditional school schedule was a relic of the agrarian past and more "time on task" would lead to higher achievement. Others placed stock in smaller classes, educational technology, or a particular instructional program. Time, technology, curriculum—each of these can be considered a lever of change employed to varying degrees by the seven organizations. In this chapter, we examine eight such levers—the structure of grades, classes, and instructional groups; the use of time; parental choice; school management; accountability; curriculum and pedagogy; technology;

and professional development. Who sought to innovate in each area, and how? And what evidence is there to indicate that such innovations accelerate student learning?

SCHOOL STRUCTURE

The most fundamental design decisions that the seven organizations confronted concerned the size and structure of their schools. Would they open "boutique" schools, enrolling just a few hundred children, or large schools with as many as a thousand students? Would they operate schools that, from the start, spanned kindergarten through high school, or would they begin with a single grade? Would the school expand to educate its students as they moved up the grades? Just as important was the question of how schools would be structured. Would they be divided into small units, to create intimate communities of students and faculty? Would they boast class sizes smaller than district schools or defy conventional wisdom and embrace classes of thirty or more students? Finally, would students be grouped heterogeneously, or would they be grouped homogenously and taught in small instructional groups?

In tackling these questions, the founders engaged considerations of efficacy, risk, capital requirements, and profitability. Small schools would be easier to site, posing less execution risk. Because the schools could secure rental space (church classrooms or a vacant store) for the first years, construction would be avoided and little or no capital required to get under way. But they would also be much less profitable, so the financial breakeven point would be delayed. A roll-out plan in which schools started small and grew one grade at a time was attractive educationally, but could be difficult to house affordably—paying for unused space would be costly, and moving from one facility to the next could prove impractical and risky. Small instructional groups might have powerful educational benefits, but would drive up staffing costs.

As the founders weighed competing considerations, they also had to take account of their customers' convictions. Two beliefs about what makes for effective schools were ascendant in the 1990s: small schools are better schools, and students learn faster in smaller classes. Choices of size and structure had to engage those beliefs. Yet the imperative of profitability (or breakeven) generally argued for large schools and class sizes.

Grade Levels. As discussed in Chapter 2, most education management organizations gravitated to the grades they saw as the lowest hanging fruit: elementary schools. There, they could post the greatest achievement gains in the least challenging environment. Operating successful high schools, and even middle schools, would require overcoming years of compounded learning deficits. Discipline problems would be greater and more costly to address. And the higher grades would require a broader range of subject offerings as well as more specialized and expensive facilities for athletics, science laboratories, and performing arts.

School Size. The charter schools that the six EMOs opened were large relative to other charters but comparable to district elementary schools. The average enrollment of charter schools in 1999–2000 was 264 and of traditional elementary public schools 443. Initial enrollment for the EMOs' schools was on average 405. In 2002–2003, the average enrollment for the five operating for-profits' schools was 564.

When the school design called for expanding each year by one grade, the school could easily swell over several years to a thousand students in grades K–12. Large by any standard, such schools could nonetheless retain a kind of intimacy, with kindergartners and high schoolers going to school together and only sixty to ninety students to a grade. The SABIS school in Springfield is an example. In 2002–2003, 1,313 students attended from kindergarten through the twelfth grade, with a total of only 241 students in the four high school grades.[6]

Local boards often pressured EMOs to open small schools. Many board members and charter school founders identified with the growing small schools movement, which contrasted the anonymity, disaffection, and lack of focus that often pervade large public schools with the connectedness and intensity of mission that advocates claim for small learning communities. That movement gained force with the decision of the country's largest charitable foundation, the Gates Foundation, to adopt as its primary education initiative "to improve high school and college graduation rates by creating small, focused high schools that help all students achieve."[7]

Whether because of board preferences or the constraints of available real estate, EMOs contemplated opening somewhat smaller schools of approximately 350 students. Most concluded these schools would not be financially viable. Revenues from the smaller number of students could not cover the fixed expenses of administrative staff, specialist teachers, and occupancy costs and such a school could not generate the "site contribution," or surplus at the school site level, to pay management fees. Indeed, Edison developed a rule of thumb that, while schools could start small, the plan had to include growth to at least six hundred students. Of the seven organizations, KIPP operates the smallest schools. Even at maturity, the schools enroll only about 360 students.

Certainly, there are many inspiring examples of small schools—whether charter schools, religious academies, or inner-city independent schools—that outperform large public schools. But is it their small scale that drives their success? Or are other characteristics that correlate with small size, including autonomy, a powerful sense of purpose, and staff commitment, responsible? If so, could these characteristics be replicated in a large, privately managed school?

Smaller Learning Communities. Edison attempted to mitigate the effects of its large schools by dividing them into smaller communities of students and teachers, where a sense of connectedness could more easily develop. Edison creates schools-within-schools, or "academies," each composed of two or three grades. Within each academy, students are grouped into "houses" of 100 to 180 students, each led by four to six teachers. The Primary Academy serves kindergarten through the second grade; the Elementary Academy, grades three through five; the Junior, six through eight; the Senior, grades nine and ten; and the Collegiate, grades eleven and twelve. Edison says the small communities help to ensure that teachers know and develop relationships with their students and that teachers take responsibility for their pupils' success.

Class Size. Of all the structural choices faced by the six EMOs and KIPP, none was more controversial than class size. Throughout the 1990s and continuing today, the American education establishment has pressed for smaller class sizes in public schools, promising achievement gains. The NEA, for example, "supports a class size of 15 students in regular programs and even smaller in programs for students with exceptional needs," and the AFT concurs: "Compelling evidence demonstrates that reducing class size, particularly for younger children, will have a positive effect on student achievement overall and an especially significant impact on the education of poor children."[8] Smaller classes made intuitive sense: teachers, with fewer children to handle, would be able to devote more attention to individual students. The public was persuaded, and reducing class size became the most popular education reform strategy. President Clinton proposed to decrease class size in the early grades to a maximum of eighteen students.[9]

Advocates of small classes cite the Project STAR (student/teacher achievement ratio) experiment conducted in Tennessee in the mid-1980s, which found substantial and lasting gains from classes of thirteen to seventeen students to which kindergarten and first grade students were randomly assigned. In 1996, after California's fourth-graders tied for last place in reading among thirty-nine states participating in the NAEP, the state enacted legislation that gave districts a financial incentive to reduce class sizes in grades K–3 to twenty students.[10] A major study of the class size reduction (CSR) initiative, conducted over four years for the California Department of Education, reported that although parents of children in reduced-size classes had "far higher" levels of satisfaction, researchers found "only limited evidence" linking gains in student achievement to the smaller classes.[11] In fact, urban districts had been damaged by the hiring of thousands of unqualified teachers to staff new classrooms. A "school-level analysis finds no relationship between CSR exposure and student achievement," the report concludes flatly. "For many people, the lack of a clear relationship between CSR and student achievement will be disappointing."[12] The report notes the failure of California to duplicate the gains of the STAR experiment, but also points out that California's goal was a class size of twenty, substantially larger than those studied in STAR.[13]

Later critiques of STAR found that sorting of students within and between schools obscured any causal relationship between class size and achievement effects. Moreover, other studies contradict the STAR findings. In her research on class size and achievement, Harvard economist Caroline Hoxby selected an experimental design that permitted the effects of smaller classes to be examined apart from other factors that may infect explicit experiments like STAR, including the assignment of particular teachers or students to the smaller classes, the "Hawthorne effect" (where individuals temporarily increase their productivity when they are being evaluated), and the existence of incentives to obtain results that might not exist if the policy were broadly enacted. (The schools may perceive that a class size reduction policy would not be enacted if the experiment fails to demonstrate gains.) Examining natural variations in class size—in the range of ten to thirty students per class—in 649 Connecticut elementary schools (where teachers were unaware of the experiment), Hoxby found no statistically significant effect of class size on student achievement.[14] Unlike STAR, actual policies like California's class size reduction arguably contain no repercussions (for example, the withdrawal of funds if the policy had no effect), which might explain why STAR showed gains that the California experiment failed to replicate.

Certainly a look at the performance of school systems internationally lends little support to an American reform strategy based on smaller classes. In a recent analysis of class size and student achievement in eighteen countries (using data from the Third International Mathematics

and Science Study, the largest international study of student performance), Ludger Wössmann and Martin West found little support for
reducing class size. That three of the five highest-performing countries
(Singapore, Korea, and Japan) had average class sizes greater than thirty
students (Korea had more than fifty) might alone give one pause. The
study aimed to look deeper, by examining the relationship between class
size and performance within the countries themselves. There were statistically significant benefits in student performance from smaller classes in
only two countries, Greece and Iceland. In these two nations, average
student performance is low (much lower than Singapore, Korea, and
Japan, despite much smaller classes), and school spending is substantially below the average of countries without class-size effects. Teacher
salaries are also low. From salary and teacher education data, the authors
speculate that these countries' teachers are less skilled and better able to
manage smaller classes than larger ones. They conclude,

> Thus, the evidence on class-size effects presented in this paper suggests
> the interpretation that capable teachers are able to promote student
> learning equally well regardless of class size (at least within the range of
> variation that occurs naturally between grades). In other words, they are
> capable enough to teach well in large classes . . . It may be better policy to
> devote the limited resources available for education to employing more
> capable teachers rather than to reducing class sizes.[15]

Reducing class size is enormously expensive, of course. Smaller classes
require not only more faculty, but also larger facilities. How the six
EMOs and KIPP have responded to the overwhelming popularity of the
class size proposition—while struggling to break even or turn a profit—
varies dramatically. While Chancellor Beacon limits class size to twenty-
five students, KIPP believes its orderly environment permits large classes
(occasionally with as many as forty-five students) to be effective. David
Levin explains, "Class size is not an issue if teachers know how to manage kids."[16]

SABIS chief executive Ralph Bistany would agree, and refuses to pander to what he sees as the American orthodoxy of aiming toward smaller classes and insists on the efficacy of larger classes. "Larger classes," the company asserts, "develop students' talents and offer an enriching diversity of ideas and approaches that contribute to raising academic standards. They also train students to work in large groups, thus preparing them better for the future."[17] Bistany sees it as SABIS's mission to demonstrate that a world-class education can be delivered affordably and scoffs at those who claim thirty children cannot be effectively taught in one classroom. "First, we need to define the word 'class,'" he says. "Every course has a prerequisite—concepts that the course is going to use but not explain. That list of concepts determines who belongs in the class and who doesn't." If the course is German, and one student is fluent and others cannot speak a word of the language, the students obviously should not be taught together, he explains. At SABIS, students in a class have the same background but neither, he hastens to say, "the same ability nor the same knowledge." So formed, it doesn't matter whether the class has ten students or fifty. "In fact, fifty is better," he adds. "We have worked with classes of seventy in countries where it is allowed, and it has worked like a charm." Students have a responsibility to their classmates to pose questions pertinent to the concepts being taught, not material that the class has already mastered. "Anybody who asks a question that is not legitimate is wasting the rest of the class's time," says Bistany.[18]

The often-promised "individual attention" of small-classes is doomed to fail, he says. "In a class of twenty, it means five minutes for every child. And before you can help him, you have to find out what his problem is. That is not teaching. That is a study hall." Conversely, large classes do not impede the progress of the brightest students. A yearlong course might encompass four hundred concepts; usually some one hundred of these are "essential concepts" that all students must master. "The weaker students must know the 'essentials.' The brightest will know 90 percent of the others" by the end of the course, Bistany explained.[19]

Chancellor Beacon's continuing emphasis on smaller classes may resonate with parents, but it is costly and unlikely to pay off in accelerated student learning. SABIS's approach, by contrast, may encounter some initial resistance from parents but seems capable of satisfying the educational model's criterion of efficiency—high performance at affordable cost.

Instructional Groups. As called for by Direct Instruction, Advantage placed elementary students into small, cross-grade instructional groups for the core subjects of reading and math and assigned students to larger, heterogeneous classes for the rest of the day. Students were grouped according to present competency—not "ability"—in the subjects of reading, language, and math, and each group of six to fifteen students (in the lower elementary grades, and as many as twenty-two students in the upper grades) was taught by either a teacher or an instructional assistant. Groupings were frequently revised on the basis of students' performance on assessments embedded in the curriculum.

TIME

When it comes to schools, time on task matters. Not surprisingly, one meta-study found that the amount of time spent learning proved a modest predictor of school achievement.[20] In its 1994 report to Congress, *Prisoners of Time,* the National Commission on Time and Learning wrote, "Time is the missing element in our great national debate about learning and the need for higher standards for all students. Our schools . . . are prisoners of time, captives of the school clock and calendar. We have been asking the impossible of our students—that they learn as much as their foreign peers while spending only half as much time in core academic subjects. The reform movement of the last decade is destined to founder unless it is harnessed to more time for learning."[21] The commission found that "only 41 percent of secondary school time must be spent on core academic subjects," and that "students in other post-industrial democracies received *twice* as much instruction in core academic areas during high school."[22] Despite the report's rhetorical flourish, it had little effect on district schools.

Then—as today—students in traditional public schools spent just six to seven hours in school each school day, for only nine months of the year. While school districts are constrained from adding instructional time—not least because union opposition and cost make extending the school day or year a near impossibility—private organizations were free to reinvent the school schedule. Edison was the first to innovate; the original school design called for adding one hour for K–2 and two hours for grades 3–12 to each day and thirty days to the school year—which, as Edison pointed out, was the equivalent of six years of additional schooling by the end of high school. While that proved impractical, Edison did extend the school day to seven and one-half hours and the school year from 180 to 200 days.[23] As a result, Edison claimed in 1999 that its students spent 28 percent more time in school each year than did students in most public schools.[24] In its contract schools, Edison sought to pay its teachers a stipend for the additional time, but it was not able to secure the union's agreement in all locations. Mosaica and Advantage also lengthened the day and year, but neither more than KIPP.

One of KIPP's five pillars is "More Time." As KIPP explains the philosophy, "There are no shortcuts when it comes to success in academics and life. With an extended school day, week, and year, students have more time in the classroom to acquire the academic knowledge and skills that will prepare them for competitive high schools and colleges, as well as more opportunities to engage in diverse extracurricular experiences."[25] At the KIPP flagship school in the South Bronx, students begin their day at 7:25 and stay until 5:00; students often stay until 6:30 to do their homework. There is also a half-day of instruction on Saturdays and three weeks of summer school. All told, the school provides 67 percent more time than regular schools. New KIPP schools are following suit. When we visited the KIPP Ujima Village Academy in Baltimore during its first year, the principal had to send along home some dozen children who at 6:45 were doing their homework. They did not want to leave.

At least as importantly, the organizations were innovative in their use of available time. The Commission on Time and Learning had decried the amount of time lost to new concerns, such as personal safety, conservation, family life, and AIDS prevention, as well as traditional nonacademic activities like gym, lunch, and homeroom.[26] Edison, Advantage, SABIS, KIPP, and other organizations dramatically increased the amount of time dedicated to academic instruction, and most importantly, to language arts. Advantage's schedule devoted nearly three hours a day to explicit instruction in reading, language arts, and spelling. Edison scheduled two to two-and-a-half hours a day for reading, writing, and language arts. To make way for more academic teaching, some of the organizations cut the time allocated to recess, lunch, and the "specials" of art, music, and physical education. Much less time, too, was given to the "projects" that consume so much time in the typical American elementary school and are frequently of more recreational than educational value.

Chancellor Beacon's Alan Olkes, who at the time oversaw academics, explained, "We are moving away from the regular 'do everything' way of schools. We are clearing the regular day for academic subjects."[27] Under Chancellor Beacon's plan, art and music would be held in the last hour of the day, from 2:30 to 3:30. Rather than employ specialists, the company would offer classroom teachers a modest supplement to teach these enrichment classes; as the classes would be ungraded, teachers would not have to be certified in these subjects to provide instruction.

It is not clear that time reforms are in all cases scalable and sustainable. KIPP experienced manageable turnover at its two original schools, but will it be able to retain teachers across its network given the extraordinarily long hours it demands of them? KIPP teachers tend to be young and idealistic. As the organization grows, will KIPP be able to recruit enough teachers who are willing to make the expected commitment? Edison, too, has experienced some resistance to its longer school day and year. At one charter conversion school, Phillips-Edison Partnership School in Napa, California, half of the teachers left at the end of the school's second year. As a result, staff now interview prospective teachers carefully, to ensure they are committed to working eight-hour days and a longer year. The first year, the school operated for 210 days; the next year it dropped back to 205, then to 190. It now plans to return, as a result of both funding cuts and the strain on teachers, to the standard 180 days. While the Napa school's teachers were highly committed to the school and to Edison, the demanding schedule remained an issue. One Napa teacher attributed to the longer school day and year the annual turnover of as many as one-third of teachers at some Edison schools. "Teachers are exhausted," she claimed.[28] High teacher turnover remains a serious and costly problem for many EMOs.

CHOICE

With few exceptions, the schools operated by the six EMOs and KIPP were schools of choice: parents selected the privately managed school for their children. Even some contract schools were operated as choice schools.

EMO founders, many of whom were businesspeople, naturally found school choice theory seductive. John Chubb and Terry Moe argued that private schools outperform public schools, all things being equal, because the political environment in which public schools must function is less conducive to educational success than is the market.[29] Chubb later described the mechanism by which market forces systematically promote the characteristics of effective schools:

> The competitive pressures of the marketplace, where families can take or leave a school, lead schools to organize in whatever ways are conducive to getting results for families. Intentionally or unintentionally, schools subject to market pressures tend to develop clear missions (parents know what the school stands for), focus on academics (parents want to see their children learn), encourage strong site-based leadership (great schools are headed by principals who take charge of student achievement), and build collaborative faculties (great schools make a team effort). Schools that fail to do these things tend to be weak performers, tend not to be favored by parents, and tend to be weeded out via natural selection over time . . .

These are only central tendencies, to be sure. Markets tolerate a certain number of lousy private schools, and politics produce many exemplary public schools. But to the extent that politics and markets cause schools to tend sharply in different directions, the central tendencies are extremely important.[30]

Choice, proponents argue, fosters commitment by parents and students, and commitment in turn enhances student learning. District schools, buffeted by myriad, conflicting external agendas, have little choice but to try to mollify everyone and offend no one. The result is that they stand for nothing. By contrast, advocates contend, choice schools can stake out strong positions on instruction, student behavior, grade promotion, and many other areas of school policy and culture. They are free to establish high expectations for their students, from arriving to school in uniform in the morning to completing their homework at night. Having freely chosen the school, parents are more likely to commit to its demands on their children and themselves.

Parents may become involved in their child's school when they perceive its mission and ways to be consonant with their own values. National Heritage Academies says that its goal is for every child to be both educated and "virtuous." The proposition resonates with many customers, especially Christian parents. "We wanted an environment that echoed our ways of teaching our children," reads one parent's testimonial on the company's website. "They are taught the same virtues we teach at home."[31] At a focus group of staff and parents at NHA's Paramount Academy in Kalamazoo, Michigan, one mother emphasized that Paramount was not a Christian school. Yet she was glad to be at a school "where everybody doesn't just accept that evolution is fact."[32] Teachers hastened to add that they do not teach creationism; Paramount was a secular school. Indeed, visitors to this and other NHA schools found no evidence to the contrary. NHA's success was in making that parent and others feel comfortable. Her beliefs, while not taught, were respected.

At Paramount, parents built the playground, participate in various committees that provide input to the school, and serve lunch to the children. If they are uncomfortable with a book assigned to their child, they may choose an alternative. The most enthusiastic parents travel as "ambassadors" to communities where the company is opening new schools, promoting NHA to other parents. In lieu of employing "student recruiters," as do other EMOs, NHA pays its parent ambassadors a stipend.

The organizations sought to tap choice dynamics in their client schools. "Choice and Commitment" is one of KIPP's five pillars: "Students, their parents, and the faculty of each KIPP School choose to participate in the program. No one is assigned or forced to attend these schools. Everyone must make and uphold a commitment to the school and to each other to put in the time and effort required to achieve success."[33] Parents, students, and teachers are all required to sign a "Commitment to Excellence Contract" that sets out their responsibilities. Parents agree to ensure their children's attendance during the school year—including summer sessions—and to assist with homework. The contract warns that failure to adhere to the commitments can lead to their child's expulsion. The EMOs similarly sought to couple parents' choice of the school with clear expectations of their role.

The EMOs and KIPP consider parent satisfaction crucial to school success. "Students learn most," Edison declares, "when parents are positively engaged in the school, when teachers are fulfilled by their work in their classrooms, and when students themselves appreciate and enjoy their school experience. Customer satisfaction is not important merely in its own right; it is important because it promotes higher student achievement."[34] Prior to opening a school, Advantage instructed its teachers and staff to view parents in a new light—as customers. Unlike in their children's former schools, dissatisfied parents had the option at any moment to no longer patronize the school. With their child would also go money, and if enough parents left, the school would have to close. Accordingly, parents should be treated with respect and welcomed in the building and classrooms at any time. Many EMOs commission outside firms to survey parents annually, to determine their assessment of the school, the quality of the curriculum, their children's interest in learning, and the quality of their children's teachers and administrators. The results are provided as diagnostic information to school staff to address deficiencies and improve parent satisfaction.

There is evidence that the choice dynamic is benefiting privately managed schools and may be successfully fostering teaching and learning. Edison reported that for the 2003–2004 year, 50 percent of parents who responded gave their child's school an "A" grade, and 33 percent a "B." Edison noted that in similar surveys of public school parents, only 24 percent awarded their child's school an "A."[35] Advantage reported that 65 percent of parents indicated that their children's interest in learning was higher than in their former school, while only 6 percent said it was lower.[36] NHA reports that 95 percent of its parents would recommend their child's school to friends who have school-age children, that 96 percent are "satisfied or very satisfied with their child's academic progress," and that 96 percent agreed that their child's school "delivers on the promise of moral guidance."[37] It should be noted that only some of the parents participated in these surveys; selection bias may influence the results, as satisfied parents may have been more willing to respond. Yet these positive findings are consistent with research on parental satisfaction at charter schools generally; parents overwhelmingly view their child's charter school as better than the child's previous school and report very high levels of satisfaction across a broad range of attributes, from curriculum to discipline.[38]

In staffing their schools, too, the organizations hoped to exploit the dynamics of choice: the charter schools' specific identities would set them apart from others, attract committed teachers, and inspire staff loyalty. While staff resistance often undermined the implementation of controversial programs like Direct Instruction in district schools, Advantage, for example, was free to recruit teachers willing to commit to the program. Some were novice teachers, others veterans disillusioned with progressive designs and seeking something more effective.

In contract settings, the marked cultures of privately managed schools could not so readily be fostered. District school staff are typically chance aggregations of employees with disparate skills and philosophies. In an effort to build a committed faculty, in most district engagements Edison secured the right to an initial interview with all staff at the school, with the understanding that the district would reassign to other schools those staff members whom Edison rejected or who wished to work elsewhere.

MANAGEMENT

The seven organizations placed great stock in the management rights and innovations they exploited in their client schools: a strong chief school executive, a redesigned administrative team, the authority to hire and fire school staff, the absence of teacher tenure, and the freedom to hire capable teachers without regard to certification or seniority. Each significant by itself, where all were in place these conditions would foster a professional culture superior to that of district-operated, unionized public schools.

Like businesses, the EMOs believed their schools needed strong and empowered leaders—for they would be personally accountable for delivering on the school's achievement promises. In the mid-1990s, few urban districts had such expectations of their principals and accorded them little power as managers. If they kept the school in compliance with the law and district policy, the central office left them alone. Many were members of their own administrative union and knew they couldn't be terminated anyway. Beginning in the 1990s, however, the standards movement began to change all of that; principals were expected to turn failing schools around.

As businesspeople, EMO executives appreciated the principal's predicament. In corporations, the chief executive hires and fires staff, controls the organization's budget, and shapes products and services to meet customers' needs and preferences. Absent this authority, how could the CEO be held accountable by the board of directors? To build outstanding schools, principals would have to enjoy the same authority: to recruit, manage, promote, and retain staff members who subscribe to the school's plan and perform to its standards, and to terminate the employment of those who do not.

The EMOs and KIPP expected school leaders to assume responsibility for the hiring and firing of the school's staff, for drafting and adhering to the school's budget, and for implementing the school's instructional programs. In turn, it was made plain that he or she would be held accountable for meeting specific objectives for academic and financial performance. KIPP's pillar the "Power to Lead" underscores the organization's emphasis on empowered principals: "KIPP school leaders . . . have control over their school budget and personnel. They are free to swiftly move dollars or make staffing changes, allowing them maximum effectiveness in helping students learn."[39]

Schools are notoriously "flat" organizations: the school staff, from custodians to teaching assistants to assistant principals, all report (at least nominally) to one person, the principal. Given the union's emphasis on lock-step solidarity, the idea that one teacher would supervise, let alone evaluate, another is apostasy. Yet in business, it is broadly held that a manager's span of control should be limited to a handful of people, because managers cannot effectively supervise, develop, and evaluate a large number of reports. Several of the EMOs reinvented the school management structure, devising alternative leadership structures and reporting lines. Edison, for example, introduced a middle-management level of "academy directors" who oversee clusters of several grades; principals meet regularly with these directors and groom them to become principals in other Edison schools. At each grade, "lead teachers" mentor, but do not supervise, the grade's teachers. SABIS created the position of "academic quality controller" to oversee the school's instructional programs and sophisticated computerized academic management system. And Advantage employed an "assistant director for instruction," whose sole responsibility was oversight of the curriculum's implementation, including the ongoing development of the teaching staff.

In charter schools, EMOs used their discretionary authority to build a cohesive, committed faculty. At Edison's school in Napa, California, teachers developed a checklist of twenty-eight "expectations and beliefs" against which teaching candidates were scrutinized. "If you truly believe the statements written below match your vision and you understand the high expectations we hold, then please consider joining our staff," it read. Candidates must "believe that students schoolwide, and thus their own class, on average, can improve 5 percentile points on the state standardized (SAT-9) tests each year." They must "meet daily with colleagues for 45 minutes for professional development, collaboration, problem solving, lesson planning, and sharing strategies. This is a foundation upon which our design is built and an essential part of the success of our school." Candidates must also commit to teach the school's core structured programs for math and reading, Everyday Math and Success for All, "as prescribed."[40] Such careful attention to "fit" in hiring, routine in the private sector, is rare in district schools.

Under some charter statutes, a specified percentage of the faculty could be drawn from outside the teaching field; the EMOs and KIPP were free to hire teachers highly educated in their content area who lacked conventional certification. EMOs also instituted differentiated staffing models. Job descriptions could be tailored to the particular requirements of the school's instructional programs, and candidates with particular interests, skills, and traits could be hired for specific roles. Jobs that demanded more or for which there were scarce candidates could pay more. And entirely new jobs could be created outside the rigid definitions of collective bargaining agreements. Advantage, for instance, hired and trained "instructional assistants" to teach under the direct supervision of classroom teachers. These assistants were similar to "teachers' aides" or paraprofessionals in conventional schools, in that they needed only a high school diploma. Such paraprofessionals are, in district settings, typically restricted to assisting the classroom teacher with small tasks and classroom management, or to working with individual students.

Teachers unions vigorously oppose linking such personnel decisions as compensation, promotions, and transfers to performance. For that matter, as Terry Moe has noted, they resist measuring teacher quality at all, whether through meaningful evaluations or measures of how much students are learning. Any policy that would cause teachers to compete with one another, as do private-sector professionals, is opposed, because it might cause teachers to have divergent interests.[41] Reg Weaver, president of the NEA, argued in June 2004 that "proposals to pay some teachers more than others do nothing to motivate all teachers and simply create a competitive environment, in contrast to efforts that foster teamwork among teachers and achieve the goal of a qualified teacher in every classroom."[42]

Most EMOs instituted detailed performance evaluations and merit pay. At Advantage, principals shaped their schools' incentive compensation programs, whereby teachers could earn both bonuses and annual salary increases. Awards were based primarily on students' academic performance (30 percent), parent and student satisfaction (20 percent), and classroom and behavior management (20 percent). Parent and student surveys were conducted annually, and both the assistant director for instruction and the school director made regular classroom observations. At KIPP schools, teachers make 15 to 20 percent more than teachers in surrounding districts, for working a longer school day and year. In addition, a privately funded program awards $10,000 to one exceptional teacher at each school annually.[43]

The EMOs and KIPP are free to fire underperforming staff, subject only to the constraints that govern private-sector employment. In districts, terminating an underperforming teacher can take years, a scandalous amount of the principal's time, and tens of thousands of dollars in legal and other expenses. Understandably, most principals do not attempt it. Knowing the practical impossibility of letting a poor performer go, most districts employ cursory performance evaluations; principals award satisfactory reviews year after year to poorly performing staff because there is no reason to do otherwise, and wrestling with the union brings no benefit. In Boston, over a ten-year period, the only teachers in a staff of 4,300 who were terminated were three or four convicted child molesters; approximately thirty "turkey" teachers (in the words of the personnel director) were rotated through the schools with bureaucratic precision, so that no school was disproportionately burdened with the district's worst instructors.[44] Still today, the NEA opposes streamlining the dismissal of incompetent teachers: "Proposals to make it easier to fire teachers do nothing to address the challenges schools face in attracting qualified teachers to take their place."[45]

In the many states where charter laws freed EMOs from the constraints of tenure and the districts' union contracts, they did not hesitate to use these special powers to improve school quality. Teachers were hired on one-year contracts and could be terminated at any time for their failure to perform. EMOs terminated, after progressive discipline, teachers who failed to perform to their standards, sometimes mid-year. Alan Olkes, former superintendent of Dade County schools and now senior vice president, human resources and school services, at Chancellor Beacon Academies, put it bluntly: "One of our key advantages is that we can hire and fire people."[46]

When a teacher was let go, colleagues often agreed with the decision and welcomed the accountability of the privately managed school. At an informal focus group of teachers from Chancellor Beacon's charter school in Weston, Florida, one teacher observed, "All of us could be making more money. But we've chosen to make a difference. In order to keep your job, you have to work harder. But no one really feels that we are at risk of being fired."[47] No one in the focus group disagreed. At Advantage's charter school in Rocky Mount, North Carolina, teachers were promised discerning evaluations and salary increases tied to individual performance. At the end of the school's challenging first year, the principal awarded identical raises to all the teachers. Everyone had worked hard, he explained. But the move backfired. Teachers were resentful that the few who performed poorly were treated as well as those who performed at a higher level. A new organizational culture of merit had taken hold, and, unwittingly, the principal had violated it in his nod to the traditional egalitarian culture.

Given the potency of the management advantages, four of the seven organizations—SABIS, Advantage, NHA, and Mosaica—operated only charter schools and did so only in jurisdictions that provided them and their principals with the requisite authority. Mosaica was awarded a district school in Chester-Upland (near Philadelphia) but never operated it; it submitted a proposal in Philadelphia proper, but it was denied. The other three have operated contracts and charters. Nearly all of Chancellor Beacon's schools were charters; the company did operate for one year five district schools under contract in Philadelphia. KIPP's schools were primarily charters, but it also operated contract schools where a structure could be negotiated with the district that would meet the requirements of the pillars, including the "Power to Lead." During the 2003–2004 school year, KIPP operated twenty-six charters and six contract schools. Only Edison aggressively sought and won contracts with school districts, which by 2002 constituted about two-thirds of the company's schools. Edison identifies its contract market as the 7,400 school districts in the United States that enroll more than a thousand students; together, these districts have annual operating budgets in excess of $300 billion.[48] Of these, Edison has focused on the eight hundred school districts with more than ten thousand students that together have an annual budget of $160 billion. In the 2001–2002 school year, Edison operated eighty-three contract schools enrolling fifty thousand students, and only fifty charter schools, with 24,000 students.[49] Of the contract schools, sixteen were contract charters.

In light of the constraints in contract schools, Edison negotiated with school districts for three prerogatives—to write its own job descriptions, to compensate according to its own system, and to insulate its schools from the shackles of tenure. Edison's design team envisioned a differentiated staffing model of resident teachers, junior teachers, senior teachers, and lead teachers, each with distinct responsibilities and compensation.

Edison sought the authority to "send back" poorly performing teachers to the district, which would place them in another school. In practice, these prerogatives were often chipped away in negotiations with the union, and Edison had to compromise. Edison says that it "got most of these most of the time."[50]

How important did the management advantages of charter schools prove to implementing the program? On the record, Edison says it makes no difference. Privately, its executives make clear that the strongest implementations are in charter schools. "You have to be able to hire and fire, or you're just playing around the edges," one remarked. Seniority provisions in collective bargaining agreements are plainly incompatible with the stability essential to turning around underperforming schools, yet never once has Edison persuaded a school district to scrap them. When one teacher exercises her right to "bump" out a teacher in another school with less seniority, the domino effect wreaks havoc on school faculties and disrupts the teamwork essential to long-term success. Consider Edison's experience in Flint, Michigan. Facing enormous deficits, the school district closed ten schools and laid off four hundred staff over a two-year period.[51] Edison, which managed three schools for the district, saw turnover of 40 percent of its school staff in 2003; more senior teachers, some who didn't want to work in the school, displaced staff trained in Edison's design.

In some contract schools, Edison's "ability to execute is compromised, no question," said an Edison senior executive. Edison is "moving into an existing culture" where some staff members resist change. There can be less commitment to "professional responsibility" than in charters; staff may be "holding their heads high even when working nine to five and no one is learning." Worse, in many such schools, according to another Edison staff member, a small number of "edu-terrorists" tightly allied with the union work relentlessly to undermine the program's implementation. Nonetheless, the strongest principals can overcome these constraints: "Good culture builders can make natural selection work for them. They are very adept at counseling [staff]."[52]

Because KIPP Bronx is a conversion charter school, its teachers remain protected, at least in principle, by the district's contract with the teachers union. But principal and KIPP National cofounder Levin deployed his force of personality and the school's uncompromising expectations to induce underperforming teachers to leave the school. Like other maverick principals, he also exploited emergency and temporary certification provisions in hiring qualified, energetic teachers who lack formal credentials.[53]

Partially offsetting the advantages of charters, Edison found, was the "inherent chaos and instability" of a charter school's first year. Every system needs to be built from scratch; operational problems are a major distraction and shift the focus away from instructional concerns. Charters also attract many teachers who "want to see if they want to work in education" and who are not committed to the school for the long term. In charter schools, "you need to overcome all of that before you can focus on education. But once you do, the advantages of charters are quite powerful."[54]

ACCOUNTABILITY

Public schools and their staffs are remarkably resilient to external pressures. Formal expectations from outside the school have little effect on teachers' and administrators' conceptions of their students and what they are capable of, and of what good teaching and learning looks like. As Charles Abelmann and Richard Elmore explain, "Schools develop their own internal normative structures that are relatively immune to external influences, and . . . teaching is an essentially isolated occupation in which teachers are left largely to their own devices in deciding important issues of what and how to teach."[55]

Indeed, even the standards movement was depicted by some educators as an affront to teacher professionalism. Susan Ohanian claims, "The proliferation of standards documents results in the deskilling and the deprofessionalization of teachers. How else are teachers to feel except helpless in the face of being told to *deliver* a curriculum that is invented by external authorities?" To Ohanian, standards are a tool of corporate hegemony and undermine good teaching. "It is crucial that we ignore the content standards and continue to nurture the children in our care."[56]

There is evidence of continued deep opposition to external accountability systems in traditional schools. A recent survey of teachers in grades four and eight found a chasm between teachers' attitudes and the intentions of reformers. Repudiating the central premise of the standards movement, nearly three-quarters of teachers subscribe to the philosophy of most schools of education that the purpose of schools is to assist students in "learning how to learn" rather than acquiring specific knowledge and skills. Only one in seven agree that educators' central responsibility is to "teach students specific information and skills." Only 25 percent of fourth-grade teachers (and 28 percent of eighth-grade teachers) place primary emphasis when evaluating student work on whether students supply the right answer or correct information. One-third of fourth-grade teachers and 29 percent of eighth-grade teachers do not agree that "a teacher's role is primarily to help students learn the things that your state or community has decided students should know."[57]

Abelmann and Elmore judge it unlikely that schools operating in what he calls the "default" mode will be

> capable of responding to strong, obtrusive external accountability systems in ways that lead to systematic, deliberate improvement of instruction and student learning ... Where virtually all decisions about accountability are decisions made by individual teachers, based on their individual conceptions of what they and their students can do, it seems unlikely that these decisions will somehow aggregate into overall improvement for the school.[58]

EMOs, run as businesses, set out to build strong internal accountability systems. As described earlier in the chapter, they made use of rewards, interventions, and sanctions—whether merit pay, end-of-year bonuses, promotion, one-year contracts, intensive professional develop-ment, progressive discipline, and, ultimately, termination—to hold ac-countable for their performance all school staff, from instructional assistants to school principals. The EMOs and KIPP all sought to hire staff who were committed to students' attainment of knowledge and skills as specified by state standards; in other respects, the organizations' approaches to accountability have varied.

One approach for bridging external standards and teacher practice is to model exemplary instructional methods and hold teachers account-able for deploying them. At Advantage, the school's accountability for meeting external standards was linked to teachers' employing specific instructional practices. Advantage rigorously monitored the implemen-tation of the Direct Instruction system, used for the critical elementary subjects of reading, language arts, and math. The company sought to persuade teachers that if they made exacting use of Direct Instruction (as well as other prescribed practices, including a student behavior sys-tem), the students in their classrooms would make remarkable—and highly predictable—gains. Because the curriculum was broken into individual lessons, weekly "lesson progress" could be monitored in every classroom, and teachers who were progressing below expected rates could be provided additional training and assistance. The full senior management team each week reviewed average lesson progress rates (strong predictors of year-end achievement on state tests) along with twenty-seven other measures of program implementation, known as the "Academic Quality Indicators." Frequent review of these data, the team believed, would enable the company to hold the school and its staff responsible for implementation of the complete school design. Quar-terly, the school directors met at the corporate office and formally pre-sented to their peers their academic and financial results.

Edison brought external state assessments into the building with its proprietary "Benchmarks" system. Each teacher brings her students to the school's Benchmarks computer lab each month. There, they respond to a series of on-screen questions delivered through a web browser; the questions are drawn from a central database of thousands of test items that precisely emulate the types of problems found on the state's criterion-referenced tests and on nationally normed tests. The Benchmarks system then compiles detailed reports for each teacher that show how far his or her class and each student has progressed toward meeting the state's grade and subject learning objectives. Chris Whittle likens the system to a pilot's navigation equipment. Previously, teachers had to fly blind. In September, they would take off toward their destination: the state's goals for student learning. During their yearlong flight, they received no information. Were they on course? Benchmarks tells teachers each month where they are and what course corrections to make—what concepts and skills their students know, and which need more work.

SABIS's "point" system and computerized "Academic Monitoring System" comprise another innovative approach to internal accountability. The system tracks precisely what has been learned on a weekly basis. Students complete brief paper tests on the curriculum that are then scanned into the school's central computer. The system provides simple but detailed reports to teachers on their students' grasp of recently taught material and pinpoints any remaining learning gaps.

EMOs are beginning to create professional cultures where staff accept—even welcome—that the school is "run like a business." A popular principal who opened one of Chancellor Beacon's successful schools was nonetheless fired early in her second year, in part because of chronic problems with special education compliance. Wade Dyke, then president of Chancellor, explained, "The line organization must be disciplined." In a focus group conducted for this study with members of the school's faculty, teachers seemed shaken by the loss of their leader. But all acknowledged the company's right to act. As one said, "If someone isn't doing what they should, [Chancellor] can do something about it." Another teacher added, "It gives you the sense that no one is indispensable—but that makes for a better staff."[59]

Teachers nonetheless disapproved of how the termination was handled. The principal was fired, as one teacher put it, in a "very corporate manner" and some teachers resented the absence of "closure." The assistant principal was also terminated from one day to the next: "There was a note and she was gone." While teachers are prepared to embrace corporate norms of accountability, EMOs must attend to the team culture of schools. In the best start-up schools, teachers work together in a tightly knit and collaborative community, putting in long hours out of commitment to the school's cause. An emotional bond connects teachers to their leader. If the leader must be wrested from the team, the EMO should be prepared to lead the staff through the change. If not, as at the Chancellor school, teachers will become alienated from the company. As one teacher said, "My heart is not ready to be slapped again."

CURRICULUM AND PEDAGOGY

At the center of every education management organization's strategy for outperforming district schools are critical choices about curricula and pedagogy—what will be taught, for how long, and by what methods. To these choices, EMO founders brought the culture and training of business. They recoiled from the chaos of public schooling, with its absence of crisp goals in stark priority and its lack of succinct plans for their attainment. Schools cannot succeed, they believed, if they continue to be charged with an ever-expanding set of peripheral tasks—smoking prevention, anger management, nutritional education, conflict management, and responsible sexuality. Schools could not continue to take on ever more, while failing to teach large numbers of students to read. While public school administrators were squeamish about defining and measuring academic success, EMOs embraced clear measures. Bluntly they asked, What are we trying to do? What works, and how do we know it? The questions were long overdue.

Educational Standards. The public imagines that the problems in America's schools stem from underfunding, a lack of discipline, or the insufficient preparedness of teachers, but assumes that the intellectual goals of schools are clear. In truth, in the 1990s there was no such clarity. "We know there is no national curriculum, but we assumed, quite reasonably, that agreement had been reached in the district or school regarding what shall be taught to children at each grade level," said E. D. Hirsch, founder of the nonprofit Core Knowledge Foundation. "The idea that there exists a coherent plan for teaching content within the local district, or even within the individual school, has been a gravely misleading myth."[60]

The lack of clear objectives for schooling was no accident. "Progressive" educators, inspired by the eighteenth-century Romantic conceptions of Jean-Jacques Rousseau, argue that children should be allowed to flourish naturally. As Hirsch has so eloquently described, much of what is wrong with progressivism in educational practice today sounds right. It sounds right that students should learn subjects whenever possible through "inquiry" rather then "rote learning" or "memorization." Will not students better retain knowledge that they have themselves "discovered"? It sounds right that students should "learn at their own pace." Should not teaching be "child-centered" and "developmentally appropriate," and embrace "individual learning styles"?[61] But in all these cases, and countless others, intuition proves a poor guide. The research evidence points away from these seductive propositions, especially for socioeconomically disadvantaged children, who arrive at school without a rich vocabulary and strong social and learning skills. Critics of educational progressivism, like Hirsch, have argued that the very term is a cruel misnomer. In truth, he argues, these approaches are more aptly considered educational conservatism, because however well intended, their effects on the children of the poor have been to deny them the essential tool of social mobility—the ability to communicate through reading and writing—and to keep them in a "natural" state of ignorance.[62]

When the Edison Project was announced in 1992, the state standards movement was in its infancy. Against the curricular chaos of American elementary and middle schools, Edison's publication in 1994 of four lucid volumes setting out standards for each academy was deeply innovative for its time. To its credit, Edison avoided the polarizing terminology and intellectual caricature that marked the education debate. It appropriately emphasized the teaching of reading, mindful of the broad failure of urban schools to teach basic skills, but was careful to stress its commitment to the aims of progressive education.

To understand Edison's achievement in developing a coherent, cumulative curriculum for the early grades, it is important to distinguish between high-quality standards, on the one hand, and "curriculum guides" and low-quality standards, on the other. Thick curriculum guides may appear rigorous, but their very length assures that teachers will omit some topics. The next grade's teachers cannot be certain what students know. Ill-conceived "conceptual" standards, intended to move beyond "rote learning," are frequently so vague as not to prescribe a specific and coherent instructional sequence. As Hirsch argues, a broad objective like "understand interactions of matter and energy" is too general to guide teachers in deciding what in particular to teach; it is the same as mandating that students "understand physics, chemistry, and biology."[63]

In the years following, other EMOs purported to have curriculum standards like Edison, but none were their equal. Edison had taken the vital first step in curricular innovation: deciding what its students should learn and be able to do, and when. Eventually, though, each state's own standards largely displaced Edison's—not always to the benefit of its quality of curriculum.

What shall we teach? Standards could provide the answer for every school, grade, and class. But what programs and practices would be deployed to attain them? Chancellor Beacon equipped its client schools with detailed standards by grade and subject but often left it to the schools to define their curriculum and select commercial instructional programs. KIPP, too, did not impose curricula or instructional programs, but its schools shared a common conception of good teaching practice that was codified in instructional guidelines for teachers. SABIS required its teachers to adhere to the point-and-prefect system that the organization had refined over decades. Advantage and Edison, by contrast, broke ranks with the education establishment and its ideology of teacher autonomy: its directives were unhesitatingly prescriptive, insisting that their teachers adopt practices and protocols deemed effective for students.

Research Evidence and Curricular Fads. Critics like Doug Carnine charge that education is an "immature profession." Carnine cites the work of Theodore M. Porter to argue that in such professions, expertise resides in the subjective judgment of the individual professional, and the client's trust in the enterprise is based on trust in that individual. By contrast, a mature profession like medicine "is characterized by a shift from judgments of individual experts to judgments constrained by quantified data that can be inspected by a broad audience, less emphasis on personal trust and more on objectivity, and a greater role for standardized measures and procedures informed by scientific investigations that use control groups."[64] Carnine faults so-called education experts for routinely making subjective decisions and ignoring research evidence when it doesn't meet their own ideological preferences.

Consider the largest educational experiment to date in the United States, Project Follow Through. In 1967, as part of his sweeping plan to move the nation "toward the Great Society," President Lyndon Johnson proposed legislation to "follow through" on the success of the popular Head Start program, which early research had found led to gains that receded in elementary school. The study, which in its first ten years encompassed 75,000 students at a cost of $500 million, aimed to identify which educational designs had the power to raise the academic performance of students from low-income families.[65] Students attending schools in economically disadvantaged communities might score at the 20th percentile on nationally normed tests. Could an education program elevate their performance to that of students nationally—the 50th percentile—and in turn break the cycle of intergenerational poverty?

Descriptions of many of the models from the project's 1977 evaluation report are eerily similar to programs in fashion today, nearly three decades later. For example, the EDC Open Education model "believes children learn at individual rates and in individual ways, and teachers should adapt approaches to encourage individual progress and responsibility in learning." The goals of the Responsive Education Model were "for learners to develop problem solving abilities, healthy self-concepts, and culturally pluralistic attitudes and behaviors."[66] Direct Instruction, by contrast, provided its schools a "technology" of teaching, with a specific operational design and polished lessons, including systematic instruction in phonics. With its constant parlay of questions and answers, Direct Instruction is highly interactive. Unison responses, provoked by signals from the teacher, ensure that all students are engaged. Correct answers are reinforced, and students' errors, which often go unacknowledged by teachers in other settings, are systematically corrected. Contrary to many accounts of the design, the program's emphasis is on the development of generalizable skills and intelligence and not on rote memorization of pieces of information. Although parent committees at more schools selected it than selected any other model, Direct Instruction contradicted the prevailing thinking in education, and mainstream educators expected very little to come of it.[67]

Cohorts of students were tracked from either kindergarten or the first grade through the third grade. Abt Associates of Cambridge, Massachusetts, compared the performance of 9,000 Follow Through students to that of 6,500 students attending a control group of nonparticipating schools. When the first results were reported, the education establishment was stunned. Not only did most of the education models fail to improve student performance significantly—let alone reach the 50th percentile—but many models resulted in substantial performance *declines* compared to control group students. Students educated in five of the models scored lower on all three outcomes categories—basic skills, problem solving or cognition, and affective development as reflected in students' self-concept and self-esteem—than would have been predicted in the absence of such "compensatory" education (in the control group schools). Only Direct Instruction (DI) and one other behaviorist model significantly elevated student performance. DI, which focused on basic skills, showed the greatest effects on all three categories of student growth. In reading, math, and language, students performed at or near national norms.[68] (Interestingly, Abt found great variability of effects from DI and other models both within and across sites. The finding presaged the vexing problem that later plagued EMOs that deployed structured programs: the wide range of academic performance across schools undermined their claims of success.) Abt's conclusion was plain: "The Direct Instruction Model is the only program which consistently produces substantial progress."[69]

Curiously, five of six designs aimed specifically at developing cognition or elevating self-esteem showed on average no effect or a negative effect on all three measurement categories. Yet students in Direct Instruction schools posted strong scores in affective measures, suggesting that academic competence promotes self-esteem, and not the reverse.[70]

The federal government moved quickly to cement the results in policy. The San Diego school system, for example, was required to choose from among the two successful Follow Through models, Direct Instruction and another behaviorist approach.[71] But the debate was far from over. In a series of journal articles, academics sought to discount the Follow Through findings. Even before the final report from Abt was released, the Ford Foundation sponsored an influential critique led by Ernest House, which appeared in the *Harvard Educational Review*. "The ultimate question posed in the [Abt] evaluation," House complained, "was 'Which model works best?' rather than such other questions as 'What makes the models work?' or 'How can one make the models work better?'"[72]

In a later report, Gene Glass and Gregory Camilli questioned the very value of experimental science in educational practice: "The deficiencies of quantitative, experimental evaluation approaches are so thorough and irreparable as to disqualify their use," they asserted. Moreover, "Test results must not be the sole or even primary indicators of success." Teaching is an art that must not be subordinated to the "technology of mass testing," which homogenizes varied program aspirations. "There is a great range of values . . . beyond what is now measurable. I am referring to such things as dignity, respect and love. And the thought that these are multivariate outcome variables that will yield their secrets to the scientific coaxing of factor analysis is a thought hopelessly held prisoner by the shackles of logical positivism."[73]

According to this view, a "bought-audience" of scholars would read the reports "when they are paid to do so," but teachers, the Follow Through reports' proper audience, would have no use for them: "Teachers do not heed the statistical findings of experiments when deciding how best to educate children," they wrote approvingly. "They decide such matters on the basis of complicated public and private understandings, beliefs, motives, and wishes. They have right and good reasons so to decide, and neither that right nor those reasons are changed one whit by appeals to the need for accountability for public funds or the rationality of science."[74]

Faced with the discomfiting findings of Follow Through, the federal Office of Education (the predecessor to the Department of Education) punted by recommending that all of the Follow Through models be disseminated to school districts, even those that contributed to a decline in student performance relative to the control group schools. Absurdly, programs that showed no evidence of improving student performance were rated as "exemplary and effective," and additional funds were directed to programs that had not been validated.[75] As is so often the case in American education, a priori ideas about how best to teach children had trumped incontrovertible evidence of what actually works in the classroom.

Project Follow Through is not the only large-scale study of instructional programs to have had little influence on district practice. More than two decades after the Follow Through findings, researchers at the American Institutes for Research found that only three of twenty-four schoolwide reform models they studied could demonstrate "strong evidence of positive effects on student achievement"; Direct Instruction was one and Success for All was another.[76] Even though the research was sponsored in part by the NEA, it failed to galvanize broad support for Direct Instruction.

When Direct Instruction is implemented rigorously, the results can be astonishing. DI enthusiasts often cite the Wesley Elementary School in Houston, Texas. Located in one of the poorest neighborhoods in Houston, 99 percent of Wesley's students are black or Hispanic, and 94 percent are eligible for free or reduced-price lunch. Yet for years, the school has performed in the top tier of Texas schools. Wesley adopted the DI curriculum in 1975, and by the early 1980s students were performing on average at the 80th percentile or higher in reading on nationally normed standardized tests. Students in comparison schools performed 40 or more percentile rank points lower. In later years, Wesley reported that some classes tested as much as three years above grade level.[77] While the success of the Wesley implementation is anecdotal, the results of Direct Instruction in large-scale studies such as Project Follow Through and the American Institutes for Research study are not. While used widely in special education, DI was in use in 1998 in only some 150 schools nationally for students in regular classes.

No topic in education has received more rigorous study than how best to teach children reading. The instructional approach called "whole language" dominated the reading wars in the late 1980s and triumphed with California's 1987 adoption of whole language guidelines for teaching English. Yet California students placed near the bottom of the states on the 1994 NAEP; 69 percent of black students and 78 percent of Hispanic students scored "below basic" in reading. By the mid-1990s, a consensus was emerging among researchers that the most successful reading programs employed systematic and explicit instruction in phonics. The California Board of Education adopted a curriculum that mandated both phonics instruction and literature in the early elementary grades; as the board of education for the most populous state in the nation, its influence on the textbook industry ensured that other jurisdictions followed suit.

At the request of Congress, the National Reading Panel was formed in 1998 and spent two years reviewing thousands of reading instruction programs, dating back as far as thirty years ago. The panel released its findings in 2000: the essential components of successful programs were phonemic awareness, phonics, vocabulary development, reading fluency (including oral reading skills), and reading comprehension strategies. These, in turn, formed the basis of the Reading First component of the No Child Left Behind Act. Armed with the panel's findings, the federal government was emboldened to link federal funds to the adoption of reading programs proven effective through research.

As the reading wars raged on, educators also struggled to agree on how to teach children math. The shock over the Sputnik launch in 1957 had led to the development of the "new math," with its emphasis on math concepts over computational skills (or what are now called "math facts"). By the late 1960s, every major math textbook was aligned with the new methods.

But the victory of the Progressives was short-lived, and during subsequent decades students and teachers experienced repeated swings of the curricular pendulum. In many schools where the new math had been implemented, test scores fell, and the 1973 book, *Why Johnny Can't Add: The Failure of the New Math,* helped incite a backlash among both parents and teachers.[78] In the 1980s, the "back-to-basics" movement stressed computational skills. Yet American students continued to lag behind their international peers on math performance. By the late 1980s, educators were increasingly decrying the drill and tedium of American math instruction.

In 1989, the National Council of Teachers of Mathematics (NCTM) released standards that emphasized "learning with understanding" and real-world applications of mathematical competencies. Individual students would not learn just one procedure for solving a mathematical problem, but rather would deploy representations and algorithms of their choice. To encourage critical thinking, NCTM favored math games, manipulatives, and activities led by students; memorization was derided.

The use of calculators was encouraged from the earliest grades, and computation was deemphasized. So were correct answers. Exposed to an ambitious, rich curriculum, students would emerge as confident problem-solvers, able to articulate orally and in writing their mathematical ideas and solutions.[79]

Like the "new math" of the 1960s, the NCTM standards were enormously influential. Before long, every major textbook publisher purported to embrace them. As states undertook the development of education standards in the early 1990s, most based their math requirements on NCTM's recommendations. But after California embraced the NCTM standards in 1992, test scores plummeted.

The NCTM standards—and their progeny of state standards and commercial math instructional programs—drew harsh criticism. Lawrence Braden and Ralph Raimi wrote in their critique of state math standards developed in the 1990s, "Learning to calculate, especially with fractions and decimals, is more than 'getting the answer'; it is an exercise in reason and the nature of our number system."[80] The standards erred, critics argued, by overemphasizing the practical application of mathematics to "real world" problems. Rather than promote an engagement in math, this approach risks depriving students of an appreciation of the formal beauty of math, the intellectual satisfactions of its internal rigor and universality. NCTM urged the practice of "spiraling," whereby topics are introduced at one point and then revisited at greater depth in subsequent years. Critics warned that spiraling risks boring students with needless repetition, introducing topics that cannot be meaningfully grasped without precursor knowledge, and crowding out important content.

Just as Edison was launching its first schools in 1995, a rebellion against NCTM's methods was gaining strength. An organization of parents in California, Mathematically Correct, decried the use of calculators in the early grades and the failure to teach basic skills, like addition, subtraction, multiplication, and division.[81] The "new-new math," as critics called it, devalued "right answers" in a discipline whose beauty and power is its capacity for certainty. In 1999, California adopted standards that set out topics that students should learn at each grade level—while leaving teachers free to choose a pedagogical approach.[82] The NCTM released a revised standards document in 2000, *Principles and Standards for School Mathematics,* which placed somewhat greater emphasis on computational fluency. Even these standards did not signal agreement among researchers. While by the turn of the century a consensus was emerging on the best way to teach children reading, math educators remained polarized.[83]

Instructional Programs. As entrepreneurs from the private sector, the EMOs' founders could be expected to be crassly empirical in their selection of instructional programs. What works? they asked. Few decisions were more important than how the schools would teach the core elementary subjects of reading and math. Establishing strong basic skills in the early grades would benefit all students and dramatically reduce referrals to special education programs. The strengthening of regular education and the consequent contraction of special education was an opportunity for reducing school-level costs.

In their choices of instructional programs for reading and language arts, the EMOs displayed a degree of pedagogic unity: explicit phonics instruction was essential to get children from disadvantaged families reading in the early grades. Advantage adopted Direct Instruction for reading, language, and math in all its schools, from kindergarten through the sixth grade. Concepts and problem-solving strategies were taught explicitly in small groups by both teachers and teaching assistants, who were trained to deliver the carefully sequenced lessons in a dynamic, fast-moving style. Urban parents, Advantage expected, would embrace Direct Instruction—for its order and purposefulness, its focus on developing strong basic skills, and its correction of student mistakes. Even its interactive call-and-response style, while disconcerting to visitors accustomed to the modern classroom, would be familiar from a central institution in urban African-American communities, the church.

In Direct Instruction there is genius—and a fatal flaw. For all its exquisite sensitivity to how children learn, DI seems deaf to the psychology of the adults on which its implementation relies. A quarter-century ago, a paper critical of DI asked, "Are teachers treated as intelligent human beings or merely as means toward technically prescribed ends and instruments of someone else's will?"[84] Still today, creator Siegfried Engelmann says, "We don't give a damn what the teacher thinks, what the teacher feels. On the teachers' own time they can hate it. We don't care, as long as they do it."[85] But holding teachers' feet to the fire to "do" DI is destined to fail. Why not engage educators as respected professionals, as collaborators in Engelmann's grand purpose?

Advantage acknowledged the frequent criticism that DI equips children with reading skills but does not expose them to enough authentic stories and novels in their entirety. NAEP results linked reading proficiency with the amount of reading assigned for students to do at home, suggesting that reading skills improve with independent reading practice. The NAEP data also revealed sharply higher reading proficiency when teachers allowed students to choose their own reading material. In light of these findings, Advantage began to supplement DI with the Accelerated Reader (AR) program. In AR, students choose from a wide range of books and demonstrate when they have finished each title by responding to a computer-based quiz. Advantage also implemented Junior Great Books, which introduces students to an array of classic stories, fairy tales, and legends. The teacher poses thought-provoking questions and guides the students in interpreting the text. The program aims to develop children's ability to communicate and think critically about complicated ideas, weigh the merits of opposing arguments, and modify their initial thoughts in light of evidence from the text. But Advantage erred by giving little priority to these supplemental programs. Junior Great Books was accorded too little time in the schedule to develop children's capacity to formulate, discuss, and defend their opinions—even though schools reported that the program was a hit with students and teachers. As for Accelerated Reader, which requires computers, software, an extensive library, and the training of staff, its implementation had barely begun in most schools when the company was sold to Mosaica.

It was a mistake, too, to use DI in the later elementary grades and the beginning of middle school. After all, Project Follow Through had left off with the third grade. At Advantage's school in Worcester, Massachusetts, the school's founder announced at a board meeting that her child had said he wouldn't stay in the school if he were "snapped at" in sixth grade, referring to how many teachers signal to their students for a unison response. Some delivery features of DI—the constant use of signals and unison responses—can seem demeaning to older children and thus simply aren't appropriate, even if students are performing academically below grade level.

Advantage struggled to train its staff in multiple, complex instructional programs. But teachers can only absorb so much in a given period, and the company could afford only so many costly professional development specialists. There were additional obstacles to implementing the supplemental designs. Since most children arrived at school with poor skills, the corporate education department was understandably protective of time allotted to basic instruction in reading, language, and math. The implementation of all instructional programs was overseen by curriculum specialists who were Direct Instruction trainers by background. Not only did some lack experience in the supplemental programs, but Junior Great Books' "shared inquiry" and "critical thinking" were fighting words to some educators steeped in the rigid culture of DI. Decades of hostility from mainstream educators had put DI's champions on the defensive: any suggestion that DI is incomplete or imperfect was an invitation to an argument.

Other EMOs also looked to reading programs that had a persuasive record of success. For reading and language instruction in the elementary grades, Edison selected Success for All (SFA), a comprehensive, structured program developed by Robert Slavin, Nancy Madden, and their colleagues at Johns Hopkins University. As of 2003, the Success for All Foundation reported SFA, with its two components "Roots" and

"Wings," to be in about 1,500 schools in forty-eight states, reaching more than 1 million children. Encompassing elementary reading, writing, and language arts, SFA is described by the foundation as a schoolwide restructuring program, because it prescribes not just instructional materials but also grouping practices, scheduling, the roles and duties of staff members, and professional development activities. The goal is to ensure that "all teachers are using effective instructional practices with every child every day" by deploying a common set of procedures, materials, assessments, and understandings in every classroom.[86]

SFA emphasizes early and intensive intervention, prevention of later academic problems, and tutoring for students who are struggling. Children are grouped homogeneously across grades according to their reading level (not to be confused with "tracking" or ability grouping), which is redetermined every eight weeks. Because students in a group are all at one instructional level, teachers can move at a rapid pace. Cooperative learning, where students work in small teams, helps develop academic skills; teambuilding activities develop social skills. In one prominent use of cooperative learning, students in kindergarten and first grade read "shared stories" to a partner, with the goal of teaching "decoding and comprehension in the context of meaningful, engaging stories."[87] By intervening early and preventing reading failure, SFA aims to diminish referrals to special education.

Success for All and Open Court, used by National Heritage Academies, adhere to many of the principles of instruction shown to be most effective in Project Follow Through: direct teaching, with specified objectives, clear explanations, correction of wrong responses, and high levels of "time on task." Both Open Court and Success for All supplement explicit, teacher-led instruction with other teaching methods—for example, cooperative learning—that their developers believe foster the range of capacities they seek to develop in children. Open Court, unlike Direct Instruction, does not make use of homogeneous instructional groups or share DI's emphasis on learning to mastery. Undoubtedly, Success for All and Open Court were more palatable choices to school districts and many charter school boards than was Direct Instruction, which was often perceived as a fringe and controversial program. Edison Schools would have been hard-pressed to sell DI to its large urban school districts, whose curriculum officers typically adhere to mainstream education philosophies.

SABIS deploys the British "Letterland" program for reading instruction in kindergarten and first grade. (In the later grades, SABIS uses its own reading curriculum.) In Letterland, reading, writing, and spelling are taught through pictogram characters, each of which animates a letter. Activities children enjoy—rhyme, art, drama, song, and movement—teach letter knowledge. For example, children sing about how letters are formed.[88] The use of Letterland reflects SABIS's admirable spirit that learning should be joyful. But students at SABIS's model Springfield school perform only slightly better through the early elementary grades than students in the Springfield district schools; only in the middle and high school grades (where accelerating student learning is regarded as more difficult) do the SABIS students race ahead.[89] Teachers at several SABIS schools wondered whether other research-proven programs might be more effective for their students, most of whom come from low-income families and arrive at school with developmental deficits. It may be that SABIS has forgone an opportunity to make still greater gains in the early grades, gains that might compound as children move toward high school graduation.

Chancellor Beacon Academies does not prescribe instructional materials to its client schools; teachers and school staff select their own materials. The company does provide teachers with detailed subject and grade curriculum standards, which teachers have found valuable for developing lesson plans. The company also provides schools with analysis of measures of achievement. But is this enough? As their five-year managers contracts with Chancellor Beacon were ending, two important clients of the company in New York State were weighing dropping Chancellor Beacon at the end of their current contracts, in part because they perceive too little value for the fees that they pay. The schools have been left on their own to manage instruction, from choosing curricula to training and coaching teaching staff. The schools' authorizer, the Charter School Institute of SUNY, agrees. In recommending that the charter of one of the schools, the Central New York Charter School for Math and Science, not be renewed, the institute cites Chancellor's limited involvement in academics.[90]

For elementary math instruction, Edison chose Everyday Math, a program developed by the University of Chicago School Mathematics Project. Everyday Math emphasizes student construction of knowledge, student selection of a single algorithm from several presented (rather than explicit instruction in one method), the application of math to real-world problems, and the use of spiraling (repeated encounters with a concept over several grade levels).

Critics of Everyday Math echo the charges levied against the NCTM standards. Matthew Clavel, a New York City public school teacher from Teach for America, says he covertly ignored much of the program when he found his fourth-grade students not only failing to learn math but also losing interest in the subject: "The curriculum's failure was undeniable," he wrote in a 2003 attack in *City Journal*. "Not one of my students knew his or her times tables, and few had mastered even the most basic operations; knowledge of multiplication and division was abysmal." He dismisses cooperative learning as a pedagogic fad that in inner-city classrooms could lead to a loss of control in the classroom. In his view, teaching a variety of algorithms for basic operations like addition without practicing any particular one does not enhance students' understanding; it creates confusion. He decried the program's emphasis on "critical thinking skills" over the mastery of facts. "Thinking can't take flight unless you do know some basic facts—and nowhere is this more the case than in math. If you really want your students to engage in 'higher-order thinking' in math, get them to master basic operations like their times tables first . . . Mastering fundamentals through practice can lift a child's confidence to do harder work."[91]

It is a testament to Edison's program implementation—its system of professional development, its staff culture of collaboration and problem-solving, and its behavior model—that in the math classes visited in Edison's schools for this research, the failures that Clavel describes were not observed. Classes were orderly, and we saw children collaborating on solving math problems. When a cooperative learning group arrived at a solution, students signaled that they were done without disrupting other groups that required more time. Students in the elementary grades seemed comfortable with unknowns, an algebraic concept, in a seeming vindication of Everyday Math's design. The program's embrace of multiple algorithms for simple operations was harder to assess. When students were observed being taught a new skill, teachers presented several methods; the presentation was confusing. To Edison's credit, the company was supportive when some schools chose to supplement the program with instruction in "math facts."[92] Edison reports academic gains that suggest Everyday Math is accelerating student learning.[93] While significant, these gains do not tell us whether another instructional program might work better.

Some EMOs, along with independent schools and home-schooling parents, have turned to an unorthodox program called Saxon Math. National Heritage, which enrolls many students who might otherwise be home-schooled, early on adopted Saxon Math for all grades. The program is the brainchild of education maverick John Saxon, a former Air Force pilot. After his retirement in 1970 at age forty-seven, he taught algebra at a community college in Oklahoma, where he was struck by his students' lack of understanding and retention of math fundamentals. Urged on by his students, he developed an algebra textbook that he later adapted for use in high schools. Over time, Saxon developed math programs for kindergarten through high school, including texts for calculus.[94]

Rather than encourage "child-developed strategies" for solving problems, Saxon presents concepts and procedures (like long division) explicitly. Topics are introduced in easily understood pieces; all previously taught material is reviewed daily. Testing is frequent and cumulative, so students receive immediate feedback and errors are corrected before they become ingrained. The goal throughout is to "automate" precursor skills, so that the mind is free to consider concepts on a higher and more abstract level.

Advantage chose Saxon Math for students performing at grade level in the upper elementary grades and higher and implemented in the elementary grades DI's math program, Connecting Math Concepts (CMC), which is philosophically similar to the Saxon program. In both programs, concepts and algorithms are presented explicitly by the teacher, introduced in a carefully crafted sequence, and taught to mastery, with the goal of reaching "automaticity." Both afford abundant practice and review. But CMC is still more structured than Saxon. Like all DI titles, CMC furnishes teachers with a polished script that has been refined and tested with students by the program's authors so that it reliably leads to understanding. Also unlike Saxon, CMC is designed to be taught to small groups of students who are at the same level of proficiency. Advantage claimed strong gains in math performance on national tests from its implementation of CMC, although student performance on state tests was compromised by CMC's idiosyncratic terminology and its sequencing, which often failed to align with state standards. The company was slow in adjusting the curriculum and providing supplemental lessons to fill these gaps.

Mosaica used Mathematics Explorations and Applications, which according to SRA, the publisher, "encourages students to look at math not as a cumbersome school subject but as a powerful and enjoyable tool for making the most of life."[95] SABIS employed its own math curriculum.

TECHNOLOGY

When Edison was launched, the one setting that continued to defy technological transformation was the classroom. The "killer application" for schools—the equivalent of word processing, spreadsheets, and databases in the office—remained to be invented, and no one could persuasively claim to have demonstrated how computers could be deployed to boost student achievement. Education management organizations were eager to make technology part of their claim to innovation. Ideally, technology would make teaching and learning more efficient. Regardless, technology was inherently exciting, and deploying it aggressively would set their schools apart from hidebound school districts. More than any other EMO, Edison invested in technology and promoted its role in client schools. From the start, "technology for an information age" was one of Edison's "ten fundamentals." In 1994, the company declared, "We intend to spark a technological revolution in education and demonstrate the equity, access, and power that technology offers students and teachers alike."[96] "State-of-the-art" technology would enhance productivity, efficiency, creative expression, and access to information, Edison claimed. In what quickly became a signature promise for the company, families were provided with a personal computer for students to use at home. In the classroom, every teacher had a telephone—an innovation for the time—and a laptop computer. Years before Internet use was pervasive, Edison's network linked classrooms, homes, and the corporate office.

The cornerstone of Edison's original technology plan was "The Common," a virtual meeting place for the Edison community of students, parents, and teachers. There, children could download homework assignments and hand them in electronically, and parents could review grade books and e-mail their children's teachers. Teachers could take attendance, select curricula, and communicate with colleagues and parents. By allowing students to continue working at home, Edison hoped the system would further extend the school day, and by providing parents with access to their children's teachers, increase their involvement in schooling. Edison designed the Common before Internet tools made such virtual communities commonplace and their functions, like web-delivered databases, easy to develop. By the late 1990s, the Common's capabilities had become broadly available to schools through web-based commercial software for school management.

As a marketing tool, the promise of free computers in every home was a strong lure for the disadvantaged districts that Edison targeted. Before

Edison opened its schools, it hired a national pollster to conduct focus groups of parents to gauge their reactions to school design elements; the pervasive use of technology, including computers in every home, received the highest ratings.[97] Certainly Edison parents, many of whom were low income and could ill-afford a computer, were enticed by the gift to enroll. The offer helped the company win the contracts that drove Edison's rapid growth. But it also provided fodder for Edison's many critics, who derided it as a cynical "chicken in every pot" gesture, a successor to Channel One's bargain of free video technology to schools that committed to play its mix of programs and commercials. Its appeal confirmed critics' worst suspicions about business's commercial exploitation of public schools.

In any event, the promise of free computers became increasingly difficult to keep. All the EMOs discovered how expensive it was to maintain computers, servers, and software applications in their schools, but Edison's challenge was an order of magnitude greater. Most EMOs installed two to four computers in every classroom, plus a laptop for each staff member. A consultant or a full-time staff member was needed to keep them working and to train teachers, many of whom were not yet fully computer literate. In addition, Edison had to maintain hundreds of computers in students' homes and attempt to recover them when they left for other schools. Another problem was the computers' rapid obsolescence. Within a few years, equipment was out-of-date, and parents pressed Edison to replace it. Edison was already spending a great deal on computers—by one estimate, $500 per student annually, versus $100 per student for the average public school.[98] With few educational returns on its dramatic investment, Edison abandoned providing computers to families in 2001. The costs of technology, according to Whittle, were "close to the entire losses of the company."[99]

The wave of EMOs that followed Edison in the mid-1990s faced a different marketplace. America Online popularized e-mail in the home, and the number of websites was exploding. Policymakers feared a "digital divide" would separate those who had access to computers and the

Internet and those who did not, including minorities and the poor.[100]
These concerns spurred a frantic drive to wire public schools to the
Internet and bring computers to the classroom. The federal E-rate program, launched in 1998, granted up to $2.25 billion in subsidies annually
to schools and libraries for Internet technology.[101] District schools and
EMOs alike were pressed to report how many computers were in each
classroom and the ratio of computers to students. Never mind that there
was little clarity over the purpose of this extraordinarily costly campaign. Was it to expose students to technology, instruct them in the use
of office applications like Microsoft's Word, or teach them how to find
information on the web? Or would the technology actually be used to
educate children?

EMOs felt obliged not only to keep up with the rush to place hardware
in classrooms but, as private-sector innovators, to outpace the public
sector, which lagged in the application of information technology.
EMOs spent heavily on personal computers, wiring, servers, and much-
touted high-speed connections to the Internet. Yet research for this book
found that in many privately managed schools, the computers in each
classroom sat turned off and gathering dust.

Today, there remains little evidence that indiscriminate investment in
computers for schools results in academic gains. In a study of the E-rate
program in California, University of Chicago researchers found no evidence that the investment in technology had any measurable effect on
student achievement, as indicated by performance on the Stanford
Achievement Test.[102] Even Edison, with its well-funded and carefully
crafted technology program, could point to little return in academic
achievement. In 1999, when Edison was flush with cash from its initial
public offering, it made a $10 million strategic investment in APEX
Online Learning, a maker of distance learning products. At huge
expense, Edison and APEX built three prototype "ed labs," where forty-
five students at a time could learn in a high-technology, multimedia
module. In the labs, designed by an architect in collaboration with a
lighting designer and graphic artists, lighting could be controlled to

direct attention and set a mood. One Edison fifth-grade teacher became a believer: "I can have discipline problems in math class but when they walk in here, it's totally different," he said. "When they're working at their pods, it's so soothing, you can just feel it in the air. They know [that] when that lighting comes on, it's time to settle down and get the work done."[103] But the capital expense of each lab and the content development costs proved prohibitive for schools, and Edison dropped the project. "We had big hopes for technology," John Chubb said. "But by and large it didn't pan out. It proved largely irrelevant for our core mission."[104]

The harnessing of technology to refashion teaching and learning eluded the EMOs. But in the quest to increase productivity, several deployed computers to manage rather than deliver instruction, an innovation in public schooling. SABIS's Academic Monitoring System runs on a sophisticated Oracle database in each school. The system produces weekly reports on students' progress. At a glance, the teacher can see which "points" are firmly understood, and which need to be reinforced. Aggregate reports tell the school's administrators how each classroom or grade is progressing toward mastering the academic standards for the year.

Edison began development of its Benchmark Assessment System, or "Benchmarks," in 1999. Chris Whittle had noted how Federal Express knows where every one of its packages is at every moment; is there a way, he asked John Chubb, that we could know where each of our students is academically in progressing toward year-end academic standards? Edison officials understand that in most schools, a question like "How is the third grade doing?" provokes a meaningless conversation. Benchmarks provides teachers with specific information on their students' progress toward the state's year-end expectations and suggests instructional remedies for areas of identified weakness. The system infuses the conversation with information and brings Edison closer to its vision of continuous improvement for its schools, where teachers and administrators mine instructional data to collaborate in improving their practice. "It's a phenomenal system, and teachers love it," the technology director for Edison's school in Napa, California, said. "Benchmarks has been an accurate predictor of student achievement."[105] Edison established its Tungsten division to sell Benchmarks as a stand-alone product to school districts in the burgeoning market for "formative assessment."

PROFESSIONAL DEVELOPMENT AND COMMUNITY

It is often said that compared to private industry, school districts spend little on staff development. In truth, large school districts spend tens of millions of dollars each year on professional development over which they have no influence: under union contracts, millions of dollars are embedded in the teachers' salary table. After rising quickly to the last "step" of automatic annual increases, teachers can increase their salaries only by obtaining course credits and higher degrees, usually from schools of education (changing "lanes"). The teachers' contract creates an incentive to obtain credits for courses that are of little value in improving the school's academic performance, because they cover dubious educational theories rather than practical skills for improving classroom teaching. What districts spend directly on professional development programs is rarely aligned with curriculum, assessment, and instruction. "Workshops" and one-time interventions usually reflect pedagogic fads that have little to do with a core instructional strategy. Yet the need to improve teachers' skills has never been greater. Comprehensive school models, like Success for All, have the most potential for raising student achievement but require close oversight and intensive, sustained training of school staff. Because few districts make this commitment, results often fall short of the programs' potential.

The weakness of professional development in district schools stems from a broader failure. As Richard Elmore has noted, teaching lacks universal standards of good practice. Teachers' decisions about what to teach and how are considered inviolable, and the normative environment of schools insists that the mystery of the teaching process be respected. As Elmore explains, it is held that such domain knowledge "cannot be clearly translated into reproducible behaviors, it requires a high degree of individual judgment, and it is not susceptible to reliable external evaluation."[106] This normative environment, Elmore contends, "is a direct result of an institutional structure that is deliberately and calculatedly incompetent at influencing its core functions."[107] School districts rarely assert a particular view of effective practice, because to do so would violate the teaching profession's norm of teacher autonomy.

Instead, superintendents focus on everything but instruction, including construction campaigns, wiring schools for computers, and modest management reforms like "school-based management." In the rare case that they do tackle instruction (with a structured program across many schools, for example), the initiative is unlikely to survive the churn of chief executives that plagues big-city schools. One study found average turnover among superintendents in urban systems to be 2.3 years.[108] Each incoming superintendent distances himself from the initiatives of his predecessor and announces some, likely ephemeral, reform gesture of his own. Teachers greet these announcements with understandable cynicism. Implementing a comprehensive instructional program that truly changes teaching practice requires years of relentless attention—by some estimates five to ten years—and steady commitment thereafter.[109]

Yet some of the most powerful superintendents in long-troubled school districts are beginning to manage instruction in their schools, fueled by the external pressures of state accountability systems and NCLB. Paul Vallas in Philadelphia and Joel Klein in New York, for example, have intervened aggressively in their lowest-performing schools, imposing specific instructional programs and providing abundant training to staff. Vallas, unlike Klein, also benefited from the infusion of competition into the district from Edison and other private providers.

EMOs once again had a distinct advantage over district schools. They could select an instructional model, invest heavily in staff development aligned with the model, and assiduously coordinate instruction. At least in their charter schools, free of the political instability of district school board elections and transient superintendents, they could sustain their commitment to the instructional design for years, continually improving its implementation and the supports they provide to client schools. Henry Levin notes that district schools typically schedule only three or four days of professional development a year and rarely evaluate the results. Levin contrasts this with the sustained investment in staff made by for-profit operators: "In my view, this is an important difference between the two sectors, since strong and cohesive professional development sessions with subsequent mentoring and assessment is one of the most promising methods for heightening school effectiveness."[110]

In 1994, before it opened its first schools, Edison set forth its professional development credo: "We believe it is an ongoing activity, one that must be site-based and intensive. Above all, our professional development program is aligned with our program of curriculum, instruction, and assessment. What we teach teachers is grounded in what they need to teach their students . . . We give teachers time and resources to explore their craft and field, and organize them in ways that enhance their ability to learn from one another."[111] Edison's teachers receive several weeks of training in the Edison school design beginning in the summer and through their first year. Many schools have stipended subject specialists and a full-time reading coordinator. Edison corporate staff provide additional training on site and assist staff with the implementation of Success for All, Everyday Math, and other programs. A regional "achievement vice president" oversees academic implementation for a cluster of schools. In this structure, technical guidance to Edison's teachers is strong and consistent.

Edison aims for two periods a day of professional development time, the first for teachers to use as they like, whether to plan lessons or further their own study, and the second to meet with their colleagues. In the daily team meetings, teachers develop recommendations to present to school leaders, collaborate to solve problems, and request additional professional development to address problem spots in Edison's program. The team model promotes the buy-in of staff to the program and the socialization of new teachers in the Edison design. The company's professional development structure, its career ladder, and extensive use of assessment data send a clear message to teachers: They are respected, part of a professional community, and collectively engaged in the school's and Edison's mission of continuous instructional improvement. The academy and house structure creates the opportunity for collaboration: "We have the power in houses to innovate and implement," said a teacher at a focus group at the Montebello Elementary School in Baltimore. "Teachers are treated as professionals."[112]

With an education model even more prescriptive than Edison's, Advantage knew that its successful implementation required an unusual commitment to teacher training and instructional management. Advantage also provided new teachers with extensive training in the school's instructional programs before the school opened. At each school a full-time professional development coordinator (PDC; later termed assistant director for instruction) oversaw instruction and coached, trained, and monitored the faculty. Each curriculum implementation specialist (CIS) worked with two schools, spending five days a month at each site and meeting weekly by phone with the school's leadership team to review lesson progress rates, mastery levels, instructional groupings, and other facets of implementation. In an unusual coaching model and a powerful rebuke to what two researchers call the "prevailing norms that maintain practice as an autonomous sphere of private discretion," the PDC and the CIS were a frequent presence in teachers' classrooms, suggesting improvements, interacting with students, and even stopping the lesson to model instruction.[113]

For their many similarities, there were key differences between Edison's and Advantage's professional development approaches. Advantage's program arose from the Direct Instruction culture, with its emphasis on the exacting implementation of polished instructional protocols. When teachers witnessed the power of the curriculum to propel their students forward, the company believed, they would become not only converts to DI but also committed to the school and company. Many teachers did become enthusiasts. Yet the Advantage corporate office struggled with the desire of school directors and teachers to exercise their own judgment and make ill-advised changes to the model. Perhaps inevitably, DI's disempowering staff culture infected Advantage's own. The corporate office conveyed that it was the repository of expertise; the task of field staff was to implement its directives and aspire to acquiring gradually its know-how. Little time was taken to explain the "whys" behind the school design and the directives to schools. Unconvinced of the design's merits, school directors could not effectively advocate it to their staff. Edison, by contrast, experienced less tension between school-level decision-making and its school design because the company had a genuine interest in placing responsibility for implementation of the school design with school staff.

An EMO's control over instruction need not come at the expense of teacher commitment and professional community. A recent study examined the degree of professional community in six charter schools operated by three for-profit EMOs.[114] At first the results seem paradoxical. The EMO that was the most prescriptive in its instructional design exhibited the highest level of professional community, including clarity of mission and purpose, collaboration, collective focus on academics, reflective dialogue about teaching, and what the authors termed "deprivatized practice," where teachers observe one another's teaching and gain constructive feedback from colleagues. The EMO emphasized teacher communication and built in daily opportunities for teacher collaboration and instructional problem-solving as core components of its model. The authors conclude, "It is *possible* for external organizations to provide the kinds of supports and relationships that can aid in the development of professional community, despite the natural tension between school-based autonomy as a support for professional community and external control."[115]

When Edison proposed to manage an underperforming elementary school in Napa, California, teachers had to agree to the conversion. Some were opposed. When they returned from Edison's training, however, they were all converts. "It was very, very exciting," one teacher recalled. "Oh my gosh! I have every book I need, every support. Way more than I ever had." Implementing the entirely new curriculum at the school was exhausting, but teachers could sense the power of the component programs. "It was very difficult to come to a school where it is very structured," a teacher said of her first year. "I came from a school where I got to make everything up. But I had no idea what my kids were learning." "There is lots of staff development," another explained. Today, everyone on staff is using the same instructional approach and a classroom management system they together developed. As a faculty, they are united in their expectations of themselves and their students.[116]

The EMOs did not hesitate to create normative environments for their students, with consistent consequences for misbehavior and explicit instruction in character, habits, and values. They understood the power of school culture—the subject of the next chapter—to accelerate learning by fundamentally altering students' perceptions of themselves and their futures.

4

School Culture

In many of the urban communities where the seven organizations ventured, they found the public schools chaotic, unruly, and not infrequently dangerous. Teachers struggle merely to maintain order, and the peer culture derogates academic achievement. Students who show an affinity for school may be teased and harassed.[1] The organizations knew that if they were to outperform the district's schools academically, their first task was to forge an effective school culture—not just in their flagship schools, but in every school they subsequently opened. Students and staff would have to feel safe. Teaching and learning could not be sacrificed to disruptive students. Academic achievement would have to be valued above all else.

At each site, the immediate task was to create an orderly environment, for few things would erode precious goodwill faster than the perception of widespread behavior problems. Such a disciplined environment would be the first sign to parents that they had made the right decision by enrolling their children. Yet the more subtle task would remain of building a culture that fostered study and academic attainment.

School Culture and Achievement

By the early 1990s, decades of well-intentioned but harmful school reforms had taken their toll. While the merits of educational progressivism in affluent suburban settings can be debated, progressive education in its more extreme forms, together with the students' rights movement, plainly undermined urban schools that served impoverished children.[2] Rather than mold the character of their students, public schools have concerned themselves with students' emotional lives and their social and ethnic identities. The schools' permissive social contracts sought to accommodate students' wishes, while teachers aimed to befriend students and provide a kind of family to them. For fear of driving students away or violating their legal rights, schools hesitated to place demands on them or enforce strong codes of discipline. Almost any behavior that was not excessively disruptive was tolerated. In many inner-city high schools, expectations for achievement were minimal. Students were permitted to languish in school, while outside they faced a world of consequences for which they had no preparation. Lacking both skills and a work ethic, they were destined to be left behind in the workplace.[3]

Catholic schools, inner-city academies, and special purpose public schools were an inspiration to the organizations' founders; these schools often created a culture of high expectations, abundant structure, and predictable consequences, in stark contrast to the diffidence and lassitude of many district schools. Following their lead, the EMOs and KIPP would create a safe and orderly environment, for learning could not coexist with fear or teaching with chaos.

Consistent Consequences

In many district schools, students receive mixed messages about what behavior is acceptable and what is not. A committed teacher who holds students to a high standard is easily undermined by another teacher who is permissive, or by a principal who fails to back her up when she sends a student to the office to be disciplined. When one child is reprimanded for a behavior that has no consequences for another, children sense that punishment is meted out capriciously, and resentment and alienation follow.

Research on student behavior finds that punishment often fails to work because it is inconsistent, delayed, or too severe.[4] The organizations codified what behaviors were expected and prescribed systems of progressive sanctions for misbehavior, including making appropriate restitution. Severe misbehavior could lead to suspension or expulsion. All developed a "code of conduct" or equivalent document; many required parents to acknowledge with their signature the school rules and expectations. Merely publishing such a code accomplished little. Implementing it throughout the school required that the staff be thoroughly trained in the system and that the school's leadership implement it exactingly.

Behavior Models

As important as predictable and immediate consequences are to establishing order, it is only the first step toward building a positive school culture. The next step is to recognize and promote good behavior. Many inexperienced teachers, facing a room of unruly students, fall quickly into the trap of attempting to control student behavior through a stream of reprimands—don't do this, and stop doing that. Many students behave inappropriately as a means of attracting attention, having learned early on that misbehavior will generate a response. Generally, when ten children are together and nine are behaving appropriately, the one whose behavior falls short of expectations will draw the adult's attention. This approach frequently engenders more misbehavior. The classroom becomes more chaotic, not less, and instruction is continually disrupted by the teacher's increasingly shrill admonishments.

The Leadership Learning Partners' Charter School in Philadelphia, managed by Mosaica, demonstrated this failed approach at behavior management, even though the school was already in its third year of operation at the time of the observation. In a first-grade class, a teacher attempted to guide students in counting the days on the calendar, but the children were out of control. "Zip it!" she cried. "Stop Talking! Quiet! Park it!" she demanded, all to no avail.[5]

Recognizing the futility of merely correcting negative behavior, some EMOs sought to provide teachers with explicit training in classroom management techniques. National Heritage's first school in New York, the Rochester Leadership Academy Charter School, was strategically critical to the company. Housed in an old downtown building, it was the company's very public first step into a large and unfamiliar market. Eighty-seven percent of the school's students were enrolled in the federal free or reduced-price lunch program, and 93 percent were black. As in many large charter schools serving disadvantaged students, getting a hold on student behavior initially overwhelmed school staff. Teachers, nearly all of whom were new to teaching, were in tears, children threw books across the classroom, and the atmosphere was poisoned with racial slurs. Students reacted to instructions with defiance. One-third of the school's teachers did not return the following fall.[6] To bring order to the school, the principal, Frances Barr, instituted in the second year a rigid "assertive discipline" system. But Barr's office was always full of students thrown out of class by the frustrated faculty. In the fall of the third year, disorder had given way to a disturbing rigor. Teachers, primarily white women in their twenties, issued canned instructions: "Feet on floor. Hands on desk. Mouth closed. Eyes forward." The atmosphere was robotic and chilling.[7]

The school's new approach to discipline was neither primarily negative (threatening punishment) nor positive (praising good behavior), but rather directive. Every opening for misbehavior had been sealed off by breaking down each activity into minute actions: when and how students walked, how they held their hands, even when they took up their pencils. Although teachers were pleased with the progress from the first year, there were many unhappy-looking children, few lighthearted interactions between students and adults, and continuing residual disruptions. Many students weren't paying attention. If one child was haltingly reading aloud, the others weren't looking at the text, but fidgeting.[8] The school's behavior system is relentless and "effective," but unlikely to build the kind of joyful engagement in learning that the school needs to succeed. The teachers seem to fear that if they loosen their grip for but a moment and be themselves, chaos will return.

For Advantage, behavior was a learned response, and misbehavior an instructional opportunity.[9] With the primary focus of the program on positive reinforcement, the company trained teachers how to encourage appropriate behavior and promote the development of good habits. They were instructed to maintain a four-to-one ratio of sincerely acknowledging good conduct to correcting misbehavior. Positive interactions were to include greeting and talking to students, making eye contact, smiling, and overtly praising students when it was deserved and could be offered in a spontaneous, genuine way. Faculty and staff regularly praised students "caught" doing the right thing.

Advantage systematized its practices through the "Green Team" plan, which it insisted be used in every classroom by every teacher. A pocket wall chart had a slot for each student. All students began with a green card, and the color of the card was changed for each progressive violation of classroom rules. Consequences for misbehavior, such as loss of recess time, were the same in every classroom. Advantage's primarily minority parents welcomed the company's approach to character development and discipline. In a 2000 survey, Advantage parents gave their highest marks to the character education curriculum: 90 percent rated it as excellent or good. The discipline policy, too, received high marks from parents: 84 percent of parents rated it as excellent or good.[10]

KIPP's token economy in its Washington, D.C., school serves much the same function as Advantage's Green Team. Students maintain a personal account; "funds" are awarded or charged by teachers for good deeds or violations and can be redeemed at the school for prizes. Such mechanical behavior systems are highly effective in bringing order to often chaotic urban classrooms and in gaining educational traction in a new school. But they can quickly become formulaic and artificial. They best serve as scaffolding for the construction of a permanent and self-sustaining culture.

Making the Transition to a Culture of Academic Excellence

Advantage's *Code of Civility: A Blueprint for Living and Learning* was intended to be at the heart of a scalable culture of academic excellence; the *Code* identified ten virtues that drove the character education curriculum. The document was to be a "blueprint for the creation of a specific environment and culture."[11] To affirm their commitment to the *Code*, parents, students, and the school's director signed a short compact. Each month, a different virtue was emphasized: responsibility, perseverance, respect, kindness, truth, citizenship, courage, self-discipline, fairness, and "true friendship." Teachers drew on literature and history to illustrate these positive character traits. Students were expected to practice what they were taught in the classroom by modeling ethical behavior.

Advantage succeeded in creating a consistent culture across its sites because the line management structure monitored the implementation of the character education curriculum and its didactic teachings of "virtues," like every other part of the school design's implementation. But, while conducive to on-task behavior, the resulting culture had an unfortunate severity—a hardly surprising result, considering both the choice of virtues and the cloying artificiality of children and adults attempting to model them on command. In addition, other qualities that are vital both to children's development and their success in later life were neglected, like curiosity, discovery, invention, and wonder.

Advantage's culture was in some ways similar to Edison's, on which it was modeled.[12] Edison schools state their objectives in codes of conduct, ask parents to sign a compact, and teach a monthly virtue. But there are notable differences. Edison's virtues include "wisdom," "compassion," and "hope." And whereas Advantage's virtues introduced children to constraint (even the strangely qualified "true friendship" discourages friendships based on "fun" in favor of those based on "virtue"), Edison's evoke the aspirations and idealism of universal education.[13] At schools where the Edison design has taken hold, students are strikingly on task. Particularly impressive is the speed of transitions between activities, a common problem area in schools; rapid transitions make more time available for teaching and learning. Children of all ages worked well together in small groups, a skill developed through the school's core curriculum, Success for All, with its frequent and effective use of cooperative learning.

The organizations SABIS and KIPP, however, truly stand out for their school cultures' success in inducing good behavior and in altering students' perceptions of themselves and their futures.

SABIS's objective is to enroll students in college. At the SABIS International Charter School in Springfield, Massachusetts, not only are students on average outperforming students in the district in math and language arts, but also 100 percent of seniors over the last three years were accepted to institutions of higher learning.[14] Student commitment to academic learning is palpable. In classrooms throughout the school, students are engaged, and there is a tone of mutual respect and academic purposefulness. In elementary classes, often nearly all hands shoot up when a teacher asks a question, with some students struggling, in their excitement, not to blurt out the answer. In high school classes, the tone is one of sincerity and calm; students are engaged in learning, with none of the acting out or alienation typical of urban high schools.[15]

This culture is in part the fruit of SABIS's efficient educational program, which leads many students to taste academic success who might otherwise have begun the spiral toward failure. But the culture is shaped at least as much by what the company calls the Student Life program. Supported by a full-time adult administrator, Student Life is a student organization whose mission is to "improve and uphold the standard of life for the students in the school, which is a miniature society of its own."[16]

Students are awarded positive points for performing tasks that contribute to the smooth operation of the school, including helping other students with academics, preparing a course for the student activity period, or helping to manage classrooms and hallways. Students serve as prefects in both the Student Life organization and the classroom. In the early grades, student prefects assist the teacher by passing out materials, collecting papers, and other classroom tasks, all of which speed transitions between activities and increase time on task. Selected for their proficiency in an academic area, prefects in the later grades extend the instructional reach of the classroom teacher through the point and prefect system of instruction. At the start of class, the concept or skill to be taught—the "point"—is identified on the board. After the point is directly taught by the teacher, students perform a quick written activity that assesses their comprehension. The prefects bring their written work to the teacher to check. If their answers are correct, the material was presented properly by the teacher, and the prefects then fan out to other students. They check for mastery and, in an effective use of cooperative learning, clarify any confusion. Only when the point is mastered by all does the teacher move on to the next point. All this happens rapidly and seamlessly. The deployment of students, from the earliest grades, as helpers, teachers, and leaders sets a tone in the classroom of cooperation, mutual respect, and academic commitment. Remarkably, it is a culture born not of the charisma of an exceptional school leader, but of a codifiable system—a set of roles and practices that, in principle, can be replicated across any number of schools.

The Student Life program was developed for the middle-class, tuition-based schools that SABIS operated abroad, and it takes years to implement. The company's International Charter School of Schenectady, New York, benefits from an unusually sophisticated principal and a capable academic quality controller, both committed to SABIS's program. Yet on opening, the school struggled with student behavior for lack of an effective behavior system—essential for operating urban charter schools that open to hundreds of students from low-income families.[17]

Visitors to KIPP's school in the South Bronx are struck by the level of student engagement. Everyone is on task. Conversations with children reveal something still more remarkable: students hold an image of their successful futures—an image that is decidedly not the typical urban fantasy imprinted from popular culture (to become a basketball hero or a hip-hop star). Except by the rarely talented, those dreams are unattainable, a truth that the public schools, by their silence, are complicit in concealing. KIPPsters, as they are affectionately called by the teachers, imagine themselves as college-educated professionals, and more importantly, can describe a realistic plan for getting there that is based not on exceptional talent but on their own choices, knowledge, and diligence.[18]

LaToya is a short, bespectacled fifth-grader who was receiving one-on-one help during lunch. When asked about her plans for high school, she said she wanted to go to a boarding school. She aspired to be a lawyer or, as she said, "chief justice." Kofi and Carlos were eighth-graders eating lunch together in a classroom. Both will attend private high schools next year. Carlos wants to go into computer graphics. Kofi, whose slight lisp and glasses might make him vulnerable in other settings, says his plans include a double major in math and science in order to become a doctor.[19]

Before they finish the eighth grade, all KIPP students have studied literature typically taught at the high school level, including works by William Shakespeare, Richard Wright, Mark Twain, and J. D. Salinger. By the end of that year, they also have completed two years of high school algebra and the equivalent of four years of science. Throughout the school building were displays that emphasized the value of hard work and celebrated students' academic achievements. In the hallway were posted some eighty letters of acceptance to college preparatory high schools, many offering generous scholarships.[20]

The school's achievements are incontestable. For seven years now, KIPP has been the highest-performing public middle school in the Bronx on reading and math tests. For the 2002–2003 school year, the school's eighth grade ranked 17th in reading and 20th in math in New York City as a whole.[21] In 2003–2004, 79 percent of graduating eighth-graders who took the CTB in reading performed at or above grade level and 86 percent did so in math, a remarkable result given that only 41 and 48 percent of these same students performed at or above grade level in reading and math, respectively, in 1999–2000, the year before they entered KIPP.[22] Consider the performance of the students' peers in District 7 (Bronx) and the New York City schools as a whole. Twenty-five percent of District 7 fourth-graders scored at or above grade level in reading in 1999–2000. By the time they reached eighth grade, only 11 percent did. Math performance followed a similar trend, falling from 27 percent to 17 percent. New York City students' reading scores also fell over the period; 42 percent of fourth-graders performed at or above grade level in 1999–2000. By eighth grade, only 36 percent did. In math, the drop was from 46 percent to 42 percent.

KIPP's latest results for its entering fifth grade are equally impressive. On average, the class performed at the 28th percentile on the SAT-10 reading test on entering in September 2003; by May 2004, they scored at the 58th percentile. In math, they climbed from the 46th percentile to the 90th percentile.[23] These data show that the school, even though it enrolls students through a lottery, attracts a student population performing on arrival above District 7 on average but similar to or somewhat below the city schools as a whole. Critics like Richard Rothstein cite these differences as evidence of a selection effect and conclude that schools like KIPP are "questionable models for raising the achievement of lower-class blacks."[24] But the unusual expectations KIPP has for students and parents—which no doubt put off some families—are precisely what make KIPP a model for urban school improvement.

In their insightful discussion of KIPP's success in New York City and in Houston, political scientist Abigail Thernstrom and historian Stephan Thernstrom examine the nature of culture in urban schools and minority families. Low-income parents, regardless of background, hold "middle class" aspirations for their children's future, including an education, a strong marriage, and a steady job. What distinguishes the culture of children of one background from another, the Thernstroms argue, are not their values but the skills and habits they have to realize these aspirations. KIPP's founders recognize this. When children first arrive at school in the fifth grade, they are taught to "dress for success," walk down the halls briskly, sit properly in their chairs without delay, stand up to greet someone, and look directly at a person when conversing. They are also taught how to organize their classroom materials.[25]

Students chant the school's rules, which include the acronym SLANT: Sit up, Listen, Ask and answer questions, Nod your head so people know you are listening and understanding, Track your speaker by keeping your eyes on the person. All the students chant:

> We SLANT at all times
> We listen carefully at all times
> We follow the teachers' instructions
> We answer when given the signal
> We stay focused to save time
> We will always be nice and work hard.[26]

In instructing students in basic social skills, and teaching them the connection between hard work and achievement, KIPP is doing nothing less than providing its socially and economically disadvantaged students with the keys to success. "We are fighting a battle involving skills and values," KIPP founder David Levin told the Thernstroms. "We are not afraid to set social norms."[27]

In KIPP schools, teachers relate the students' behavioral choices to their futures. First, KIPP teaches students that there are no excuses and few second chances in the world outside the school's doors. If you break the rules or don't do the work, the consequences are swift and certain. The Thernstroms witnessed Levin refusing to compromise when a student had failed to earn a ticket to a Yankee game. "You can't argue your way into privilege," Levin explains to a class. "You've got to earn it step-by-step."[28]

Second, KIPP teaches that "earning privilege" is about gaining knowledge—a curiously neglected word in the education establishment today, with its emphasis on "learning how to learn." At the KIPP Bronx school, the teacher asks, "What room is this?" In unison, the students respond: "This is the room that has the kids who want to learn to read more books to make a better tomorrow." The KIPP Ujima Village school in Baltimore was early in its first year when the school's twenty-something director, Jason Botel, spoke to students. He was agitated. "We work hard to get you to college," he said of his faculty at the "life skills" meeting that ended another demanding day. "We get frustrated when we don't get your attention for your benefit. Is that clear?" "Crystal," the students responded.[29]

David Levin explained to the Thernstroms, "We are giving the kids the skills and confidence to take them to someplace better."[30] KIPP is neither preaching abstract "values" nor exhorting its students to excel. It is teaching every child that to gain knowledge is to gain power—exactly as the KIPP name says. The Thernstroms conclude, "It's an optimistic message about America, and about the rules that govern social mobility—the climb out of poverty to greater affluence. 'There Are No Shortcuts' on the road to success, although doors are open for those determined to walk through them . . . Skills and persistence will pay off."[31]

KIPP Bronx's dean of students, Jerome Myers, who grew up in Harlem, understands how important it is to create a powerful alternative culture within the school's walls. "I can relate to the students here. I know what it's like for them at home. And I tell them, 'Don't use excuses.'" His students, he explains, face tremendous challenges: "We have kids whose parents or siblings are incarcerated—some will be the first in their families to graduate from high school. They have to fight to be successful because they are going in a completely opposite direction from others in their lives."[32] But unlike in so many urban public schools, the children's backgrounds are not invoked to excuse weak teaching and low student performance. "All those things that schools list as reasons they don't succeed—the home, the environment—we don't care about that," says Frederick Shannon, KIPP's master teacher.[33]

One of the most memorable aspects of a visit to KIPP Bronx is the school's String and Rhythm orchestra. Every child plays an instrument, and the results are dazzling. The teacher, Jesus Concepción, who received his master's degree in conducting from Julliard and has taught at KIPP for three years, said that none of the students had received music instruction before. Instruments are assigned, and students may take them home to practice, but none of the children receive individual instruction at school or in private lessons elsewhere. At one point, he tells the students to practice their parts independently for thirty seconds, and a great din follows. A moment later, with his single clap, the room falls silent, and the next phase of the rehearsal begins. "OK, now, let's be musical," he said. "Violins, give it to me, let me feel your energy." The force of the music, in the crowded room, is overwhelming. As the conga players tackled their solos, we saw in their faces an expression of pure joy.[34]

After the class, Concepción explained: "In the class you just saw there is no 'talent'—it is all learned skills." Yet the full orchestra has performed at Carnegie Hall, completed a thirteen-city national tour, and performed at the inaugural ceremonies for Mayor Michael Bloomberg. KIPP believes that the discipline and confidence developed in the orchestra is transferable to the academic disciplines, and in turn, the students' lives outside of school. "The orchestra," KIPP says, "provides a clearly observable example for the entire school of the type of greatness that can be achieved if one is willing to put forth the required desire, dedication, and discipline."[35]

The seven organizations all tried to shape a permanent culture at its client schools that would support high achievement. Elements of a best practice emerge from their experiences: a code of conduct with clear and predictable consequences for misbehavior, implemented consistently and fairly schoolwide; a behavior system that explicitly teaches children good habits, recognizes and rewards good behavior, and serves as scaffolding while the final element is constructed—a permanent and powerful school culture that prizes academic achievement and endows each student with a vision of future success, in college and beyond. Students need to learn that a better life is available to them through dedication and discipline. Many school leaders understand that their task must include reshaping students' attitudes about themselves and their future.

Only KIPP makes this goal primary and has a specific and scalable plan for achieving it.

Few private organizations had before attempted to run public schools. As each organization set out to open its first schools, it was confident in its strategy, but mindful of the many obstacles ahead. Each organization believed its school design would accelerate student learning. Only time would reveal the strengths of each organization's strategic choices.

Even with a sound model, they faced daunting execution risks. Could key staff, knowledgeable in both schools and operations, be recruited for the corporate office? Would it be possible to obtain financing for constructing or renovating facilities? Could schools be enrolled on very short timetables, and capable teachers recruited? These execution risks were largely anticipated by entrepreneurs and their funders. Others, like tensions with client boards, or the complexity of working in multiple jurisdictions, were at best underestimated.

The challenges the six EMOs and KIPP encountered as they strove to turn their business plans and school designs into reality are the subject of the next chapter.

5

Execution

When the founders of the six education management organizations and KIPP pitched their plans to venture capitalists and philanthropists, many investors were captivated. By the year 2000, investors had gambled three-quarters of a billion dollars on the organizations and their bold claim that the private sector could improve public schools—and in the case of the for-profits, make money in the process.

But running public schools proved to be a very tough business. Edison, for one, has burned through $500 million in capital since its founding in 1992, at last reporting its first profitable quarter in 2003. National Heritage Academies, little known to Wall Street and operating out of the media spotlight, claims to be making a profit. But expansion into urban markets is testing the company's model—the company was forced to close its flagship school in Rochester after the charter was not renewed.[1] The only nonprofit of the seven, KIPP, is opening new schools throughout the country but relies on millions in ongoing philanthropic support and what may prove an unsustainable level of staff commitment.

What common obstacles did the organizations face? And what were their most damaging missteps? Which strategic choices eased their way and contributed to academic and financial success? And which hindered their progress?

Venture Climate of the 1990s

To understand the experiences of the EMOs, one must recall the exuberant business climate of the late 1990s. The stock market was soaring, "dot-coms" were the rage, and start-ups that were little more than concepts could command enormous prices.

In the "old economy," companies needed a meaningful history of revenues and earnings before they could successfully complete an initial public offering of their stock. But the new companies were often unprofitable and frequently had minimal revenues. To take these companies public, management had to have a "story" to justify their exorbitant offering price. Their Wall Street bankers, in light of the prices some newly public companies were obtaining on the market, were emboldened to deploy methods for valuing stock issues that once would have embarrassed them. Rather than justify the company's offering price on the basis of present or future earnings (its capacity to create value), investment bankers began to invoke the company's projected revenues in support of the initial price.

Using this method, a company that had negligible current revenues but projected millions in sales next year might be priced at some multiple of those future revenues. The specific multiple was justified by reference to other, already public, companies in the same broad industry. Just as a real estate broker backs up the listing price for a house by pointing to the prices recently paid for comparable houses, investment bankers justified the price for one company with the multiples of revenues at which other companies were trading (by dividing their market capitalization by their annual revenues).

The passion on Wall Street for Internet stocks, and the extraordinary shift in how new companies were valued, had broad implications for all entrepreneurial companies. The exorbitant gains that some investors were realizing in technology companies made returns that venture capitalists would previously have celebrated—for example, a 40 percent annual rate of return—suddenly seem unattractive. One company,

Theglobe.com, saw its stock climb 606 percent in its first day of trading.[2] Why invest at all in traditional industries—retail, pharmaceuticals, service businesses—when instead you could make truly spectacular gains in Internet companies?

In every industry, entrepreneurs sought to adapt their business plans to this sea change in investors' expectations. The cultural and business pressures to join the party were enormous. Dot-com millionaires, barely out of business school, were a staple of the popular media. Friends became rich overnight, and colleagues gave up respectable jobs to join start-up companies where they were showered with stock options.

For traditional entrepreneurs who were slogging away at building "real" companies, the choices were two. Even though they didn't run Internet companies, they could try and sound like them. One choice was simply to add ".com" to their names and concoct a web component for their enduringly traditional business, and some did. Another strategy for evoking the potential of technology companies was to adopt their rhetoric of transformative ideas, unlimited potential, and exceptional growth. For EMOs, that meant growing faster and thinking bigger. Then they could be valued like technology companies, raise money cheaply, and go public quickly. One booster of the school management business, analyst Scott Soffen of Legg Mason, predicted, "In the near term, you're going to see growth not unlike the Internet."[3]

Two characteristics of the K–12 industry made it easy for EMOs to adjust their stories to the capital market's new appetites. First, the market was potentially enormous, with annual spending on public schools (excluding construction and debt service) of nearly $350 billion.[4] (Never mind that the actual market of available charters and districts that would consider contracting was a small fraction of that figure—dramatic scale was central to the pitch.) Second, the revenues of several companies had grown at a striking rate in their early years, and it seemed plausible that such growth could be sustained. A Merrill Lynch analyst averred that Edison "can grow both its revenues and earnings at nearly 70% [a year] for the foreseeable future."[5] While companies in many industries resorted to financial projections that venture capitalists called "hockey sticks," where revenues suddenly and improbably leap upward, school management companies could point to a history of dramatic jumps in revenue over the first years of operation. When each school an EMO opened added millions in revenues to the company, it was easy to project $100 million or even $500 million in revenues in a few years.

Entrepreneurs are by nature wont to overpromise, and in the new economy the pressure to do so was enormous. EMOs succumbed. When Edison Schools went public in 1999, one analyst projected revenues of $1.8 billion by 2005.[6] Pressed to make good on this promise of spectacular growth, Edison entered into undesirable contracts and sought huge awards in New York City (five schools were designated, but the company failed to secure the requisite votes from parents to move forward) and Philadelphia. Advantage Schools, too, raised over $25 million in private equity in 1999 and $33 million in 2000, primarily from Chase Capital and Credit Suisse, on a business plan that promised a rapid buildup in client schools and revenues. After Edison went public, Advantage's investors pushed hard for the company to go public quickly, so they could reap their returns in the overheated market for initial public offerings. But the IPO window closed abruptly in mid-2000. Lacking a means to cash out of their investment, Advantage's investors sold the company to Mosaica Education in the fall of 2001 and invested in the combined company.

Beacon Education Management made plans to go public in the summer of 2001, and the company hoped to raise as much as $33 million. But in August the company aborted the offering, citing market conditions. Education investors showed little interest in the unprofitable company that had posted a $2.7 million loss in fiscal 2000 and projected twice that amount for 2001. Consequently, in January 2002, Beacon merged with Chancellor Academies to form Chancellor Beacon Academies.[7]

The effect on EMOs of this brief, but profound, aberration in the capital markets cannot be overstated. Even in ordinary times, the pressure to grow and generate returns for venture capital investors is enormous; the company's mission, culture, and quality of service can be jeopardized. In the mania of the late 1990s, however, the bar had been raised. In hindsight, the rise in expectations damaged an emerging industry struggling to gain its footing. "Our growth rate made quality of execution very difficult," one Edison executive conceded.[8] Excessive growth undermined quality of service—and, ironically, the creation of long-term value for investors.

It is too soon to know which education management organizations will ultimately succeed. But many lessons can be learned from their early travails. In some cases, key assumptions in their business models proved faulty. In other instances, the model was sound, but the company stumbled in its execution. In this chapter, eleven major challenges the organizations faced in realizing their plans are examined, from disciplining growth and financing school facilities, to managing relationships with school boards and state regulators.

Disciplining Growth

School management companies have been likened to other multisite service businesses such as retail and hotel chains. Like these operations, education management companies consist of a growing number of service delivery locations (the individual schools), overseen by a central corporate office. The analogy is limited, but instructive. Several common causes of failure among site-based businesses are risks for school management companies as well. One cause is inadequately refining and developing the first, or prototype, site before rushing to replicate it. Another is expanding too quickly. Companies may fail to exercise discipline in the selection of new sites and open weak sites in marginal locations that underperform financially and fail to replicate the success of the prototype. A third is failing to build up the company's capacity to manage and support new locations adequately, including providing the necessary infrastructure of executive management, line management, information technology, and accounting.

Most education management companies made at least one of these mistakes in their early years. Among the six EMOs, none had CEOs who had run site-based businesses like retail, hospitality, or multisite health care. The pressure to reach financial breakeven through the proliferation of sites—and end the companies' voracious requirements for cash to fund ongoing losses—was enormous.

Some organizations, like Edison and Advantage, sacrificed discipline for growth when they entered low-spending markets and signed financially marginal contracts. After essential costs such as teacher salaries and rent, marginal schools were only able to pay a fraction of their expected management fees, which in turn covered only a portion of the costs of the corporate office attributable to supporting the school. At the financially weakest schools, the EMO not only received no fees but also had to subsidize the schools' continued operations, sometimes to fulfill contractual commitments to the schools' boards to fund deficit operations.

The consequences to the corporation of opening financially underperforming schools were devastating. Short of terminating management contracts or closing the schools, the EMO had no choice but to continue to operate them at a recurring loss. Just one school's deficit—or negative "site contribution"—could cancel out the positive site contributions from two or more profitable schools. Consequently, the number of additional schools required to reach profitability increased. So did the annual losses of the EMO, and the amount of venture capital required to fund them. Worse still, investors' confidence in both the company's business model and the management team was shaken.

Advantage opened its first two schools in low-spending states because that was where charters were available. The management team was persuaded that both the Rocky Mount Charter School in North Carolina and the Phoenix Advantage Charter School in Arizona could make money. But there was very little margin for error at either site, and both schools operated at a perennial loss.

Perhaps the best example of undisciplined expansion was Edison's decision to manage nine schools in the Chester-Upland school district in Pennsylvania, which was being run by a state-appointed control board. In Chester-Upland, among the most troubled school districts in the state, Edison inherited an intransigent teachers union, decrepit facilities, and a history of academic failure. While more disciplined EMOs passed up the opportunity, citing poor economics and ambiguous authority for the EMO, Edison accepted the control board's unfavorable terms. In Chester, Edison saw an opportunity to demonstrate the power of its school design in the most challenging of circumstances. As Thomas Persing, the chairman of the Chester school board, remarked, "I told Chris Whittle he wasn't going to make any money here. But he said that if Edison could take Chester—urban, troubled, black—and show academic success, he could use it as a marketing tool and really make big money."[9]

The company endured a miserable first year. Media coverage was relentlessly negative; Edison faced persistent criticism as it struggled to implement its model. Far from earning a site contribution, the company was pouring millions into the project. "We have lost our shirt in Chester in every sense of the word," Whittle remarked, "and we continue to go forward."[10] Edison successfully renegotiated its contract to double its compensation for services to $4.4 million annually, but even with the increase, it remained saddled with a financial loser. Whittle acknowledges that the district may never be profitable. "There's a difference between hemorrhaging money and just struggling by," he remarked in an interview. "In Chester, I think struggling by is where we'll be."[11]

Edison may have justified Chester as a loss leader, but the effect on the company of a handful of unprofitable clients was dramatic. The company continued to post large losses at a time when its depressed stock price precluded raising additional cash from the public. In August 2002, Edison told investors that Charles Delaney would become vice chairman and impose new financial discipline on the company. "I represent profit," Delaney told Wall Street analysts. "We need much better discipline on every deal we do. We've done some bad contracts."[12] Not only did Edison forgo marginal new projects, it sought to exit unprofitable contracts. The company's CFO, in an investor conference call, declared, "The management team is totally focused on showing the company can make money."[13]

Looking back today, the resolute drive to expand seems reckless. The truth was that ideal opportunities were few, and making sound evaluations of new projects proved unexpectedly difficult. In some relatively high-spending states, including Massachusetts and Michigan, the cap on the number of charters that could be awarded had already been reached. Other states passed charter legislation that contained insuperable barriers. One such provision requires local school boards to sign off on all charter school proposals, which can be like requiring Burger King to obtain the consent of McDonald's before opening a new location. In Kansas, for example, local boards are the sole authorizer of charters; applicants must demonstrate support from district employees, and there is no appeal to a state agency.[14]

When EMOs could obtain charters, it was often difficult to find appropriate client boards, suitable real estate, or an authorizer that would be receptive to a partnership with the particular EMO and its educational philosophy. Not surprisingly, EMOs were tempted to experiment wherever charters were available, even in relatively low-spending states. As costs for staff and real estate were also lower, there was still a prospect of earning a modest management fee. But there was no margin for error. When expense projections proved optimistic, these sites failed to perform financially, yielding weak or negative site contributions.

Site profitability was not the only concern; stewarding the company's precious cash was equally critical. Later, some organizations turned to modeling each proposed school's return on invested capital. Only projects that were projected to generate an adequate rate of return were given the green light. But lack of confidence across the organization in the many assumptions that the finance department used in its financial projections often undermined consensus on a project's viability. Edison said its approval model was "noisy," primarily because occupancy costs were unknown at the time projects were evaluated; other EMOs said they wrestled with the same problem.

Chancellor Beacon benefited from unusually sophisticated investors who had studied the market thoroughly before making their play. "Warburg [Pincus and Company] never pushed for an immediate IPO. They took a long term-perspective," said Wade Dyke. Nonetheless, "there were a lot of internal pressures to grow," remarked Octavio Visiedo. "We knew people didn't put in $15 million and just wait and see what happened." When the company set out to open many new schools in just its second year, it put "incredible pressure on this organization," he said.[15]

KIPP and other nonprofit education management organizations are less directly affected by the capital markets, but growth is no less an imperative. In attempting to meet its early growth targets, KIPP also opened financially marginal sites. KIPP's Hamilton today says, "In the end, we worry less about the breadth of the diaspora than in the conditions in which we are starting schools. So, for instance, in Atlanta, they ended up giving us $1,000 less per pupil than we thought we were going to get . . . In California, the numbers are so bleak, we worry about the long-term viability of the [KIPP] schools."[16]

Managing Multiple Jurisdictions

When statutory caps, political opposition, weak economics, and the difficulty of securing customer boards made management contracts difficult to obtain, the organizations had to look far and wide for viable projects. Many took on schools wherever they could be found, creating networks of schools operating in vastly different regulatory and political environments. By each organization's fourth year of operating schools, Advantage worked in eleven states (including the District of Columbia), Chancellor Beacon in nine, KIPP in fourteen, Edison in twelve, Mosaica in five, and Sabis in two. By contrast, NHA operated in just one, its home state of Michigan.

Supporting a smattering of client schools in distant states proved enormously costly. Customer boards, especially in the first year of a new school, often gauged the organization's value to the school by the presence of corporate staff on site. Associated costs—airfare, for one—could be anticipated. But there was a greater problem with working across many jurisdictions. EMOs had to modify their standard curricula to align them with the standards in each state in which they operated and then develop and deploy unique test preparation programs. In effect, companies had to develop what venture capitalists call "one-off" products for each state. Customized designs diminished the potential for scaling the business, increased corporate staff, and delayed the financial breakeven point.

Cultural differences exacerbated the challenge of long-distance relationships. Corporations were already likely to be distrusted by many people working in public education. Subtle regional differences of class, race, religion, and political ideology—even of personal style—made the development of trusting and effective relationships between the six EMOs and KIPP and their local customers that much more difficult. "It makes it hard for us to give good advice or counsel when we don't know their milieu," Scott Hamilton said of KIPP's far-flung school founders.[17] Both boards of trustees and regulators in southern states, for example, expected education management companies from the Northeast to adapt to their ways. Imagine a school board in North Carolina that opens its meeting with a prayer; its EMO is squeamish about the public school's obligation to the separation of church and state. Now turn to Texas, where "citizen" legislators are almost expected to pursue their private interests. A state representative thinks nothing of standing to benefit from a charter school while lobbying for the grant of its charter; its EMO, accustomed to the rigid ethics laws that govern "professional" legislators, cannot hide its disapproval. Successfully navigating these cultures was difficult without bringing on regional staff who had lived in the area, could earn the trust of the client, and would mediate between the corporation and the community.

Because its geographic expansion was slow and deliberate, National Heritage Academies could take the time to attend to such regional and cultural differences. It opened its first thirteen schools in its home state of Michigan between 1995 and 1998. Only then did it carefully expand, opening four schools over two years in North Carolina, a state likely to be receptive to NHA's conservative moral focus. The company's initial regional strategy greatly simplified execution and the development of a respected brand.

Attending to Secondary Customers

Although an education organization's ultimate clients are students and their parents, as the industry is structured today its primary customers are charter and district school boards. They hire the company and, should the organization fail to perform, can fire it. In the highly regulated and intensely political environment of privately managed public schools, the six EMOs and KIPP have also had to attend to an array of other parties who wield power over their schools: charter authorizers, state education regulators, local politicians, city officials, and the local media.

The organizations' executives have frequently underestimated the importance of these "secondary customers." A supportive charter authorizer can award additional charters and help grow the business; a hostile one can fail to enforce a management agreement with a client school. A favorable regulator can assist the company in coming into compliance with abstruse state attendance and financial reporting requirements; an adversarial one can put the company on probation and ensure that it appears on the front page of the paper the next morning. A newspaper reporter can offer a balanced portrayal of a new school struggling to get on its feet—or slam the company in a story that will be forever tethered to it in Internet searches. EMOs have often failed to invest the time and effort to cultivate relationships with secondary customers or to develop information systems to meet their needs.

Each state has its own regulatory requirements and reporting expectations for public schools. State bureaucrats insist that EMOs adhere to them and generally cannot be humored into accepting instead an EMO's internal reports for student information, finances, special education, and the like. Manually reformatting data is bad enough, but the problem runs deeper. For example, each state might have different rules for when a student would have to be removed from the list of enrolled students, yet the EMO may have also sought to apply a consistent policy across its schools. EMOs typically keep track of all students with a single database, working with uniform definitions. Further, some states require that periodic enrollment and attendance reports be submitted electronically through the state's own student information software. To comply, the EMO must either enter information each day into two incompatible software systems or write custom software that links its central system with the state's software.

When it comes to meeting these requirements, squeaking by is one thing, but doing an excellent job—filing reports on time, providing thoughtful narratives in annual school reports, creating electronic linkages to state systems, and so on—is another. As companies entered new geographic markets, corporate staff scrambled and often failed to submit the myriad reports on time. Internal data systems were strained and distrusted. The inability to produce high-quality, timely reporting "products" frustrated both the overtaxed company staff who produced them and the EMOs' customers. Staff turnover was often high, but those who left frequently took with them crucial expertise for which the learning curve for replacements was steep. Even Edison, with its enormous investment in corporate infrastructure, concedes that in the early days it was not "even close" to having the right systems and products in place to work across many jurisdictions.

EMOs have struggled with the best way to organize to meet the needs of their primary and secondary customers. Advantage Schools first established departments of client services and regulatory affairs. The client services department functioned as the liaison to client boards, sending representatives to monthly board meetings and preparing summaries of action items from the meetings. The regulatory affairs department, meanwhile, sought to identify and summarize regulatory obligations across jurisdictions and assist the company and each school in complying with them. In each department, individuals were responsible for a portfolio of schools.

As the company expanded, it established a traditional regional management structure. New regional directors assumed responsibility for relationships with customer boards and supervised school directors. As part of the restructuring, Advantage eliminated the client services department. The regulatory affairs department was retained, but its members were each assigned to work with a regional director. The finance department hired financial analysts who also each worked on a specific region. While logical, this organizational structure did not deliver the kind of informed and attentive service that both primary and secondary customers expected. Regulators continued to cite the company for noncompliance.

The inattention of EMOs to their secondary customers may have stemmed from the organizations' entrepreneurial philosophy. Founders believed that public education was vastly overregulated; both charter schools and private management promised freedom from the rules and bureaucratic oversight that had public schools consumed more with compliance than with results for their students. As the charter movement matured, founders feared that state officials would seek to "re-regulate" charter schools and subject them to the same debilitating constraints as traditional schools. In this light, regulators were a threat. They should alternately be ignored and cajoled, just as the best urban principals had long bent district rules to protect their successful schools.

Suspicion of regulators was not entirely unwarranted. While New Jersey offered the highest per-student spending of the fifty states, so hostile was the state department of education that most companies came to the conclusion that doing business there was impossible.[18] The department never formally approved any of Edison's surplus model management contracts; when Edison altered its fee structure, this too was rejected. Edison's legal counsel repeatedly asked the department to identify its specific concerns with the contracts; the department declined. Other

EMOs fared no better. The department scoured regulations for possible roadblocks. The state hobbled the EMOs' ability to manage schools when it took the position that charter school boards had to approve day-to-day actions like disbursements and personnel actions. By decreeing the cost of Advantage's academic implementation and professional development staff working at the school to be "non-instructional spending," the department was able to rule the company out of compliance with the state's required spending ratios. EMOs were improbably deemed not "professional service contractors" but "vendors," like custodial and transportation companies, and their contracts were therefore limited to two-year terms.[19] Mosaica's executed contract with one school was declared invalid after two years. The department "literally refused to deal with us, prohibited us from attending meetings, and wouldn't return phone calls," recalled Michael Connelly of Mosaica. "We don't deal with vendors," he was told. By excluding the companies from meetings between state personnel and managed schools' principals, the state was able to undermine the relationship between principals and the companies that recruited them. "You're our buddy; Mosaica is your enemy" was how Connelly characterized these interactions.[20] By barring Edison from its meetings with charter boards, the state similarly drove a wedge between Edison and its customers.

Many other states' officials bore no animus toward EMOs. While ideology—stoked by painful experiences in hostile jurisdictions like New Jersey—initially caused EMO managers to resist regulators, authorizers, and other public bureaucrats on whom they depended, they came quickly to respect the expertise and professional commitment of many officials.

At Advantage, ambivalence to secondary customers, embedded in the organizational culture, was hard to eradicate. As senior managers learned the difficulty of building exceptional schools, they came to respect the agencies they had once scorned. But it was difficult to build within Advantage's ranks a spirit of customer service toward its authorizers and regulators. The change in attitude came too late. Many education officials—who were also national opinion leaders in the school reform movement—had by then soured on the company.

Securing School Facilities

By far the greatest challenge to the education management business has been securing facilities. Contracts with school districts came with a school building, but the facility often required costly improvements. Districts that turned over their school buildings to education organizations only rarely agreed to provide the funding to refurbish the facility or install the company's technology package. Technology could be leased, but because the organization didn't hold title to the underlying building, borrowing for leasehold improvements was difficult.

Charter schools presented a far greater problem, as a facility had to be found or constructed. The EMO may only have offered to help the client secure a school building, not to pay for its purchase or improvement. But once a commitment was made to parents and the community to open a school in September, some EMOs felt obligated to deliver and advanced the funds to buy, build, or improve a facility. Were the EMO instead to drop the project or even delay by a year, the damage to its reputation would be great, especially if parents had already enrolled their children in the school. When the management company could not line up an outside lender for school construction or renovations, the EMO became the lender of last resort. The management company would advance its own funds for the construction, while awaiting, at least in theory, the loans to reimburse it.

One building alone could draw down millions in a company's venture capital dollars. In Somerville, Massachusetts, SABIS purchased a building for $3.2 million to house the Somerville Charter School, investing $1.8 million of its own funds and borrowing $1.4 million over ten years from the owner.[21] The company then invested further to convert it to a school. Residents blocked construction, arguing that the for-profit SABIS was not entitled to zoning exemptions provided to public schools and nonprofit corporations (even though the school was a public entity). The city further delayed construction by requiring lengthy environmental reviews. Unable to open the school on time, SABIS was obliged to hold classes in a restaurant's function rooms. After the relationship soured and the board voted not to renew its contract with SABIS, the school moved and left SABIS unable to recoup its investment.[22]

In a few cases, the landlord of an existing commercial facility loaned the company or the school a portion of the cost of improvements or built these costs into the lease rate, as was common practice with commercial "tenant improvement" allowances. At the end of the lease, the owner benefited from an improved asset. The landlord of a vacant brick warehouse in Worcester, Massachusetts, leased the building to Advantage's Abby Kelley Foster Regional Charter School. The landlord loaned Advantage much of the money required to convert the building into a school. Advantage used its own contractors and managed the construction. Advantage leased the building back to the school at a rate reflecting the base rent plus the cost of the borrowing for the improvements. In still other cases, facility improvements were "leased" from a leasing company, in the same way as computers and furniture.

When agreeing to lay out the cash for a building or improvements, an EMO often intended to be "taken out" of this investment by a third party, such as a local bank or real estate investor. But obtaining such permanent financing proved enormously difficult. After all, the EMO was usually a start-up with little credit history and no certainty of its own survival. In the mid-1990s, few lenders understood what charter schools were or how to assess their credit risk, including the risks of underenrollment and charter revocation or nonrenewal at the end of the typically five-year term. When lenders could not be secured, the EMO would transfer title of the improvements to the school and structure a loan to the school.

In addition, committed financing sometimes fell through. In 2000, Edison advanced $15 million to build the New Covenant Charter School in Albany, New York. The city demolished an existing community center and pool and made the land available to Edison, which constructed the complex and leased it back to the city.[23] Albany's Industrial Development Agency planned to issue bonds for the full cost of the project and take Edison out, but a financing was not completed until 2005. For a company with precariously little cash—its cash balance hovered at $30 million in late 2002—the financial impact of its Albany commitment was considerable. If Edison had less money locked up in Albany and other loans to its client charter schools, it would not have been obliged to raise cash at an extravagant price to fund ongoing operations.

Even when some outside financing was obtained, it was often for significantly less than the value of the building, reflecting the investors' perception of risk. Lenders required collateral with a market value significantly in excess of their exposure. The "loan to value" percentage, a measure of the amount financed as a percentage of the market value of the asset, was frequently no more than 80 percent. On a school with a total price tag of $5 million, $1 million of the company's venture capital would remain in the project.

Using venture capital—expensive money, when investors expected a rate of return of 40 percent or more—to fund school building construction is hardly a viable financial model, when cities and towns finance through tax-exempt bonds at 5 percent or less and with state reimbursement. Consequently, early on some companies posted less than a dollar in annual revenues for every dollar of invested capital. Advantage Schools, for example, raised more than $72 million in total venture capital and private equity by late 2000 to site and open nineteen schools. Contracts with four of the schools were terminated, resulting in total annual revenues from remaining schools of less than $60 million before the company's sale in 2001. Similarly, Edison Schools raised approximately $500 million in equity to open 130 schools (by Edison's count) and reach annual revenues of $426 million.

These are, of course, not attractive achievements by venture capital standards, and the facilities hurdle was one of the principal reasons that private equity for school management companies largely dried up in 2001, although the newly consolidated entities, Mosaica (Advantage) and Chancellor Beacon, received additional backing from their already committed investors.

In recent years, EMOs have succeeded in committing less capital to charter school facilities. Partly this is a result of their new discipline: they and their investors have chosen to slow growth rates sharply rather than commit scarce equity capital to real estate. Some companies have become more skilled at structuring facilities deals so as to avoid tying up their own funds. Mosaica stands out as the leader in tapping bond financing for school building projects; by 2004, it had completed twelve such deals totaling $100 million. Mosaica's two most senior executives, Michael Connelly and Gene Eidelman, brought to their jobs experience in commercial real estate development, finance, and corporate law. In each state, they sought out a public or quasi-public entity authorized and willing to issue the bonds. The process has still not become standard; every deal remains a "one-off." "The inability to routinize capital structures in real estate is the single biggest obstacle" to the industry, says Connelly.[24]

EMO founders anticipated, of course, the problem of building, refurbishing, and financing school facilities, and it was a central concern of their investors. Both banked on steady improvements to the external regulatory and financing environments. Private-sector lenders would become more comfortable with charter schools and their underwriting risk. Banks would find Community Reinvestment Act credits a powerful incentive to loan money to urban school projects. Real estate developers would build and lease back school facilities, especially where the new schools would prove an amenity to their residential developments. Wall Street would help devise clever financing packages for multiple schools (pooled facilities), including real estate investment trusts and sale-leaseback deals. States and the federal government would adopt legislation of one kind or another that would ease the facilities challenge for charter schools. In time, tax-exempt bond financing would become commonplace.

These expectations proved optimistic. Debt, in any form, for constructing charter schools remains hard to come by. Private developers have played an important role in financing and building Chancellor Beacon's schools in Florida, where overcrowding in district schools is severe.[25] But cooperation among housing developers and education management organizations has failed to take hold more broadly across the states and has had no effect on central city locations, where EMOs operate most of their schools.

Several states, including California and Minnesota, have passed laws that provide modest financial assistance for charter school facilities, but they fall short of what is needed. In California, districts are now required to provide charter schools with facilities to accommodate all of the in-district students in "conditions reasonably equivalent" to those of the district. But school districts recognize autonomous charter schools as competitors, and some have turned to the courts in an effort to avoid the requirement. Aspire, for one, has been reluctant to exploit the law's provision for fear of harming its relationships with districts, which authorize its charters. Another California measure promises charter schools in low-income areas up to $750 per student in aid for leasing costs. Yet these monies are paid as a reimbursement after the close of the fiscal year; given the vicissitudes of annual appropriation by the legislature, charter schools cannot responsibly budget for this support. A third California initiative authorized $400 million in state bonds for charter schools, with the schools obliged to pay only half of the bond's value over a twenty- to thirty-year period. Requests from charter schools have far exceeded awards under the program, and schools that obtain financing are required to comply with state regulations that cause school construction costs to skyrocket. Aspire was awarded $47 million, almost one-half of the initial disbursement—to build just two schools. Half of the award is in the form of an outright grant, and the other half is financed at the state bond rate of approximately 4 percent. The effective borrowing rate is low, but the cheap capital came with strings: Aspire was obliged to work with the state's architect, conform to state seismic standards, and secure formal approval of building plans. Turnaround times were long, and title to the buildings will be held by the district in which the schools are located. "I can build these schools for half of what it's costing us with state money," complained Charles Robitaille, Aspire's director of real estate.[26] Were Aspire to build the schools for the price the state envisioned, the debt service burden on each school for the borrowing would be crippling. In another venture, Minnesota's Lease Aid program assists eligible charter schools by providing 90 percent of approved leasing costs up to a designated amount per student ($1,200 in 2003), but the law is subject to annual appropriation, inhibits schools from buying or constructing buildings, and leaves charter schools still unable to tap the state's full faith and credit.[27]

Still more progressive are the policies of the District of Columbia. Leveling the playing field with district schools, the district grants charter schools a per-pupil facilities allowance equal to the school system's per-pupil capital spending, averaged over five years.

Sticking to the Financial Model

As EMOs opened schools and built the capacity at their corporate offices to support them, many were unable to adhere to their financial plans. At the school level, revenues fell short of plan and expenses exceeded budgets, resulting in lower than planned fees paid to the management organization. Corporate office expenses also exceeded budgets, as the EMO struggled to build and finance school buildings, adequately support client schools, manage relationships with client boards and secondary customers, comply with regulations, and operate under unrelenting and often hostile media scrutiny.

School-Level Challenges. When EMO executives were undisciplined in their approvals of new school projects or their assumptions proved faulty, they found themselves managing schools saddled with bad fundamentals—low capitation rates, a limited pool of area children, or an expensive facility—and unable to pay their contractual management fees. Yet good site fundamentals were no assurance that a school would perform well financially. Difficulties arose as the model was implemented, among them sustaining enrollment, collecting grants, and managing unanticipated costs for facilities, staffing, board expenses, and corporate operations.

Maintaining Full Enrollment. Most EMO schools had waiting lists. But when schools performed poorly financially, weak enrollment was most often the cause. When delays with permits or construction forced the EMO to postpone the school's opening by more than one or two weeks, some parents pulled their children out and returned them to district schools. When the school eventually opened, enrollment levels might have fallen by one hundred or more students. In West Chester, Pennsylvania, the school district obtained a court order barring the opening of Mosaica's Collegium school. When the school opened forty-five days late, there were only thirty-seven students in a building designed for 450. By the end of the year, however, enrollment had climbed to 150 students, and the following fall there were 500.[28]

Rebuilding enrollment in the first months was possible if the school was well received and had a strong principal. But if the opening was rocky and the principal could not communicate a persuasive vision to the community, the school could languish the entire year with empty seats. The cost to the EMO in lost revenue would be enormous; at a $6,500 capitation, a shortfall of 150 students translated into close to a $1 million variance from budgeted revenues. When it came to meeting the company's financial plan, Jeff Poole, NHA's vice president of operations, attested, the biggest risk was not expense variance, but meeting plans for revenues, "which is enrollment, which is parental satisfaction, which is leadership."[29]

Collecting Grants. Large school districts rely on federal grants, smaller state grant programs, and private contributions to supplement state and local dollars. Many of the new companies underestimated both the amounts available from these sources and the difficulty of collecting them. Some state departments of education dragged their feet on making federal entitlements like Title I available to charter schools. Funds often had to flow through local education agencies (LEAs) to the charter schools. "We have consistently had trouble collecting our entitlements monies. The LEA sits on the entitlement dollars and doesn't pass them on to the school," said Wade Dyke of Chancellor Beacon.[30] EMOs often failed to understand the complexity of applying for the funds, complying with program rules, and meeting reporting requirements. In other cases, like the federal E-rate program for subsidizing school connections to the Internet, EMOs simply did not apply. School districts deployed long-time staff who knew where the pots of money were and how to tap them. The junior staff members assigned by EMOs lacked this specialized expertise and left hundreds of thousands of dollars on the table.

Some EMOs' site models assumed the schools would also receive private grants from individual, foundation, and corporate donors. The expectation was reasonable; big city schools regularly secured large gifts. But it proved difficult for EMOs to persuade donors to give to schools that were supported by a corporation presumed wealthy (and that had received millions in venture capital investments). Would they not be subsidizing the corporation? When they did award grants, they were often for items like playground equipment or library books and supplemented the school's resources rather than defraying the EMO's costs.

Site-Level Overspending. The EMOs had far less difficulty adhering to school expense budgets than to revenue plans. Most school expenses were predictable and, in principle, flat over the course of the year. Nonetheless, there were execution problems.

By far the largest expense control problem was the annual cost of the school facility. Many external factors contributed to facility cost overruns. Unexpected environmental problems required expensive mitigation and delayed the start of construction. Permitting roadblocks, usually the result of political action by the project's opponents, delayed the planned launch of construction; when work then had to be accelerated with triple shifts and other measures, costs skyrocketed.

When Advantage Schools prepared a charter application on behalf of the trustees of the Mystic Valley Advantage Regional Charter School in Malden, Massachusetts, a facility had not yet been found. By necessity, the application's budget contained only an estimate of annual occupancy costs. After a far-reaching search, the board and Advantage settled on the only available property, a former parochial school. Untouched for decades, the building required extensive improvements, including asbestos removal, sprinklers, new windows, and entirely new wiring and plumbing. When the building's one tenant, a daycare provider occupying one classroom, was served notice by the archdiocese of the termination of her at-will lease, she said she would defy the orders to vacate—even after Advantage offered six months' rent in a new location. It took a lengthy court procedure to evict her. Meanwhile, under Massachusetts tenant law, utilities to her classroom could not be disrupted and no demolition work could begin. Construction, then, did not begin until August. To compensate for lost time, Advantage's contractor moved to triple shifts. The school opened in late September, delayed by several weeks. But the school's board, holding the EMO to the occupancy costs estimated in the charter application, refused to buy back (even when aided by a loan from a local bank) the tenant improvements performed by Advantage at their actual cost. The management company ended up with a significant loss.

Borrowing costs were equally unpredictable. When schools were themselves able to borrow money for facilities, it was from unusual sources, such as a building's owner, venture leasing companies, or quasi-public government agencies that made loans in the public interest to borrowers that failed to qualify for commercial loans. The cost of borrowing—at 12 percent or more—was often higher than planned and the term of the loan shorter, with amortization schedules rarely exceeding ten years. Payment on these loans came out of the client school's budget, cutting into funds available for salaries, school expenses, and management fees to the EMO.

Construction cost overruns and financing failures caused variances to the EMO's profit and loss statement, but it was the balance sheet that was hit the hardest. When EMOs' cash balances were depleted, less was available for working capital and pre-opening expenses associated with new schools. The companies then had to raise more equity capital from venture and institutional sources than expected, diluting the ownership position of founders and managers. Often the credibility of the management team with the company's investors was damaged.

The largest expense in a school is staff: teachers, aides, and other personnel. Personnel cost variances resulted from changes in class sizes, unexpected costs of providing special education, and the failure to adhere to staffing models.

SABIS encountered stiff resistance at its Foxborough, Massachusetts, school to its large classes—despite the academic success of the same model at its sister Massachusetts school in Springfield. SABIS had planned two classes for the school's fifty-eight eighth-graders based on a review of students' knowledge gaps, but the school's administration mistakenly assigned them to three, requiring a third teacher and the allocation of a third classroom. SABIS insisted they be consolidated into two classes of twenty-nine students each and that the third room be used for another kindergarten class. The EMO's educational philosophy supported the use of large classes, and adding a class of kindergartners would meet parent demand and bring new revenues to the school. But eighth-grade parents were irate.[31] If EMOs acquiesced to clients' insistence that they pare down class sizes and hire unbudgeted staff, it created revenue and spending variances. If instead EMOs stuck to their guns, it often came at the price of client relations. Ultimately, SABIS lost the Foxborough school over the board's involvement in day-to-day operations.

Another frequent cause of staffing expense variance was the provision of special education. Large urban school districts manage special education costs by assigning students who require particular services to schools that have the necessary specialists on staff. Charter schools are also generally required by law to provide services to all students, regardless of disability, but they lack options for serving them cost-effectively. For a small charter school, just a few students requiring full-time aides or other services can result in a large expense variance. In other cases, the EMO's well-intentioned plans to "mainstream" most special needs students in regular classrooms (as urged by many educators) proved unrealistic. When Edison opened the Renaissance Charter School in Boston in 1995, it hired only one special education teacher for six hundred students, intending to implement a "responsible inclusion" model. Even with teachers' aides, the model proved grossly unrealistic. In 1997, the Office for Civil Rights of the Department of Education found that the school had discriminated against one kindergartner during the school's first year by "shortening his school day, suspending him, placing him with a teacher not trained in special education, and finally forcing his mother to withdraw him from the school."[32] By the time of the ruling, the school had grown to more than a thousand students, operated three learning centers, and employed nine special education teachers, a Spanish-English bilingual psychologist, two social workers, and occupational and speech therapists.[33]

Each school's financial model made assumptions about not just the number of staff but also their seniority and associated costs. When staffing a school, principals were not always able to adhere to the model, particularly in a region with teacher shortages or when hiring late in season. Hiring even small numbers of unplanned teachers with high levels of experience—and at relatively high salaries—would cause the school to be widely off budget.

Another obstacle to controlling costs at the school level was unbudgeted expenses incurred by the board. The most common were legal expenses, the board's "discretionary account," patronage positions at the school, a paid staff member reporting to the board (such as a president or executive director of the school), and contracts with favored vendors. Such expenses created two problems for management companies. First, they could easily add as much as $100,000 to site costs. Second, they often posed ethical problems, as when a board member insisted that a local concern in which the member had a financial interest provide the school meals or construction services at above-market rates. Board members were often unsophisticated about such conflicts of interest and determined to have their way. Resistance on the part of the EMO risked serious damage to the relationship, particularly in the critical early months when the school was preparing for launch.

Disciplining Corporate-Level Spending. A great uncertainty in the initial business plans of the EMOs and of KIPP was the cost of the corporate office. How many staff, and how much in related expenses, would prove necessary to support the network of schools? Five years into running schools, Edison understood the challenge of reducing administrative spending. "Claims that half of school spending is wasted on administration is hyperbole," Whittle said. He estimated that the average district spent about twenty-seven cents of every dollar on the central office; he would reduce that to eight cents. Most of the savings (twelve cents) would be pushed back into the classroom, with seven cents left over in profit. By implication, school-level spending at Edison would consume eighty-five cents, rather than the seventy-three cents that districts spent.[34]

But Edison continues to spend at a much higher level than Whittle predicted. Across the industry, the corporate office has proved more expensive than anticipated. Staffing models significantly underestimated the administrative burden of mandated programs like special and bilingual education, teacher and staff credentialing, regulatory compliance, and financial reporting. Added staff were almost exclusively engaged in managing the complex external environment of regulation and politics, and not in providing educational or other value to individual school sites. State departments of education were increasing the regulatory burden on charter schools, adding to the cost of compliance.

Caught up in enthusiasm for the new "autonomy" promised by charter school advocates, founders failed to consider that charter schools still faced most of the administrative burdens of traditional schools—and altogether new compliance and reporting requirements as charters. Actual corporate spending ran higher than expected, delaying profitability and increasing losses and capital requirements.

Had the schools simply been private schools, only a fraction of the staff would have been required. Consider accounting. For equity investors and lenders, the EMOs had to account for their schools' and corporation's finances according to generally accepted accounting principles (GAAP) and provide periodic financial statements. For client schools and regulators, EMOs had to prepare statements according to state government financial reporting and accounting rules, which were unique to each state and not based on accrual accounting, the bedrock of the private sector. Some states even required that transactions be run through their customized financial software. In addition to the corporate auditors, each school hired its own local auditors, which had to be supported, and charter authorizers and state education departments also undertook further reviews and audits. Each state had its own teacher retirement system, with its own rules and reporting requirements. Federal monies, too, such as for Title I, came with their own compliance and accounting requirements, which were also different from one state to the next, as grants were often disbursed through state education agencies. All these requirements contributed to the burgeoning headcount at the corporate office.

Each state's charter and other statutes necessitated small but onerous differences in the financial and legal structure of an EMO's schools. While many EMOs preferred that teachers be employed by the corporation, some states required that they be public employees of the school, which was either a nonprofit corporation or a public agency, depending on the state. Rather than offer a single retirement plan, EMOs had to cope with 401(k) plans for their own employees, 403(b) plans for their individual schools, and a welter of state retirement systems.

Accounting rules for EMO finances continued to evolve, further burdening the finance and legal departments at the corporate office.

Navigating Accounting Rules

A private corporation managing a network of public schools was an entirely new idea, and in the late 1990s questions arose at several EMOs about the correct way to report financial results. New guidance from accounting authorities required each EMO to analyze particular features of its management contracts to determine how revenues and expenses should be recorded. For both Edison and Advantage, this necessitated a restatement of not only the current fiscal year but past periods as well. Because contracts varied across schools as well as companies, the new rules proved to be another impediment to scaling the business. "Brutally difficult" is how Edison describes accounting in an EMO; even by 2003 (when the company was spending $60 million a year on its corporate office), Edison found financial management "still very hard, but getting easier."[35] Chancellor also struggled with its books. "Growth caused so much pressure, then we added Beacon. We didn't have the systems in place."[36] Only some time after the merger did the company switch from the small business accounting software Quickbooks to financial software appropriate to a mid-sized company.

The accounting questions pertained to what accountants call "revenue recognition." Under accrual accounting, accountants recognize revenues for the goods or services the company sold during the period, whether or not it has received payment for them, and records expenses it has incurred even if it hasn't yet paid out cash for them. By matching revenues with expenses in the period the activity occurs, accrual accounting provides a clear picture of the company's actual profit or loss during the period. The accounting profession has developed detailed rules for how revenues and expenses should be recognized, and the Financial Accounting Standards Board (FASB) and other standard-setting bodies continually elaborate on these rules. The consolidation of revenues and expenses from subsidiary organizations is governed by additional rules.

In May of 2002, the Securities and Exchange Commission (SEC) announced that it had entered into a settlement with Edison regarding its accounting and revenue recognition practices.[37] While Edison did not "contravene Generally Accepted Accounting Principles," the commission nonetheless found that Edison "inaccurately described aspects of its business in SEC filings" and "inaccurately stated that Edison 'receives' all Per-Pupil Funding."[38]

The commission said that Edison had not disclosed that a substantial portion of its revenues consisted of payments that never reached Edison. These funds were expended directly by the school district on teachers and other service providers. Under the required reclassifications, Edison's net earnings were unaffected; while revenues were reduced in the restatement, so were expenses. Edison was not fined. "The Commission's action today shows that technical compliance with GAAP in the financial statements will not insulate an issuer from enforcement action if it makes filings with the Commission that mischaracterize its business, or omit significant information."[39]

In Edison's management contracts with school districts, it assumes operational and educational responsibility for particular schools in exchange for funding comparable to the district's spending on other schools. While Edison is usually responsible for all of the costs of running the schools, the company frequently arranges for the district to pay for certain expenses, such as teachers' salaries, and to deduct these from what would be paid to Edison. In six of Edison's sixty-two contracts, the SEC ruled that revenues should be reported net of teacher salaries. In those contracts, Edison could not be considered the "primary obligor" of the cost of teachers because the district retained a level of control over their salaries and other terms of employment.[40] As part of the settlement, Edison agreed to report "gross student funding" in its financial statements, to report client-paid expenses and Edison's expenses separately, and to restate revenues for previous periods. Under the reclassification, Edison's revenues dropped by close to 7 percent for both of the previous two years.

The commission found that Edison's systems had not kept pace with its growth to sixty-two school districts and twenty-two states and faulted, in particular, its practices for invoicing clients.[41] The announcement of the investigation undermined the company's credibility with Wall Street and contributed to the dramatic decline in its stock price.

Other organizations, starting later and better advised, structured management contracts to avoid such accounting problems. National Heritage Academies and Mosaica, for example, made school staff employees of the corporation wherever legally permissible.

Avoiding Overpromising

When most EMOs were getting under way, their founders generally shared the expectation of the charter school movement—that well-run charter schools would outperform traditional urban schools. The business development teams of many EMOs were charter school and market-oriented missionaries, and they captivated their prospective clients with vague but thrilling talk of building "world-class schools" and a conviction that every obstacle along the way could be overcome. The audience was often school reform activists—parents, ministers, business executives—who were disaffected with the local school system and receptive to the EMO's reform rhetoric. But when founders promised the world in sales presentations, they unwittingly created specific expectations on the part of enthusiastic but often naive charter school board members. Client boards later remembered every claim and took each as a commitment. In the heady early months after the charter was awarded, trustees of managed schools would enthusiastically echo—and often amplify—the management organization's promises. When the school later endured a difficult launch, and many of the promised features of the design had not yet been realized, it was the trustees' reputation in their own communities that was on the line. It was their neighbors who accosted them in the supermarket with questions and complaints about their child's new school. There, it was easy to blame the management company, co-opt the school principal, and begin the downward cycle of board and EMO hostility that crippled many school projects. When the company opened a school in a temporary facility of classroom trailers rather than a renovated warehouse, or computers were delivered but not connected to the Internet when the school opened, or teachers were trained in the school's core curricula but not supplementary programs, board members considered the EMO to have failed to meet its commitments. "If the computers weren't there yet, something we'd all write off as start-up stuff—parents didn't see it that way," recalls Gene Eidelman. "You're liars!" parents and board members would say.[42] In light of the hurdles along the way, EMO staff felt victorious in opening a school to hundreds of students in a matter of months. The customer saw only the chasm remaining between the promises that echoed in the community and the current reality of the school.

In hindsight, Advantage erred by communicating to boards that it would take virtually the entire responsibility for building and opening a school that would then perform to specific, measurable standards. When the board was given no responsibility for the realization of the school— other than to hold the company accountable—it could only blame Advantage for problems that inevitably arose. On the critical task of the school building, Advantage's commitments were more ambiguous, but there too the board heard only that the company would take full responsibility. In sharp contrast, Mosaica and Chancellor Beacon were judicious in the promises they made. Commitments were not made for academic outcomes but for initial inputs. Mosaica benefited from value propositions that shrewdly combined specific but readily achievable commitments with gauzy promises. Mosaica pledged a longer school day and year and a high ratio of computers to children—commitments that were expensive but otherwise easy to realize. It enlivened these commitments with seductive but vague aspirations: its schools would "open portals of opportunity" and serve as "a community pillar."[43]

"A lot of the promises Advantage made were unattainable," reflected Michael Connelly. "Mosaica made far fewer promises."[44] In contrast to

Advantage, Mosaica told client boards it would share with them responsibility for (and ownership of) the realization of the school; officials emphasized that the company took on responsibility for real estate with reluctance. Connelly explained, "We always said [to the boards], 'We don't want to do this.'"[45]

Chancellor Beacon's promises of smaller class sizes were particularly appealing to parents in states—Florida and Arizona—with overcrowded schools, and such commitments were easy to deliver on opening day. Never mind that the literature on class size and achievement was inconclusive. Chancellor's assurances that it would "offer students a challenging and exciting academic experience within a nurturing, supportive environment" resonated with its middle-class parent customers—and were, once again, difficult to measure.[46]

A survey of EMO contracts found that companies varied widely in their contractual commitments for academic performance. While Advantage and SABIS often committed to specific academic achievement gains, Chancellor Beacon's contracts examined in 2003 stipulated only that the company shall make "reasonable efforts" to meet the performance criteria set out in the school's charter, including annual gains.[47] A sample of Edison's contracts gave no specific levels of academic performance to be attained, but rather stated vaguely that the board may "measure the success of the Charter School on the basis of student achievement, compliance with State Standards and by measures of student and parent satisfaction."[48]

Yet while promising too much jeopardized client relationships, prudent commitments didn't assure stable contracts. Chancellor Beacon proceeded cautiously at its five contract schools in Philadelphia. By February of its first year on the job, Octavio Visiedo's assessment of his company's performance was "nowhere near a homerun. It's a single." The schools were in much worse shape than they had expected, causing the company to accelerate its plans and hire more staff. But he described Chancellor's relationship with district chief Vallas as "excellent." In a meeting, Visiedo had found Vallas to be "very receptive, appreciative of [Chancellor's] approach."[49]

Yet in April, Vallas terminated Chancellor, claiming the firm had done little to make the schools better: "They were not fulfilling what we felt to be their obligations . . . They had not really established a presence in the schools."[50] Chancellor claimed that the district had urged them and other contractors to take things slowly during the first year, and that they had deliberately chosen to "get in and see the landscape" before making more extensive changes in the schools' second year. Chancellor insisted it had met its primary promise of smaller class sizes from the start.[51] The company announced it was considering contesting the termination, but it never filed suit.

Nor did academic performance guarantee stability. One of Edison's first contracts was to operate a school in Wichita, Kansas, beginning in fall 1995; it soon operated four schools for the district. Edison put in a good performance. When students arrived at the first of the four schools, Dodge-Edison Elementary, they were performing on average between two and eleven percentile rank points below district students on the Metropolitan Achievement Test (MAT-7). Four years later, students were consistently performing on average at levels above the district, in some grades and subjects by as much as fourteen percentile rank points.[52] In January 2002, a principal at another of the Edison schools was accused of helping students cheat on standardized tests; the district voted to take back that school and one other, even though the principal had been inherited from the district and Edison had participated fully in the investigation. Later that year, the district took back the remaining two schools, despite their record of improved performance under Edison's management. "They're just not delivering on the promise, not only here, but across the nation," school board president Chip Gramke said.[53] Superintendent Winston Brooks claimed that ending the contract would save the district over half a million dollars a year. Brooks acknowledged the district had benefited from the competition: "They are one element of several that started the district's achievement climb."[54] In fact, the district implemented Success for All, the reading curriculum Edison brought to Wichita, in five other schools, and a longer school day and year in three elementary schools.[55]

Managing Academic Expectations

Even when EMOs were careful with their promises, academic expectations for privately managed schools ran high. Charter schools implicitly claimed superiority to district schools. But charters operated by EMOs—and still more takeovers of district schools—represented an even more pointed challenge to the status quo. The private sector had thrown down the gauntlet to the public schools.

EMOs did little to temper expectations. Rarely did they provide a schedule for the new school's complete implementation, offer a yardstick for sizing up reported gains, or emphasize that a fair judgment on a new school could only be reached after several years. It takes time to refine a school, realize gains from the institution of new curricula and pedagogical programs, and reach the level of excellence to which the school's founders aspire. Test results often decline in the first year, as teachers and students adjust to new methods. In time, the school gains its footing. A recent study of California charter schools found that schools that had passed their five-year milestone posted annual gains greater than the average district school.[56]

Even when deploying powerful designs, EMOs faced considerable challenges in implementing them successfully on site. Beyond their apparent simplicity, schools are complex production functions. Before anything else can happen, behavior systems must be implemented consistently throughout the school and a pervasive school culture, supportive of high achievement, established. Then teachers need to be persuaded of the benefits of unfamiliar, and sometimes controversial, methods and extensively trained in them. Finally, the school's management must continually collect and analyze performance data, diagnose instructional problems, and hone instruction.

To put the EMOs' challenge in perspective, consider the difficulty of improving performance in traditional public school systems that serve low-performing students. A new superintendent would be lauded for getting the school district on course for any discernible improvement in achievement, even an average annual gain of one percentile point. EMOs often had to post gains many times that to be considered successful in fulfilling the schools' charters. Even Edison's reported gains of five or six percentile rank points across its network of schools attracted more skepticism than admiration.

Many EMOs found themselves holding a portfolio of schools of widely varying quality. Generally a few schools—benefiting always from a strong leader—posted exceptional gains, but many others performed no better (and sometimes worse) than the surrounding schools. When privately managed schools lacked a focused leader or were locked in conflict with the board, the quality of implementation was poor and staff turnover high, and the schools developed a reputation for mediocrity. Fixing these schools required perseverance and patience; client boards were seldom inclined to either.

The media, which delight in controversy, as well as the many opponents of private management, have been eager to reach a quick verdict on new privately managed schools. EMO staff, in presentations and casual conversation, would at times omit the caveats and details that kept claims honest; this failing provided the media another opportunity to portray EMOs as dishonest profit-seekers. For example, Advantage Schools publicized the power of its reading program to raise student achievement in the early grades. When a reporter from the *New York Times Magazine* attended an enrollment seminar and heard a company vice president make an impassioned claim—"Every single one of our kindergartners in both schools is reading! Every single one! I don't get up here and say it unless it's true"—it was an invitation to discredit her and the company: one exception disproves an absolute.[57] The reporter traveled to the company's school in Rocky Mount, North Carolina, which had opened the year before. He yanked individual kindergartners out of class and required that they read on the spot a text they had never seen, with words like "ghostie" and "haunted" that would intimidate even many older readers. In his account, the reporter doesn't mention that two pupils in the lowest-level reading group read the book cover to cover, noting only that two others struggled with his impromptu exam.[58]

Of course, "reading" is a complex notion. The vice president should have included the phrase "at grade level." What it means for a kindergartner to read—to decode regular words and understand simple sentences—is nothing like what is expected of a literate eighth-grader. Kindergarten students at the Rocky Mount school were tested on arrival in the fall and again in the spring on the Iowa Test of Basic Skills. Total language skills rose 40 percentile rank points, from the 47th percentile to the 87th.[59] While these facts were provided to the *Times*, it did not report them.

Failing to meet academic commitments five years out was an abiding concern for EMOs. But there was a more immediate threat: some opponents of private management were eager to cast short-term test results as evidence of a new school's failure. In Albany, New York, an Associated Press story that ran in June of the Advantage school's first year was headlined "Albany Charter School on New Test: Ninety-one Percent Fail." The state education commissioner Richard Mills was quoted as saying that the school needs "to have a very serious conversation" about its low test scores.[60] The same day, the headline in the front-page story in the *(Albany) Times Union* was "Charter's Scores Renew Criticisms—Poor Results Prompt New Covenant Officials to Reconsider Firing Management."[61] Only at the end of the story does the reporter acknowledge that the school's academic focus was already generating results and that the fourth-grade tests represented a baseline for measuring the school's future gains. "The test was administered in January—only four months after New Covenant opened—and therefore says more about the education students received at the school they came from, parents, teachers, and officials said."[62] In truth, the students were gaining rapidly, as spring testing would later reveal.

Unfortunately, education reporters at city dailies are often young and inexperienced; the beat is among the least prestigious, and capable reporters often move on to other more desirable assignments. "In the course of a decade, you end up dealing with ten different reporters" from the same news outlet, Whittle lamented. "You're constantly having to reeducate."[63] Early negative coverage by the media put new schools at risk in their earliest stages of operation by eroding the confidence of parents, board members, and regulators in the management company.

Had EMOs communicated a timetable for the implementation of each component of the school design, it would have created realistic expectations for achievement gains and for the training of the faculty in the school's many and complex curricula, with clear priorities established for core programs, like reading. Thus forewarned, trustees could have served as ambassadors for the EMO, rather than critics, as they fielded inquiries from the media and the inevitable complaints from quarrelsome parents during the school's early months.

Weathering State Tests

For decades, districts had administered nationally standardized tests—including the Stanford Achievement Test, Iowa Test of Basic Skills, and Metropolitan Achievement Test—which embodied longstanding, if implicit, mainstream conceptions of what students should learn at each grade level. In the mid-1990s, states were implementing their own tests, which initially often reflected regional, idiosyncratic expectations of what students should know and be able to do and were shaped by passing pedagogical or ideological influences. While national norm-referenced tests reported students' performance relative to the national average of all test-takers, new state criterion-referenced tests measured achievement of individual students against state curriculum standards.

State tests posed a problem for management organizations. The tests' assumptions about what students should know at each grade level and what skills they should be able to demonstrate were often very different from the scope and sequence of the EMO's curricula. What's more, even when students had in fact learned the skills being tested, the students might fail to demonstrate their knowledge: unfamiliar terminology or the format of the questions could cause confusion. Education management organizations often initially failed to grasp the political importance of these high-stakes state tests and to take the steps required to ensure that students did well on them.

Some EMOs wrongly assumed that if students performed well on national tests, they would demonstrate their newly acquired competencies on state tests. John Chubb, Edison's chief education officer, said his initial hypothesis was, "Smart kids would perform well on both."[64] An Edison booklet created in 1994 for potential school board clients declared, "Students who perform well on Edison's rigorous assessments will perform well on other assessments, too."[65] Chubb later reflected, "It quickly became apparent that you had to demonstrate your worth on whatever the local test was, and [school board] clients quickly focused on that."[66]

Some EMO executives were openly dismissive of the tests and attempted—unsuccessfully—to cast doubt on the tests' validity and downplay their importance to client school boards. Others were merely skeptical about the new tests or underestimated their imminent significance. Advantage's chief education officer, Theodor Rebarber, questioned the quality of many of the states' new standards and worried that Advantage's curriculum would be degraded if it were aligned with them. As late as 2000, Advantage was under pressure from its client boards to demonstrate alignment with state standards and corresponding state assessments. But that same year, the Fordham Foundation, led by Rebarber mentor Chester Finn, judged in its annual report that twenty-one states' academic standards in most subjects were "vague, vapid, and misleading (or missing)."[67] Standards of poor quality, the report warned, could harm market-style reforms, including charter schools. The new schools were being held strictly accountable for attaining standards that "are not altogether worth reaching. Bad standards could force otherwise exemplary charter schools to become worse."[68]

Principals knew it was pointless to challenge the tests. "Edison had all sorts of lofty concerns," Chubb said. "But the principals knew the kids would get slaughtered on the tests."[69] Embracing the new reality was difficult and costly. Companies that worked in multiple states had first to adjust their curricula—in essence, create a new curriculum product—for each state. Second, they had to develop new curricula to fill in the gaps between their own curricula and state expectations for what students would learn in each subject and grade. Finally, they had to ensure that students became both familiar with the idiom of state tests and able test-takers. Edison worked closely with school staff to bring together—to "align and embed"—state standards, testing, and daily instruction. Few education departments of EMOs had the staff to undertake this volume of work and do it well and quickly.

The press chronicled every turn in the standards movement, from the early controversies about curriculum standards to the latest test scores of school districts. In 2002, with the graduation requirement looming over high school juniors, Massachusetts Comprehensive Assessment System (MCAS) scores were the subject of three hundred separate *Boston Globe* articles. Because the tests had high stakes both for students—who could ultimately be denied a diploma if they failed—and for schools, the media quickly cast a spotlight on schools that performed poorly.

Edison Schools and the Boston Renaissance Charter School, the largest charter in Massachusetts with 1,300 students, severed their contract in May 2002, three years before it was set to expire. Both sides cited weak academic performance, including low scores on the Massachusetts tests, along with the school's desire to manage its education program on its own. In 2001, the school had posted higher failure rates on the MCAS than did the Boston Public Schools as a whole; 22 percent of the school's eighth-graders had failed the English exam, compared to 21 percent in the district, and 69 percent had failed the math exam, compared to 55 percent of the district's students.[70]

Opened in 1995, Renaissance was one of Edison's first four schools and generated $9 million in annual revenues for the company.[71] Chubb said that test performance would have been stronger had Edison full control over instruction.[72] Under an arrangement for sharing power, the school's principal reported to both Edison and the trustees. "For our side, working under the arrangement where we didn't have the full authority to do the job was less than ideal," he said.[73]

There were serious consequences for those EMOs that did not catch on to the importance of state tests. Students did not do well unless EMOs or their client schools aligned curricula with each state's testing program, identified knowledge gaps, developed new lessons to provide students with the missing skills or knowledge, and prepared them for the kinds of questions the tests presented. EMOs that operated in many states faced a vastly greater challenge than those with schools in just a few jurisdictions. Today, the idiosyncrasies of state testing regimens continue to pose unique challenges for national organizations. One recent study found vast disparities in the percentage of students found to be proficient in reading on the National Assessment of Educational Progress (NAEP) and on states' own tests. For example, 18 percent of students in Mississippi were proficient according to the NAEP, while 87 percent were judged proficient on the state's test. While students in Louisiana posted similar results on the NAEP, with 20 percent found proficient, just 14 percent were proficient on that state's test.[74]

Avoiding Conflicts with Local Boards

In a true market structure, parents could choose from among schools run by local boards and schools owned and operated by education companies. Public funds would follow the student. Higher education is structured this way today, with both independent institutions and growing networks of for-profit postsecondary providers competing for students and tuition dollars.

But under the current regulatory structure, EMOs operate at a distance from their true customers, parents. Whether for a district or charter school, the EMO enters into a contract to provide management services to the school's governing board, which remains a legally separate entity from the management company. In many cases, the school's staff are public employees of the charter school or district, rather than the management company, and the governing board retains by statute the ultimate oversight over all aspects of the school.

This structure gives rise to immense problems. Companies, their client boards, and principals vie for control over the new school. When the school's board lays claim to a school as truly its own, the law is in its favor. The EMO, for its part, naturally seeks as much authority as possible to ensure it can generate financial and academic results and protect its financial investment in the school. But even when the local board is willing to delegate much of its authority for day-to-day management to the contractor, state regulators and charter authorizers often prevent it. Many charter laws require officials or charter authorizers to approve any comprehensive management contract. They have used that authority to ensure that contracts in their judgment comport with the statute. When boards planned a stark delegation of responsibility to their contractors, regulators insisted on inserting language throughout the contract that rendered the EMO's powers ambiguous by subjecting them to "the board's ultimate oversight."[75]

In North Carolina, Advantage negotiated a contract with its client board in Rocky Mount that gave the company broad authority over the charter school's day-to-day operations, including the hiring and firing of school staff. To prevent the school's opening, the Nash–Rocky Mount school board filed an appeal of the North Carolina Board of Education's charter award, claiming that the hiring of the for-profit Advantage was impermissible under the state's charter law. The North Carolina

Department of Public Instruction sought the guidance of the state's office of attorney general. To strengthen its hand in defending the department, the attorney general recommended that clauses in the management contract defining Advantage's authority include the words "subject to the ultimate authority of the board."[76] Advantage had little choice but to agree to the changes. "The [charter school] board was always responsible for the school and we still are," charter school board chair Robert Mauldin said after the matter was settled. "Advantage Schools is under contract to manage the school in the way we direct."[77]

When state law required principals to be employed by the board or when boards accepted only recommendations from the EMO for the appointment, the EMO was at risk of running a school with a chief executive it had no confidence in and could not replace. When tensions arose between the board and management in the course of launching the new school, the board naturally sought to draw the principal to its side. For the principal, it was an easy choice. When the board had the final say over your job, why side with the management company hundreds of miles away whose power was in question? It took courage to defy trustees who were in and out of the school every day, disparaging the management company and telling you what to do.

With such a muddled chain of command, it was probably inevitable that boards and EMOs would fight, from the earliest days of their marriage, over the most basic components of the new schools. Where should the school be housed and at what cost? What instructional programs should be used? Who should lead the school? Once the school was launched, there were new opportunities for conflict, often more personal and bitter. Common areas of conflict were the hiring of school staff, the transfer of payments to the EMO as required by the management agreement, and the letting of contracts.

EMOs typically planned an expansion over time of the school's grades and enrollment, in part to meet the organization's goals for site profitability. Yet even when the charter application reflected this growth plan, after the school opened a board might challenge the wisdom of expanding as planned. At its school in Syracuse, New York, relations between Beacon Education Management and the board were strained after a rough launch, discipline problems, and changes in the school's leadership. The expansion plan called for adding a seventh and eighth grade. Angering Beacon, the school's new principal prepared on behalf of the board an amendment to the school's charter to maintain the school's K–6 structure.[78] The authorizer, the principal said, "reinforced" his position. In an interview, he was emphatic that the board, rather than Beacon, was his employer.[79] With the announcement of the change in plan, enrollment dropped precipitously, and Beacon and the school had to work to build enrollment back up the following summer.

EMOs knew that charter authorizers wanted to see "community members" on the boards of the charter schools they approved, so EMO staff recruited—often with little diligence—parent activists, local church leaders, and their friends and colleagues. Once a charter was awarded, authorizers were reluctant to question the board's practices. "There isn't much oversight of charter boards, and there should be. They can be engaged in the grossest mismanagement and there are no consequences," lamented one executive.[80]

Trustees "start off on the right track, with the right purposes," one senior EMO executive acknowledged. "But then they get involved in little things. In parents' eyes, they are responsible, and they feel quite important." Yet few have any preparation to serve as fiduciaries of millions of dollars of public funds flowing through the school's accounts. "A lot of board members haven't seen payments of $100,000 before, and then there's a transfer payment from the state of $750,000," said another official. Holding up transfer of the funds to the management company, notwithstanding the terms of the management contract, was a way to exercise power.

At the SABIS International School of Cincinnati, the chair of the board was in the school every day, a SABIS manager said. "Parents came up to her, asking about this and that. She wanted to be a prima donna, so to speak. 'I want to see these reports,'" she'd demand of SABIS's business manager and academic quality controller, requiring that they drop whatever they were doing. SABIS asked that she not disrupt the school's staff, to no avail.[81] After the trustees terminated SABIS's contract, the state transferred $588,252 to the school, corresponding to the six-hundred-student enrollment in the school under SABIS's management. The board broke its lease and abandoned the company's $7.5 million school building, moved the school to a undisclosed "secret location," and reopened to some fifty students. The state obtained an injunction forcing the school to reveal its location; when state officials appeared at the school, they were prevented from entering the building. The state went to court and eventually recovered the funds.[82]

Ralph Bistany has noted the illogic of approving an EMO-affiliated charter application, premised on the school design and expertise of the EMO, and then later permitting the board to terminate the contract unilaterally and continue to hold the license to operate the school. SABIS's experience in Cincinnati, while unusually colorful, was not uncommon. A charter school serving the middle and high school grades in Kansas City, Missouri, withheld payments from Edison; the management contract was later terminated. After Edison had left the scene, the Kansas City school district, which sponsored the school, engaged the auditing firm of KPMG to assist in the district's oversight of the school. In addition to inadequate financial records, purchasing systems, and internal controls, KPMG found numerous problems with related party transactions, in violation of the board's stated ethics policies. Many board members were employed by organizations to which the board had contracted for services.[83]

Many trustees were well-intentioned but unsophisticated when it came to their ethical responsibilities as public agents. Some saw nothing wrong with lobbying the principal to hire a friend, or decreeing that male kindergarten teachers could not be hired, or insisting that the EMO do business with a particular firm at above-market rates. When the EMO demurred, mindful of the law and the responsibilities that came with managing public funds, the board perceived it as highhandedness. It was downhill from there. Soon enough, relationships among all three parties running the school—board, EMO, and principal—deteriorated. The project, once fueled by optimism and drive, was now shot through with bitterness. Sometimes the relationship could be healed, often it continued under the weight of distrust, and not infrequently the contract was terminated. Avoiding conflicts with customer boards was the "single biggest problem we've had," Mosaica's Connelly reported.[84] Other CEOs said the same.

Enforcing Contracts

As the charter movement matured, authorizers came under pressure to demonstrate that they held their portfolio schools accountable for academic performance. "Accountability" was the theme of charter conferences everywhere, and this focus had special implications for management companies and their contracts. Authorizers held the recipient of the charter, the school's board, responsible for results; in their judgment, the board should be free to take whatever actions were necessary for the school to meet the terms of its charter. But the authorizers' insistence on the board's unfettered authority to make good on the charter was at odds with the EMO's premise of a long-term agreement. Under the terms of the contract with its management organization, the board did not have the authority to terminate the management contract at its discretion. In negotiations with client boards, EMOs typically insisted on limiting the right of the board to terminate the contract and on having several years to generate a return on their invested capital. Under the agreement, only in the event of the EMO's breach of contract, bankrupcy, or malfeasance could the contractor be summarily fired.

Despite these provisions, many boards threatened to terminate their management contractors, citing poor performance. From the board's perspective, it was responsible for holding the EMO accountable for its performance. The EMO's failure to deliver on all of its promises and to fulfill the commitments set out in the charter application was inexcusable. In the face of such threats, an EMO's options were limited: it could lobby the school's authorizer to compel the school's board to abide by its contract, but such appeals nearly always fell on deaf ears. Authorizers, charged with holding the local board accountable to the terms of the charter, were understandably loath to interfere with actions the board judged necessary to fulfill its commitments. They reflexively backed the boards. Appealing to state regulators was also no solution. State education agencies were often reluctant administrators of charter programs enacted by reformist legislators and tended to assume the worst of management companies.

To cite but one example, the relationship between Edison and one school board deteriorated after Edison had invested over $3 million in facilities upgrades, technology, curriculum materials, and furniture in a leased school building. Edison threatened to evict the school when scheduled payments were not made. The board refused to communicate with company officials and barred Edison's staff from entering the building. Edison continued to honor its side of the contract and attempted to provide full services to the school, incurring more than $2 million for personnel and other school expenses for which it received $326,000 from the board. Well over $1 million in management fees also went unpaid. Edison eventually commenced legal proceedings against the board, threatening to terminate the contract and evict the school from the building, for the school's right to occupy was coterminous with the management contract.[85] In a five-page letter to the board's president, Edison implored the board to come to the table to "repair the relationship" and cited the company's "devastating financial exposure."[86] An Edison official wrote,

> Please, I implore you on behalf of all affected stakeholders at the school, to respond to this letter with a firm date in the next two weeks when we can meet to work this out . . . This matter can and should be resolved

amicably and quickly through reasonable discussion. That is our highest aspiration and hope. We can only proceed in this spirit, if it is shared by you and your board. I pray that it is.[87]

When Edison's appeal to the board president failed, the company asked the general counsel of the charter authorizer to intervene and "broker a mediation" because "the future of the school is in grave jeopardy." "I do understand," Edison's counsel wrote, "that, as a general rule, it is not in the province of [the authorizing university] to throw itself into the middle of a contract dispute. With respect, however, this is something more. Indeed, I would think it highly appropriate for the charter authorizer to get involved where, as here, a very successful charter school is in jeopardy of closing down. Indeed, I can think of no more important role for the charter authorizer than to use its good offices to save a great school from perishing unnecessarily."[88] The authorizer declined to get involved.

If state officials were unwilling to hold trustees of charter schools to their contracts, EMOs could litigate. Most found this option unattractive; entering into a public fight with a client school would be a public relations nightmare. Regardless of the circumstances, the public would be sympathetic to the local board, who would claim to be acting in the interest of the children against the out-of-town, profit-seeking corporation. Moreover, charter schools rarely have any assets, so the threat of an EMO suit was largely idle and a damage award unlikely. And while the company had little chance of recouping its legal costs, the charter could pay its lawyers out of the school's public operating funds.

Only in the politically charged climate of school management would a vendor's actions to enforce a business agreement be regarded as unseemly. Consider a food services provider that has gone unpaid by a big-city school board. No one would be surprised if the provider threatened to litigate. The board's legal counsel would be quick to advise the board to settle—both parties would expect the contract to hold up in court. A food services company taking on a big-city school board for breach of contract has none of the public relations perils of an EMO litigating a charter school board.

Faced with limited options, most EMOs have chosen to do everything possible to maintain their engagement in the school. With the contract on the line, they have often agreed to renegotiate, resulting in lower fees, elimination of contract renewal provisions, loss of supervisory authority over school personnel, reduction in responsibilities, and shortened contract terms. SABIS purchased and renovated one short-term facility and completed the construction of the first building of the permanent campus of the Somerville Charter School. In time, the school posted impressive gains in state test scores; in two of the three grades tested in spring 2001, students scored above the state average in both English and math. Yet on June 30 of that year, SABIS's management contract expired, summer vacation began, and the board had not negotiated the contract's renewal. SABIS in good faith continued to fund payroll and reopened the school in September. In November, the matter unresolved, it told the board it was willing to make radical changes to its management contract. Despite the fact that the board owed SABIS several months of school payroll and expenses, the company offered to relinquish its right to retain school operating surpluses, to develop a plan for the board to purchase the school buildings in the future, and to limit SABIS's financial control to just its own management fees. The board did not renew the contract and eventually moved the school to another location. SABIS has not been paid, continues to own the two properties without tenants, and is in litigation with the board.[89]

When concessions have failed to sustain the engagement, EMOs have sometimes sought to arrange a quiet departure billed as a mutual decision rather than litigate a client for breach of contract. In March 2002, an Advantage client sought to end its relationship, notwithstanding its five-year contract. The school's sponsor, a major civic organization, was embarrassed by the school's poor marks in a report from the city, based in large measure on an indifferent performance on the Iowa Test of Basic Skills administered to students just eight months after the school opened—results that should have served as a baseline for the school's future achievements.[90] There was no arguing the point; the board had made up its mind. Rather than litigate a client, Advantage chose to terminate the contract at the end of the school year and agreed on the language that both parties would use to describe the separation.

Typically, Edison chose to withdraw from conflicts with a board— either by capitulating to demands or by walking away—rather than protect its contractual rights. "It was so important to keep contracts," one official explained, "that we would capitulate." In Sherman, Texas, the district claimed that Edison was too expensive, stopped paying Edison, and began to discuss canceling its contract. With its IPO pending, Edison offered to work the remaining two years of the agreement without compensation. "He [Whittle] was just really desperate to make sure the deal didn't end abruptly," said the district's retired assistant superintendent.[91] Whittle concedes he was sensitive to the effects of a contract cancellation: "We were trying to hold customers, and they were our first customers."[92] In other cases, Edison judged that it would suffer less damage to its brand by "amicably" separating than by battling a hostile board. By late 2002, however, Edison had changed tack: it was not so desperate to retain clients that it would accept extortion. "We cannot continue to carry clients who don't pay their bills," said Deborah McGriff, an Edison officer, at a company presentation.[93] When necessary, Edison will now sue clients who breach their contracts. "We'll take more punches than probably anyone," Whittle says. But "people have to know that we're not going to roll over for incredible abuse."[94]

In 1999, urged on by superintendent Waldemar Rojas, the trustees of the Dallas school district voted 5–4 to enter a five-year agreement with Edison for the management of seven elementary schools.[95] By the third year of the contract, three of the five trustees who had voted for the contract were no longer on the board, and the district's new superintendent, Mike Moses, called for the termination of the contract. The schools had not sufficiently improved under Edison, he charged, while invoking budget constraints as the primary cause for the termination. State law and a provision in the management contract, he asserted, permitted the district to end the agreement. In August 2002, the trustees voted unanimously to end the agreement.[96] Just prior to the vote, John Chubb said it would not be so easy for the district to terminate the contract for financial reasons. The provision "is not intended to let districts pick and choose what contracts they want to be in," he said. "It means to provide relief in times of extraordinary stress."[97] At the time, Dallas was one of Edison's largest contracts. Yet ultimately Edison decided against filing suit against the school district.

Two EMOs took a tough stance from the start—but at a cost. SABIS's CEO, Ralph Bistany, aggressively protected the company's contractual rights and was not hesitant to litigate clients who did not honor their agreements. SABIS sued the Chicago Charter School Foundation over its termination at the end of the school's second year, the board at its former Somerville school, and its original board in Cincinnati. Only when speaking of the SABIS Foxborough Charter School board does SABIS stress that the separation was amicable. The approach has not as yet made for a strong business. By late 2003, SABIS had ongoing management contracts with only seven independent charter school boards.[98] Mosaica's posture is still more aggressive. "We have a contract; if you break the contract, we will seek redress," maintains Connelly.[99] By 2004, Mosaica's reputation for its litigious stance with clients had reportedly become an obstacle to recruiting experienced educators to the management team.

The failure of authorizers and state regulators to hold schools accountable for their contractual commitments has far-reaching implications for private-sector involvement in public schools. It also damages the charter movement, because it permits trustees, who are public fiduciaries, to break the law with impunity. SABIS's Bistany defends his aggressive stance with client boards and questions the public-policy merits of current charter laws, which interpose lay boards of trustees between EMOs and parent customers. Why should individuals with few qualifications—no financial, managerial, or educational expertise, and often limited education—be appointed as trustees? As custodians of millions of dollars in public funds? "You can't create a new industry this way," Bistany explained. "My interest is to awaken people that these laws are not right."[100]

Private funds will not again flow into public education if Wall Street believes its investments in schools are not protected. While just one school termination could result in a charge of $500,000, a succession of write-offs from terminated schools could cause an EMO to "miss its plan" repeatedly and fail to perform financially. In a business where investors were skeptical from the start about the potential for profit, write-offs from lost schools struck hard at investor confidence and management's credibility. Privately, one Edison executive describes school management as "the least commercial world one could possibly imagine."[101] Investors dislike surprises and punish stocks severely for them. Could management of schools, they asked, be a predictable business?

The difficulty of enforcing management contracts, school terminations and associated write-offs, and worries about the industry's underlying stability caused investors to back away from K–12 education investments. Investors wrestled with whether to risk new money in their existing EMO investments or merge their investments with other EMOs. Combining operations—whether or not the companies were culturally or educationally compatible—created immediate scale and, with that scale, the promise of profitability. It was in this climate that Advantage Schools was sold to Mosaica Education, Beacon Education Management merged with Chancellor Academies, and LearnNow was sold to Edison Schools. Other companies struggled to raise additional funds, including Charter Schools USA.

This chapter has highlighted the chief business problems that EMOs, and in some instances KIPP, commonly encountered. The absence of funding for charter school buildings put privately managed schools at an immense financial and practical disadvantage to district schools. Building and financing schools for hundreds of children, often in urban cores, under extraordinary time pressure and in the face of fierce political resistance, burned through equity capital and diverted top executives from the task of implementing quality education programs. Operating schools by way of service agreements with local school boards, too, whether district or charter, proved a far cry from owning and operating schools directly. The arrangement rarely fostered the accurate implementation of an educational program and the efficient operation of the school; if anything, it was a hindrance.

The pressure to meet investors' expectations for short-term profitability caused management to expand rapidly before the school's design was perfected in a small number of locations; the capital market's reckless focus on top-line growth only exacerbated this pressure. While expanding rapidly into multiple states, each with its own regulatory environment, EMOs stumbled as they sought to meet disparate reporting requirements and develop relationships with regulatory, authorizer, and media "customers" who held the power to ease or obstruct their work. Few of these failings are inherent to private management of public schools; most are consequences of the particular regulatory setting that education entrepreneurs encountered in the 1990s.

Whereas some EMOs became mired in conflict—feuding with customer boards, failing to satisfy regulators, and defending themselves against a hostile media—two organizations, National Heritage Academies and KIPP, pursued business models and made strategic choices that mitigated some obstacles to execution.

KIPP's focus on leadership has set it apart from the six EMOs, which struggled to identify and recruit the kinds of leaders they needed at both the school and corporate levels. School leaders are the subject of the next chapter.

6

School Leaders

Everywhere, effective schools owe much of their success to strong principals, and nowhere more so than in schools that serve the disadvantaged. When students defy their demographic destiny, an extraordinary school leader is invariably leading the charge. Marva Collins drove the celebrated Westside Preparatory Academy in Chicago, Thaddeus Lott the Wesley Elementary School in Houston, and David Levin the KIPP school in the South Bronx. All three schools served inner-city children and were celebrated as "miracles" for their extraordinary academic results. All were led by charismatic, driven leaders who rallied students and teachers to their audacious plans.

Education management organizations knew they could not rely on finding such extraordinary individuals. How could the business be brought to scale if every school they opened required an exceptional leader? Some client schools would be blessed with stars; most would have to succeed with merely competent principals. And surely what EMOs could consistently provide their client schools—a well-chosen school design; competitively selected staff; heavy investment in staff training; and in charter schools, freedom from the worst constraints of district schools—would alone sharply raise student achievement.

Yet one of the starkest lessons from the experiences of the six EMOs and KIPP is the importance of a strong principal to the success of each new school. The difficulty of the principal's job was increased, not diminished, by private management. Strong leaders for new schools were difficult to find, especially in time to meet the frantic school opening schedules that marked the early industry. Many schools opened with weak principals and then fell into a pattern of mediocrity and leadership instability.

The difficulty of recruiting qualified leaders was not limited to the school site, but extended into the corporate office as well. Regional executives and senior management often lacked the requisite blend of education and operational expertise.

School Principals

One firm conclusion from three decades of research on effective schools is that principals matter: exceptional schools benefit from dynamic leaders who announce ambitious goals for student achievement and inspire the deep commitment of staff to realizing them. School leaders forge a powerful school culture that is widely shared and warmly endorsed. In the successful middle schools she studied, Joan Lipsitz found in each a principal with vision, unusual clarity about the school's purpose, a coherent philosophy, clearly articulated and shared goals, strong instructional leadership, respect for staff members as professionals, a climate of positive attitudes and expectations, high levels of effort by the staff, and encouragement of staff ingenuity.[1] The effective schools she studied

> make powerful statements, both in word and in practice, about their purposes. There is little disagreement within them and little discrepancy between what they say they are doing and what they actually do. As a result, everyone can articulate what the schools stand for . . .
>
> *Each [school] has or has had a principal with a driving vision who imbues decisions and practices with meaning, placing powerful emphasis on why and how things are done. Decisions are made not just because they are practical, but for reasons of principle.*[2]

Lipsitz's vivid description anticipated the leadership challenge the organizations would face as they sought to build not just one school but a network of high-performing schools. Could they find principals who were strong leaders, yet would adhere to the organization's school design and accept responsibility for meeting its academic and financial goals?

The task was made all the more difficult by the growing shortage of principal candidates, especially in challenging urban and rural settings. Half of urban districts say they lack qualified school principals, and the problem is worsening. Nationwide, principals' average age is fifty, and some 40 percent will be eligible to retire within a few years.[3] At the same time, the job of the public school principal is becoming more demanding. The state accountability movement and most recently the federal No Child Left Behind Act have radically changed the focus of the job. Not only have principals assumed new responsibilities for security, technology, budgeting and finance, public relations, and political matters; they have also been charged with producing unprecedented levels of academic achievement. The principal is expected to shape a vision of educational transformation and rally staff and students toward its attainment. Fail, and they risk losing their jobs. Today's principals cannot simply administer; they must lead.

Principals: The Record

Given the manifest importance of strong school leaders, it is surprising how varied has been the level of engagement by the seven organizations in recruiting them. Most education management organizations develop new schools by identifying where they can obtain a charter to open a school in partnership with a local board of directors, or where they can secure a contract with a school district to manage an existing school; schools are built opportunistically around the charters and management contracts that business development staff secure. Recruiting a school principal to lead the school is, like finding a facility and hiring the staff, merely an execution task that follows. By contrast, KIPP forms new schools around KIPP fellows, individuals who apply to open KIPP-affiliated schools and who participate in a yearlong training program before opening the school's doors to new students. The selection and development of leaders for new member schools is the national organization's primary activity; strong leadership is the key to the "Power to Lead." According to the KIPP website, "The principals of KIPP Schools are effective academic and organizational leaders who understand that great schools require great school leaders."[4] When research has abundantly shown the connection between powerful school leaders and high-quality schools, KIPP's approach amounts to a critical difference in strategy.

Edison claims success in screening candidates with a "surprisingly subtle" psychological test developed by Gallup that identifies leadership traits. Future principals participate in Edison's Leadership Institute. With the benefit of its size, Edison now places strong emphasis on "growing its own" principals by promoting academy directors from existing schools. Edison provides an incentive for current principals to develop future school leaders; the company awards the principal a bonus when a staff member is promoted out of his or her school.[5]

As did Advantage, National Heritage uses search firms to identify candidates at $10,000 to $30,000 per hire. Its principal training program has the candidate "shadow" strong NHA principals, gain familiarity with government reporting and compliance obligations, and make site visits at various NHA schools. Mosaica employs a small consulting firm that employs industrial psychologists to evaluate principal candidates using both interviews and written instruments. Instructional leadership is less important in the company's view than administrative skills; accordingly, principals are called "chief administrative officers."[6]

Given Chancellor Beacon's many low-spending markets, the strongest leaders are often unaffordable. CEO Octavio Visiedo emphasized the importance of recruiting "team players." "I look for people who will push back and give their opinion and then sign on to be the biggest advocates—I can't deal with renegade principals."[7] But the Chancellor Beacon school sites examined for this research suffered, like the schools of many EMOs, from weak directors or vacancies. One strategically important school in an affluent Florida community, for example, was being led by a corporate staffer who had stepped in as acting principal after the company had fired the principal early in the school's second year. And when the academically troubled Options Charter Public School in Washington, D.C., recruited Chancellor to manage it in 2001, Chancellor hired a principal whose only previous educational leadership experience was in correctional facilities.[8] Chancellor fired him after the company learned he had served prison time for credit card fraud; the school then terminated Chancellor for the "hiring fiasco" (while crediting the company for its earlier work in stabilizing the school).[9] Two other schools were led by principals who, while affable, were not academic leaders. Their schools were orderly and their faculty engaged. But when asked to assess the progress of their schools, they responded with generalities ("we're off to a strong start, but we have a ways to go"), rather than a thorough evaluation of the school's instructional strengths and weaknesses, supported by specific data on student performance.

A SABIS official professed, in an interview, that a weak school director could be overcome: the company's proprietary school design, including its curriculum, are what makes SABIS's schools work.[10] Yet the company's struggles to replicate the success of its flagship Springfield school suggest otherwise. Ralph Bistany conceded that he has "not solved this problem yet" and said SABIS was developing its own specialized recruiting function for school directors.[11]

Across the six EMOs, the record of principal success is poor. Among them, they hired and fired several hundred principals in the early years of the industry, and it was common for a principal to last only a year or less. At Advantage, fewer than half of principals were still on the job two years after they were hired. Chancellor Beacon says its success rate is only about 50 percent.[12] NHA reports that 70 percent of principals have been successful hires; even so, about one-quarter of principals turn over each year.[13] Mosaica claims "75 percent of principals are good hires, but they might choose to upgrade" even these.[14]

Edison too has experienced heavy turnover among principals. Consider its schools in New York, the company's home state and a key market. The New Covenant Charter School in Albany, which Edison took over from Advantage in 2000, was by 2005 on Edison's third principal. Serving in an interim capacity, she was the school's fifth since inception. The Charter School of Science and Technology in Rochester, which opened in 2000, was on its fifth principal by 2005. The Buffalo Charter School for Applied Technologies and the city's other Edison school, Stepping Stone Academy Charter School, both opened in 2001 and had two principals in two years.

Daunting Requirements

As the record of failure accumulated, the six EMOs became more fully aware of how high were their expectations for school leaders. In 2000, Advantage codified the skills and traits it sought in school directors:

> The School Director will be a visible, forceful education advocate within the community and will demonstrate a self-reliant, entrepreneurial approach to school leadership and management. With a "can-do" attitude and relying on real-life experiences, the Director will guide the school through the critical start-up phase with composure and humor. The Director will leverage his/her strong working relationships with Advantage Corporate, community leaders, students, teachers and parents to support high student achievement, to develop a dedicated staff, and to recruit and hire additional staff as needed. This will occur as the Director meets key financial goals and ensures that the school remains in compliance with applicable legal requirements.[15]

The specification also delineated the successful candidate's personal and professional requirements: "The ideal candidate will have significant administrative experience, a business-like approach to school management, and will enthusiastically implement the Advantage school design."

The school director must be "passionately committed to children," "have strong interpersonal skills and must balance competing interests with skill and tact," and have "a master's degree in education, business, [or] administration . . . and prior experience as a Teacher and as a Principal, Assistant Principal, Head of School, or Assistant Head of School."[16] Needless to say, candidates who fit the specification were a very rare find.

The Advantage example reveals how paradoxical are the requirements for school principals in education organizations. One set of requirements argues for hiring "self-starters"—enterprising leaders who are confident in their judgment and accustomed to exercising it. Especially when opening a charter school, principals must function like entrepreneurs, rapidly hiring dozens of staff members, overseeing the completion of the school building, appeasing impatient parents, and generally lurching from one crisis to the next. The other set of requirements calls for loyal, diligent managers who take pride in the care with which they implement the company's school design and protocols. The first type of candidate might bristle at being told what to do or how to do it; the second might flounder in an unstructured environment where each day brings new problems for which there are no ready solutions.

While each EMO wrestled with these conflicting requirements, for KIPP the choice between the two was clear. Scott Hamilton invoked Freud. "Most people in education are 'erotics,'" he lamented—people who want to be liked and avoid conflict. School principals ought instead to be "narcissists," driven leaders who want not to be loved but admired and who, through their gifts of charisma and oratory, attract followers to their bold plans. In education, narcissists are few and far between. "The people who are drawn to this profession are not necessarily leaders who don't give a rat's ass about conformity, about whether people like them or not," says Hamilton.[17]

The best schools have fiercely committed principals who are able to exact an extraordinary engagement from their staffs. In independent charter schools, the principals are often also the founders; the schools are in fact "theirs." It is hard to rival the level of investment we feel for what we have ourselves created. But for EMOs to invite principals to shape their own schools was perilous; "ownership" might come at the expense of fidelity to the organization's model. They had to find another way. How would EMOs induce such commitment in their principals? How the different organizations wrestled with these paradoxical requirements was as varied as their models and organizational cultures. Consider the cases of five organizations: Advantage, Beacon, SABIS, KIPP, and National Heritage.

ADVANTAGE AND GUIDELINES

Advantage's human resources vice president was impatient with the contradictions in the school director's job requirements. Until they were resolved, it would be impossible to recruit school directors on whom the senior management team members agreed. A cultural divide within the corporate office would fester, and dangerously mixed messages would be sent to principals.

One way to reconcile the corporation's expectations would be to distinguish those areas where the school director was permitted latitude in decision-making from those where she was expected to adhere to the company's way. If she wanted to do something different, she would consult with corporate. More than once Advantage tried to draw this line, but the efforts only provoked disagreement among corporate factions. The education department produced draft guidance to school directors, but its stingy conception of a director's authority outraged the "entrepreneurial" camp. According to the guidance, school directors could not change the curriculum in any subject, or even alter the school schedule or student groupings (without the consent of the corporate "curriculum implementation specialist"), but they were free to take any actions with respect to parental involvement. Many school directors found such limits on their authority demoralizing: the company, they felt, did not trust them and did not value their expertise. Few could hide their irritation from senior staff and even teachers, exacerbating a school-corporate divide.

But the education department's position was not without merit. The company had selected its curricula on the basis of evidence of their effectiveness. The department knew that outcomes from Direct Instruction and other structured programs are highly sensitive to the quality of implementation. There was ample evidence in the research on DI, for example, that the failure to group correctly or to regroup frequently on the basis of assessments erodes educational gains. If students are incorrectly grouped, some will be bored, having attained mastery of the material being taught, while others will be frustrated by material that relies on concepts they have not yet mastered.

The department correctly likened the professional culture they sought to establish in the schools to that of medicine. A surgeon, they argued, would take pride in the skill by which he followed established procedures, and the clinical results that he thereby obtained for his patients. Educators needed to move away from a culture that valued teacher invention, regardless of the outcomes, toward one that prized results.

The line-management chain at Advantage, including the chief operating officer and the regional directors, naturally favored the entrepreneurial view. They heard primarily from their school directors, who complained about micromanagement by the education department, wanted more authority, and promised better results from it. Exhorted by the school directors, understandably eager to accommodate them, and inclined generally to the American corporate philosophy of empowering managers, management grew increasingly hostile to the education department and its concerns. Ultimately, the conflict forced out both the chief education officer and the vice president for academic implementation, who could no longer tolerate what they perceived as disrespect and lack of authority. The irony is that these senior educators had designed and implemented the one part of the company that was unquestionably working: the academic program was producing strong annual gains in student achievement.

BEACON'S INTERNAL CUSTOMERS

Michael Ronan, CEO of Beacon Education Management before its merger with Chancellor, described how he worked to ensure the loyalty of school directors. Inspired by the culture of Southwest Airlines, Ronan had adopted the successful upstart as an explicit metaphor for Beacon. Employees flew Southwest, decals of the airline's wings were taped to computers in the corporate office, and a conference room was even painted in the Southwest colors. Ronan's goal was to create a customer service culture within his organization. "Every opportunity we have to do something for our parents, our principals, and our students, we have to do it," he said. Corporate staff were instructed to respond to e-mail and return all phone calls within twenty-four hours. To Ronan, principals were "internal customers" to whom corporate staff aimed to provide good service; in every conversation with them, he would ask, "What do you think about that?" Even his most senior executives were to follow his example, asking school staff, "How can I help you?" rather than dictating to them what they should do.[18]

Ronan's approach was a good match for Beacon's early business model, in which the company served an educationally diverse group of client schools. The company could afford to provide its principals substantial autonomy in exchange for accountability for academic results, a bargain that Beacon expected would build trust and loyalty among them. Yet as the company changed strategies and sought to impose the Lightpoints curriculum on all of its new schools, the customer service analogy for the relationship between corporation and schools became strained. The corporate office was not only looking to assist, it was also trying to direct. Ronan's personal style could overcome these tensions, but the people he hired to run important new state markets, where Lightpoints was being implemented, could not match Ronan's finesse.

EARNING TRUST AT SABIS

Both contemporary American business culture, which pretends to consultative decision-making and informality, and the collaborative ideology of district schools are foreign to the hierarchical, formal culture of SABIS. Power is held closely by the company's intergenerational owners, ways of doing business are entrenched, staff refer to "Mr. Bistany" and "Mrs. Saad," and even principals are treated unabashedly as employees. In the course of interviewing prospects, the company explains the "SABIS way," and candidates assent to follow it.

In the SABIS culture, school directors are not granted broad authority from the start; they gradually earn the trust of the company's executives and with it increased authority. "First show that you can perform, then tell me your ideas," Ralph Bistany tells his school directors. He "doesn't even want to hear any ideas until eighteen months" after they start with the company, "because otherwise he'll have to keep hearing the same stupid things again and again." With characteristic candor, he adds, "Invention is very rare."[19]

As jarring as SABIS's style is to American management sensibilities, its approach is not illogical. SABIS has refined over decades a school design that when properly implemented has reliably brought results. Accordingly, any modifications would likely degrade performance, not improve it. This is especially true of proposals from school directors steeped in what SABIS deems the emotionally appealing but erroneous tenets of American educational practice.

A minority of educators will commit to learning SABIS's ways; to most, this conception of leadership will seem parsimonious. Consider the fate of two of SABIS's Massachusetts schools. From the start, the successful Springfield school benefited from strong leadership. The first principal, Michael Glickman, was an experienced public school educator who gave unwavering support to his staff and was tenacious in his pursuit of the school's academic goals. His highly capable successor, Maretta Thomsen, who had served as the school's assistant director, sustained his leadership and continued to refine the school. Both leaders bought into the SABIS culture; they became expert in its practice and earned Bistany's deep respect.

But this dynamic is unlikely to be realized at most sites, for most principals will expect their power to be ascribed rather than earned. From the start, they will make "judgments on the fly" that alter the model; they will sooner indulge teachers' expectations of autonomy and creativity than uphold the SABIS system. SABIS attributes this freelancing to both the principals' desire to appear strong in front of their staff and their socialization in the American education culture. Witness Springfield's sister school in Foxborough. Floundering under the wrong leaders, Foxborough never gained the academic traction of Springfield and in 2003 severed its ties with SABIS. During site visits for this book before the break-up, staff members appeared demoralized and were outspokenly hostile to SABIS and its design. The principal privately disparaged both the school's board and SABIS. This was no secret to SABIS's executives: the principal "created a 'we-them' culture," one said.[20]

KIPP'S SOLUTION: LOOSE-TIGHT

KIPP addresses the ownership problem with what might be termed a "loose-tight" approach. KIPP recruits strong entrepreneurial leaders who are provided great latitude in how they operate their schools. Yet each must adhere to KIPP's core principles—embodied in the five pillars—or lose their KIPP affiliation. Most notably, "Focus on Results" requires KIPP schools to "relentlessly focus on high student performance on standardized tests and other objective measures . . . Students are expected to achieve a level of academic performance that will enable them to succeed at the nation's best high schools and colleges."[21]

At KIPP, quality is not assured through a line-management hierarchy. The organization does not prescribe specific curricula or pedagogical methods, schedules, teacher credentials, or other components of the school, and in no sense does the school leader report to KIPP. (Under the contract for its school in Albany, New York, KIPP does not have the explicit authority to terminate the school leader, although its broad authority to dictate "corrective action" at an underperforming school could be interpreted to include this right. KIPP also has the right to terminate the agreement and deny the school continued use of the KIPP name if the school comes under the direction of a new leader whom KIPP has not approved.)[22] Instead, KIPP relies on its extraordinary care in selecting and training the school's initial leader, immersing each in the ideology and practice of KIPP. KIPP's claim to being something different is legitimate. Its "leadership program," the website explains, "provides aspiring school leaders with the knowledge, skills, and support needed to successfully lead high performing public schools. Once established, KIPP Schools receive continued support from KIPP's national organization to ensure they successfully adhere to KIPP's core operating principles."[23] To evaluate each school, KIPP hires an outside organization to conduct a multiday inspection, modeled on the British school inspectorate system. The inspection at the end of the school's second year marks the end of the three-year KIPP Leadership Program.

The problem of ownership is greatly diminished in the KIPP model: school directors see the schools as their own. Unlike at the EMOs, executives at KIPP National do not regard school staff as their employees and do not describe the schools possessively. It helps that the KIPP culture constantly underscores the primacy of the school's leader, without a trace of ambivalence.

While most EMOs approached the recruiting of the principal as just another execution task (albeit a critical one), KIPP built its schools around its leaders. KIPP appears to be succeeding academically because its highly educated teaching force functions effectively with minimal direction. It is unclear whether the KIPP model would work were KIPP to prescribe best practices in curriculum, schedule, and other aspects of the school.

TEAMWORK AT NATIONAL HERITAGE ACADEMIES

National Heritage Academies' model, by prescribing an academic design and instructional programs, might have posed a problem for securing strong leaders and engaged staff. But from the start, NHA forged a corporate culture built on teamwork and shared values. Its unique regional strategy allowed the company to convene all its principals once a week to identify and resolve common issues. Later, its principals in New York flew in to Michigan once a month to join their Michigan peers. Frequent "face time" among the corporation's executives and school leaders inoculated the organization against the "us-them" hostility that plagued many of its competitors.

NHA's efforts to foster commitment to the company's mission were not limited to management. To nurture a sense of corporate family, NHA executives established a tradition of festive company gatherings where top executives mingled with school staff, celebrated the company's and schools' achievements, and conveyed their sincere appreciation to teachers. Unquestionably, the company benefited in this effort from its earnest Midwestern culture and explicit focus on ethical teachings. Many staff, alienated from the public schools, identified with the company's moral values.

Teachers in most EMO-run schools cast themselves as employees of the school and not infrequently criticize the EMO, just as district teachers reflexively complain about the central office.[24] In contrast, at a focus group held at the Rochester Leadership Charter Public School in New York, many of the teachers considered themselves to be working for NHA. The company, they felt, was "very supportive," "family-like," "good at team-building," and "made an investment in the faculty of their schools." Specifically, they cited NHA's many activities for staff, including an annual Christmas party held at a nearby hotel with centerpieces, linens, a DJ, and individual gifts for the teachers. Any teacher who wished to attend the company's annual gala in Michigan would be flown out and lodged at company expense. Wouldn't the teachers, earning

modest salaries, rather have the money the corporation spent to enter-
tain them? No, they said.[25] At NHA's Paramount Academy in Kalamazoo,
Michigan, teachers demonstrated the same ingenuous commitment.
One teacher said that she had never wanted to be part of a charter
school, but after NHA's kick-off gala and summer training, she realized,
"They want me to be a great teacher."[26] Rituals like NHA's that express
appreciation for teachers and celebrate their achievements are surprisingly effective for overcoming the corporate/school divide.

"The building principal is the key to our success or failure," an NHA
vice president said. "We look for someone who is a very effective coach
and has good relationships with parents and teachers. They must always
be prompting, developing, praising." NHA recognized that "it takes a
very strong person," but there were limits: "We're not hiring entrepreneurial people. We're hiring people who are very good at catching the vision
and implementing . . . We aren't looking for people to create; we want
them to implement. We track, share and implement those things that
work."[27] Whereas KIPP passes on its formula to new schools through
ideas, NHA replicates its approach by transferring specific practices.

Like other companies, including SABIS, Advantage, and Edison,
National Heritage struggled with the tension between precise implementation and principal autonomy. The issue was on the agenda for an
upcoming conference of school principals and NHA management. The
goal was to come to agreement on what principals could and could not
do—to define the "banks of the river" for the school's captain. NHA
wanted leaders who would push up against the banks. If a principal
wanted to change a component of the design, NHA would ask, Is it going
to improve academic results? If the principal could make the connection
clear, NHA would give its full support.[28]

Sourcing Principal Candidates

Identifying exemplary candidates for principal proved difficult. Each of
the three types of candidates—district principals, heads of independent

schools, and nontraditional candidates from the private sector who had not served as principals—had distinct disadvantages.

DISTRICT PRINCIPALS

EMOs often held a dim view—not entirely unjustified—of the pool of candidates from public school districts. District principals had rarely had the opportunity to attend distinguished colleges or universities and their focus was rarely instructional leadership. The public school principal's day is given over to "attending to parent issues, community-related tasks, discipline, and facilities management," and not to instructional leadership.[29] Even when they cast themselves as instructional leaders, rarely could they claim specific gains in student performance under their watch. Among educators, the most able leaders are seldom attracted to district principalships: the job responsibilities hold little appeal, and many are deterred by the requirement of completing vapid education school courses in administration and pedagogy.

Of course, within urban districts there was the occasional dynamic principal who despite overwhelming odds had raised student performance. The problem for EMOs was that with few exceptions such principals were mavericks. They were successful precisely because they broke the district's rules and gamed its systems to get what they needed for their students. One EMO rejected the expert rule-breakers outright: "We can't use those maverick-type world beaters who don't want to take any direction. People who come out of the public school system who have been successful are inherently rule-breakers. That's the only way to get things done there. We need people who want to, and can, work as part of a team—a personality trait that conflicts with doing whatever you need to do to get it done."[30] While EMOs admired these successful urban principals, they worried how such leaders, accustomed to flouting the rules, would fare in an EMO's system of schools. Would they be able to work as part of a team?

Despite their hesitations, EMOs that were opening central-city charter schools were drawn to principals from urban districts. Urban principals could work comfortably across the boundaries of race and class and could forge deep ties to the school's community. But there were obstacles to recruiting them. First, continued hostility to charter schools, and still more to private management firms, from teachers unions, superintendents, and many government officials had a chilling effect on recruiting. Unions had painted charter schools as the enemy of public education. For a district principal to sign on to a charter school required courage; the move would be seen as a betrayal of the district and as contributing to its decline. Second, the exclusion of charter schools in many states from public pension systems deterred district principals who were not yet fully vested.

Of those principals who are willing to leave the security of a school district, how many are qualified to lead urban charter schools to academic excellence and financial viability? How many have the breadth of financial and general management skills necessary to succeed in jobs far more expansive in scope than they have likely ever held before?

INDEPENDENT AND PAROCHIAL SCHOOL HEADS

Like the leaders whom EMOs sought, heads of private schools are accustomed to the twin demands of academic quality and financial discipline. Yet the EMO principal's job requirements are very different. The EMO school principal must devote considerable time and attention to ensuring compliance with statutory mandates, like special and bilingual education, that do not apply to independent or parochial schools, and must fulfill the burgeoning reporting requirements—annual reports, audits, and enrollment and attendance filings—to which even charter schools, under ever-increasing scrutiny, are subject.

Urban public school students also present instructional challenges that arguably make the independent school headmaster's job look easy. Children at urban charter schools typically arrive performing in the bottom quartile on nationally standardized tests, and charter authorizers and state regulators expect to see sharp and immediate improvements in scores on high-stakes state exams—a Herculean task.[31] Such expectations are utterly foreign to private school headmasters, as are the immense challenges of establishing discipline in a new inner-city school. And in joining an EMO, private school heads would often have to accept lower pay, longer hours, limited staff and financial resources, and the loss of perquisites.

Nonetheless, many at Advantage, for example, held in high esteem leaders of independent schools, who to them embodied a tradition of academic excellence that would enhance the company's brand. SABIS's Bistany had no such regard for private schools. As "value-added" is the measure of schools, "there are no good private schools. The first thing they tell you is they select their students. So they can't be doing a good job."[32]

Principals from parochial schools, with their reputation for strong discipline and sound instruction, were a logical choice for EMOs. Their experiences with such principals is as yet too slight to merit any firm conclusions. But the early years of NHA's Rochester Leadership Academy Charter School, led by a capable and experienced former principal from the city's Catholic schools, demonstrate how overwhelmingly difficult it can be to open a large new school and create a school culture de novo. Urban public schools and private schools—and their demands on school leaders—differ markedly.

NONTRADITIONAL CANDIDATES

A third source was "nontraditional" leaders: candidates who had not run schools but had a record of leadership in business, nonprofit organizations, or the military.

The Broad Foundation and the Thomas Fordham Institute, in *Better Leaders for America's Schools: A Manifesto*, recently urged schools to consider recruiting "CEOs" who may neither have run schools nor be knowledgeable about instruction: "School boards should seek people with manifest leadership capabilities bolstered by a solid track record of leadership success. School-specific knowledge and skills can follow."[33] Education management companies did experiment with recruiting individuals from other backgrounds to run their schools, in pursuit of the very leadership traits the *Manifesto* extols. Most often, these individuals failed; with little knowledge of schools, they were unable to gain the trust of staff and parents and could not credibly oversee, develop, and evaluate educators.

When teachers at a new school brace themselves for opening day, they are poised to make a judgment: Will the principal command their respect and loyalty? In large measure, the answer turns on the leader's command of the ordinary, moment-to-moment tasks of operating a school. If the principal is not from their world, she can lose their trust rapidly and irretrievably. Parents, too, have an intuitive sense of a principal's confidence and rapport with staff and children. When they gamble on a new and unproven school and weather its inevitable early glitches, it is the seasoned principal who can best put them at ease.

The truth is that principals who have not been educators have no idea what to look for when entering a classroom and are ill-equipped to assess or coach instructional staff. Hiring nontraditional candidates might work if the school also employs a proven instructional leader to focus on the classroom, while the nontraditional head (perhaps titled the executive director) attends primarily to general management. But seldom can schools afford two senior executives.

Disenchanted with the pool of public school principals, SABIS was by 2003 increasingly interested in the potential of noneducators. "We want someone who says, 'OK SABIS, teach me,'" one executive explained. "That's difficult to embed in [educators] who are used to making decisions." With candidates from industry, "you get pluses of organizational and skills, but you're missing educational understanding, expectations of parents."[34] Given the complex charter school regulatory environment in which SABIS has had to work in the United States, principals who could ably manage litigation risk, special education compliance, regulatory detail, security, and other nonacademic matters were attractive. SABIS's school director in Cincinnati, Derrick Shelton, later promoted to regional director, had served on the Cincinnati police force and in the military. SABIS found his background an ideal fit: he was accustomed to taking direction. Shelton didn't hesitate to pick up the phone to call SABIS if he had a question about the SABIS program, for which company executives especially admired him.

Other EMOs reached different conclusions about nontraditional principals. Early on, Advantage hired as principals two educators with significant exposure to Direct Instruction; neither had served as principal before. Both were committed to the school's success and brought an understanding of the curriculum's often counterintuitive design. The company anticipated that their enthusiasm for the often controversial program would prove a decisive advantage, as some faculty bridled at the demands of its unorthodox, highly structured methods. In actuality, both were quickly overwhelmed by the day-to-day challenges of starting up a new school, for which they had neither the leadership qualities nor the management skills. They also lacked the practical knowledge critical to running a school—how to solve discipline problems, how to move children on and off buses—school processes that are rarely codified but that principals know. As they struggled, exhausted and on the defensive, they increasingly projected their authority inappropriately. Within months, they had lost the respect of their faculties. Coaching and support from the corporate office was of no use. Both were gone before the end of the first year.

From the six EMOs' experiences in hiring principals, a profile of the successful leader of a managed school, serving primarily disadvantaged children, emerges. The effective principal is a highly focused instructional leader who thrives on data, analysis, and intervention. That leader is almost invariably a seasoned educator, having previously served as an urban principal or assistant principal, with specific knowledge about the day-to-day practice of running a school. KIPP's principals are a notable exception. What they lack in experience, they make up in idealism and drive. They will be tested as their schools mature and enrollment is not sixty or eighty students, but several hundred. Will they, who have on average only five years of teaching and lack experience managing a staff, be able to mature quickly enough on the job to succeed?[35] In any event, the KIPP school leader profile would not be an option for most EMOs and their business models. Taking on a school with five hundred or a thousand students and managing a staff of forty is a different matter altogether; veteran urban teachers would not brook taking direction from a principal twenty-five years their junior.

A Challenging Timetable

Candidates with the requisite skills and traits were scarce, and the EMOs struggled to find leaders for their new schools. Not only were there few qualified candidates, but also principals had to be recruited in a matter of months. Often, an EMO would make the decision to open a school as late as March or April, when the chartering authority had granted final approval and the EMO had identified a viable facility. That left only four months to find an exceptional principal—and most experienced principals had already accepted positions for the fall.

If the search failed to find a star, the school would either have to launch with a mediocre principal or postpone its opening by a full year. Neither option was attractive. Opening late posed ethical and practical problems. Parents may have forgone other schooling options for their children, and staff other jobs. From a business perspective, the company would have to write off investments in pre-opening costs, including marketing expenses for enrolling students and costs for recruiting staff and the school director. A few such delays could devastate the organization's financial results for the period, undermine confidence in the management team, and lead investors to question once again whether managing schools could be a predictable, stable business.

But EMOs discovered that opening under a weak director locked the school into mediocrity. "Upgrading" the director later was seldom easy; trustees were likely to side with the principal, even while recognizing his or her inadequacies. "We've been handcuffed in many situations from making changes," one EMO executive lamented. Of a strategically critical but undistinguished school, he said, "We've been trying to change the principal forever."[36] Even if the board could be convinced to support a change, recruiting high-quality principals midyear (who were under annual contracts) was a near impossibility. The seasonal nature of principal recruiting and the urgency of removing a failed principal would necessitate the hiring of an interim director, often pulled from the corporate office; by the time the school was at last ready to make good on its promises, it would be on its third leader. Frequently, a school that opened with the wrong director cycled through a series of replacement principals. At some point, board members would fear that another announcement would seal the school's poor reputation. One board member of a troubled Chancellor Beacon school in New York State told a school staff member, "If we brought in another director, it would look like the school was a failure." On the issue of instead keeping the mediocre principal, she said, "Even if we had to pay $87,000 for him to sit on his fanny, that's what we would do."[37] NHA rightly concluded it was always better to delay than to open with the wrong principal. The company wouldn't open a school without a top-flight manager. But even NHA found it difficult to adhere in every instance to that policy.[38]

Regional Directors

When an education organization is small, with just a few schools, principals report directly to a founding officer, like the chief academic officer or the CEO. That officer also personally manages the EMO's relationship with each school's board, the EMO's client. As the network of schools expands, however, the organizations must hire regional directors to oversee clusters of schools, generally with responsibility for managing clients and the schools' academic and financial performance. Structuring and staffing this level proved just as vexing to many education organizations as finding the right principals. "It's a huge conundrum," said one Chancellor Beacon vice president.[39]

In EMOs, regional directors serve as the vital interface between the corporation and the schools and are a key link in the "line-management" chain. Each has profit-and-loss responsibility for a large fraction of the company's business. If a school is underperforming financially or academically, it is the regional director's responsibility to correct it. Should regional directors have business skills—operational and financial expertise in managing multiple sites—or should they be experienced educators? Someone with an educational background, it was thought, could manage academic problems, but would probably have no record of meeting financial targets, choosing and grooming managers, or solving complex operational problems. Yet someone with a business background might be good at "operations" but have little ability to address academic issues. And which could most effectively manage the often fragile relationships with the schools' boards of trustees?

Former district superintendents were the obvious choice for regional directors; they would bring experience in supervising principals, overseeing schools, and managing school board politics. Edison went this route from the start, investing in a costly layer of former superintendents and principals. Chancellor also hired experienced educators as "regional area directors," each with five to seven schools, who in turn reported to senior vice presidents, each with eight to twelve schools.[40] At Beacon, the first schools reported directly to Michael Ronan. As it absorbed schools acquired from JCR in 1999 and expanded into new markets, Ronan turned to former superintendents to serve as regional directors. Most proved unsuccessful in the company's lean, entrepreneurial environment. "They couldn't do anything—get a building, write a grant, nothing," remembers one key former manager at the company. "They were good talkers with the boards, and that's it."[41]

Other EMOs spurned superintendents; they were associated with the stereotype of failed urban school systems and were perceived to be bureaucratic, ineffective, and overly political. Advantage's chief operating officer sought out individuals with operations experience in for-profit companies; in his view, corporations were adept at developing and training good managers, and school systems were not. Educational knowledge, in his view, was unnecessary or even detrimental; line management and operational skills, along with demonstrated success at meeting regional profitability goals (in whatever industry) were what mattered. Accordingly, his first hire as a regional vice president came from for-profit health care and had no experience in education. Her tenure was remarkable for its failure. To her credit, she eventually concluded that she lacked the domain knowledge to be effective and resigned.

Advantage's investors exerted an unhelpful influence. Resorting to first principles rather than the particulars of a new industry, they advocated for regional directors with corporate regional management experience and a background in operations, rather than educators with experience in running schools. Even the company's one outside corporate board member, the capable CEO of Bright Horizons Children's Centers, a public for-profit child care company, hewed to this view. In his company's structure, the education department was subordinate to the operations function, which oversaw the centers through the line-management chain of regional directors and center directors. What he overlooked was that day care centers, unlike schools, were operationally complex but essentially recreational; the success of the company did not rely on exacting implementation of an instructional model and the posting of exceptional gains in test scores.

In selecting regional directors and establishing a line management structure, a key question was, Who should manage the relationship with the client board? Edison officials had taken for granted that if the company created great schools its clients would love them. The assumption proved false, as the alarming loss of clients in 2002, including Dallas, drove home. Another Edison executive said that in Philadelphia, the company's largest market, "happy parents and high academic performance aren't enough to guarantee keeping the school."[42] The same problems were affecting Edison's charter business. President for Charter

Schools Joe Keeney explained, "Schools could have great student achievement but their client board did not know who Edison was." In 2003, Edison woke up to the importance of managing its client school boards. "We wanted to create Edison schools, but our partners wanted something else," John Chubb said. "We didn't see until recently that we were ignoring our clients."[43] To staunch the loss of clients, Edison took a bold and risky move and convened a conference for existing charter clients to "talk them back off the ledge." Keeney recalls, "They didn't know what Edison's value-added was. We had to resell them on everything we did."[44]

Edison, like many EMOs, expected principals to be loyal ambassadors to school boards—but like many EMOs it was often let down. "We assumed that the principal worked for and represented us at board meetings," Keeney said. "That was a hugely flawed assumption—the principal is really torn" between Edison and the board. Edison's ability to command the principal's loyalty was limited, because the principals see "board members in the community as much as they see Edison . . . The board wouldn't like it if all the principal did was sing Edison's praises." Keeney noted, too, that under Edison's management agreements, the principal is an employee of the board, not of Edison. Rather than fight for the principal's total allegiance, as did SABIS and Advantage, Edison accepted the reality of the principal's status. Edison would now communicate directly—"overcommunicate," as Keeney put it—with its client boards. Edison required regional operating vice presidents to attend every client board meeting and reduced the span of their control.[45]

KIPP is reorganizing with the goal of better serving its schools. Previously, disparate central office functions like operations and facilities maintained separate contacts with the schools. "If you asked 'how's the school doing?' you couldn't get an answer," said John Alford, KIPP's national director of trailblazing. In the new structure, "school liaisons" will each be responsible for a handful of schools. Expected to be "listeners" and "problem solvers," KIPP has charged them with walking a fine line with their school directors: "We don't want someone to tell them what to do, but yet [we do want the liaison to] be aware of their strengths and weaknesses." Will the KIPP culture sustain this nuance? "The school director is king—or queen—is a belief that everyone respects," says Alford optimistically.[46]

The Officer Team

Never before had K–12 public education been combined with business, let alone with real estate or venture capital. There were few professionals with experience in working across these disparate domains. Worse, experts in one domain could be suspicious of, if not hostile toward, experts in another. Not a few educators were suspicious of business-people, and some businesspeople were dismissive of educators. Real estate developers were cast as "shifty" and not to be relied on for straight answers, finance people as "bean counters" who were prepared to put money before children, and educators as sanctimonious autocrats who didn't respect financial imperatives. In some organizations, such attitudes undermined trust at all levels, from the senior management team—where cohesion was essential—on down.

Some venture capital investors pressed CEOs to recruit executives from industries they thought analogous. Education management seemed like other "site-based" businesses that provide a "high-touch service," like for-profit health care companies, or even the hospitality industry of hotels and restaurant franchises, and specialty retail chains, like boutique shoe stores. Investors favored officer candidates who had service business backgrounds. If candidates had once served on their town's school board or finance committee, that was considered a bonus.

Ironically, some senior managers hired were not only unable to add value to education decisions, they were ineffective at solving operational problems in the schools and corporate office. In hindsight, the notion that someone who had run a shoe company could be an effective CEO of an urban education company seems ridiculous. But at the time, it reflected the prevailing attitudes of Wall Street. EMOs were perceived to be generic, operationally intensive companies. The service they "delivered" just happened to be education, rather than shoes or meals.

Today, nearly every education organization is saddled with a portfolio of schools of varying quality. Those that excel are led by stars. In this is a clear lesson. No amount of focus on recruiting, selecting, training, and acculturating principals is too much. At the corporate level, EMOs erred in thinking that any part of an education company's activities was generic. Nearly every task required knowledge of schools. Managing human resources required a background in the complexities of teacher certification, state pension programs, and countless other public-sector employment rules. Solving food-service problems could not be undertaken without an immersion in the intricate rules of the National School Lunch Program. Collecting revenues to which the school was entitled required mastery of not only the arcane discipline of federal grants and grant compliance, but also state and local politics. Indeed, politics—urban politics, racial politics, school politics—infused nearly every problem.

7

Politics and Schools

When private organizations proposed to run public schools, they threatened one the most powerful forces in American politics, the teachers unions. The EMOs and KIPP promised parents superior schools, and many responded—particularly urban, minority parents whose children were consigned to the weakest city schools and were falling the furthest behind. The organizations found support, variously, in conservative Republican politicians, business leaders, radicalized education activists, and African-American and Latino community leaders fed up with dangerous and dysfunctional schools. The National Education Association and the American Federation of Teachers, and their local affiliates, as well as their allies throughout the education establishment, often fought vigorously to prevent districts from contracting with Edison Schools, which they naturally perceived to be the greatest threat. They also often worked to prevent individual, privately managed charter schools from opening. When despite their overwhelming resources the unions failed, they and others sought to depict the schools as academic failures and to overturn their contracts.

In these struggles, each side rallied its constituents. The unions and their traditional allies were able to appeal to a potent strand of American ideology—the common school—and to depict private management as an attack on public education itself. They understood that private management aroused a deep and inchoate resistance, emotional and normative, in the public at large.

America's Confidence in the Public Schools

Confidence in the public schools, as an institution in American society, has declined sharply since the 1970s. In 1973, 58 percent of adults surveyed said they had a "great deal" or "quite a lot" of confidence in the public schools. By 2003, only 40 percent said they did.[1] In a 2000 poll, 61 percent said they were somewhat or completely dissatisfied with the quality of education students receive in kindergarten through the twelfth grade.[2] Yet, as is often noted, parents of school-age children continue to give much higher marks to their own child's school than to others. Seventy-eight percent said they were somewhat or completely satisfied, and only 18 percent were somewhat or completely dissatisfied.[3]

In truth, parents have little basis for their satisfaction with the schools. Not only do high school students perform very poorly on internationally administered tests, but three-quarters of American employers and professors report that job applicants and first-year college students lack basic skills.[4] Even so, some apologists persist in claiming that the system is functioning adequately for middle-class, suburban students. Few would say the same of urban public schools that educate primarily disadvantaged minority children. White and black parents are both concerned about the problem of minority underachievement, but white parents are predictably more complacent than blacks, whose children are far more likely to be locked in low-performing city schools. Fifty-four percent of black parents polled in 1998 perceived underachievement in public schools by black students to be a "crisis" that must be addressed quickly, while only 33 percent of whites did; 52 percent of white parents saw it as a "serious problem but not a crisis."[5] In the urban communities that the organizations often targeted, many parents had lost faith in their public schools.

The Myth of the Common School

While Americans have deep concerns about the overall performance of the public schools, their devotion to the myth of the common school has not waned. Here "myth" refers not to a falsehood, but to the enduring resonance of an idea in American life. Americans, as Terry M. Moe has observed, "simply like the idea of a public school system. They see it as an expression of local democracy and a pillar of the local community, they admire the egalitarian principles on which it is based, [and] they think it deserves our commitment and support."[6]

So successfully has the public school lobby equated universal education with the present public school system that any proposal to alter that status quo is portrayed as an assault on public education. As Charles Glenn has observed, "The common school has functioned above all as a statement of national intention and a symbol of national unity, and those who have laid a hand upon it have, correspondingly, been perceived as disturbers of the peace and of the national dream."[7]

One indication of this devotion is found in the level of agreement to the following proposition: "The public schools deserve our support even if they are performing poorly." Sixty-eight percent polled supported this statement, and only 29 percent disagreed.[8] In another poll, when asked which statement came closest to expressing their overall view of the public school system, only 6 percent chose "we need to completely replace it," while 64 percent chose "there are good things, but it requires major changes," and 28 percent chose "it's basically okay, but does require some minor changes."[9] The strength of the public school ideology may explain both the public's support for ever-increasing spending and its uncertainty about proposals, like school vouchers, that opponents can most readily depict as an attack on public education.

The power of the public school ideology was glimpsed in the early 1990s in the debate over enacting charter school laws. Proposals for charter schools were most successfully attacked by appealing to fears that they would cream the best students and drain money from the public schools; conversely, they were most successfully promoted by assuring policymakers and the public that charter schools were in fact "public schools."

Opponents of private management of public schools, like those resisting school vouchers and charter schools, often portray it as an effort to make schools less public—"to privatize" the schools. This is a deliberately vague term and, in the absence of explanation, is likely to be understood as a reduction in the state's responsibility or engagement in public education. One prominent critic of private management, Alex Molnar, decries "the political bankruptcy and the almost boundless cynicism of many corporate initiatives in schools." His scorn is not limited to the privatizers themselves but rather extends to "superintendents, principals and other people who work in schools aiding and abetting them. And it's a shameful derogation of their responsibility, and their moral standing is correspondingly undermined."[10] This portrayal of private management by opponents inevitably gives rise to useful misconceptions: that the schools or their management organizations may charge tuition, that the schools can select their students or exclude students, that the schools themselves will operate at a profit, and that the schools or the companies will not be held accountable to state authorities as are district schools. All of these apprehensions are patently false, but pervasive.

Opponents also understand that many are repulsed by the idea that executives and shareholders could "get rich" from running public schools. The primary actors in public schools, teachers, are broadly perceived as underpaid and beleaguered, an image teachers unions promote assiduously. The chance for personal financial gain by EMO staff is easily contrasted with this image of altruistic service. A corporation is assumed to be "rich" and its executives "greedy," even when its executives make no more money than district administrators and work harder, and when the EMO has negligible resources compared to the school district or the teachers unions.

Similarly, public schools are cherished as a "business-free zone" insulated from the profit motive and crass commercialism. Interestingly,

EMOs often succeed in opening minds to contracting by exposing both the degree of existing private involvement in the provision of public schooling and the absence of commercialism—branded products, advertising, and so forth—in EMO-run schools. Public schools have long purchased goods and services from private companies—building contractors, architects, food service providers, custodial companies, textbook publishers, special education providers, and professional development consultants—that make a profit from schools ("off kids") and thereby enrich their executives and stockholders. Few would argue that the public agencies should assume responsibility for these functions or that they would be provided at higher quality and lower cost by government employees.

The broader question, of course, is whether the troubled education sector can continue to forgo the involvement of everyone for whom financial prosperity is important. We don't condemn such aspirations in most every other walk of life. Yet when Benno Schmidt left Yale to join the Edison Project, Jonathan Kozol asked, "If it is idealism that motivates him, I don't understand why he has to commercialize his intelligence. Why not set up a nonprofit foundation and not give deference to the almighty dollar?"[11] The assumption is that, when it comes to the schools, seeking profits is morally inferior to governmental or nonprofit activity, regardless of the consequences for children.

Many recoil at the idea of private management, Chris Whittle believes, because "American schools don't teach economics very well. They have this simplistic idea that if you're making a profit, it's coming at the expense of the children. It's never that you're changing the cost structure so that children are getting more. That never even crosses anybody's mind."[12] But even John Chubb acknowledges that for-profit schooling will suffer from market imperfections: "Consumers are not always good judges of quality, and they may not notice when profit taking compromises service. Consumers may not always insist on high quality, thereby providing a market niche for a shoddy alternative." But in time, he argues, the market will "deny profits in the absence of value."[13]

Opponents also invoke support by appealing to values of democratic and local control of schooling, and to the vague notion—however peda-gogically questionable—that every public school must be "community-based," which in turn is linked to the notion (still more dubious, but a cornerstone of current ideology) that "every child learns differently." Critics of private management contrast this commitment with the specter of corporations like "McDonald's" running "cookie-cutter" schools, invoking the image of a low-cost, unhealthy product adminis-tered identically in hundreds of locations.[14] Of course, American capi-talism has also given us a great diversity of high-quality products at remarkably low cost; many families would be delighted to receive a high-quality educational service for their children and would feel indifferent to whether it was also provided similarly in other locations.

At the deepest level, our response to business's management of schools may arise from concerns about corporate hegemony. When national companies propose to run schools, it may seem like the latest encroach-ment by corporate America on community life, a kind of corporate im-perialism to be resisted, whatever the failings of the beleaguered public schools.

Two Struggles

Two case studies illustrate the ceaseless challenges that politics presents to private organizations delivering a public education: in Albany, New York, the intense politics of race, poverty, and local control enveloped the New Covenant Charter School, thwarting Advantage's implementation of its educational program. And in San Francisco, Edison's dramatic turn-around of a long-neglected school prompted a powerful political back-lash from school board members determined to drive the EMO out, but parents organized and successfully fought to save Edison Charter Academy.

ALBANY

When Republican governor George Pataki signed New York State's char-ter school law in 1998, he was eager to establish a school in Albany that would become a showcase for his administration's education policy. In what to everyone involved seemed a near ideal opportunity, the Albany chapter of the venerable Urban League would partner with Advantage Schools to establish the New Covenant Charter School in the impoverished African-American community of Arbor Hill. Three-quarters black with a median household income of less than $16,500, the neighborhood was a stone's throw from the ornate state capitol.[15] From Advantage's perspective, the project would benefit from the enthusiastic support of the governor's office and the involvement of the charismatic president of the Urban League of northeastern New York, Aaron Dare.

In late June 1999, the school's founders chartered a bus to bring community residents to see Advantage's school in Jersey City, New Jersey, where Mayor Bret Schundler gave them a tour. The school had opened the year before in a complex of modular classrooms while the city constructed a permanent facility. Dare returned to Albany impressed. "We want to adopt the whole philosophy," he told a reporter. "We're about to raise the standards and turn the system on its head."[16]

The project got a late start. Only in mid-July was the school's charter given preliminary approval by the Board of Trustees of the State University of New York (SUNY).[17] There would be perilously little time to build and open the school, and the price of failure would be immense. Moreover, New Covenant was embroiled in politics from the beginning. The school district warned that the sudden loss of 550 children would wreak havoc and force a tax hike.[18] And when district officials notified families that they would not receive bus service to New Covenant because the school had missed an application deadline, three hundred primarily African-American parents, long angry with the district, confronted the city school board.[19] The board of regents, appointed by the Democrat-controlled state assembly, rejected the charter application. By the time the Board of Trustees of SUNY, whose members are appointed by the governor, voted unanimously to give final approval to the plan, essentially overruling the regents, it was already mid-August.[20]

Foolishly, Advantage pressed ahead, believing it had the tools to succeed. It had reserved modular buildings identical to those in Jersey City, and there was no shortage of parents eager to enroll their students in the school. When the Urban League requested that it assume responsibility for constructing the temporary facility, Advantage reluctantly agreed. The League was engaged in a well-publicized real estate development program, and in the spirit of an Amish barn-raising, local community members rather than Advantage's out-of-town contractors would be put to work building the school. Advantage provided specifications for a temporary facility capable of sustaining its school design, site plans used for the Jersey City installation, and information on portable classrooms it had reserved for the school. But the League said it could obtain other portables at lower cost. With the school opening date approaching, the school was far from ready. Hurricane Floyd dealt the school another blow, delaying the connection of electricity.

When the school finally opened on September 21, parents were elated. But it was immediately apparent that the ramshackle facility was grossly inadequate. Classrooms were too few and too small, administrative offices were virtually nonexistent, and there was no indoor space for recess, lunch, or a library. Advantage had also failed to find an acceptable school director, so a top educator from the company had to fill in.

Even by the standards of urban charter schools, New Covenant had enrolled an exceptionally low-performing population: students arrived scoring on average at the 16th percentile on national norm-referenced tests.[21] The school was immediately beset with serious discipline problems, exacerbated by a crowded and dysfunctional physical plant and inexperienced teachers. Tensions arose between parents, who were nearly entirely black, and teachers, who were primarily white. The staff grew angry and demoralized. To make matters worse, the school's troubles were splashed across the front pages of the capital city's dailies.

Aaron Dare, articulate, ambitious, and just thirty years old, was immensely popular in the community, and the League, with its bold agenda of neighborhood transformation, was seen as a beacon of hope. As parents grew increasingly dissatisfied and enrollment declined, Dare and the school's board publicly announced that they were in discussions with other management organizations. The tensions of race, class, and geography, never far from the surface, intensified. In a none-too-subtle code, the League depicted Advantage to parents and the media as out-of-towners who didn't understand the community.[22] Advantage sought unsuccessfully to distinguish its role of operating the school from that of the League—building the facility.

Meanwhile, the League was collapsing financially. A for-profit affiliate had built the school, which it leased to New Covenant. Advantage lent $100,000 to the League's subsidiary, notes on which the League repeatedly defaulted without notice. When the affiliate failed to pay the school's contractors, they threatened to picket the school, lien the property, and begin to dismantle the facility. In desperation, the League turned to Advantage for help. Advantage arranged to infuse $560,000 of its own funds into the subsidiary, via the school. Meanwhile, the League made no secret that it was in talks with a new organization headed by Rev. Floyd Flake, a former congressman, to replace Advantage. It withheld hundreds of thousands of dollars in public funds from Advantage, while the company continued to front the school's payroll and operating expenses.[23]

By January, Advantage had hired a permanent school director and seemed to have patched things up with the school's board. The school's PTO president reported, "The parents feel that we're moving forward and their concerns are being met."[24] Then in June, the media reported the school's results on the state's fourth-grade test: New Covenant students had scored among the lowest in the state. Buried in the story was that the test was administered only four months after the school opened.[25]

Testing in the spring revealed that the academic performance of New Covenant students had in fact grown considerably over the course of the troubled first year. On the Stanford and Woodcock tests, students had gained on average 22 percentile points, rising from the 16th percentile to the 38th percentile. In reading in grades K–2, student scores rose an average of 37 points, from the 24th percentile to the 61st.[26] PTO president Seliatu Layeni said her daughter, a kindergartner, was studying first-grade math and could read by Christmas. "Not just sounding out words, but reading Dr. Seuss books and understanding them," she said. But Layeni also criticized Advantage for its "Eurocentric" history curriculum and failing to teach "the whole child."[27]

In August, the Charter School Institute of SUNY revealed in a scathing report that Dare had misused $89,000 of the school's money. Dare resigned from the school's board.[28] The state's education department, an agency hostile to charter schools, alleged in a second report several violations of the charter.[29] SUNY reconstituted the board, asked Advantage to leave quietly, and made way for Edison to be hired in its place.

Under Edison, the school continued its rocky course. Eleanor Bartlett, a member of the state board of regents and a broadly respected former interim superintendent of Albany, became principal. Edison fronted an astonishing $15 million of its own money to build the school's permanent facility in just nine months. The mayor required that, in exchange for the land, the school include a new community center with a swimming pool. The city required that Edison use city contractors and that the facility be built according to state school building requirements, which like those of most states needlessly add millions of dollars to the cost of school buildings. After two years of operating in trailers, the school opened in its new building in September 2001.[30] The projected debt service on the borrowing was enormous, and it would have to be paid out of the school's operating funds. For a planned bond offering to be viable, Edison would need to ramp up enrollment to increase revenues.

After two years, Bartlett resigned, in part over disagreements with Edison concerning enrollment growth and control of the school.[31] Earlier she had submitted her resignation, but the board had persuaded her to stay. "I work for two entities, the New Covenant board of trustees and Edison Schools. My contract is with Edison. I guess I've come to be characterized as defiant down at Edison," she remarked at the time. "I am defiant . . . I'm not going to say that 900 [students] here is right, because it's not. It's too many."[32] It was a conflict over control, she said—whether New Covenant would be a community school or be controlled by Edison. In June 2002, the charter school's teachers unionized, a first for the state. The bond financing was finally completed in 2005, and Edison was able to recoup its cash. Yet test scores remained dismal. Many of the students who transferred in arrived several grade levels behind and with discipline problems.[33] Still, state officials were warily optimistic that the school was on course to long-term success.

SAN FRANCISCO

At a raucous, five-hour meeting of San Francisco's board of education in late June 1998, pugnacious superintendent Bill Rojas secured a 5–2 vote to turn over one of the city's worst performing elementary schools to Edison. "Shame on you!" shouted Kent Mitchell, president of the teachers union, pointing to board members and Rojas. "So you are now saying the administration has no idea how to fix that school! Shame! Shame! Shame!" he said to thunderous applause.[34]

Coincidentally named Thomas A. Edison Elementary, the school was notorious throughout the district for its unruly students and dismal academic performance. In eight years, it had had nine principals. Even two "reconstitutions"—in which the school's entire staff was assigned to other schools, a new faculty assembled, and extra money and assistance provided—had failed to turn it around. Despite its location in the middle-class neighborhood of Noe Valley, the Spanish-tiled school served primarily black and Latino students from low-income families.[35] The school had long been a dumping ground for disruptive students and for parents who failed to navigate the city's Byzantine open enrollment system. The average fifth-grader read at a second-grade level. Only 20 percent of all students scored at or above the national average in reading.[36]

A previous principal, Ken Romines, had written a book about his struggles to improve the school, a tale of urban educational dysfunction studded with incidents of chaos and violence—a parent who punches

Romines in the stomach, teachers who physically threaten one another, a child who partly loses her hearing after classmates kicked her unconscious, a razor-wielding student who slices her teacher's hand.[37] "Our appeals for assistance from the district when the school had broken toilets, crumbling hallways, rat infestation, Latino teachers refusing to teach African-American children and routine violence fell on deaf ears," wrote one parent.[38] The district had long ago turned its back on the school. "It was a disaster," Rojas explained, looking back in a 2000 interview. In Edison Schools, "I found somebody . . . who thought they could turn it around. It didn't seem like much of a risk."[39]

At the June meeting, frustrated black and Latino parents urged the board to allow Edison to manage the school. But many community activists and union leaders opposed the plan, accusing the board of "abandoning students to the free market." Union leaders saw the action as the first step toward privatizing the school district and vowed they'd remember it the next time they went to the polls to elect the school board.

Under the plan, Edison had just two months to reopen the school as a district-authorized charter school and implement its school design. Barbara Karvelis, the school's existing principal, gamely signed on to lead the transformation, and teachers agreed to work Edison's longer school day and year for only a modest stipend over the district's pay scale. Like many managed schools, Edison Elementary endured a rough first year before the turnaround began. On California's Standardized Testing and Reporting System (based on the SAT-9), test scores climbed from the spring of 1998, before Edison began, to the spring of 2000: in 1998, just 11 percent of second-graders and 20 percent of fifth-graders had scored at or above the 50th percentile in reading; two years later 39 percent and 34 percent, respectively, did so. In math, the gains were as dramatic: in 1998, 21 percent of second-graders and 26 percent of fifth-graders scored at or above the 50th percentile, while in 2000, 58 percent of second-graders and 47 percent of fifth-graders met or exceeded that mark.[40]

But as test scores rose, so did teacher dissatisfaction. "I remember visiting the school that first year and thinking, 'I could never work here,'" said Mary Hernandez, a school board member and Edison supporter. "I told Edison, 'you've got to let them have a life.' And sure, there were all the pressures and stress of a start-up, but it didn't get better the second year."[41] In May 2000, twenty-seven of thirty-three teachers signed a letter to the district school board calling on it to intervene in talks with Edison over working conditions and threatened to resign en masse if they failed to negotiate better pay. Burnout and discontent had set in. The school board required Edison to cut its school year by fifteen days, and Edison agreed to increase teacher salaries by 10 percent more than was sought by the teachers union. The school day was also shortened. Yet more than 60 percent of the school's teachers did not return in the fall. Edison acknowledged that it had failed to pay sufficient heed to the complaints of its teachers.[42]

In the November 2000 school board election, two Edison opponents gained seats. Both Mark Sanchez, a public school teacher, and lawyer Eric Mar, whose wife was a schoolteacher, were on record as opposed to Edison. "I would vote to immediately revoke the charter," said Mar. "For-profit schools like Edison have no business in our public schools."[43] Veteran board member and long-time Edison opponent Jill Wynns, who had previously attempted to revoke the school's charter, announced that she now had the votes to take back control of the school. Edison, she said, threatened the collective efforts of teachers to raise standards throughout the district. The New York company, she asserted, could not understand the needs of a racially mixed student body in San Francisco, and test score improvements were simply evidence that Edison was teaching students to pass the test. By contracting separately with teachers and establishing its own standards, according to Wynns, Edison undermined the efforts of the district's teachers to improve the quality of education citywide.[44]

In reality, Edison had attracted 120 more students, increased instructional time, and raised scores at every grade level. The school was cleaner and the classes more orderly. Thanks to a grant from the Fisher Family Foundation, more than two hundred personal computers had been provided to families for children to do their homework. A charismatic new principal, Vince Matthews, had strengthened staff morale, teachers were earning salaries significantly above the district scale, and they could earn bonus incentives. Parents appeared broadly satisfied, and the state gave Edison high marks. "They're doing great as far as I can see," said Bill Padia, director of the policy and evaluation division of the California Department of Education.[45]

At a three-hour board debate on the school's fate, not one parent spoke against the school. As both sides girded for the board fight, Chris Whittle remarked, "If you don't run good schools, you get fired. In San Francisco, we may get fired for running a good school."[46] "The fact is, it's really a miracle," said principal Matthews, who is black. "Nobody's ever seen anything like this before. Instead of trying to learn from it, the district is trying to shut it down. You have a school that's never worked for African-American and Latino kids, and now it is, and the district wants to take it away from them. I just find it so sad."[47]

Edison's school board opponents attributed the school's improved test scores not to its academic program but to changes in its student population. The company, they alleged, coerced low-performing students to attend other schools. One prominent critic, Margaret Brodkin, executive director of Coleman Advocates for Children and Youth, insisted that Edison had systematically advised parents of low-performing students to select other schools. "They're weeding out difficult kids," she alleged to the *New York Times*.[48] Neither Brodkin nor the school board provided any specific evidence that students had been forced out. Under the district's open enrollment program, parents could apply to a school of their choice anywhere in the city; students whose parents did not choose were assigned to a school. By March 2001, Edison had increased enrollment from 370 students to 550, as parents chose to enroll their students in the charter school. Many saw this newfound popularity as a sign of success, while critics pointed to the makeup of the student body as evidence of the school's wrongdoing. Before Edison assumed control, the district had assigned many students from the Mission neighborhood, which is largely poor and Latino, and from Hunters Point, a low-income, primarily black neighborhood several miles away; Latino enrollment was 45 percent and black enrollment 38 percent.[49] Under Edison, more families from the nearby Mission had chosen the school, increasing Latino enrollment to 53 percent by 2001; black students from Hunters Point, meanwhile, were no longer bused there by default, lowering black enrollment to 30 percent. With the spiraling cost of housing in the city, the percentage of black students in the school district as a whole had fallen, though by a lesser amount.[50]

Board members repeatedly announced their intention to revoke the school's charter. In February 2001, the board had directed the district's superintendent, Arlene Ackerman (Rojas's successor), to undertake an "investigation" of the complaints against the school, including that it "materially violated its Charter, failed to meet or pursue all the pupil outcomes identified in the Charter, failed to meet its financial obligations, and violated the Education Code and other provisions of law."[51] Her preliminary report made numerous accusations, which were effectively countered by Diallo Dphrepaulezz of the Pacific Research Institute.[52]

Among other charges, the district report cited complaints of "higher teacher turnover" and the charter's unrealized plan for "long-term relationships among teachers, students, and families." Yet it acknowledged that the school had also suffered turnover before Edison took it over. (Indeed, Romines wrote in his book that turnover was "excessive—50 percent to 70 percent" of staff left each year of his tenure as principal.)[53] Moreover, the report conceded that teachers interviewed for the investigation said that the school had addressed the causes of turnover and that teacher satisfaction was now much higher. Second, the report took issue with the school's provision of bilingual education through an immersion model. The district had responded with defiance to the passage of California's Proposition 227 prohibiting transitional bilingual education, because it took away local control. Edison's immersion model was consistent with the new law and popular with the school's Latino parents; it also fulfilled the district's own objectives of eliminating segregation in schools, programs, and classrooms and improving the academic performance of all students, especially English Language Learners.[54] Third, the report took up the explosive charge that Edison was counseling academically low-achieving students to leave the school. It noted several "allegations" of such counseling, but all were from current and past employees of the district—except for one from the district's Special Education Advisory Council. Again, the report hedged. "The District's data does not clearly indicate that these incidents are occurring at a statistically significant level," the report dodged. "However, the anecdotal evidence indicates a perception that potentially at-risk students may have been counseled to leave Edison."[55] Board member Mark Sanchez conceded, "We don't have any names" of parents; he also acknowledged that the district had no written accounts of parents attesting to "counseling out" or racism.[56]

Fourth, the report noted that the percentage of Latino and educationally disadvantaged youth had increased, while the percentage of African-American students, students eligible for free and reduced-price lunch, and special education students had declined, as if this were prima facie evidence of "discrimination" and noncompliance with the school's obligation to achieve "racial and ethnic balance," rather than the return of children from the neighboring communities to a long-shunned school. In fact, according to the district's own office of Student Nutrition Services, which qualifies students for the free and reduced-price lunch program, the percentage of eligible students in the school declined only slightly, from 83 percent in 1997–1998 before the charter to 77 percent in 2000–2001.[57] Poverty levels for students in the city as a whole dropped in the late 1990s, as parents were driven out of the city by soaring rents.[58] In absolute numbers, the school educated only two fewer black students in the spring of 1999 than it did prior to the charter; in the two subsequent years black enrollment dropped by only fifteen students.[59] With regard to enrollment in special education, it ought to be a sign of success when the number of students labeled "special needs" declines in urban schools.[60]

The day after the report was released, the board held a tumultuous three-hour meeting. Some four hundred parents and students attended, mostly in support of Edison. Nonetheless, the board voted six to one to begin the process of revoking the charter and ordered the school to "cure deficiencies" within ninety days.

Gloria Lee, who lives across the street from the school, attended the meeting. "It's true that there is a philosophical issue for parents of whether they want to send their students to a school run by a for-profit company, but what the school board really needs to focus on are student test results and whether the students are learning," she told a reporter.[61] Lupe Hernandez, a parent of an Edison first-grader and Mission resident, worried about what would happen if the charter were revoked. "I just want a good school for my son. Previous to the charter, Edison was a really bad school. There was truancy, trash, the school was ground zero for trouble. It's really different now. It's not a perfect world at Edison, but it's good."[62]

To the disbelief of her neighbors, Kitty Clark, a Noe resident and single mother, transferred her daughter from the well-regarded Alvarado Elementary School to Edison for the fourth and fifth grades, where she was one of only fourteen white children. After two years at Edison, her daughter was placed in the honors program at the Roosevelt Middle School. "My evaluation of Edison is 100 percent positive," she said in an interview. "I can't speak highly enough about the teachers and the program. The students get lots of individual attention, and Edison has art and music programs, which the district can't support in most schools."[63]

A group of Edison parents, led by Linda Gausman, Lupe Hernandez, and Heather Mobley, formed Parents to Save Edison Charter and launched a website to mobilize community support. At first they assumed the board was misinformed, so they enumerated the school's successes at public meetings. As one parent urged the board not to revoke the charter, board president Jill Wynns read the newspaper, infuriating parents. "It was obvious at that point that they had their minds made up," Gausman said. "Our children were their last concern, and we knew that we had a fight on our hands."[64]

At the school board's May meeting, Edison supporters filled the gallery. Just three opponents were present: Brodkin, her husband, and a former teacher from the school. When the meeting ended and the crowd dispersed into the hallway, Brodkin interrupted Benno Schmidt's conversation and claimed that Edison was the worst performing school in the district. The diplomatic Schmidt remained calm. But Brodkin grew shriller. "I don't want you to make a profit off of our children. I don't want my tax dollars going into your pocket," she continued, as she reached up and fingered the pocket of his jacket. "You don't want textbooks in your schools?" he asked. "You don't want computers?" "Not so you can make a profit out of it," she responded. Schmidt, normally professorial, finally lost his temper: "And don't lie about us, we haven't counseled out one child!" Brodkin screamed back, "You counseled out 50 kids!" "You're full of shit," he responded.[65]

Parents took the offensive, organizing a public march on the board and circulating a petition among parents and teachers urging renewal of the school's charter. "We wanted to get [the board] on record as being obstructionists by watching them defy the wishes of every parent and teacher at the school," explained Mobley.[66] All but one teacher signed the petition and 80 percent of parents—a remarkable feat considering that families came from many corners of the city. On June 5, over three hundred parents, teachers, and supporters marched to the district headquarters chanting, "We will not be ignored!" and "Our children, our choice." The crowd burst into the board's meeting and presented the petitions to a stunned Wynns. Then came a campaign of e-mails, faxes, and letters.[67]

One June 28, in a 4–2 vote, the district severed ties with Edison but allowed Edison Elementary to seek a charter from the California State Board of Education. But the school's victory came at a high price. The company agreed to not add grades beyond the current fifth, to surrender over $300,000 in funding from a desegregation consent decree, to not support any future parent or teacher petitions, and to pay rent to the district for the school's building. The board also precluded Edison from managing additional district schools. On July 12, the California Board of Education voted to transfer sponsorship of the school's charter from the city to the state.

Laura Baker, parent and president of the charter school's board, reflected on the fight in August 2003:

> Our feeling was, How can you ignore the fact you failed so many times with these kids? Now somebody's come in here and turned it around . . . They entered into a contract with you for five years. At the end of two years you're going to say, "Oh gee, well you did it, but we don't really like *how* you did it and we have people here who are quote-unquote 'philosophically opposed to for-profit education'?" That was the big buzz word. And that was a crock, because every single person that does business with the SFUSD is a for-profit corporation—the man who sells them the paper, the person who sells them the Xerox machine, all those people are for-profit companies and they make big profits off of doing business with the San Francisco Unified School District. So to say that they're philosophically opposed to for-profit education is just a joke. They were opposed to the fact that somebody else was controlling the purse strings. And was able to do it better than they did.[68]

Wynns draws a very different conclusion. The privately managed school, she says,

> was such a poisonous presence in our school district that *it had to be gone,* as gone as it could be, which was not all the way . . . And that took courage and strength and that's a good thing to have done. I mean, in a way, who would have done it, if not the San Francisco School Board? It could have taken years for the truth to come out. [Edison] could have pulled the wool over the public's eyes for a lot longer . . . So now I think

people should say, "It failed. Privatization doesn't work." What does work? The hard work of slow, incremental reform that engages the community, the teachers, the professionals, and the parents . . . We know it works. We know it takes time, money, and hard work. And in San Francisco, and I think all kinds of other places around the country, a huge amount of energy has been diverted away from focused reform toward fighting political, ideological battles that must be fought once people like Rojas and Chris Whittle engage them. You can't give up.[69]

A failure? After a miserable year in 2000–2001, which the school attributes to the distraction of the political fight, scores at the school soared in 2001–2002. The school posted its highest gains ever in all four tested subjects. Overall average gains across all grade levels in reading were 8.3 percentile points, in math 6.8 percentile points, in language arts 8.3 percentile points, and in spelling 7 percentile points.[70] Second-graders nearly doubled their national percentile ranks in reading, from 22 to 40, and rising from 24 to 44 in math.[71] Enrollment continued to climb, and 90 percent of teachers returned to start the 2002–2003 year. That year, California dropped the SAT-9 and administered only the California Standards Test (CST). With 100 percent of its students taking the CST, the percentage of Edison's students who performed at the "proficient" or "advanced" levels gained on average 11 points from just the year before in English/Language Arts and math and more than 15 points in English/Language Arts over 2001 (math results were not reported for that year).[72]

So powerful is the myth of the common school, and so inseparable in the public's mind is public education from its longstanding institutional structure—of local school boards, school districts, and public employees—that private management will continue to encounter deeply felt, if unexamined, resistance in the public at large. Opponents will continue to portray private management as an assault on public education itself—

and the democratic ideals for which it stands. In San Francisco and in Philadelphia, as in cities around the country, politicians and school board members who supported private management were attacked for "abandoning" public schools and "abdicating responsibility" for making them work. EMOs were not going to "make a profit off our children." Schools would not be "sold off to the highest bidder" and taken away from "our community." Corporations would not "cash in on our kids." Some will charge that EMOs have "counseled out children," but this can be refuted. Others will claim that the schools "are not educating the same population," as though attracting families from diverse ethnic and socioeconomic backgrounds back to public education is evidence of failure, rather than the very realization of the common school ideal. Still others will perversely insist that some children not be permitted something better than others. In the court of public opinion, these will ultimately be losing arguments.

In time, the public may begin to distinguish its commitment to public education from an allegiance to its present institutional form and bring an open mind to alternative structures where "public" is no longer equated with "government-run." Emerging organizations, like the Black Alliance for Educational Options and the Hispanic Council for Reform and Educational Options, will challenge longstanding political alignments in the politics of school reform. In local chapters throughout the country, they will insist that low-income minority parents enjoy the same access to school choices as parents of greater economic means. Competition, they will recognize, strengthens rather than weakens public schools. At the same time, enlightened district executives like Philadelphia's Paul Vallas will see private management as a powerful lever for reform in their own schools, rather than a threat to their authority.

The story of the Edison Charter Academy reveals the power of parents to protect their children's school when it has begun to set down a record of achievement. As parent activist Linda Gausman explained it, "The unions were silent because they were fearful of taking on something that had made parents so happy. The school board expected their natural allies to rush to their aid, but they didn't, because they would not publicly stand up against a unified group of parents."[73] In many locations, however, the academic record of privately managed schools is still too equivocal to be a powerful political weapon. Opponents have been able to dismiss Edison's academic performance, for example, as a "mixed record." But in any system of schools, it is unreasonable to expect uniform results. Some schools will do far better than others. The media's responsibility is to look deeper and report the central tendency of that distribution—the fair measure of academic performance in any system of schools. Are students in privately managed schools in fact learning faster than their district school peers? Chapter 8 examines the evidence.

8

Academic Results

Are schools affiliated with the six education management organizations and KIPP academically more effective than traditional public schools? In this chapter I consider the evidence.*

Each organization administers different tests and reports results uniquely. Some report publicly on the performance of their client schools as a whole. Typically, these reports focus on test scores but may include other measures of school quality, such as attendance levels, graduation rates, and the results of satisfaction surveys of parents and students. Data on student demographics are often provided, including the percentage of students from low-income families (as reflected in the percentage eligible for free or reduced-price lunch under the federal program) and schools' racial and ethnic composition.

---

*I thank Herbert J. Walberg, emeritus research professor of education and psychology at the University of Illinois at Chicago and presently distinguished visiting fellow at the Hoover Institution at Stanford University, for finding evaluations of achievement other than those submitted by the EMOs, proposing criteria for assessing the evaluations, and for initially compiling, analyzing, and appraising information about the evaluations. The analysis in this chapter is based on his preliminary work and my own reading of the evaluations.

This review looks at school performance strictly in terms of achievement test data, the most objective measure of school quality. Whether charter or contract, public schools managed by private organizations participate in state-mandated testing regimens; districts have generally required schools under contract to EMOs to administer the same tests the district uses. Unfortunately, there is today no single test that all states and districts administer, which makes comparisons of student performance across schools and districts difficult.[1]

Education researchers analyze data from both national and state tests to reach conclusions about the relative academic effectiveness of education programs. Like education evaluations generally, studies of achievement in privately managed schools vary enormously—in the research questions they pose, the number of schools and grades they cover, and the periods studied. They may examine the results from one test or several and use statistical methods to incorporate results across these different measures. One study might look at the performance of students at a given time relative to a comparison or "control" group of demographically similar students in other schools. Another study might compare gains in the performance of students over time with their grade-level peers nationally. Naturally, the scope of the study and the quality of the research design have distinct implications for the robustness of the findings.

Assessing Evaluations of Managed Schools

In assessing evaluations of the seven organizations, it is useful to understand the standards for educational evaluation. Researchers agree not only on the features of the ideal study (as well as the challenges to conducting it), but also on the particular strengths and weaknesses of other, more practicable designs. Trade-offs must be made among various considerations of scientific validity and practical feasibility. Control groups are problematic, test-taking consumes instructional time, and data collection can be expensive for researchers and burdensome for schools.

STUDY DESIGN

Of the thousands of education evaluations, few have been "true experiments," where researchers assign students randomly to program and control groups and changes in the program group can confidently be attributed to the program. In a quasi experiment, nonrandomly assigned program and control groups are compared. To the extent that the groups differed initially, the results are less reliable. Quasi experiments may be strengthened by controlling statistically for the characteristics and initial status of the two groups. Baseline achievement measures are the most valuable statistical controls, for they allow gains to be compared across groups from the start to the end of the study period. Controls for characteristics such as socioeconomic differences between the groups help to isolate the effects of the program itself.

When no control group is available, a study may compare gains in performance of the students receiving the treatment over a period of time to what might have been expected. One expectation might be that students keep pace with their grade-level peers nationally. At each administration of norm-referenced tests (NRTs), such as the Stanford, Iowa, and Metropolitan, the publishers create a "norm" comparison group composed of a diverse sample of students nationally in the same grade taking the test at the same time. This "norming" allows the results for the program group to be expressed as percentiles in relation to all students taking the test. Students who remain at the same percentile rank from one year to the next are learning at a pace comparable to their peers nationally, while students who gain in percentile rank are learning at an accelerated pace.

State tests are typically criterion-referenced tests (CRTs), where an individual student's performance is measured against specific learning objectives. Individual results are presented in raw scores or with reference to threshold of performance—that is, a passing line. Average group results can be compared to the average for the entire tested population, such as all fifth-graders in the state.

Before proceeding to examine the research, a final note: the organizations have particular educational objectives for their programs. They choose achievement tests and other assessments to measure the degree to which they have accomplished these objectives. Consumers of the evaluations, including parents, policymakers, and the media, have disparate objectives for schooling and may prefer a measure of student performance that reflects their own goals. The content of the various tests (their breadth and representativeness) is not typically a concern of the researcher, whose analysis begins with test score data. Performance on a single test may not, at the end of the day, correlate with everyone's definition of school quality.

PURPOSE AND SCOPE OF THE REVIEW

This chapter presents an analysis of existing research on student achievement in schools managed by the seven organizations. Each organization was formally requested to provide data on academic performance at its schools, including reports on student performance prepared by the organization and by independent researchers on behalf of the organization.[2] KIPP and five EMOs—Advantage, Chancellor Beacon, Edison, National Heritage, and SABIS—provided such self-evaluation reports. Mosaica did not provide any information.

To identify evaluations conducted by other organizations and researchers and to ensure that no relevant studies were overlooked, multiple Internet searches, with various search engines and search methods, were performed. Among the studies found, six evaluations were specifically concerned with one or more of the seven organizations, focused on academic achievement, and, if in a series, were the most recent available. Along with the six evaluations found on the Internet, the chapter considers all six self-evaluations, so that all the organizations that provided information are represented. This small body of evidence is analyzed critically. How well do the studies meet standards of educational evaluation? Taking the studies as a whole, what tentative conclusions can be ventured?

The Self-Evaluations

Here the six self-evaluations are considered, including both their achievement claims and the limitations of their methods and presentation.

SABIS INTERNATIONAL CHARTER SCHOOL, 2002 ANNUAL REPORT

While SABIS has not published a report on achievement aggregated across all its client schools, it has published annual reports on individual schools. The company submitted several such reports for this analysis. They present a wealth of school information, including program descriptions, standardized test scores, and other measures of academic performance. Among those submitted, the most recent and the most comprehensive was the 2002 school report for SABIS International Charter School in Springfield, Massachusetts.[3]

SABIS test scores are reported for the school's 1,226 students that were in grades two through eleven. The racial and ethnic makeup of the student population was 37 percent white, 35 percent black, 26 percent Latino, and 2 percent Asian. Forty-nine percent of students were participating in the National School Lunch Program, eligibility for which is based on both household income and family size. Among student achievement measures reported by the Springfield school are average SAT scores and passing rates on the Massachusetts Comprehensive Assessment System (MCAS) tests. On the MCAS test, passing rates for SABIS Springfield students exceeded those for students in the Springfield district schools in all subjects in five of six grades tested. Passing rates for SABIS students on the tenth-grade MCAS (required for graduation) exceeded those for district students by a wide margin in 1999, 2000, and again in 2001.

One stated objective for the SABIS school is student performance on nationally standardized tests equal to or better than that of students in the Springfield district.[4] The 2002 report includes scores on the Iowa Test of Basic Skills (ITBS) for both SABIS students and Springfield students dating back to 1996. Scores on the ITBS are reported in terms of grade-level equivalents. The achievement of SABIS Springfield students continued to accelerate in the middle and high school grades, while the district's students' growth flagged.[5] The results may highlight the strength of the SABIS design in the upper grades, a weak area for many American urban public school systems.

SABIS did not undertake any statistical analysis of the test score data. On the basis of test scores and other performance measures, the report concludes that the academic program at the SABIS Springfield school is successful. Every student in the class of 2001 was admitted to at least one institution of higher education, 75 percent to four-year colleges.[6]

CHANCELLOR BEACON ACADEMIES, *2001–2002*
ANNUAL EDUCATION REPORT

Chancellor Beacon submitted a report on the performance of its schools on norm-referenced standardized tests and state tests in the 2001–2002 school year. The company hired the Center for Resource Management, an educational research firm, to verify the student achievement outcomes reported. At the time, Chancellor Beacon operated forty-two schools, two of them private, serving 14,873 students in urban and suburban locations. Information is included for thirty-nine schools in eight states and Washington, D.C., and for students in grades pre-K–12.

Because schools administered different tests and used different scoring methods, the data are not aggregated, and no systemwide results are reported. Most of the schools did report fall and spring scores in bar graph form, but without the numerical information necessary to calculate gains and losses. Achievement results appear mixed. Among schools that reported scores in reading for both the fall and spring tests, roughly 65 percent appear to show gains. Among those schools that reported both sets of scores in math, roughly 55 percent showed gains. Missing data and the lack of a research design—calculations of gains, use of a control group, statistical controls—make any conclusions tentative at best.[7]

MAKING THE (BETTER) GRADE: A DETAILED STATISTICAL ANALYSIS
OF NATIONAL HERITAGE ACADEMIES

Gary Wolfram, president of the Hillsdale Policy Group, conducted an evaluation of student achievement at schools run by National Heritage Academies titled *Making the (Better) Grade: A Detailed Statistical Analysis of National Heritage Academies on Student MEAP Scores.*[8] Although not prepared by the EMO and obtained through the Internet search, this study was prominently featured in the annual report that NHA submitted and is considered here as an EMO self-evaluation. All the schools in the study were in Michigan. On average, approximately 22 percent of students enrolled in these schools were eligible for free or reduced-price lunch. The study sought to compare the performance of students who had attended one of the company's twenty-two schools for two years or more with students who had been in one of NHA's schools for less than two years. Using a variety of statistical techniques, Wolfram analyzed the scores on Michigan's state test, the Michigan Educational Assessment Program (MEAP), from January 2001. More than three thousand students were tested in grades four, five, seven, and eight in subjects including reading, math, writing, social studies, and science. Not all grades were tested in all subjects.

Wolfram found that students in the former group (at NHA more than two years) outperformed the state on 80 percent of the tests. The latter group (at NHA less than two years) scored below the state average on every test. From the statistical analysis, Wolfram concludes, "The longer a student has been at National Heritage Academies the more likely he or she is to score in the highest category of any MEAP test, and the lower is the probability that he or she will score in the lowest category."[9] The researcher also concludes that the "evidence shows a history [at NHA's schools] of moving students from below the state average to above the state average in a short period of time."[10] Among the limitations of this evaluation are the use of application dates as a proxy for enrollment dates, the failure to control statistically for socioeconomic status, and low adjusted R squares in the regression results (which indicate a lack of confidence that the independent variables fully account for changes in the dependent variable). Although the researcher employs a number of analytical techniques, no strong causal link is demonstrated between longer attendance in an NHA school and greater achievement, as Wolfram concedes.[11]

EVALUATING SUCCESS: KIPP EDUCATION PROGRAM EVALUATION

The Education Performance Network at New American Schools issued in October 2002 an evaluation of KIPP's first three replication schools in their first year of operation.[12] At the time, each served only the fifth grade. The three schools—in Washington, D.C.; Gaston, North Carolina; and Houston, Texas—enrolled between seventy and eighty fifth-graders. The schools served urban students from low-income families; the percentage of students eligible for free or reduced-price lunch ranged from 80 to 86 percent. Researchers Harold C. Doran and Darrel W. Drury asked, What percentage of students is making normal educational growth each year? Have KIPP students made statistically significant achievement gains as compared with gains made prior to enrollment? Have KIPP students outperformed their traditional school counterparts? Because each school administered different tests, the report offers only findings for schools individually. In each case, the primary goal was to compare achievement gains shown by individual students while at KIPP to gains they had made at the school previously attended. The researchers' hypothesis was that any student gains from grades three to four would not be statistically significant, while student gains from grades four to five would be.

At the KIPP DC/Key Academy in Washington, students gained 23.5 normal curve equivalent (NCE) points in math and 12.1 NCE points in reading from the fall of 2001 to the spring of 2002 on the Stanford Achievement Test, Ninth Edition (SAT-9), exceeding normal educational growth. DC/Key students showed larger gains than did students of any other middle or junior high school within the district.[13] There were no previous year student-level test data for this portion of the study, however. The fifth-grade gains were statistically significant, but because there were no previous gains to look at, only half of the hypothesis is confirmed.

At the Gaston College Preparatory School in North Carolina, the percentage of students who passed the state reading test increased dramatically from the previous year. Ninety-three percent of students passed the test in 2002, whereas only 57 percent of the same students had passed the test the year before, while at other schools. In math, 90 percent of KIPP students passed the test in 2002, while only 81 percent of the same students had passed the test the previous year. From an evaluation of gains, the researchers find support for the hypothesis in the reading data (because the students made statistically significant gains at KIPP and not previously), but not in the math data. Math gains were statistically significant at the students' previous schools as well as at KIPP.[14]

At the 3D Academy in Houston, Texas, 98 percent of the school's students passed the math portion of the 2002 Texas Assessment of Academic Skills (TAAS) compared to 89 percent of fifth-graders in the Houston Independent School District. In reading, 88 percent of KIPP's students passed the test compared to 84 percent of students in the district. On the SAT-9, scores of KIPP students exceeded those of the district students in math, were the same in reading, and were slightly lower in language. Students made statistically significant gains on the SAT-9 from grade four to grade five and prior to attending KIPP; no support for the hypothesis was found.[15]

Limitations of the evaluations include missing data, the use of proxies for some baseline data, and the relatively small sample sizes in each school. The three schools were studied separately, and comparison groups varied. The KIPP evaluations also suffer from the limitations of pretest-posttest evaluations without control groups. Even a large rise in achievement may be attributable to factors other than program effectiveness.

The study concluded,

The first year data from all three schools provide positive evidence to support the effectiveness of the KIPP instructional program. Observed academic gains exceed what could have occurred by chance and exceed the performance of respective district performance. Each school increased levels of academic achievement performance for students, regardless of background or label . . . The results of the statistical analyses for Gaston and 3D are statistically significant and indicate impressive academic gains for the students enrolled. Although partial support for the a priori hypothesis was found at Gaston, with no support at 3D, this does not disqualify the remarkable academic achievement gains observed. Rather, it suggests that KIPP students continued to increase in achievement at KIPP.[16]

As of 2004, KIPP was still in the planning stages of a second evaluation of its schools.

ADVANTAGE SCHOOLS, *ANNUAL REPORT ON SCHOOL PERFORMANCE: 1999–2000 SCHOOL YEAR*

In the spring prior to its acquisition by Mosaica, Advantage Schools published a two-volume report on student performance for the previous academic year, 1999–2000. At the time, the company operated fourteen urban schools in eight states, serving more than 7,500 students in grades K–7; 71 percent of students were eligible for free or reduced-price lunch. Advantage administered national standardized tests in the fall and in the spring.[17] Test scores are reported and analyzed for the 5,874 students for whom scores could be matched. Detailed information on individual schools is given, along with results aggregated for the network as a whole. The report did not include results for its schools on state tests, such as the MCAS and MEAP.

Across the entire network of schools, for all grades and subjects, there were no statistically significant declines in scores on the SAT-9 and the

Woodcock Reading Mastery Tests—Revised (WRMT-R). The data cover twenty-four distinct grade-level tests; in nineteen of these, statistically significant gains were made. Across all grades and subjects tested, the company reported that students had gained 9.1 points in national percentile rank during the year, or 5.2 NCE points. Like many EMOs, Advantage found that results varied widely across schools. The strongest school reported average gains of nineteen percentile points, but the weakest school reported average gains of only three points.

While the study is methodologically conscientious, all data are included, and gains are tested for statistical significance, the study design lacks a comparison group. The report's conclusions must be interpreted in light of the limitations of such pretest-posttest evaluations discussed earlier.

EDISON SCHOOLS, *FIFTH ANNUAL REPORT ON SCHOOL PERFORMANCE, 2001–2002*

Edison Schools has since 1998 reported annually on the performance of its students in each school by describing their average gains on norm-referenced tests, criterion-referenced tests, or both.[18] In the fifth report, for the 2001–2002 school year, current achievement data, and wherever possible multiyear trends, are reported for 136 schools at 112 sites. (Edison counts elementary schools, junior academies, and high schools separately, even when they are in the same building.) These mostly urban schools served a student population that was 83 percent minority; 73 percent of students were eligible for free or reduced-price lunch. These individual school data represent approximately 74,000 students in grades K–12.

Tests administered include the SAT-9, ITBS, TerraNova, and state criterion-referenced tests. Edison gave each individual school with complete data a positive or negative rating, which indicates whether or not the school had on average gained or lost ground on its principal test since opening. The baseline score (score when Edison began managing the school) for each subject at each grade level is subtracted from the respective 2001–2002 score; these differences are then averaged. The school's classification (positive or negative) is determined by the sign of this average. The company reports that 84 percent (79 out of 94) of its schools are achieving at higher levels than when they began.[19] Edison also found the gains for Edison schools to be greater than those reported by the districts and states in which the schools are located. For forty-one of the Edison schools in which at least 90 percent of the students are African-American, the company reported average annualized gains of 4.7 percentage points on criterion-referenced tests and 4.4 points on norm-referenced tests.[20]

For each school, annualized gain scores are derived by dividing the average gains made over the entire period each school has been open by the number of intervals between test administrations. For example, at the San Jose–Edison Academy in West Covina, California, which opened in the fall of 1998, gains were calculated from SAT-9 scores. In the spring of 1999, second-graders scored on average at the 47th percentile in reading; by the spring of 2002, second-graders were performing on average at the 73rd percentile, a three-year successive cohort gain of 26 points. In math, the average score for second-graders in 1999 was at the 57th percentile. In the spring of 2002, second-grade scores averaged at the 87th percentile, a gain of 30 percentile points. This represents annualized national percentile rank (NPR) gains of 8.7 points in reading and 10 points in math.[21]

The report presents system-level achievement for Edison schools as the average of annualized gains, across the schools, first for criterion-referenced tests and then for norm-referenced tests. Schools are treated equally; larger schools or schools that have been open longer are not weighted differently.[22] Edison excludes from this system-level analysis schools no longer under contract to Edison, schools with enrollment changes greater than 15 percent from the prior year resulting from expansion or contraction of their contract (rather than from student mobility), and schools for which complete data were unavailable. The system-level analysis is calculated on results from 66 of Edison's 136 schools.

To provide a context for the company's achievement results, Edison measured the performance of its students against a comparison group. Unfortunately, Edison does not identify the schools that form that group, explaining only the methods by which they were selected. Using a national database, Edison identified all the schools within the districts in which the 66 Edison sites were located. For each Edison school, comparison schools were included in the control group if their demographic characteristics (race, ethnicity, and income) fell within a defined percentage band of the characteristics of the Edison school. The resulting comparison group was made up of 1,102 schools.

Edison reported that its students gained on average 3.5 percentage points annually on criterion-referenced tests, versus 1.4 percentage points for students in the control group schools, and 5.5 percentile points on norm-referenced tests, versus 2.7 percentile points for comparison group schools.[23] The report concludes, "The gain rates of Edison schools nationwide are of a magnitude and consistency that clearly distinguishes them from the gain rates of comparable schools: the Edison gain rates are higher, educationally meaningful, and statistically significant."[24]

Edison's study was a quasi experiment in which pre- and post-tests were used to measure gains against a comparison group. With respect to standards for statistical analysis, this study is the most rigorous of the six self-evaluations. Among the study weaknesses are the many schools left out of the system-level analysis (Edison explains the rationale for the exclusions), the lack of gain calculations in many of the school profiles, incomplete information on the composition of the control group, and the absence of an accompanying technical report.

Edison's annual reports have generated substantial controversy. Its critics have focused on several vulnerabilities. Schools Edison had lost were excluded; if the client terminated for low performance, the exclusion would inflate Edison's performance systemwide. Edison inappropriately averages, they charge, results from different tests. Some claimed that the effects are too small to be notable. Even after several years under Edison's management, schools continue to perform at levels below those of the state and even the districts in which they are located.

In response, Edison highlights the low starting point of the schools for which they are contracted. Initial test scores for Edison students on norm-referenced tests are at the 25th percentile, on average, compared to district school scores, which are at the 37th percentile.[25] In the report, Edison argues that its schools should not be judged by absolute performance:

> Most of the schools in which Edison works have had traditionally low levels of achievement. Indeed, Edison is asked to work in schools and communities often for the precise reason that achievement has stubbornly resisted efforts at improvement . . . The more appropriate measure of achievement in Edison schools is not the *level of achievement,* but the *amount of improvement* . . . Has the school gained relative to state standards or national norms?[26]

The Outside Evaluations

An Internet search found six additional evaluations that met the criteria stated earlier for inclusion in the study.

EDISON READING ACHIEVEMENT TEST-SCORE ANALYSIS

Edison Schools commissioned Robert Mislevy, a researcher at the Educational Testing Service, to analyze the company's data on reading achievement in grades K–3 in a series of yearly reports.[27] Data were drawn from four schools opened in Edison's first two years of operation, 1995 and 1996. The four longitudinal studies, the most recent of which includes results for the 1997–1998 school year, had similar but not identical designs. Each compared the performance of students in Edison's program with control groups composed of students from district-run schools. In each case, the design used analysis of covariance in an attempt to control for initial differences between the groups. The tests administered were the Peabody Picture Vocabulary Test (PPVT), Durrell Analysis of Reading Difficulty, and Woodcock Reading Mastery Test—Revised (WRMT-R).

Mislevy's analysis presents results in average grade equivalents and also reports effect sizes.[28] Results were mixed: positive for the school in Wichita, Kansas; mixed for Mount Clemens, Michigan; and negative for Sherman, Texas. No difference was found between the groups in Colorado Springs, Colorado.

The studies are a cautionary tale in educational evaluation. While the basic research design is sound, the narratives of the studies call attention to deficiencies in the makeup of the control groups. The formation and management of the control groups were left to the school districts. Pretest scores for the control groups were sometimes higher; some control groups suffered from high levels of attrition; and the racial, LEP classification, and poverty characteristics of the program and control groups often differed as well. In Wichita, attrition for the control groups was approximately 60 percent and 35 percent for the Edison program groups.[29] In the Sherman study, the author warns that "substantial differences were found between the Washington-Edison and Control group distributions of background characteristics and pretest scores. These differences challenge the interpretation of posttest differences as estimates of program effects, even after statistical adjustment."[30]

A letter to Mislevy from James Harrison, who administered the tests in Sherman, highlights the attrition problem. The district's testing coordinator had sent letters to parents seeking participants for the control group; those who agreed were then scheduled for testing. There were numerous no-shows, and it was difficult to obtain the necessary number of control group students. "Toward the end of the 2nd week of testing, it is my suspicion that demographic matching became less important than simply providing the right number of children," Harrison wrote. The control group was 74 percent white with 6 percent characterized as ESL, in contrast to the Edison population, which was 54 percent white and had 16 percent of its students characterized as ESL.[31]

The American Federation of Teachers has commented extensively (and negatively) on the Mislevy studies, using the most recent results to characterize early reports of positive effects as "inflated."[32] The AFT notes that positive effects were often statistically insignificant and had diminished by the third year of the Mislevy studies. The union casts Edison's results as no better and perhaps worse than those seen in implementations by school districts of Edison's chosen reading curriculum, Success for All. The AFT also reported that Edison cancelled the Sherman evaluation after a disappointing first set of results.[33]

AN EVALUATION OF THE MICHIGAN CHARTER SCHOOL INITIATIVE: PERFORMANCE, ACCOUNTABILITY, AND IMPACT

The Michigan Department of Education commissioned Jerry Horn and Gary Miron, researchers at the Western Michigan University's Evaluation Center, to report on Michigan charter schools.[34] In *An Evaluation of the Michigan Charter School Initiative: Performance, Accountability, and Impact,* the authors offer a thoughtful and detailed look at operational and policy issues then facing the state's charter program. The study does not, however, provide a methodologically sound analysis of charter school performance, let alone of EMO-run schools.

Horn and Miron obtained MEAP data from the Michigan Department of Education for the state's 171 charter schools as well as all other public schools. MEAP is administered to students in grades four, seven, and eleven in math and reading, and grades five, eight, and eleven in science and writing. The study analyzed the MEAP data from 1995–1996 through 1998–1999 (and some data for 1999–2000) to compare charter school performance over time to that of the district, in terms of both absolute scores and gains.[35]

By 1999–2000, nearly three-quarters (71 percent) of Michigan's charter schools were operated by EMOs, compared to 10 percent nationally.

Among the schools included in the report are three schools operated by Edison, thirteen schools by National Heritage, and ten schools by Beacon Education Management (before its merger with Chancellor Academies). These figures are accurate for the 1998–1999 data but may not be for prior years covered by the study; the authors indicate that the test score data reflect an increasing number of schools over the study period. Subject schools are not specifically identified.

The study concluded that the schools operated by National Heritage Academies performed well on the MEAP in both reading and math. These results were qualified by the acknowledgment that NHA students were performing well in their previous schools and that NHA's suburban schools had relatively homogeneous student populations. Beacon schools, for their part, showed mixed results on the MEAP tests. And the study places the three Edison schools among those with the poorest MEAP scores in reading and math, both in terms of absolute scores and gains over time.[36]

Horn and Miron's conclusions about EMOs are of little value in assessing student achievement. Annual test score data are for a changing mix of students and schools, yet the authors infer trends from these data and then use these trends to rank the performance of several EMOs. There is no attempt to control statistically for either demographic differences among school populations or initial performance. Given the varying demographic profiles of EMO students, the focus should be on students' gains attributable to the EMO's program.

The study has even more fundamental weaknesses, however. Grade- and subject-specific graphs show trend lines for "percent passing" for several EMOs, including Edison, NHA, and Beacon. But the study does not present the data needed to quantify these gains; indeed, nowhere in the report are any numerical data for EMOs—scores or gains— reported. In the core subjects of reading and math at the two grade levels reported, the graphs unambiguously show that Edison's passing rates increased on three of four tests over the study period, while the percentage passing in writing declined. Nonetheless, the authors do not hesitate to propose "Safeguards to Limit the Negative Impact of EMOs" in their recommendations.

UPDATE ON STUDENT ACHIEVEMENT FOR EDISON SCHOOLS, INC.

The most recent of several AFT-sponsored studies of Edison, *Update on Student Achievement for Edison Schools, Inc.* looks at eighty Edison schools in numerous states.[37] F. Howard Nelson and Nancy Van Meter first present the findings of the California Department of Education and Texas Education Agency comparing student achievement in Edison's schools to that in similar schools, followed by the findings of the authors' own analysis. The executive summary states,

> More than seven years after the first school opened its doors under Edison's management, the company has amassed a revealing track record. Edison Schools Inc. can boast of some successes, but it must also account for a substantial number of schools that have significantly lagged behind comparable public schools . . . When it comes to Edison, the magic bullet of private management of public schools is not hitting its target. This is not an excuse or justification for poor performance in traditional public schools, where it exists. It is to say, that, in most cases, the private companies are doing even worse.[38]

The AFT report analyzed changes in rankings for Edison's schools on performance indices calculated by California and Texas. For California, the study reports the state's ranking of seven Edison schools against demographically similar schools in the state for three school years. The analysis focuses on year-to-year changes. Only in passing does it concede that the majority of the Edison schools improved their ranking over the two years. Indeed, the data table shows that four schools each gained either two or three decile ranks, two schools each declined by one decile rank, and a seventh school posted no change in rank. In short, Edison's record of elevating its schools' performance on the California index was plainly positive.[39]

The AFT's presentation of data on Texas schools does more to conceal Edison's record than to reveal it. As with the California analysis, the AFT draws attention to single-year changes and then focuses on the wrong measure. Texas compares each Edison school with thirty-nine demographically similar schools by categorizing the magnitude of annual TAAS gains in reading and math (first quartile is the ten schools with the highest gains, fourth quartile is the ten schools with the lowest gains). The study lists each Edison school by year and gain category. By moving from absolute performance to changes in gains, the AFT skips over the gains themselves and sidesteps the fundamental question: whether the school's performance has improved or declined over the entire period of Edison's management.[40] As Edison explains, the AFT analysis

> says nothing about its overall record of gains—which is what the AFT wants to criticize. A school may make top-notch gains one year and slower gains the next, relative to comparable schools; but, over a multi-year period, the gains of that school may be the best of the comparables. Had the AFT bothered to aggregate the long-term gains of Edison schools they would have found that this is often the case, especially in Texas.[41]

The Texas data the AFT presents does not permit such an analysis of the schools' overall record of gains. But it does allow a comparison of year-to-year gains in Edison schools with such gains in the state's demographically similar schools. More often than not, Edison schools' annual gains were in the first or second quartile. Of sixty annual gains results in reading and math for the eleven Edison schools, thirty-five of the annual subject gains were in the first or second quartile, whereas twenty-five were in the third or fourth. In short, if anything, the AFT data support Edison's contention that its students in Texas were learning at an accelerated rate compared to students in demographically similar schools.[42]

The authors' own research analyzed pre- and post-test scores on various state assessments in Edison schools for 2000–2001 and contrasted these results with those for comparison schools in the same state that had similar low-income populations and the same grade levels. Nationwide student achievement data were drawn from the Education Trust database, and achievement data in math and reading for Edison and comparison schools were ranked into a decile scale for analysis. The study asserts that Edison's student achievement claims are exaggerated and that, in fact, Edison schools are performing below average in most states. Nelson and Van Meter also dispute Edison's claims of success with distinct student populations, in particular, African-American students. The only caveat the study offers in this regard is "extremely modest evidence" that schools with predominately African-American students were more likely than comparison schools (chosen without regard to ethnicity) to improve their ranking in math under Edison's management.[43]

Edison Schools rejected the AFT findings on several counts. The first concerned the makeup of the comparison group. "The AFT . . . compares Edison schools to comparable schools selected only on the basis of economic status. Race and ethnicity—well known influences on achievement—are completely ignored. Moreover, Edison schools are compared to schools all over their respective states, and not to the schools most like them, located within their own school districts." Secondly, Edison objected that the AFT did not account for the low starting point of Edison's schools in its comparison of performance levels. Finally, although the AFT study had responded to earlier criticisms by including data on gains, rather than just absolute scores, Edison termed the analysis inadequate as it looked only at single-year gains rather than gains aggregated and averaged over several years.[44]

AN EVALUATION OF STUDENT ACHIEVEMENT IN EDISON SCHOOLS OPENED IN 1995 AND 1996

Funded by the National Education Association, *An Evaluation of Student Achievement in Edison Schools Opened in 1995 and 1996* looks at ten of the eleven schools opened by Edison during its first two years of operation.[45] The eleventh school, Dillingham Intermediate School in Sherman, Texas, was omitted because it was a school-within-a-school, and test data from Edison's program could not be disaggregated from those of the district. The most ambitious of the outside studies, the 273-page document consists of ten separate studies using similar but not identical research designs. First, for eight schools, the researchers examined results for one or more grade-level cohorts of students over varying periods on nationally normed tests (the ITBS, MAT-7, and SAT-9). To their credit, they examined test records to match individual students over time. The researchers did not provide any comparison group for the analysis of these longitudinal gains; the progress measure was limited to that embedded in the normed scale of the results. The researchers concede that this "represents a major limitation of this analysis." National norms serve as a "point of comparison; but because we cannot control for the characteristics of the students considered in the national norms, this is somewhat limited."[46]

Second, the researchers analyzed successive cohort comparisons of scores on state criterion-referenced tests relative to district and state performance. Two statistical tests, chi-square analysis and odds ratio analysis, were performed. CRT scores are grouped by each state into categories of performance, and each has its own such categories. For example, in Colorado the four categories are Unsatisfactory, Partially Proficient, Proficient, and Advanced. To perform an odds ratio analysis, the researchers had first to collapse the results into those passing and those failing the test, summing scores across multiple categories to create this dichotomous outcome. The odds ratio is the proportion of students who fail the test in the program group relative to the proportion of students who fail the test in the comparison group. When the quotient is one, students in both the program and the control group face equal odds for failing. When the result is less than one, program group students are less likely to fail, and researchers can infer that the program is having a beneficial effect. A confidence interval is constructed around the quotient; if the interval includes one, the result is not considered statistically significant.

To reach overall conclusions on Edison's effects in each school, the researchers distilled their findings from their NRT and CRT analyses into between five and eighteen "trends" per school, with each trend cast as "positive," "mixed," or "negative." The researchers summed the number of positive findings, the mixed findings, and the negative findings to reach an overall conclusion about the ten schools. Of ninety-nine "trends," fifteen were positive, sixty-one were mixed, and twenty-three were negative. The executive summary concludes, "The majority of the trends, both norm- and criterion-referenced, were mixed, indicating that students in Edison schools are achieving at levels similar to students in the comparison groups."[47] The authors interpret their findings to mean that

> the expectations of district and charter school boards that contract with Edison as well as the expectations of parents who enroll their children in an Edison school are not being met. These groups believe that an apparent goal behind Edison's school model is to have achievement gains that exceed the gains at comparable schools.[48]

The analysis was flawed. First, the researchers lay out principles for data analysis and then fail to follow them. In comparing Dodge-Edison's performance with the Wichita Public Schools, the researchers use NPR points rather than NCEs, even though NPRs are not an equal interval measure and cannot be used to compare gains at different points on the scale.[49] As the researchers themselves caution in the discussion of their methodology, "NCE scores are a preferred method for measuring and comparing gains made by a school over time. Percentile ranks in a normal distribution clearly do not represent the same score scale distance between equal differences in PR [percentile rank] values."[50]

Second, even though the schools had been open for four or five years by the time the study was released, longitudinal gains were rarely calculated off of results from more than one or two years of data, or compared with those of a comparison group.

Third, the comparison groups for criterion-referenced tests were students throughout the district and state, not students with similar demographic backgrounds and initial levels of achievement. For example, for the Reeves school in Miami-Dade County, the researchers inexplicably found "suitable comparison" groups in the district and the state as a whole, yet the Edison school had 81 percent black students in 1997–1998 versus the district's 33.4 and the state's 25.3 percent. The percentage white for the three was 1, 13, and 55.8, respectively.[51]

Fourth, the use of an odds ratio analysis, by collapsing performance categories, conceals progress below the passing line. This is particularly misleading when applied to scores of low-achieving students, who may have progressed out of the lowest categories but still fall short of the passing threshold.

Fifth, the researchers labored to discern "mixed" or "negative" trends even from data that unequivocally showed otherwise. For example, at the Roosevelt-Edison school the performance of third- and fourth-grade students was examined. In 1998, the result of the odds ratio for Edison third-graders in reading was 2.344, meaning that the odds of failing at Edison were much higher than in the district schools. The ratio fell to 0.591 for 1999, indicating the reverse: district students were now more likely to fail the test. The authors admit, "This is a dramatic improvement for Roosevelt-Edison students relative to students in the rest of the district."[52] Yet in a summary of results for the school, 1998 is assigned a negative one (−1) and 1999 a zero (0), for, improbably, a "mixed" "trend" by their accounting. The researchers discount the district comparison, favorable to Edison, and base the trend sign primarily on a less favorable (and inappropriate) comparison to the state as a whole. The study is littered with such instances, where the researchers discern unfavorable "trends" in positive data.

Sixth, clear gains for Edison students are concealed not only by the tendency to look at gains over just one year, but also by the rejection of year-to-year gains where the calculated effect size was less than 0.20.[53] Calculated effect sizes very often fell below the bar, resulting in a "trend" termed "mixed." The choice of one-year gains often arithmetically assured effect sizes below Miron and Applegate's threshold for inclusion.

Finally, the number of trends developed for each school varied widely, so some schools weighed more heavily in the totals than others. For instance, Boston Renaissance, a school with poor results according to this evaluation, was accorded eighteen trends, while a stronger school, Dodge-Edison, had only seven trends.

The study's release was accompanied by a press statement titled, "Edison School Test Scores Do Not Reflect Claims." In Edison's response to the evaluation, John Chubb assails the study: "Despite the mountains of statistics designed to give it an aura of legitimacy, the study is a political attack piece . . . stacked to support its predetermined conclusions. It examines trends at only 10 of Edison's 113 schools, and even then completely omits critical data that fail to support the conclusions it labors so hard to reach." Chubb decried the study's use of the term "trends": "The conclusions of the Western Michigan study are hard-wired into the study's design. Much of the study's analysis of so-called achievement 'trends' involves comparisons of absolute levels of achievement in Edison Schools with levels of achievement in so-called 'comparable' schools on state tests . . . No responsible analysis would evaluate low performing schools by ignoring their progress."[54]

The researchers issued a rebuttal to Chubb, defending their choices regarding the data included and the statistical methods they employed.[55] The rebuttal addresses some of Edison's objections but does not resolve the issues raised here.

ACHIEVEMENT PERFORMANCE REPORT: DALLAS-EDISON PARTNERSHIP SCHOOLS, 2001–02

A study of seven Edison schools in Dallas, all serving a low-income population, was conducted by the Division of Evaluation and Accountability of the Dallas Independent School District (DISD) and released in August 2002.[56] The researchers employed a pre-post design with a control group composed of eighteen of the lowest-achieving schools in the district. Rather than comparing gains directly, the study measures achievement relative to "effectiveness indices," which are essentially expectation levels that the district calculates for all its students based on their demographic, socioeconomic, and school-related predictors of performance.

The study concluded,

> Based on this analysis, continuously enrolled students in the seven Dallas-Edison schools over the past two years have had positive cross-sectional achievement gains on all TAAS assessments and on the Stanford-9 mathematics assessment. They also had positive two-year cohort gains on SAT-9 mathematics and TAAS reading and mathematics assessments. However, as of summer 2002 the Edison students, in the aggregate, neither have met nor exceeded the performance of comparable students from comparable schools in terms of matched cohort achievement gains or effectiveness on all assessment comparisons except the TAAS Writing Effectiveness Indices for 2001 and 2002. Consequently, there currently is not sufficient evidence establishing that the implementation of the Edison Schools Inc. program in Dallas offers their students a value-added component as great as, or greater than, the current achievement growth of students in similarly low performing PK/K–6 elementary schools in the Dallas Independent School District.[57]

In August 2000, Superintendent Bill Rojas had brought Edison into the district to begin managing seven chronically low-performing schools under a five-year contract. That summer, the DISD school board terminated Rojas and, shortly after, hired Mike Moses as his successor. After two years running the schools, Edison announced its gains in a statement titled, "Edison Schools Reports Second Successive Year of Large Test Score Gains in Dallas, 6 of 7 Edison Schools Up Significantly over Two Years." The May 2002 announcement compares test scores of students in the Dallas-Edison schools on the Spring 2002 TAAS to the previous year's scores and over the two-year span:

Compared with 2001 scores, students in the seven elementary schools managed by Edison improved 6.9 percentage points in reading, 11.6 points in math, and 6.1 points in writing. Students in the Dallas Independent School District (DISD) . . . improved 6.7 points in reading and 6.8 points in math, but declined slightly by 0.3 in writing . . . In the two years Edison has been working at the schools, student performance has improved an average of 10.5 percentage points in reading, 16.5 points in math and 13.0 points in writing. By comparison, DISD, also with impressive gains over the past two years, improved 10.0 points in reading, 13.6 points in math and 2.4 points in writing.[58]

Edison goes on to state that the progress shown at its schools demonstrates that the company has in fact delivered on the promise made in its contract with the Dallas school district.

In June 2002, the district produced a draft of a report that compared Edison's progress to a comparison group of students in district-run schools. This early version of the district's report also reached positive conclusions about Edison's performance: "For all practical purposes, the Edison Schools have matched the growth of the district in TAAS achievement over two years when comparing similar students from similar schools." It also states, "This report shows that both Edison and the rest of the district have made substantial but equal gains."[59] District students made slightly better gains in reading and math, though the difference was not statistically significant, and they showed much smaller gains in writing than did students in the Edison schools.

Upon reviewing the June draft, John Chubb objected to the composition of the comparison group, and the district's evaluator agreed to apply an alternate method for selecting comparable schools and students, to share the methods by which the new comparison group was formed, and to permit Edison to verify the comparable student matches. In August 2002, before Edison had this opportunity, the DISD released the final report at a public meeting of the school board. In the revised report, Edison's performance was measured against a comparison group with larger gains than the one used in the June draft and the district concluded that Edison had not met the terms of its contract. Within a few weeks, the DISD board had voted to terminate Edison's contract at the end of the school year.

"PRIVATIZATION IN EDUCATION: A GROWTH CURVE ANALYSIS OF ACHIEVEMENT"

The most statistically rigorous of the six outside evaluations, the study "Privatization in Education: A Growth Curve Analysis of Achievement" was conducted by researchers in the Miami-Dade County Public Schools' Office of Educational Evaluation.[60] The researchers compared the progress of two groups of students in a single Edison elementary school to that of students in other district schools with similar demographic performance and pre-test performance. This quasi experiment followed 114 second-graders through the fourth grade and 159 third-graders through the fifth. Most of the students were black and from socioeconomically challenged families.[61] Test data covered a three-year period from 1996–1997 through 1998–1999.

Research methods included a pre-post quasi experiment, using repeated test scores and a growth curve analysis. While the study controls for most potential threats to statistical validity, it involves only one school and a homogeneous population, which limits the extent to which the conclusions can be generalized to other locations.

The study concluded, "Significant levels of growth were achieved across the three-year period in both subject areas for all groups of students." The research "failed to reveal any significant differences in reading achievement levels or rates of growth that could be attributed to membership in either the project or control group." Regarding math, the authors write, "The levels of mathematics achievement at the end of the three-year period were not significantly different in either group." The third-graders were an exception. Their "rate of growth in mathematics over time was greater for the project students than for the control students."[62]

In a letter to the district, Edison notes that students at the school—like their control group peers—made "real achievement gains" against national norms as evidenced by same cohort and successive cohort gains on the SAT-8, as well as gains on Florida's writing test. Edison also points out that over the course of the study period, the Florida Comprehensive Achievement Test (FCAT) became the primary measure of school performance for Miami-Dade County schools. Edison's fourth-grade reading results on the FCAT grew thirteen scale points from 1998 to 2000, and fifth-grade math results grew twenty-eight scale points. (These were the subjects and grades the state tested.) By comparison, results for all students in the district over the same period showed on average a decline of two scale points in reading and a gain of five scale points in math. Edison acknowledges that these comparisons do not apply formal statistical controls.[63]

The chapter began with the essential question, Are schools affiliated with the seven organizations academically more effective than traditional public schools? While there are many indices of school quality, from levels of parent satisfaction to rates of college acceptance, only performance on state and national achievement tests provide objective measures of students' knowledge and skills.

In contract settings, EMOs are brought in to take over chronically failing schools; pretests reveal that their students typically arrive performing well below the average for the district. Privately managed charter schools, too, have enrolled primarily low-performing students, as tests administered in their first months document. In assessing the efficacy of these schools, the proper focus is not the level of student performance but the gains they are making. Are their students learning faster than their peers in traditionally managed schools?

Given the stakes, this ought to be the question the organizations answer for their customers. Mosaica submitted no information on the performance of its schools. The remaining organizations, in self-evaluations reviewed for this chapter, all claimed positive effects in the core subjects of reading and math. Some studies claimed positive effects in other subject areas (such as writing) and in other measures of school quality, including attendance rates, college acceptance rates, and school climate.

The self-evaluations vary widely in quality. While the vendors cast their performance claims as definitive, the evidence they offer falls short of scientific. Chancellor Beacon offered some indication of performance levels but no data on gains. SABIS provided detailed information in individual school reports, but no aggregated data on its network of schools. Edison has each year published the most complete and rigorous report on performance, but even these fall short of what policymakers and the public need to fully evaluate the company's effectiveness. A forthcoming study from RAND is likely to corroborate Edison's claims of achievement growth.

In its fifth annual report, Edison claimed average annualized gains of 3.5 percentage points on state CRTs and 5.5 NPR points on NRTs.[64] These gains might seem modest, but their cumulative effects for disadvantaged students can be dramatic. Over several years, students in Edison schools with strong implementations can rise on average from one quartile of performance, by comparison to test-takers nationally, to the next. Consider the Chamberlain Campus of the Edison-Friendship Public Charter School in Washington, D.C. When the school opened in the fall of 1998, second-graders scored on average at the 31st percentile on the SAT-9. Three years later, fifth-graders scored at the 50th percentile, the national average, when given the exam in the spring of 2002. Similarly, in math, the second-graders in the fall of 1998 scored at the 25th percentile, whereas fifth-graders in the spring of 2002 scored at the 63rd percentile.[65] Such a marked change in achievement level, if sustained, will have profound consequences for the students' futures.

KIPP's claims are more dramatic than Edison's, though limited to just three schools, each serving fewer than one hundred students. KIPP reported gains for a single grade over one year that were in some cases several times those of Edison. But it remains to be seen whether KIPP will continue to realize these gains across its more recently opened sites and as each existing school expands to serve several grades. National Heritage Academies also boasts that, according to its analysis, students who had been in its program longer were far more likely to perform above the state average on Michigan's state test than students in the program only a short time.

Despite their claims of accelerated learning, none of the organizations has as yet conducted an evaluation of sufficient rigor and transparency to satisfy private management's many skeptics. In fairness, the reports prepared by the organizations to date have sought primarily to communicate information to community stakeholders, including parents and school boards, particularly in the case of single school annual reports. To serve that purpose, the presentation needs to be straightforward and easily understood. But if opportunities for private management are to expand, the organizations will have to make their case persuasively through robust analyses.

At first glance, all six outside evaluations appear to have rigorous designs, yet none meet the causal-validity standards of psychological and social research. None permit policymakers to conclude definitively that privately managed schools produce superior, inferior, or indistinguishable achievement results relative to comparison groups. No report is sufficiently extensive in scope, nor are there a sufficient number of reports, to make confident conclusions about any one organization or the seven organizations as a group.

Taken at face value, the outside evaluations show a mix of positive, negative, and neutral effects. Unsurprisingly, given the educational levels of students at enrollment, the studies find that Edison schools are posting scores below the district and state averages. To the limited degree that the studies address progress, they conclude that Edison schools were making gains that were no better or, in some instances, worse than those made by comparison groups.

Two of the studies were rigorous efforts to assess aspects of Edison's performance. But even these had severe limitations. Mislevy examined only reading achievement and at just four of Edison's earliest implementations. Problems with the districts' formation of the control groups and their response to attrition also threatened the validity of Mislevy's conclusions. The Miami-Dade study by Shay and Gomez, while methodologically impressive, studied only 273 students in just one of Edison's now 136 schools. It also ignored the school's performance on the FCAT, which had become the primary measure of performance for the state and for Edison.

In the remainder of the studies, politics seems to have overwhelmed dispassionate research. Just as the EMOs and KIPP found positive effects on student achievement, studies undertaken or funded by their long-standing critics, such as the American Federation of Teachers and the National Education Association, reached negative conclusions. Their findings, nearly all unfavorable to Edison, are highly dependent on questionable study design decisions, are simply not supported by the analysis, or both.

The Dallas study found that Edison's students had indeed made gains in all three subjects tested, but students in comparison groups also posted solid gains. An initial version of the Dallas Independent School District's report on Edison's first two years of management found that Edison had made solid gains in reading and math, as had students in the district's comparison group, and had made superior progress in writing. But before the district released the final report, it altered the composition of the control group; in the new analysis, gains for the control group exceeded gains for Edison's students.

In the Michigan study, which focused primarily on charter schools and not on private management, the authors provided only graphs of achievement for EMO schools, from which gains or losses could be estimated. While the study was critical of Edison's performance, the graphs show a positive trend. In the core subjects of reading and math at the two grade levels reported, the graphs unambiguously show that Edison's passing rates increased on three of four tests over the study period.

Like many of the studies critical of EMOs, the AFT-sponsored Nelson and Van Meter study belabors the obvious: Edison's schools score lower than the state average. The authors purport to also focus on gains in two states, California and Texas. For California, the study focuses on year-to-year changes and concludes the schools had not improved. Had the study calculated gains over the full period for which it reports data, the authors would have drawn a different conclusion: four of the seven gained either two or three decile ranks on the state's performance index, a fifth held its standing, and two lost ground but only by one decile rank each.[66] For Texas, the AFT study sidesteps the critical question of annual gains altogether by focusing on the largely irrelevant question of whether the gain in a given year was larger or smaller than in the previous year.

The most ambitious study, funded by the NEA, looked at ten of Edison's first eleven schools. The Miron and Applegate study purports to examine gains, but the analysis is so error-ridden as to discredit its conclusions. Despite the apparent sophistication of the research design, all comparisons are to dissimilar groups, namely district or state test-takers. More importantly, the study presents an abundance of raw data showing longitudinal gains, which the analysis then labors to exclude from the study findings.

Taken as a whole, Mislevy, Shay and Gomez, and the four studies prepared or funded by Edison's critics fail to refute Edison's claims that its students are learning at an accelerated rate. Indeed, at least three and perhaps five of the six instead offer an inadvertent corroboration. A close reading suggests that a reanalysis of the underlying data, without the methodological deficiencies, would likely support Edison's claims that while students are performing in absolute terms at levels below those of the district or the state, they are making greater gains than students in comparable schools.

Education management organizations and independent researchers should continue to investigate and evaluate the achievement and other effects of EMOs. Existing research is lacking both in amount and quality. The emerging education industry and experts in educational evaluation need to reach consensus on standards for comparing the performance of privately managed and traditionally managed schools, so that policy-makers and parents can make informed decisions about the participation of private organizations in public education.

9

Business Results

Can money be made managing public schools? Can nonprofit school management organizations achieve financial self-sufficiency? To answer these questions, in this chapter I consider the six extant organizations. Which of the five for-profit companies are profitable, or have the best prospects for becoming so? Can the nonprofit KIPP reduce its dependence on philanthropic support, or even in time become self-sustaining?

Next, the future of the industry is addressed. If the first generation of EMOs has generally proven a poor investment, can a new generation of education companies, pursuing better business models, attract new private capital and promise a competitive rate of return on investment? What level of investment would be required in a new company to reach profitability?

The Organizations: Financial Prospects

The five for-profit organizations are all privately held (Edison went private in November 2003) and do not release financial information. As explained here, however, two claim to be profitable: Mosaica and National Heritage Academies. Edison has reported one quarter of profitability and projects profitability for the 2006 fiscal year. Chancellor was not yet profitable at the time of its sale to Imagine, and SABIS is still losing money in its operations but is committed to succeeding over the long term in the charter market.

Two of the five EMOs, pursuing very different business models, appear to have the best prospects for sustained profitability: Edison Schools and National Heritage Academies. KIPP is reporting impressive early academic gains but, with the small site contributions paid by network schools, will continue to rely on major philanthropic support through at least fiscal year 2012.[1]

EDISON SCHOOLS

Founded in 1992, Edison has yet to report an annual profit. From inception through June 2003, the company chalked up $282 million in losses.[2] In fiscal 2003 (beginning July 1, 2002), with its stock price collapsed and unable to raise new capital on the public market to fund continuing losses, Edison undertook financial disciplines overdue in a company long accused (often unfairly) of profligate spending. Once Charles Delaney took an active role in the company's management as vice chairman, new school projects were subjected to strict tests of profitability, cash was preserved, and financial controls were tightened.

The company has shed some unprofitable management contracts and renegotiated others, including its contract to operate nine schools for the Chester-Upland district in Pennsylvania. While the company was criticized for losing schools, Edison claims that, not including a major contract in Dallas, the site contributions from the terminated contracts were only $3.8 million, representing less than 5 percent of the company's total site contribution. At the corporate office, Edison let go about 10 percent of its employees, by trimming functions.[3] Meanwhile, enrollment in Edison's summer school programs, a highly profitable business for the company, grew sharply from the previous year.[4] And Philadelphia, for all its challenges, added 13,000 students to Edison's core business.

Growth and new fiscal discipline led to a sharp rise in EBITDA (earnings before interest, taxes, depreciation, and amortization) from the previous year. Edison had forecasted EBITDA for the 2003 fiscal year of $26 million, compared with negative $51 million for fiscal 2002. Instead, Edison reported $21.5 million, still an impressive performance for a company with a long history of falling far short of its financial commitments. Even though revenues in fiscal 2003 declined slightly from the previous year, owing in part to accounting changes, Edison posted its first profitable quarter, with a net income of $10.2 million, compared to a loss of $48.9 million for the same quarter the year before.[5] Without raising new capital, the company also managed to maintain a cushion of about $30 million in cash throughout the year (slim for a company of its size). "This is an important day," exulted Chris Whittle, announcing the news in an investor conference call.[6]

But investors were unmoved. Edison's stock price, which had traded as high as $36.75 in February 2001 and as low as fourteen cents in October 2002, barely budged, whatever announcements Edison offered of its financial progress. By May 2003, with the turnaround nearly complete, the stock traded at a dollar. Founder and CEO Chris Whittle had little choice but to take the company private. In July 2003, Whittle announced that Edison's board had accepted a bid by Whittle and Liberty Partners, a private equity firm, to buy out the existing shareholders at $1.76 a share and retire the company's debt. Edison predictably identified as factors in its decision the difficulty of raising capital at its low share price and the stock market's excessively short-term focus. But it also cited its customers' perceptions of its stock price. Operating in the intensely political atmosphere of public schooling, the company feared a further loss of clients: "Edison's stock price has been inaccurately perceived by school districts, charter schools and others as indicative of the Company's ability to perform its obligations . . . The Company's ability to execute its educational mission will be enhanced if school districts, charter schools and others are not distracted by perceived implications of Edison's stock price."[7]

The experiences of recent years—the bitter opposition to its school contract in Philadelphia, the collapse of its share price, the withdrawal from the stock market—have only deepened management's determination to prevail. "There's no question that we had a near-death experience last spring," remarked Benno Schmidt, the company's chairman, to the *New York Times* in 2003.[8] Management has endured years of vilification, first by the education establishment, and then by Wall Street. Ninety-five percent of the value of their stockholdings evaporated, and they nearly lost not only the company they had devoted ten years of their careers to building, but their reputations as well. What holds the team together, interviews reveal, is a sense of public purpose—that it is engaged in a virtuous fight. "I don't think whether we're private or public has any effect on our standing in the national debate over educational reform," Whittle declared. "I think we're going to be a very important voice."[9]

It is likely that Edison will post its first profitable year in fiscal 2006. For fiscal 2004, the analyst closest to Edison had projected revenues of $467 million for the year, EBITDA of $43 million, and a net income of $2 million.[10] But the company incurred large one-time charges from "going private" in that year, depressing its results. On the path to profitability, serious challenges await. Edison continues to suffer the loss or adverse renegotiation of school management contracts. Its schools in its home state of New York are troubled; the state recently declined to renew the charter of its Rochester school, citing poor academic performance. The company's school design is a decade old and needs to be renewed. These problems aside, Wall Street asks a larger question: Is there a large and expanding market for school outsourcing? Edison says yes. The school accountability movement continues to drive education policy in the states, and the federal No Child Left Behind Act will only intensify it. As the states' and NCLB's accountability provisions continue to kick in, states may require districts to "restructure" chronically failing schools. One of NCLB's "restructuring" options for underperforming schools is contracting for private management "of demonstrated effectiveness."

Edison will be in a uniquely strong position to capture these opportunities, because it has the most persuasive and least anecdotal claims of academic gains. These claims are likely to grow stronger each year, as Edison's program implementation continues to improve and the range of implementation quality across school sites is narrowed.

In the summer of 2004, the state of South Carolina hired Edison to assist the long-troubled Allendale County school system. In a new approach the company dubs "Edison Alliance," Edison departs in key ways from its usual practice. Normally, Edison assumes management responsibility for district staff and, in installing Edison's comprehensive system, must jettison what is already in place in the schools—books and practices, good and bad alike. A downside of that approach, Edison says, is that it inadvertently sends a message that everything the school is doing (and that it may have struggled to achieve) is a failure. Instead, Edison will help Allendale align its curriculum and teaching with the state's standards and deploy the Benchmark Assessment System to track students' academic progress.[11]

Edison is successfully moving beyond its core business of comprehensive school management to offer school districts related and highly profitable services. Under NCLB, underperforming schools may be required to allocate a portion of their Title I funding toward the provision of tutoring and other services to struggling students. Edison is well positioned to provide such supplemental services through its new Newton Learning division, which offers after-school, summer, and tutoring programs tailored to the requirements of NCLB. Additionally, Edison's Tungsten Learning division licenses the company's intellectual property, including the Benchmark Assessment System.

Edison is unlikely to realize Whittle's 1991 dream of operating a thousand campuses with a million students by 2010. But he may yet realize his goal "to reshape education in America by providing state-of-the-art schools to communities nationwide and a state-of-the-art example for others to follow."[12]

NATIONAL HERITAGE ACADEMIES

With Edison's New York flamboyance contrasts National Heritage's Midwestern modesty. While Edison spoke of transforming public education and building a billion-dollar company, NHA quietly assembled a stable and profitable company. Even today, it credits its success as much to good fortune as to strategic insight.

Whichever the case, NHA has avoided most of the execution pitfalls that plagued its competitors. The company grew slowly at first, operated exclusively charter schools, housed students in new and low-cost buildings, and expanded only cautiously beyond its home state of Michigan. In its choice of markets, it stuck to states supportive of for-profit management (limiting political resistance to its activities) with relatively high per-student spending (average is $7,000 versus Edison's $6,400). Sensibly, it operates only schools for K–8, avoiding the risky and costly high school grades. High per-student spending together with moderate costs have resulted in strong site profitability. Shrewd choices in how the business is structured—for example, hiring all school staff as NHA employees, except where not permitted by law—avoided accounting problems.

There is an irony to National Heritage's success as a business. When early on the company was looking to raise equity capital from institutional investors, it was repeatedly turned down. Investors were wary of the controversy over religious teachings and a conservative ideology that had been depicted unflatteringly on the front page of the *Wall Street Journal*. The concentration of schools in one state exposed the company to too much political risk—the Michigan charter law could be gutted or repealed outright. The lack of institutional money in the company alienated prospective blue chip investors. And finally, NHA's real estate model, in which the company purchased and held the school properties, was not regarded as viable.

In fact, these very features propelled NHA's early success. Shared values created vibrant school communities, where parents are engaged, staff committed, and relationships with customer boards harmonious. Proximity greatly reduced costs; permitted many of the company's charters to be awarded by a single, supportive authorizer, Grand Valley State University, which was receptive to private managers and developed a trusting partnership with NHA; and built trust between school leaders and corporate executives—in the first three years, all the principals could meet in person once a week on an hour's drive. Management projected humility and restrained from making boastful promises. The company readily delivered schools strong on character and values and with a pervasive atmosphere of civility, its primary value proposition. NHA made sound curriculum choices, like the Open Court reading program, and by sticking initially to one state could easily align its academic program with Michigan's state test. Finally, by not seeking attention and staying regional, the company stayed largely under the political radar.

The company built essentially the same affordable but inviting school facility in every location ($2.8 million and an additional $1.2 million when the school expands), financed by the company's angel investor and chairman. The tens of millions of dollars of real property—the school buildings—on the company's balance sheet secured a loan package sufficient to fund years of continued construction. Today, NHA is in the enviable position of not needing the investors who once rejected its business plan.

Rather than taking on schools in far-flung states, NHA pursued a disciplined regional growth strategy, mastering one regulatory environment before venturing into another. Limiting the number of jurisdictions in which it operated greatly simplified the demands on the central office and kept corporate overhead low. With only the founder's money to spend, a frugal corporate culture was sustained. While National Heritage would not disclose specifics, these characteristics all support NHA's claim to have reached profitability in the 2000–2001 school year and to have continued to make money since.[13] Provided that the company maintains its disciplined growth, NHA is likely to be robustly profitable in the years ahead.

Still, National Heritage faces risks going forward. As yet, the company's claims of offering a superior education are unproven; as reviewed in Chapter 8, NHA's analysis of achievement results, like those of the other organizations, falls short of the standards of strong science. Second, NHA educates a student population that is far more affluent than Edison's; only 37 percent of NHA's students are eligible for free or reduced-price lunch, compared to Edison's 73 percent. NHA's students are also primarily white (61 percent), compared to Edison's 12 percent.[14] NHA's home market of Michigan is lucrative, but charters have become much more difficult to obtain. A statutory 150-school cap on the number of charters that can be granted by university authorizers has been reached, although one Native American statewide community college is not subject to the cap and continues to grant charters. Further, NHA's foray into urban, primarily black, schools is recent, and its ability to adapt to this profoundly different setting is unproven. Recently, the State University of New York declined to renew the charter of the company's flagship school in Rochester. (Many EMOs would have fought such a decision. Characteristically, NHA graciously accepted it and pledged to ensure an orderly closing.) In 2003, the company researched and developed the framework for a promising new school design for urban settings, but the model is only beginning to be deployed.[15] Will NHA establish a reputation for raising achievement in schools that serve the urban poor and win the business it needs in that market to meet its goal of doubling in size in five years?[16] It also remains to be seen whether NHA's association with evangelical Christianity will assist or impede efforts to attract new charter school board clients.

KIPP

KIPP's approach has striking advantages for a school's launch and operation. As a nonprofit, KIPP has avoided the virulent political opposition that profit-making in public education arouses. Second, KIPP took five years to build a powerful and distinctive brand at its first two schools (prototypes, in effect) before attempting to roll out the program nationally. That brand, in turn, attracts KIPP fellows who identify with its mission and values. During a year of training and internships at KIPP schools, KIPP fellows reliably assimilate the organization's culture.

Choosing to open each school to just three classes in a single grade gave the school leader time to find and finance a permanent facility and recruit exceptional staff. In short, it gave the school several years to solve the problems that EMOs often confronted in a single summer. Finding three classrooms—in a church basement, for example—is a trivial task compared to building or improving a facility for hundreds of students— especially under unreasonable pressures of time and budget.

KIPP's fellows program has attracted young, enterprising school leaders from top universities, who in turn hire a staff of highly educated teachers much like themselves. The school's principal can lavish great care on the selection of the first three teachers, who set the tone for the school and drive its initial achievements. The small size and careful selection of staff make possible the establishment of a radically new culture of high expectations for students and facilitate a focus on academic results. Establishing an orderly climate and building a school culture with ninety students is an entirely different challenge from opening a school for five hundred. In the larger setting, the school leader's focus will be on averting crises and attempting to achieve stability, while in the small school it can be directed from the start both to honing teaching and learning and to shaping the school culture.

Finally, KIPP fellows have recruited to their boards mentors and community members eager to be a part of the KIPP phenomenon and who can be expected to support the school leader in bringing the lauded program to their community.

Early on, KIPP received invitations from communities around the country to open schools. The Fishers and other philanthropists have given millions in support of its mission. KIPP has created high academic expectations for its schools, and their boutique size and elite teaching corps should permit them to deliver strong results.

But is KIPP sustainable? It may not be the network's goal to become self-sustaining, but can it rely indefinitely on millions of dollars in annual philanthropic support? And will continued dependence on private largesse, by tilting the playing field, weaken its claim to be a model for reforming public education?

If nothing else, KIPP's financial model can illuminate the choices of emerging nonprofit EMOs. KIPP's 2002 financial projections called for its reliance on donations and grants to be reduced from $15 million in school year 2003–2004 to $5.3 million in 2012.[17] Without changes to the model, that seems unlikely. The fees paid by schools are extremely low: 1 percent of school revenues in the first year, and just 3 percent of revenues subsequently. Edison and National Heritage, by contrast, are generally entitled under their contracts to keep the difference between their schools' revenues and costs. For Edison this "gross margin" is approximately 15 percent; for National Heritage it is probably higher. Compounding the problem of low fees is KIPP's small initial school size and slow expansion. A typical school opening with 80 students and growing to 320 would pay just $6,071 to KIPP in its first year and $60,854 by its fifth. Compensating for such low fees, KIPP's plan called for opening some 230 schools over a ten-year period. Even so, total fees paid by the schools would come to only $10.6 million in the tenth year.[18]

Under that plan, twenty-five new schools were to be launched each year. That quickly proved excessive, however, and KIPP scaled back the pace of its openings. In 2003, KIPP opened seventeen schools with difficulty. "We realized we had no business doing 17 schools, and there was no way we could do 25," said John Alford, who heads up new school development.[19] With just twenty KIPP fellows in training, KIPP said it was having difficulty finding high-quality candidates among applicants. Even if positive media coverage for its schools continues, KIPP will be challenged to identify and train the new leaders it needs. Further, invitations to the organization to open KIPP schools have slowed, and the charter market appears to be drying up, says Scott Hamilton.[20] KIPP's nonprofit structure has not provided full immunity to political opposition; in Lynn, Massachusetts, the mayor, city council, school committee, and district administration all spoke out against the KIPP Academy Lynn Charter School. The city council thwarted the school's opening by trying to establish a new permitting requirement for charter schools, which eventually was ruled illegal.

To sustain even its current pace of new school openings, KIPP must scout for opportunities throughout the country—with all the attendant challenges of a national roll-out. Navigating the complexities of real estate acquisition, build-out, and financing will require specialized skills that few of its young principals have. Even though the schools start small, each will soon serve more than three hundred students and will face challenges, similar to those faced by the EMOs, of securing permanent facility financing.

KIPP initially assumed that school leaders would themselves successfully take on, with the benefit of a year of planning and a small initial size, most tasks related to siting, building, and operating their new schools. But KIPP soon found that the national office in San Francisco had to provide more support to its schools and needed a much larger staff than the model anticipated or is found in most EMOs' business development offices. By early 2003, a staff of six "trailblazers" worked regionally to locate opportunities to open schools by developing relationships with state regulators, community leaders, politicians, and district officials. The trailblazers prepared charter applications, identified facilities, built community support for the new school, and met with school districts. The national office also found itself providing extensive support to school leaders in the areas of academics, organizational culture, community development, and especially, operations. Operations staff assisted principals in opening and managing their schools, including addressing issues of budgeting and finance, facilities, human resources, procurement, and compliance.[21]

For these reasons, KIPP's corporate office staff in 2002 was already about twice the size projected in its earlier business plan. KIPP's financial projections assume no growth in national office support staff between the 2003–2004 school year and 2012, despite an increase in the projected number of schools from 35 to 235. If all KIPP National provides is pre-opening services and then over three years weans the sites of corporate support, this assumption might be realistic. But schools will need ongoing support services. And if they don't, will they be willing to continue to pay fees?

The EMOs have had to intervene relentlessly in their schools, parachuting in supplemental academic and operations support staff to maintain a standard of quality, ensure compliance, and make good on their promises to the community. Even with the raw talents of the typical KIPP fellow and the benefit of thorough training, a few KIPP principals will stumble early on, and others will fail to develop the management skills to oversee the school as it grows to more than three hundred students and $2 million in annual expenses.[22] KIPP National will have to intervene. Invoking KIPP's contractual right to revoke the license of the school for its failure to meet a detailed set of standards may not prove a practicable quality-control strategy. The KIPP brand may not be insulated from damage simply by decreeing that the school no longer has a legal affiliation with KIPP; the board of the school and the community will look to KIPP to repair the school, not disown it. Moreover, where KIPP National holds the contract with the school district, or a charter with the state, KIPP will not have the option of separating itself from the school, and closing it will be politically unacceptable.

KIPP's culture would not stand for raising license fees, and even Scott Hamilton says it would be wrong.[23] But let's consider what would be necessary if the organization decided that, like for-profit EMOs, it had to become self-sustaining. To close the growing gap between license fees from the school and likely levels of national office expenditures, a fee of not 3 but perhaps 10 percent might prove necessary. KIPP's value proposition, comprised of a leadership development program and ongoing participation in the KIPP network, would not justify such a fee at the outset, let alone one paid out in perpetuity, well after most of the value has been received. An EMO that provides a comprehensive curriculum, professional development, and central operational services, including financial management and human resources, would not face such resistance.

SABIS

SABIS has an immensely powerful school design that could contribute greatly to the improvement of American public education, especially in the middle and high school grades where our students slip in comparison to their peers in other countries. SABIS is comfortable operating high schools, and data on achievement growth in upper grades at its K–12 charter school in Springfield, Massachusetts, are impressive. The company's school design and practices are distinctive and innovative. It is vital that their potential be realized at scale.

But the company's strengths are also at the center of its difficulties in this country. SABIS's approach, with its rational school practices and traditional management philosophy, was bound to clash with the American public school culture—its fads, progressive orthodoxies, and tradition of assigning responsibilities to actors (from school board members to teachers) unequipped to exercise them competently. In entering the market, one wishes that SABIS had been better advised on when to accommodate and when to hold firm.

Two aspects of the company's approach may require a change in course: school leadership and client relations. First, SABIS must overcome any ambivalence toward strong principals. Upholding the principal's primacy takes nothing away from the company's curriculum—to which their prized Springfield school is testament. The current enthusiasm for nontraditional candidates who are "good at taking orders" may prove a distraction, not a solution. Second, SABIS's record of managing client relationships is spotty, and it has lost nearly half the schools it has opened. In response to what it perceives as a pattern of wrongdoing and financial exploitation by charter school boards, SABIS has sometimes assumed a kind of fortress mentality. Rather than give trustees, as Carl Bistany puts it, "a red carpet welcome" to the schools they govern, SABIS has asked some trustees to state their purpose and schedule an appointment.[24] Board members, appropriately, have limited say in day-to-day operations. The frustration of SABIS's executives is understandable. Yet without a new approach, SABIS may continue to lose schools even where it is serving its client well—damaging the company's brand and resulting in large write-offs. Until regulatory changes obviate client school boards by permitting management organizations to hold charters directly or redeem vouchers, the company must embrace the tradition of local control of schools and accept that it works at the pleasure of its client boards. With these adjustments to the market, SABIS can yet fulfill its tremendous promise for American schooling.

CHANCELLOR BEACON

In 2003, Chancellor Beacon reported that it was breaking even and would make a profit in fiscal year 2005.[25] But one source close to the company says that goal remains elusive. The long-term prospects for Chancellor's educational and business models are uncertain. Will Chancellor's progressive focus and limited prescription to its member schools produce achievement results superior to those in district schools, an outcome that will ultimately be necessary to secure new business and ward off competition? The company's choice of low-spending states, coupled with a value proposition of smaller class sizes, will constrain site profitability and Chancellor Beacon's ability to offer competitive salaries. Already, teachers interviewed for this book were unhappy that promised raises were not awarded, and many said they would not remain for another year without increased compensation.

Chancellor Beacon's investors, led by Warburg Pincus, have sold the company to Dennis Bakke, reportedly for less than half the value of their original investment. In its newly decentralized structure, where services previously performed by the central office will all take place at the school level, what will be the value the company provides to client schools? And why would the schools be expected to outperform district schools? If one thing has been learned from the governance reforms of the last two decades—radical decentralization in Chicago and New York, "school-based management" in the early 1990s, and charter schools today—it's that devolving authority to school personnel to make decisions and then holding them accountable for their actions is an insufficient plan for addressing a school's problems. Building a network of schools that consistently outperform their district competitors will also require equipping each school with exceptional—and probably proprietary—tools and practices.

MOSAICA

Of the five EMOs, Mosaica is run most like a business. Its core competencies of real estate development, finance, and litigation have served the company well, given the challenges of the present regulatory environment. Mosaica's management team has ably steered the company to profitability, avoided unprofitable projects, and tapped long-term debt financing for its client's schools.

Mosaica's real estate model could be instructive to other management organizations. The company was wise to distinguish to its clients its dual roles as education service provider and "reluctant" landlord, and to assure them that its goal was to transfer ownership of the building to the school as soon as practicable. Carefully vetting new projects, it invested $1 million in equity in each facility and secured temporary financing for the balance of $2 to $2.5 million. Within two years from the school's opening, an operational history established, Mosaica generally arranged for permanent financing of the facility through the sale of tax-exempt bonds and the transfer of title to the client board at "fair market value." The company recouped not only its equity but collected a handsome "development fee" of $250,000 to $500,000 as well. Each deal had to be handcrafted, paying close attention to legal structure and artfully securing issuers in each new state. By late 2003, it had completed twelve transactions in three states and the District of Columbia, for a total of over $100 million. By rapidly recycling its equity from one project into the next, Mosaica successfully limited its commitment of venture capital to real estate.

In the short term, Mosaica's well-intentioned Paragon curriculum will continue to appeal to many school boards, teachers, and even charter authorizers, just as progressive educators have always won over parents and policymakers with their seductive promise that learning will be made "fun." But in the long term, Paragon, now the company's center-piece, may prove more an impediment than an asset. "We spend a lot of time trying to convince people it's not just an arts and crafts pro-gram and has real content," CEO Michael Connelly reports.[26] The cur-riculum is untested, and schools showed an uneven commitment to its implementation.

As industry competition intensifies, charter awards and contracting decisions will be driven not by pedagogic aspirations, but by evidence from large-scale studies that a company's chosen curricula are effective and by rigorous analyses confirming that an EMO has raised student achievement in its schools. Yet Mosaica's website provides few details about student achievement and no underlying data. So far, Mosaica's management team appears to be the least focused on instruction and academic results among leaders of the EMOs and KIPP.

Private Management of Public Schools: A Good Investment?

The financial performance of the six companies generally fell far short of their commitments to investors. Most notably, Edison's stock price col-lapse soured education investors not only on the company, but also on for-profit K–12 management generally. Wall Street, which values stabil-ity and predictability, is chary of the political controversy that continues to surround private management of public schools. Nonetheless, there are important pockets of investor interest. Some private equity funds—

which buy stock in later-stage privately held companies—have shown renewed interest in the K–12 market. National Heritage Academies says it has been aggressively pursued by major private equity investors. When Chris Whittle sought a private equity fund as a partner in his proposal to take Edison private, he attracted multiple bidders. In time, new for-profit education management organizations will emerge. Can they, learning from the lessons of their predecessors, deliver an attractive return to their equity investors?

Large philanthropic investors, including the NewSchools Venture Fund, the Gates Foundation, and the Broad Foundation, are investing tens of millions of dollars in nonprofit charter management organizations and school networks. Beacon founder Michael Ronan has received funding to develop a CMO called Lighthouse Academies, which is opening charter schools in the Northeast and the Midwest. Can such nonprofit managers become self-sustaining?

Critics of for-profit education argue that the travails of the EMOs—especially Edison—confute the premise of for-profit education management: that with enough schools over which to spread overhead costs, the company will show a profit. Heidi Steffens, a senior policy analyst at NEA, and Peter Cookson, former professor at Columbia University's Teachers College, have argued that "economies of scale don't apply to the business of schooling." Schooling is labor-intensive; the single largest cost is teachers' salaries: "Short of hiring cheap labor (underqualified teachers) or replacing teachers with computers, neither of which is recommended as a way to create successful schools, there's simply no way to dramatically reduce labor costs."[27] Yet the experiences of the six organizations do not support this conclusion. There is ample opportunity to deploy personnel more efficiently in schools, if one is willing to look beyond the constraints of union work rules and the sacred cow of small classes.

Steffens and Cookson further contend that economies of scale work in businesses with "uniform products," but "schooling is not one-design-fits-all."

Replicating a successful school at multiple sites is not like replicating a successful restaurant or bookstore. Schools' raw materials (students) are highly individual and unpredictable, the product of forces external to the school. The central control required to create schools that look and feel and educate like all a company's other schools stands in direct contradiction to the need for every school to respond to its students and community, its "customers."[28]

This argument rests on the faulty premise that every school must be fundamentally unique. Certainly, the educational needs of elementary students from an affluent suburb are different from those of inner-city students, even while their schools' aspirations for achievement ought to be the same. But a program highly effective for children in Detroit would likely work as well in Los Angeles, Chicago, or Washington, D.C. Strong design features—like Direct Instruction's early reading programs, school uniforms, or character education—won raves from urban parents in every location they were properly implemented by the organizations. The educational—even moral—imperative is not to ensure that every child's education is conceived anew, but rather that every student benefits from sound, proven practices.

To the extent that private managers have the wisdom to focus on settings to which their designs are well-suited, there is no evidence that then adapting these designs to multiple locations will contribute to central overhead. Principals and teachers need to have discretion to fit the school design to the academic, emotional, and social conditions of their students. Private managers may struggle with this tension between local discretion and fidelity to a central model. But this is a concern for the organization's culture, not its finances. Edison, for one, has managed this challenge skillfully, building into its model the values and structures to accommodate this tension at each location without incurring adaptation costs. As we have seen, corporate overhead costs for the six EMOs and KIPP spiraled from regulatory and political features that are not intrinsic to "the business of schooling": the failure to provide capital funding for buildings, the incoherence of curriculum standards and tests from one state to another, the inconsistencies of regulatory and reporting requirements, and the relentless political and legal challenges to private management.

Yet two of the five EMOs are now making money, two have been acquired, and another is likely to become profitable imminently. As Henry Levin notes, the real issue is whether EMOs can provide a return on capital that is competitive with other investment opportunities.[29] The combination of an unfavorable regulatory environment and poor execution added to operating losses, delayed profitability, and increased capital needs. As seen in Chapter 5, many of the EMOs spent heavily on school real estate, greatly increasing capital intensity. (Edison invested $200 million in charter schools.) A few early investors lost their money, and others face poor liquidity options in the current general climate for initial public offerings and, specifically, because of Edison's failure as a public company. Whether certain of the EMOs will ultimately generate an adequate return for their investors will depend on future demand, regulatory reforms, improved access to real estate debt, and the tenor of the capital markets.

Future EMOs

There is no longer any doubt that EMOs can operate profitably, and the failure of the first companies to generate strong returns for their investors should not dissuade future investment in the K–12 education industry. The excessive capital requirements of the first EMOs can be traced directly to two regulatory defects: lack of capital for school facilities and the EMOs' inability to protect their investments in the schools they operated and often built—because the charters were held by the schools' boards, and authorizers failed to enforce management agreements. When boards breached management agreements, millions of dollars in facility investments; loans; technology, furnishings, and instructional materials; pre-opening expenses; and uncollected rent and management fees had to be written off. When EMOs' financial histories became pocked by lost schools, breached contracts, and resulting write-offs, commercial lenders and developers only became less comfortable lending to client schools.

Under what conditions could new EMOs, learning from the mistakes of their predecessors, attract investment and generate a competitive return? Consider a hypothetical new operator of charter schools that benefits from just one key improvement in the regulatory environment: its charter schools, like other public schools, can borrow the money to build the school's facility, either by issuing public debt, or by borrowing from commercial sources enabled by credit enhancements from the states or the federal government. None of the company's capital is required for this purpose. Given this modestly improved regulatory environment, a detailed financial model using conservative assumptions indicates that EMOs could provide their investors with an attractive rate of return. Such returns need not await the ideal environment, where charter schools are funded on an equal basis with traditional schools. It requires only that client schools be able to borrow the money to build schools without tapping the capital or credit of the EMO.

Conclusion

Of the many questions with which we began, we now return to the most essential: Have the organizations provided their students a superior education? Will they ultimately succeed? How can the private sector contribute more effectively to the improvement of public schooling?

Accelerating Student Learning

Private managers of public schools brought the business world's focus on measurement, accountability, and intervention to K–12 education. Some critics insist that privately run schools look much like traditional public schools. But the best private managers had little interest in chasing the chimera of educational "innovation": their focus was tapping practices known to be effective. In their school designs, each deployed an array of reforms that together would boost educational productivity. Most lengthened the school day and year and devoted more time to the core academic subjects. Abandoning the union's insistence that all teaching jobs be equivalent, they created professional environments where teachers were evaluated on the basis of their students' learning and could work their way up a ladder of responsibilities and rewards. Most deployed structured instructional programs chosen on the evidence of their effectiveness; many invested heavily in professional development fitted to these programs and hired specialists to oversee their exacting implementation. Some wrote ambitious software to track their students' mastery of essential knowledge and skills and to gauge their progress toward state standards. And the organizations did not hesitate to create normative environments for their students, with consistent consequences for misbehavior and explicit instruction in character, habits, and values. Commercialism did not permeate their schools—even corporate logos, when they could be found at all in EMO-run schools, were at most a discreet presence.

As detailed in Chapter 8, a final verdict on the academic performance of privately managed schools cannot yet be reached. Data on academic performance are sparse, and the best studies available fall far short of controlled experimental studies. Nonetheless, amidst this ambiguity, we can venture some tentative conclusions.

First, by choice or assignment, the EMOs and KIPP have taken on one of the most intractable problems in American society: persistently failing schools. Whether by contracting to turn around district schools or by opening new schools that offer parents a much-needed alternative, the organizations have focused on educating low-performing students, often from inner-city neighborhoods burdened by concentrated poverty and social ills. Opponents of school choice warned that charter schools and profit-motivated operators would "cream" the most capable students, leaving school districts with the grim task of educating the poorest-performing children. Yet there is evidence of the reverse selection effect: privately managed schools (and independently operated charter schools) have proven especially attractive to parents whose children have struggled in district schools.

Second, when students arrive performing in the bottom quartile of their peers nationally, success must be measured not by absolute performance but by gains over time. Are students in some privately managed schools learning faster? Especially for schools that serve low-performing students, "value added" analysis offers a true measure of school effectiveness, isolating the effects of schooling from other factors, including race, poverty, and prior achievement. State and federal policies today embrace measures for school accountability that resemble—but fall short—of true value-added systems. The No Child Left Behind Act requires schools to make "adequate yearly progress" toward the objective that all students be grade-level proficient in 2013–2014. But under NCLB, schools are judged by comparing the performance of successive cohorts—for example, one year's third-grade class with the previous year's—even though the two groups of students may be very different (a particular problem when examining the performance of individual small schools). Further, NCLB's emphasis on the percentage of students attaining "proficiency" on tests obscures the progress of students who either fall short of the passing bar or who have already cleared it. Many schools are labeled "failing" even when their students are learning faster than their peers in schools with higher absolute achievement levels. Far fairer would be to track the progress of individual students over time. Accordingly, sixteen state school officers urged the secretary of education in 2004 to permit value-added measures to satisfy the accountability requirements of NCLB.[1]

On this question of relative gains, the limited evidence points in the private managers' favor. In a recent study, rare for its independence, Tom Loveless at the Brookings Institution examined charter school performance in ten states. The EMO-run schools, the report concludes, typically serve low-achieving students. Compared to schools with similar demographics, they were performing at absolute levels below independent charter schools and still further below traditional schools. "EMO-operated charters," Loveless observes, "apparently are not brought in to manage schools in recognition of schools' success, but to intervene in the case of school failure."[2] But the EMO-run schools posted on average significantly greater achievement gains over the period of the study than both independent charter schools and regular public schools. Loveless concludes:

Importing management expertise from the private sector should be explored further as an option for improving low-achieving schools. The results presented here are quite positive for EMOs. The findings raise doubts about a strain of thought in the charter school movement: that anyone can successfully start and operate a school if he or she merely possesses abundant energy and a love of children. In the extreme, this form of romanticized amateurism dismisses the importance of educational expertise. That appears unwise. Future research should focus on identifying the broadest range of policies and practices that are capable of creating achievement successes out of achievement failures.[3]

The study's findings are consistent with the reports of several organizations that document the low performance of their students on arrival and gains over subsequent years. Some might view an annual gain of several points on a national norm-referenced test as unimpressive. But if a student's performance is elevated by five percentile rank points over each of five years—say, from the 25th percentile to the national average—his or her fate, in statistical terms, will have been profoundly altered.

Third, and contrary to the claims of some critics, reading and math gains did not come at the expense of children's overall development. In fact, the seven organizations offered classes in the arts that urban schools had often sacrificed. There is no evidence that they created "test factories" or even that schools devoted much time to preparing students for tests.

Fourth, as described in Chapters 5 and 6, the organizations struggled with overwhelming challenges: securing and financing school facilities, fundraising (both equity and debt), political hostility, conflicts with their school board customers, regulatory complexity and compliance, and their own sometimes reckless growth expectations. Management bandwidth—the time, focus, and resources of executives and their staff—was sapped by these nonacademic concerns.

The situation may be changing. The advantages of private management—the entrepreneurial drive to succeed, the stability of instructional approaches, and the continual upgrading of leadership and staff—are beginning to bear fruit. The industry has learned much about how to structure and account for its business. The capital markets are once again valuing companies for their earnings and not their claims to top-line growth. The pressure to open many new schools at once has relaxed, and management has been able to devote greater attention to the quality of implementation of the school design at each site. Edison and other organizations have become increasingly sophisticated about the choice and training of school leaders, have better aligned their educational programs with state standards and assessments, and have refined their professional development practices. This newfound focus on quality will translate into stronger and more consistent implementations and accelerating achievement gains. Consider Edison. In its seventh annual report on school performance, for the academic year 2003–2004, Edison reported its strongest gains ever. On state criterion reference tests, the percentage of students at its school achieving proficiency increased by an average of 7.4 percentage points over the 2002–2003 school year.[4]

In the years ahead, the academic performance of the six organizations (and others in the industry) will likely become starkly differentiated. Organizations with weak programs will have difficulty supporting claims of offering a superior education; those with strong designs sustained over years at client sites will present ever more robust evidence of their effectiveness. In time, those organizations that are focused on educational implementation and quality may be able to overcome ideological resistance with incontrovertible academic results.

Education as a Business

While skeptics continue to assert that K–12 education will never work as a business, two EMOs have quietly begun to make money.[5] By 2004, Mosaica and National Heritage had become profitable, and Edison, after a decade of losing money, had posted its first profitable quarter; it is expected to be profitable in fiscal year 2006.

But what of the industry's long-term prospects? As argued in Chapter 9, the skills that propelled some management teams to profitability may be of less value as the external environment of customer needs and regulation evolves. In the late 1990s, political savvy and business skills proved the key competencies. EMOs that were expert at securing charters and district contracts, financing real estate projects, and structuring and enforcing management contracts could open schools and in time turn a profit. But by century's end, the environment in which the EMOs had developed was no longer. After the technology bubble burst in 2000, Wall Street, once drunk on grand "stories," slunk back to companies with predictable earnings. The growth in charter schools continued nationally, but licenses to open new schools were less freely awarded. Experienced authorizers conceded that the academic record of their portfolio schools was mixed. In major markets like New York State, charters remained available, but only to applicants with a history of building high-achieving schools. Prospects for wholesale privatization of school districts reached their zenith in Philadelphia.

Although new proficiency standards and sanctions were merely legislative blueprints when many EMOs were launched, in many states they took full effect during the late 1990s, creating an unprecedented focus on academic quality and improvement in school districts everywhere. With the signing of NCLB in 2002, the standards and accountability movement was enshrined in federal policy and became the nation's de facto school improvement strategy. "Adequate yearly progress" quickly became the new currency of the public school establishment. State education agencies at last began reporting academic outcomes, rather than monitoring only "inputs"—spending levels, class sizes, and racial quotas. Superintendents once consumed with compliance and reporting were compelled to manage the school's core function, instruction.

As these trends continue, the essential competency for private managers will be instructional management. Under NCLB, schools that fail to make adequate yearly progress are subject to a series of escalating interventions. In the fifth year of this sequence, school districts must take one of five actions, one of which is to contract with a private management company of demonstrated effectiveness. Organizations that have a powerful school design, the capacity to implement it exactingly across multiple locations, and a record of elevating student achievement ought to be in great demand by districts, charter school boards, and state education agencies. Private managers that can point only to weak or inconsistent results will find themselves struggling to retain clients.

The Future of Private Management

The next wave of education management organizations is learning from the experiences of the last. The NewSchools Venture Fund has funded several charter management organizations and plans to launch more. The Gates Foundation and the Walton Family Foundation are among the largest supporters of charter schools, emerging CMOs, and school networks.

The CMO strategy mitigates several of the challenges of private management, but not all. Aspire has struggled no less than the EMOs with the problem of securing and financing facilities and, burdened with excessive borrowing at several sites, has chosen to blend facility costs across schools, in a kind of cross-subsidization of school costs. Growth is no less an imperative for Aspire than for earlier EMOs. To reach breakeven, Aspire projects it will need to reach a total of thirty-five schools under management; under more pessimistic assumptions, self-sufficiency will only be obtained with ninety schools. Both scenarios require an increase in management fees from 7 to 8 percent of school revenues; the first relies on $11 million of additional philanthropic support and the second, $25 million.

With a lean central office befitting a nonprofit, Aspire may not have the capacity to take on its ambitious Los Angeles project while several of its first schools still need close attention. Its Monarch Academy in Oakland, California, an elementary school, has posted impressive gains, but several schools (especially those serving the upper grades) are still struggling.[6] The progressive design's capacity to produce strong annual gains consistently (particularly in high-poverty locations) is unknown. If it must be overhauled, rank-and-file staff are likely to resist the change. Yet with a seasoned educator at the helm, a committed management team, and thoughtful backers, Aspire has the ingredients to succeed.

Meanwhile, there is again a smattering of iconoclastic investors interested in the for-profit K–12 market. A next-generation organization could combine the best practices of the EMOs profiled in this book—KIPP's focus on leadership development and its culture of transformation; SABIS's point and prefect system (including computerized academic measurement systems); Edison's balanced pedagogy and emphasis on professional development and instructional management, including formative assessment (benchmarking); National Heritage's client relationships and cluster strategy; Mosaica's shrewd execution of real estate transactions; and Advantage's program for reliably equipping children in the early grades with strong foundation skills. With these strengths, its potential would be extraordinary.

Implications for Policy

As the charter movement matures, it is called to account. First, charter authorizers must demonstrate that charter schools are on average educating students to a higher standard than traditional public schools. Second, charter schools must proliferate rapidly enough that they cannot be dismissed as a marginal phenomenon that only benefits a small minority of students—an unjustifiable distraction of money and intellectual capital from the task of improving the majority system.

The first task is made harder in many states by early awards to "innovative" proposals that were not based on research-proven practices. Most of these schools have since failed to elevate student achievement and now depress the performance of authorizers' portfolios. It won't work to claim that these early awards should be excluded from consideration. The solution is to award new charters judiciously to schools that offer a near certainty of performing to a high standard, thereby elevating the portfolio's average. Many authorizers have observed that their strongest performers are certain "moms and pops" that benefit from extraordinary founders and school leaders and that deploy proven, research-based designs. But authorizers now receive few such high-quality proposals.

In every community, there are few savvy, driven school founders who forgo seductive theories for evidence-based school designs and who possess the broad-ranging skills to make good on their audacious plans. The time and energies of such exceptional leaders are deployed over years in building schools that rarely reach more than a few hundred students. Proliferation is impossible if it relies on such rare talent, and if that talent is directed toward the realization of just one school.

Management organizations—when they bring an exemplary school design and relentless focus on instructional implementation—can offer a solution: new systems of public schools, managed by or affiliated with a private organization and operating under a "brand," aim to leverage a common core of human and intellectual capital to benefit not one, but many schools and thousands of students. But the current structures of local school boards and management contracts—which reforms proposed earlier would obviate—needlessly thwart the establishment of large numbers of high-quality schools. Charter laws were intended to spawn individual schools, each with its own lay board, not foster systems of privately managed schools. Recognizing this, authorizers must take steps to mitigate these constraints, while forcefully advocating for changes in state policy.

For EMOs to succeed fully, two impediments must be removed. First, states must level the financial playing field of district-operated public schools and charter public schools. Charter schools, including those operated by private organizations, should not have to pay for school facilities out of operating revenues while districts occupy school buildings built at public expense. In recent years, several states and the federal government have taken the first steps toward redressing this inequity, but these will fall short because they are appended to an underlying school finance system that is itself inequitable, deeply regressive, and antiquated. Jon Schroeder, an advocate for charter schools, notes that the school district as at once a taxing jurisdiction, a political subdivision, and an attendance zone is an anachronism.[7] Once students cross such traditional boundaries, the district-based school finance system is obsolescent. School choice is expanding. Interdistrict choice laws allow students to attend schools outside their districts. New charter schools are opening, often created not by the local school district but by a variety of authorizing entities. In some cities, parents are abandoning assigned schools and exploiting public or privately funded voucher programs to attend private schools. Ultimately, we are driven toward state financing of public education, with both operating and capital funds following students to whatever public school they choose.

One solution to the problem of charter school facilities financing is for each state to establish a charter school facility commission to administer capital for charter school buildings. Once awarded a charter, the school's board would submit a detailed proposal for its facility to the commission, including location, architectural plans, the intended financial mechanism (whether the school would be leased or owned, and if the latter, whether public bonds would be issued or private loans obtained), and the annual per-student cost of the proposal. The commission would evaluate both the facilities proposal itself and the charter school's viability—its board, business plan, enrollment levels and projections, financial performance, and academic record. The commission's enabling legislation would require that, for each approved project, the municipalities from which the school's students are drawn, in partnership with the state, fund the facility's cost in the same proportion that they would fund such costs for a district-run school. The playing field would at last be level.

School boards are the second major impediment to private management. Some thoughtful critics of public education identify school boards as the weak link in the structure of public schooling; they proved a problem as much for private managers. A few schools benefited from able boards that powerfully contributed to their success. The Edison Friendship School in Washington, D.C., a collaboration of an established community organization and Edison, is one example. But Friendship was the exception. Time and again, to satisfy charter laws' requirements for community control, EMOs hastily cobbled together weak boards that later destabilized school implementations and undermined educational quality. For that, EMOs are rightly criticized. But the greater fault lies with a policy that requires boards in the first place.

In the case of contract schools, elected school board members who embrace private management (or other reforms powerful interests find threatening) risk being punished at the polls. Superintendents who contract with EMOs may find themselves out of a job when a new board takes office, as did Bill Rojas in San Francisco. Like other serious initiatives to improve urban education, private management relies on a long-term commitment, which the political structure of districts rarely provides. Board coalitions and superintendents come and go, and the district lurches from one often symbolic reform to another.[8]

Charter school boards have been no less an impediment to the implementation of an organization's school design, and thereby to the quality of teaching and learning. Boards and organizations connected to board members have sometimes insisted on undertaking responsibilities they lack the capacity to fulfill. When charter schools are struggling to get on their feet, board members are understandably tempted to play the blame game, distancing themselves from start-up problems and the management organization. The politics of race and class often sound an ugly supporting note, as board members resort to fanning age-old grievances as a way of enhancing their power and insulating themselves from the school's problems. School principals and staff are soon torn between two bosses, the EMO and the board. As the struggle for control intensifies, the board may withhold from the management company public payments, or worse, it may extort the company, demanding changes in the contract.

Much has been learned in the first decade of charters about how to build a regulatory structure that promotes high-quality schools. In August 2004, one rogue private operator, the California Charter Academy

(CCA), announced that its sixty "campuses" would close, leaving some ten thousand students scrambling for alternatives. The operator was mired in questions regarding inflated attendance figures, conversion of private and religious schools to charters, flimsy "independent-study" programs, and possible conflicts of interest. CCA had exploited California's permissive chartering environment: enticed by oversight fees, the 150-student Oro Grande Elementary School District had granted CCA only one charter yet within a short time found itself with oversight responsibility for twenty-four sites spread over hundreds of miles. Some charter school founders had joined the CCA network when they were unable to obtain authorization from their local district.[9] In 2002, California addressed the problem by passing legislation requiring nearly all new charter schools authorized by school districts to be located within district boundaries.[10] But the issue is not primarily one of geography. Many school district authorizers still lack the capacity to oversee independent or privately managed charter schools. Nationally, the best authorizers have proven to be state agencies and universities that dedicate expert staff to fulfilling their oversight responsibilities.

The public interest would be better served in California and elsewhere if sophisticated state-level authorizers awarded charters directly to private managers. Accountability for school performance would be clarified, investment risk and control would be in the same hands, and the long-term stability that is essential for the implementation of any comprehensive school design would be assured. Private managers and their schools would be directly accountable through choice to parents and to state authorizers, who have the impartiality and expertise to gauge the organizations' performance evenhandedly. To ensure parents and local stakeholders a voice, the organizations could be required to form, for every school they operate, a community board that would serve in an advisory capacity.

If the intermediary of school boards cannot be eliminated altogether from the regulatory structure, authorizers should permit the organizations to hold a majority of seats on their client schools' boards and allow several schools to be spawned from a single charter where appropriate. Failing that, they should require school boards to act responsibly as public fiduciaries and honor their management contracts. When they don't, authorizers should intervene. Finally, authorizers must be militant in fighting the re-regulation of charter schools by state education agencies.

In return for such policy enhancements, private managers must commit to full transparency in the reporting of academic results. We need better and more comprehensive research to determine if privately managed schools are in fact outpacing district-run schools, and the organizations themselves could do much to facilitate this analysis. Investors spent millions to open their companies' first prototype sites; yet astonishingly, few invested even small sums in the test administration and psychometric analyses needed to find out how well their schools were working for their students. When Mosaica bought Advantage, the computer belonging to Advantage's former director of assessment, which contained all student test data and analyses, was redeployed to a school site. Five years of academic data were lost.

Some of the most promising organizations, including SABIS and KIPP, have not consistently reported the performance of their schools; each school follows its own testing regimen, and disparate claims are made for each. Every organization should require its schools to administer the same national test in the fall of the school's opening and subsequently each spring, so the performance of its schools and students can be assessed with a common measure. All data should be meticulously maintained in a database with student identifiers, so that the longitudinal progress of student cohorts can be gauged. Private managers should make it a priority to publish annual studies of their schools' performance that meet the standards of rigorous educational evaluation.

To reduce costs and increase credibility, the organizations could form a membership organization charged with maintaining an industry database of longitudinal student results and demographic data. Rigorous annual reports on the "value-added" performance of each private manager would underscore the industry's commitment to academic excellence, permit clear comparisons of results, and strengthen claims of accelerated learning. As all data would be available online, independent researchers could develop their own analyses of student learning at privately managed schools.

Recommendations to Future School Entrepreneurs

As the five EMOs and KIPP continue to evolve, the next class of social entrepreneurs is today conceiving new education organizations, including EMOs, CMOs, and school networks. Looking back over my experiences and those of my colleagues, I can offer several hard-learned lessons.

First, focus every school's organizational culture on instruction, data, and results. I found few principals of managed schools who were effective instructional leaders. While the EMOs all promised academic excellence, their schools were often run by people whose primary focus was not the quality of instruction. Few were fluent in the instructional programs on which they relied. Most offered blithe claims that "things were going well," but very few could coherently cite test results in support of them, let alone real-time data that revealed which classrooms and grades had gained traction with an instructional program and which others were as yet languishing. If the next EMOs are to make good on their claims to academic excellence, they must deploy school leaders who are consumed with instructional quality and the data by which to manage it. In their schools, the "talk" must be about instruction and achievement.

Accordingly, invest heavily in the recruitment and development of exceptional school principals, as described in Chapter 6. The task is not to find a principal for a school, least of all just months or weeks before it opens, but to build schools around great principals—leaders committed to the organization's mission. While the KIPP fellows program represents the best practice in the selection, training, and acculturation of school leaders, each new organization will have to wrestle with the profile of its ideal candidate. KIPP's young, energetic missionaries with little managerial experience may prove effective in opening schools that start small; employ primarily young, highly educated teachers like themselves;

and build up enrollment slowly over time. But if the goal is to open larger schools that serve hundreds of students, the EMOs' experience is instructive. They generally found that the most effective principals were experienced educators: instructional leaders who thrived on results and data, with practical knowledge about day-to-day school operations. Whichever path is chosen, one lesson is certain. When a private manager cannot find the right leader, it should postpone the school's opening, however great the cost or the inconvenience to parents.

Strong privately managed schools also have a number two leader focused solely on instructional implementation—the coaching of staff, student groupings, assessment, and the precise implementation of the structured programs that are the main engine of student attainment. Constantly in classrooms, this instructional manager provides discerning critical feedback to teachers on their lesson construction and delivery.

With instruction paramount, an effective line-management structure requires regional directors who are also educators. A dual reporting structure, where school directors report to both a regional operations manager and a regional education manager, defies conventional wisdom. But for education organizations it can be a sound choice. At the corporate level, founders would be wise to resist calls from investors to hire for line-management roles executives who have experience with multisite service businesses but know little or nothing about schools.

Second, build the business in a few select jurisdictions. Ideally, the organization would operate schools for the first several years in just one region. If opening charter schools, the organization should aim to obtain one or more charters that each permit several campuses. Short of that, a single board holding multiple charters would also simplify the business and reduce risk. Whatever the approach, the goal would be to operate a number of schools in close physical proximity, under a single set of rules, and licensed by just one entity. NewSchools Venture Fund's sponsorship of regional "charter management organizations" is a step in exactly this direction.

Third, resist the temptation to apply for a charter and immediately open a school under the organization's flag. Entrepreneurs should take at least a year to plan, not only to hone the school design but also to develop essential central-office infrastructure. Information and reporting systems for finance, student information, staff compliance, and academic management must be designed and tested. When public funds are at stake, even minor failures to provide timely and accurate financial information to primary and secondary customers can damage relationships, sometimes irretrievably.

Fourth, take the time to perfect the prototype school before opening additional sites. Despite the evident financial disadvantages of delaying, the business plan should forecast additional schools only in the prototype's third year. One year of operation is not enough to fine-tune the school design, improve the corporate support systems, and distill the lessons from the inevitable execution failures at the prototype school, before rushing to replicate the design in other locations. In truth, opening schools in the second year requires full-throttle engagement no later than January, leaving only four months to attend to the first site before displaying it to potential customers. By that point, the reference site will still only be limping along.

Aspects of forging an exceptional school, such as the formation of a powerful school culture of student achievement and staff collegiality, follow their own timetable. Entrepreneurial zealotry can't accelerate them. But management's patience will be greatly rewarded. An impressive prototype—and an enthusiastic local board—will begin to build a powerful brand that creates invaluable momentum for the organization.

Fifth, vet new projects exhaustively before committing capital or staff time. Education organizations must avoid a common pitfall of multisite businesses: opening locations with poor financial or demographic fundamentals, only to find themselves saddled with locations that chronically lose money. A retail chain can close a store with few consequences, but education organizations cannot easily back away from—or worse, close—a school. Management must adopt a disciplined process for evaluating and approving new school projects. Enthusiasm for a customer, project, or market must not sway a sober assessment of the site's fundamentals: the regulatory context, the project's economics, the community's demographics (which drive enrollment risk), and the quality of the school's board of trustees, the customer.

At a certain point, proceeding with a project ties up scarce capital. An annual capital budget should be drawn up and allocated only to worthy projects. Once a project has been approved, the commitment of capital should be staged against milestones in the project's development, such as the grant of the charter, a signed management agreement, an executed lease, and minimum enrollment.

Sixth, develop a plan for overcoming the "us" and "them" divide between the school and the corporate office. Here, National Heritage Academies represents the best practice. Management successfully fostered a sense of corporate family through small gestures that had a surprisingly large impact. Edison, too, powerfully conveyed respect for its classroom teachers in the structure of its school design, especially its innovative model of professional development, teacher collaboration, and career ladders.

Seventh, attend to "secondary customers." As argued in Chapter 5, relationships with charter authorizers, state regulators, local politicians, and the media all need to be actively managed. By identifying this as a priority, and assigning staff to attend to these relationships, the organization can earn goodwill that will prove invaluable when problems arise, as they inevitably will. In conceiving of regulators and authorizers as customers whose needs must be met, private managers can identify the "products" provided to secondary customers: financial statements, annual charter school reports, electronic data submissions, annual financial audits, federal grant applications, teacher certification compliance reports, school staff background checks, and much more. School staff should not be expected to prepare these on the fly; the consequences of poor quality and late filings are too great. All data—student, enrollment and attendance, financial, and academic—should be contained in a data warehouse from which reports can be prepared automatically and submitted electronically.

Finally, actively manage expectations of all stakeholders, including the local media. Emphasize that value-added gains should be the primary measure of quality; first-year scores, rather than providing an early verdict on quality, establish a baseline by which to gauge the school's performance.

Future entrepreneurs would do well to adopt "exceed expectations" as their organizational creed. Humility proved a great asset in the education business. It earned National Heritage stable and trusting relationships with its client boards, authorizers, and regulators, the foundation on which every education organization is built. At every opportunity, at every level of the organization, the next school managers should set conservative expectations: school openings will be difficult and taxing. The academic program will take time to deliver results. Schools will initially not be fully enrolled. Not every school leader will succeed. There will be unpleasant surprises and setbacks.

Fortunately, the investment community has learned how difficult it is to build strong schools. Business plans that propose to hone a very small number of schools before expanding the franchise can expect a good reception. Entrepreneurs should have the discipline to present financial projections that reflect a scaled-back version of what they believe is achievable.

Vouchers and School Supply

Publicly funded school choice plans, where eligible parents may select a school of their choice, public or private (including church-affiliated schools), are in place today in Cleveland, Ohio; Milwaukee, Wisconsin; Florida; and Washington, D.C. A decision by the Supreme Court in 2002 eased the way for additional voucher programs by ruling that Cleveland's program did not violate the Establishment Clause of the First Amendment. The program, the court found, had neither the "purpose" nor "effect" of advancing or inhibiting religion; public monies reached religious schools only as a result of the independent choices of private individuals.[11] But impediments to vouchers remain in the states; some three-quarters have constitutional provisions establishing a church-state separation or barring the use of state money to fund religious instruction.[12]

Voucher proponents, like the *Economist,* contend that the state "has little skill" in the supply of education. "Its role should become that of regulator, not schoolmaster."[13] Whatever the merits of vouchers as education policy, opponents are correctly concerned that most present programs in practice limit parents' choices largely to the public schools or to available seats in church-affiliated schools. In Cleveland, the face amount of the voucher varies by income, but in 2004 was at most $3,000—far less than the cost of most independent schools, but in line with religious schools, which are heavily subsidized by churches.[14] While the Court denied that the Cleveland program amounted to state-sponsored religious instruction, nearly 97 percent of vouchers are taken to church-affiliated schools.[15] At about $5,900 per student, the value of the voucher is higher in Milwaukee, but still too low to induce EMOs to open schools.[16]

It is clear that so long as the face amount of school vouchers remains far below what the district spends on per-pupil operating and facility costs, competition will be marginal, and schools will not feel the press to improve. We now know under what circumstances the private sector will expand supply by opening new voucher-redeeming schools. The EMOs learned, often painfully, what their true cost structures were, and at what minimum level of per-student funding they could successfully operate. To induce new supply, the voucher amount must be the *full* per-student spending of the district, which itself must be funded adequately. Naturally, "adequately" is a function of local costs and other factors, but in broad terms annual funding of at least $7,500 (excluding the cost of facilities) is a reasonable estimate of the true cost to provide a child with a high-quality education.

In the spring before Advantage Schools was sold, my colleagues and I caught a glimpse of what might have been. Test scores showed some of our schools racing ahead, while many others had yet to gain their footing. But on average our students, despite their disadvantaged backgrounds, were learning faster than their peers nationally in nearly every subject and grade.[17] At the best-led schools, the children's progress was truly remarkable. Who knows how far they might have traveled had we stayed the course?

In building a business, we had stumbled. The company's plan was flawed and our execution of it troubled. By the time we had learned our lessons, it was too late. I wish we had been able to see the project through.

Fortunately, in writing this book I've come to know other education organizations that pursued their plans more ably. I might quibble with one or another aspect of their designs, but their overall capacity for improving public schooling—especially for urban students—is unmistakable. Vested interests that exploit the public's unexamined allegiance to an outmoded structure for public schooling should not prevent the promise of private management from being realized.

Every year, the public school system fails millions of children. In many inner cities, the public schools not only betray our shared ideals. They are our national shame. In the search for public remedy to the seemingly intractable problem of chronic underachievement, private action may have the greatest promise—it should be welcomed, not decried. "The deepest effect of opening a market to competition," Paul Grogan has written of urban schooling, "is that it engages the energies of people and institutions outside the monopoly—people who previously used their gifts elsewhere."[18] The first education entrepreneurs were sobered by the difficulty of the task. Yet some can now point to signs of modest success. Policymakers should clear the way of needless obstacles and permit this experiment in public education to continue, so that we may in time take its true measure.

Acknowledgments

Notes

Index

Acknowledgments

My first debt is to the staff of the private education organizations that are the subject of this book. At the schools we visited, administrators and staff extended a warm welcome and arranged for us to observe classes and speak with teachers. The founders and executives of the organizations were no less gracious, offering hours of their time to reflect on their experiences. I thank all for their assistance and candor.

I am grateful to John G. Ruggie, director of the Center for Business and Government at John F. Kennedy School of Government, Harvard University, and Dow Davis, executive director. The center offered the ideal setting in which to undertake this project. I am indebted to my colleagues at the center, John D. Donahue and Richard J. Light, for their sage guidance and enthusiastic support from the project's inception; to fellows director Elizabeth Bulette for her warm welcome and constant support in what was often a solitary enterprise; and to Miranda Daniloff Mancusi for advice in preparing for the book's publication. In my third year at the center, Michael R. Sandler, who for years has encouraged research on private involvement in public schooling, generously provided the support for my fellowship.

I am thankful for the financial support that made the project possible. Phoebe Cottingham of the Smith Richardson Foundation brought clarity to an inchoate research plan; the foundation provided the core funding for the research. I thank also Bruno Manno of the Annie E. Casey Foundation and Joseph Dolan of the Achelis & Bodman Foundations. The findings and conclusions presented in this report are mine alone and do not necessarily reflect the opinions of the foundations.

The examination of academic outcomes would not have been possible without the collaboration of Herbert J. Walberg, emeritus research professor of education and psychology at the University of Illinois at Chicago. An expert in educational evaluation, he identified, qualified, and evaluated studies of academic performance of students in privately managed public schools; his research provided the basis for Chapter 8. I am privileged to have worked with him.

Longtime colleague and friend Lisa Simon Cohen was a true partner in the project. She ably performed much of the field work, helped organize the book and shape its thesis, and in the drafting stages, offered daily counsel. Her unflagging belief in the project was a constant inspiration. Colleagues Jana Reed and Lisa O'Brien both made invaluable contributions during the research phase.

I benefited at various points from able research assistants. I thank Heather Ampel, Niraj Kaji, Kenneth Klau, and Emily Potts, as well as undergraduates Mike Press, Jesse Oberst, Adam Perlman, Simon Rich, and Genevieve Sheehan. I am especially grateful to Benjamin Hall, who coordinated the other students' efforts.

Several friends and colleagues have taken the trouble to help me think through portions of the book or comment on early versions of the manuscript, including Jess Brallier, Matthew Clark, William Edgerly, Chester Finn, Nathan Glazer, Michael Joseph Gross, Chris Kelaher, Doug Lemov, Stig Leschly, Diane Ravitch, and Thomas Toch. I also wish to thank the anonymous readers who reviewed proposals and the manuscript on behalf of foundations and my publisher; their discerning comments and suggestions greatly strengthened the book. I am grateful too for the guidance of Chris Kelaher of the Brookings Institution and David Miller of the Garamond Agency.

My editor Kathryn Ciffolillo was indefatigable in her quest to bring organization, logic, and clarity to an unruly manuscript. It is impossible to imagine completing the book without her constant good humor and extraordinary skills.

I am especially grateful to my editor at Harvard University Press, Elizabeth Knoll. With charm and resolve, she pressed me to submit a final manuscript that would engage readers of diverse backgrounds and convictions on a charged topic. Susan Abel and Julie Carlson further strengthened the manuscript and meticulously prepared it for publication.

Lastly, I wish to thank my former colleagues at Advantage Schools, who worked so tirelessly in pursuit of the organization's mission.

Notes

Introduction

1. Alex Molnar, David Garcia, Carolyn Sullivan, Brendan McEvoy, and Jamie Joanou, *Profiles of For-Profit Education Management Organizations, Seventh Annual Report, 2004–2005,* Commercialism in Education Research Unit, Education Policy Studies Laboratory, Division of Educational Leadership and Policy Studies, Arizona State University, Tempe, April 2005. Molnar includes organizations that run a single school. A 2004 National Center for Education Statistics report estimated home-schooled students at 1,100,000, on the basis of data from the National Household Education Surveys Program. Advocates contend the figure is today closer to 2 million.

2. While parents may choose to enroll their children in private schools, government provides little financial assistance to them, other than in the form of tax relief to private schools as nonprofit entities.

3. Diane Ravitch, "American Traditions of Education," in Terry M. Moe, ed., *A Primer on America's Schools* (Stanford, Calif.: Hoover Institution Press, 2001), 5–8.

4. Ibid., 2–8; Theodore R. Sizer, *The Age of the Academies* (New York: Teachers College, Columbia University, 1964).

5. Sizer, *Age of the Academies,* 1.

6. Ravitch, "American Traditions," 6.

7. Sizer, *Age of the Academies,* 25.

8. Ibid., 43.

9. Joseph White, in a debate at the 1973 NEA convention, National Education Association, *Addresses and Proceedings, 1873,* quoted in Sizer, *Age of the Academies,* 43.

10. Charles Leslie Glenn Jr., *The Myth of the Common School* (Oakland, Calif.: Institute for Contemporary Studies, 2002), 4.

11. Glenn, *Myth,* 168, quoting Horace Mann's *Twelfth Report to the Massachusetts Board of Education,* 1848.

12. Ravitch, "American Traditions," 10, quoting Lloyd P. Jorgensen.

13. John E. Chubb and Terry M. Moe, *Politics, Markets, and America's Schools* (Washington, D.C.: Brookings Institution, 1990), 6.

14. Craig E. Richards, Rima Shore, and Max B. Sawicky, *Risky Business: Private Management of Public Schools* (Washington, D.C.: Economic Policy Institute, 1996), 20. For more information on the structure of public education in other nations, see Charles L. Glenn and Jan de Groof, *Finding the Right Balance: Freedom, Autonomy, and Accountability in Education* (Utrecht, The Netherlands: Lemma, 2004).

15. The National Commission on Excellence in Education, *A Nation at Risk: The Imperative for Educational Reform* (Washington, D.C.: U.S. Department of Education, April 1983), p. 5.

16. Eric A. Hanushek, "Spending on Schools," in Moe, *A Primer on America's Schools,* 72.

17. Caroline M. Hoxby, "What Has Changed and What Has Not," in Paul E. Peterson, ed., *Our Schools and Our Future . . . Are We Still at Risk?* (Stanford, Calif.: Hoover Institution Press, 2003), 101–102. Per-pupil spending is generally determined by dividing total expenditure by enrollment, but Hoxby favors using average daily attendance because enrollment numbers systematically overstate the schools' population. Districts retain students on their rolls who have switched to other schools. Hoxby draws attendance and spending data from the National Center for Education Statistics. Spending is expressed in 2002 dollars.

18. Eric Hanushek et al., *Making Schools Work: Improving Performance and Controlling Costs* (Washington, D.C.: Brookings Institution, 1994), 38; 1999 *Digest of Education Statistics* (Washington, D.C.: U.S. Department of Education, 1999), table 87, www.nces.ed.gov.

19. Hoxby, "What Has Changed," 103.

20. Ibid., 96–97. Spending is stated in inflation-adjusted 2001 dollars.

21. NEAP scores, known as "The Nation's Report Card," are a broadly respected, if imperfect, national measure of student achievement.

22. *Digest of Education Statistics 2002,* table 112, www.nces.ed.gov.

23. *Digest of Education Statistics 2001,* table 124, www.nces.ed.gov.

24. Paul E. Peterson, "Little Gain in Student Achievement," in *Our Schools and Our Future,* 45. Admittedly, the SAT is a less reliable measure than the NAEP, because the percentage of high school seniors taking the test rose over the second half of the last century.

25. Title I was passed as part of the Elementary and Secondary Education Act of 1965. U.S. Secretary of Education Rod Paige observed after the release of NAEP scores in 2001, "We can no longer use the social experiences or conditions of children as the excuse for the low performances of children. After spending $125 billion of Title I money over 25 years, we have virtually nothing to show for it. Fewer than a third of fourth-graders can read at grade level." See "Poor Readers Have Gotten Worse, U.S. Study Shows," *Los Angeles Times,* April 7, 2001. It is open to question whether a greater investment would have narrowed the gap. Fact Sheet on Title I, part A, August 2002, www.ed.gov.

26. Fact Sheet on Title I.

27. Herbert J. Walberg, "Achievement in American Schools," in Moe, *A Primer on America's Schools,* 46–47.

28. U.S. Department of Education, NCES, National Assessment of Educational Progress (NAEP), 2000 Mathematics Assessment, www.nces.ed.gov.

29. *Digest of Education Statistics, 2002,* table 111, www.nces.ed.gov.

30. National Center for Education Statistics, *The Nation's Report Card,* online database, www.nces.ed.gov/nationsreportcard, accessed July 29, 2005.

31. Hoxby, "What Has Changed," 101–102.

32. "Beating the Odds IV: A City-by-City Analysis of Student Performance and Achievement Gap on Assessments" (Washington, D.C.: Council of Great City Schools, March 2004), 39.

33. Expenditures are adjusted by OECD for purchasing power parity. Data for the United States include expenditures for both public and private institutions. For some countries, the data are for public expenditures only, which in some cases flow to private institutions. Organization for Economic Cooperation and Development (OECD), *Education at a Glance, 2003* (Paris: OECD, Sept. 2003), table B1.1.

34. Mean scores on PISA mathematical literacy scale for 2000. Ibid., tables A6.1 and A6.2.

35. Now known as the Trends in International Math and Science Study.

36. "Highlights from TIMSS," www.nces.ed.gov.

37. Hanushek, "Spending on Schools," 80.

38. Charlene K. Haar and Myron Lieberman, "NEA/AFT Membership: The Critical Issues," Washington, D.C., Education Policy Institute, www.educationpolicy.org. According to the authors, "Their ranks include preschool and support personnel, college faculty, retirees, students, health care employees, government employees, other groups."

39. Terry Moe, "Teacher Unions and the Public Schools," in Moe, *A Primer on America's Schools.*

40. Diane Ravitch, "Testing and Accountability, Historically Considered," in Williamson M. Evers and Herbert J. Walberg, eds., *School Accountability* (Stanford, Calif.: Hoover Institution Press, 2002), 16.

41. Achieve, Inc., *Staying on Course, Standards-Based Reform in America's Schools: Progress and Prospects,* 2002, p. 4, www.achieve.org. Council of Chief State School Officers, "State Content Standards."

42. See www.educationpolicy.org. Union contributions to Democratic candidates are well documented.

43. A teacher, Ray Budde, had proposed in the 1970s that school boards award contracts, or "educational charters," to teachers who would devise new educational approaches and be held accountable for their results. Budde published his ideas in the report "Education by Charter: Restructuring School Districts" (Andover, Mass.: The Regional Laboratory for Educational Improvement of the Northeast Islands, 1988).

44. Chester E. Finn Jr., Bruno V. Manno, and Gregg Vanourek, *Charter Schools in Action: Renewing Public Education* (Princeton, N.J.: Princeton University Press, 2000), 18. The original text appears in Albert Shanker, "Restructuring Our Schools," *Peabody Journal of Education* 65, no. 3 (Spring 1988): 97–98.

45. "Charter School Laws across the States, 2003: Ranking Scorecard and Legislative Profiles," Washington, D.C., Center for Education Reform, www.edreform.com.

46. Finn, Manno, and Vanourek, *Charter Schools in Action,* 14.

47. Generally, charter laws provide that students outside the district or region may also attend the school, but preference is given to students from the

district in which the school is located. None of the schools operated by EMOs selected their students, because charter laws prohibit it.

48. "Latest Charter School Laws Scorecard Released," press release, Washington, D.C., Center for Education Reform, January 14, 2003, www.edreform.com.

49. These conditions were that the new charter school be an autonomous legal entity and receive the full per-pupil spending of the district from which its students were drawn, that tenure laws be waived, that teachers need not be certified, that the charter authorizer be independent of district school boards, and that there be no cap on the number of charters that could be awarded in the state (or that the cap be high). Only Arizona's law satisfied all of these conditions, but each of the others met enough of them that the law was favorable to EMO operation. Advantage Schools, *Business Plan, 1997* (Boston: Advantage Schools, 1997).

50. "Charter School Laws across the States, 2003."

51. Paul E. Peterson and Bryan C. Hassel, "School Choice in Milwaukee: A Randomized Experiment," in Peterson and Hassel, eds., *Learning from School Choice* (Washington, D.C.: Brookings Institution Press, 1998).

52. Molnar, Wilson, and Allen, *Profiles*, 2005.

53. KIPP website, www.kipp.org, accessed April 25, 2005.

1. The Organizations

1. "Agreement between the Chelsea School Committee and Trustees of Boston University," May 3, 1989, www.bu.edu/chelsea/, accessed October 10, 2003.

2. Average SAT scores for Chelsea in 1989 were 664 (Boston University/ Chelsea Partnership, *Twelfth Report to the Legislature,* September 1, 2003, 16), with 24 percent of seniors taking the exam, compared to the state average of 905. National Center for Policy Analysis website, www.ncpa.org.

3. Muriel Cohen, "BU Will Face New, 'Tough' Chelsea Board," *Boston Globe,* November 17, 1989; Jordana Hart, "Chelsea Schools Progressing, But Dissent Persists," *Boston Globe,* November 12, 1995; Jennifer A. Kingson, "Ailing School System Seeks Control by Boston University," *New York Times,* July 30, 1988.

4. Boston University/Chelsea Partnership website, www.bu.edu/chelsea/, accessed April 26, 2005.

5. Raynolds quoted in Gus Martins, "State Education Commissioner Raps Chelsea Panel for BU Plan," *Boston Globe,* December 23, 1988; Willie and Silber

quoted in Lee A. Daniels, "Doubts Abound on Boston U. Plan to Run Schools," *New York Times,* August 10, 1988.

6. For the Howe quotation, see John Silber, interview with the author, April 1, 2004. Silber said: "That included Doc Howe at Harvard who made the statement that no university should be running a school." For Silber quoting *Henry V,* see Sam Allis, "Reflecting on Chelsea," *Boston Globe,* February 9, 2003.

7. For the Brennan quotation, see Robert L. Turner, "Silber and the Chelsea School System: Trust But Verify," *Boston Globe,* May 23, 1989. On the contract, see "Agreement," 4, 11.

8. 421 Mass. 598, 659 N.E. 2d 277; "Day of shame" quoted in Renee Graham, "As Protests Persist, BU and Chelsea Cement Pact," *Boston Globe,* May 4, 1989.

9. 421 Mass. 598, 659 N.E. 2d 277.

10. Boston University/Chelsea Partnership website, www.bu.edu/chelsea/principl.htm, accessed October 10, 2003.

11. Greer and Heichman are quoted in Susan Chira, "The Lessons Learned When College Officials Run Public Schools," *New York Times,* July 11, 1990.

12. Hart, "Chelsea Schools Progressing." See also Matthew Richer, "Busing's Boston Massacre," *Policy Review* 92 (November–December 1998).

13. National percentile rank on the California Achievement Test; see "The Boston University/Chelsea Partnership," *Fifth Report to the Legislature,* September 1, 1996, 18. For state tests, see Boston University/Chelsea Partnership, *Twelfth Report,* 10.

14. The 1998 *Boston Globe* ranking is from www.boston.com/mcas/rank_overall.htm, accessed May 1, 2004.

15. John Gehring, "Boston University–Chelsea Match Endures," *Education Week,* November 24, 2004; Silber interview, April 1, 2004; Allis, "Reflecting on Chelsea."

16. Allis, "Reflecting on Chelsea"; Silber interview, April 1, 2004.

17. Kim Weidman, "World Language," *Chelsea Record,* December 23, 2003; on money raised, see Silber interview, April 1, 2004.

18. For attendance, see Boston University/Chelsea Partnership, *Fifth Report,* 22; Boston University/Chelsea Partnership, *Eleventh Report to the Legislature,* September 1, 2002, p. 17, www.bu.edu/chelsea/, accessed October 10, 2003. For high school dropout rates and the AP program, see Boston University/Chelsea Partnership, *Twelfth Report,* 19.

19. Boston University/Chelsea Partnership, *Twelfth Report,* 6, 14.

20. For SAT scores, see ibid., 5, 16. The 2001 MCAS ranking was 207 out of 211. See the *Boston Globe* 1998 MCAS listing.

21. "Agreement," 3; Silber interview, April 1, 2004; on progress under NCLB, see Gehring, "Boston University–Chelsea Match Endures."

22. Robert Gaudet, *Effective School Districts in Massachusetts: A Study of Student Performance on the 1999 MCAS Assessments* (Boston: Donahue Institute, University of Massachusetts, March 2000); Boston University/Chelsea Partnership, *Eleventh Report,* 11: "The Beacon Hill study shows that given the percentage of students who scored in the Advanced, Proficient, and Needs Improvement categories on the 2001 MCAS (that is, the percentage of students who 'passed' the MCAS tests), Chelsea High School tenth graders were first in Massachusetts for performing beyond demographic predictions; fourth graders were second out of 266 districts; eighth graders were 28th out of 236 districts."

23. Ibid., cover letter from Irene Cornish, Superintendent of Schools.

24. Both quotations by Silber are from John Silber and Doug Sears, interview with the author, April 1, 2004. The quotation by Sears is from Doug Sears, interview with the author, May 3, 2004.

25. Hart, "Chelsea Schools Progressing."

26. Sears interview, May 3, 2004.

27. Silber and Sears interview, April 1, 2004.

28. Ibid.

29. Ibid.

30. Ibid.

31. Ibid.

32. Ibid.

33. Madeleine L'Engle, *A Wrinkle in Time* (New York: Ariel Books, 1962); Craig E. Richards, Rima Shore, and Max B. Sawicky, *Risky Business: Private Management of Public Schools* (Washington, D.C.: Economic Policy Institute, 1996); Gail DeGeorge and Christina Del Valle, "The Green in the Little Red Schoolhouse," *Business Week,* October 14, 1991.

34. Quoted in Elizabeth Conlin, "Educating the Market," *Inc.,* July 1991.

35. Ibid.

36. Ibid.

37. Ibid.

38. Golle in 1990 was quoted in Steven A. Holmes, "In Florida, a Private Company Will Operate A Public School," *New York Times,* December 7, 1990; in 1991 he was quoted in Conlin, "Educating the Market."

39. Bennett and Geiger are both quoted in Troy Segal et al., "Saving Our Schools," *Business Week,* September 14, 1992.

40. The Golle quotation and information on EAI's going public are from Conlin, "Educating the Market."

41. Test scores are from Segal, "Saving Our Schools." For Golle's promise, see Joe Rigert and Carol Command, "Education Firm Oversells Its Record; Company Has Made False Claims, Failed to Meet Goals," *(Minneapolis) Star Tribune,* June 4, 1994; for Golle's claims regarding future performance, see Jim Jones, "EAI to Manage Some Baltimore Schools," *(Minneapolis) Star Tribune,* June 10, 1992; on how he planned to achieve it, see William Tucker, "Foot in the Door," *Forbes,* February 3, 1992, 50.

42. Rigert and Command, "Education Firm Oversells Its Record." On EAI's investment in facilities and computers, see Thomas Toch, "Do Firms Run Schools Well?" *U.S. News & World Report,* January 8, 1996.

43. Rigert and Command, "Education Firm Oversells Its Record."

44. Shanker quoted in George Judson, "As It Moves to Privatize Schools, Hartford Is Keeping Some Controls," *New York Times,* July 22, 1994. On the Hartford contract, see Toch, "Do Firms Run Schools Well?"

45. Rigert and Command, "Education Firm Oversells Its Record." For the quotation by the parent, see Kirk Johnson, "Hartford to Slow Company Role in Schools," *New York Times,* June 21, 1995.

46. Richards, Shore, and Sawicky, *Risky Business,* 62.

47. Lawrence W. Reed, "Ideas and Consequences: Mixing Public and Private," *The Freeman,* July 1996.

48. Susan Feyder, "CFO Becomes Latest to Leave EAI," *(Minneapolis) Star Tribune,* December 23, 1995; George Judson, "Hartford Plans to End the Private Management of Its Public Schools," *New York Times,* January 24, 1996; Allie Shaw, "Eagan School Celebrates Its Survival: Parents Raise Money to Buy Their Close-Knit School after Its Parent Company Folded," *(Minneapolis) Star Tribune,* March 15, 2001.

49. Paul T. Hill, Lawrence C. Pierce, and James W. Guthrie, *Reinventing Public Education: How Contracting Can Transform America's Schools* (Chicago: University of Chicago Press, 1997), 122.

50. N. R. Kleinfield, "What Is Chris Whittle Teaching Our Children?" *New York Times,* May 19, 1991. Kleinfield comments, "One magical day, it [13–30] found bliss when it agreed to develop a magazine for Nissan in which the car maker was the sole advertiser. This single-sponsorship notion caught fire and

life went along beautifully. Still, the company was obscure until 1979, when it bought and revitalized *Esquire* magazine."

51. James B. Stewart, "Grand Illusion," *New Yorker,* October 31, 1994, pp. 64, 66–67.

52. Paul B. Brown and George Gendron, "A Gathering of Entrepreneurs," *Inc.,* November 1, 1989.

53. Whittle quoted in Thomas Toch, "Homeroom Sweepstakes," *U.S. News & World Report,* November 9, 1992; on the Time Warner deal and "Whittlesburg," see Stewart, "Grand Illusion," 71; Mark Landler, "Financial Triage at Edison," *Business Week,* August 1, 1994.

54. Toch, "Homeroom Sweepstakes."

55. Thomas Toch, "Whittling the Future School," *U.S. News & World Report,* August 16, 1993; Whittle is quoted in Stewart, "Grand Illusion," 72; Shanker is quoted in "Revamping America's School System," *St. Petersburg Times,* May 16, 1991.

56. Deborah Sontag, "Yale President Quitting to Lead National Private-School Venture," *New York Times,* May 26, 1992, A1. Emphasis in original.

57. Toch, "Whittling the Future School."

58. Stewart, "Grand Illusion," 74–80.

59. Peter Applebome, "Entrepreneur Gets $30 Million to Establish For-Profit Schools," *New York Times,* March 17, 1995; Rene Sanchez, "A Flicker of Grander Plans: Edison Project Under Way at Four Schools," *Washington Post,* September 5, 1995, A3.

60. Terzah Ewing, "Edison Schools' IPO Is Overshadowed as It Can't Sway Interest from Dot-Coms," *Wall Street Journal,* November 12, 1999, C18.

61. Queena Sook Kim, "Edison Sees Golden Opportunity in Philadelphia," *Wall Street Journal,* February 15, 2002.

62. See Susan Snyder and Dale Mezzacappa, "Philadelphia's Mayor Wants Plan to Privatize Schools Dropped," *Philadelphia Inquirer,* November 9, 2001; and James M. O'Neill, "Pennsylvania Residents Protest Proposed Privatization of Philadelphia School," *Philadelphia Inquirer,* November 11, 2001.

63. Feldman is quoted in "AFT: Privatization Plan for Philly Schools Is Wrong Rx for School Improvement," press release, Washington, D.C., American Federation of Teachers, November 12, 2001; for student protests see George Stawley, "Students Protest Plan to Privatize Philadelphia Schools," *Associated Press,* November 21, 2001; Michael Rubinkam, "Students Form Human Chain to Protest Privatization," *Associated Press,* November 30, 2001.

64. D. C. Denison, "School of Hard Knocks in the Bull Market," *Boston Globe,* May 26, 2001, E1; Schmidt quoted in Diana B. Henriques, "Edison Stays Afloat by Altering Course," *New York Times,* July 3, 2003, C1.

65. "Philadelphia Schools Scaling Back Corporate Role," Associated Press, June 30, 2003.

66. Ibid.

67. "Edison Schools Posts First Quarterly Profit," *New York Times,* September 13, 2003, C2; Whittle quotation is from Chris Whittle, interview with the author, September 8, 2003.

68. "Edison Schools Applauds Philadelphia School District's Historic Leap in Student Achievement," press release, New York, Edison Schools, August 24, 2004.

69. John C. Eason, "On a Personal Note," *Enterprising Educators* 8, no. 2 (Winter 2000).

70. Thomas Mauhs-Pugh, "Charter Schools, 1995: A Survey and Analysis of the Laws and Practices of the States, Including State-By-State Summaries, Cross-State Comparisons, Descriptions of Existing and Proposed Schools, and Lessons Learned," *Educational Analysis Policy Archives* 3, no. 13 (July 1995). On the outcomes of the judge's decision, see Eleanor Chute, "A New Page on Revisionist Tale: Outcomes Debated as School District Assumes Control," *Pittsburgh Post-Gazette,* June 29, 1998, A1.

71. DeLoache quoted in Charles Mahtesian, "The Precarious Politics of Privatizing Schools," *Governing* 7, no. 9 (June 1994): 46; company spokesperson quoted in David Strow, "For-Profit Company to Manage Charter School," *Triangle Business Journal,* April 28, 1997, www.triangle.bizjournals.com, accessed July 1, 2003.

72. Michael Ronan, interview with the author, November 26, 2002.

73. Ronan quoted in "School Choice: A Marketplace for Education," Policy Dialogue, Pioneer Institute for Public Policy Research, www.pioneerinstitute.org, accessed November 25, 2002; and in Sarah E. Reynolds, "Thinking Outside the Box: How to Have Creative, Effective Public Education," *Worcester Business Journal,* December 23, 1996.

74. Ronan interview, November 26, 2002.

75. Beacon Education Management, Inc., S-1 Registration Statement, filed with the Securities Exchange Commission on May 8, 2001, in author's possession; Raymond Hennessey, "Going Public: With Beacon, Customers Are Debtors," *Dow Jones News Service,* July 26, 2001; William C. Symonds et al.,

"For-Profit Schools," *Business Week,* February 7, 2000; Steven Syre and Charles Stein, "Boston Capital: Beacon Gets an Education with Offering," *Boston Globe,* August 7, 2001.

76. Ronan interview, November 26, 2002.

77. For "fourth largest school system," see Council of Great City Schools, "City-by-City Statistics, 2000–2001," www.cgcs.org, accessed October 2, 2003 (the three largest districts are New York, Los Angeles, and Chicago); Visiedo quoted in Kent Fischer, "Public School Inc.," *St. Petersburg Times,* September 15, 2002; biographical data are drawn from the Co-nect website, www.co-nect.net, and the South Boston Harbor Academy Charter School website, www.sbha.org.

78. "Chancellor Academies and Beacon Education Management Merge," *Business Wire,* January 8, 2002.

79. Octavio Visiedo, interview with the author, February 12, 2003.

80. Chancellor Beacon Academies website, www.chancellorbeacon.com, accessed August 22, 2002.

81. Visiedo interview, February 12, 2003.

82. Visiedo quoted in ibid.; Dyke quoted in Wade Dyke, interview with the author, February 12, 2003.

83. Biographical data drawn from the Chancellor Beacon Academies website, www.chancellorbeacon.com, accessed August 22, 2002; Visiedo quotation is from Visiedo interview, February 12, 2003.

84. Visiedo interview, February 12, 2003.

85. "Kissimmee Charter Elementary Celebrates National Charter School Week with Days of Appreciation," press release, April 20, 2004, www.chancellorbeacon.com.

86. Bakke quotations are from "AES's Dennis Bakke: A Reluctant Capitalist," *Business Week Online,* www.businessweek.com, December 13, 1999, accessed July 15, 2004.

87. Bakke quoted in "Chancellor Beacon Academies Merges with Imagine Schools, One of Nation's Largest Operators of K–12 Public Charter Schools," Coconut Grove, Fla., Chancellor Beacon, press release, June 8, 2004.

88. Historical information drawn from SABIS website, www.sabis.net, accessed August 13, 2002; "Historical Note," at the International School of Choueifat, Lebanon, website, www.isc-lebanon.com.

89. SABIS website, www.sabis.net, accessed August 13, 2002; and www.isc-lebanon.com.

90. Quoted in Muriel Cohen, "Large Classes, Discipline—and Profit: New Charter Schools Emphasize Tradition," *Boston Globe,* July 7, 1996, A37.

91. Nanette Asimov, "Can Profit and Education Mix? Questions Arise over New Kind of Public Schools," *San Francisco Chronicle,* March 9, 2001.

92. *2000–2001 SABIS International Charter School Annual Report* (Eden Prairie, Minn.: SABIS, 2001), 4.

93. Absolutely all—100 percent—of its students, including special education students, were tested using the Iowa Test of Basic Skills; see ibid., 6. For MCAS scores in English, math, and science, see ibid., 13, 25. For enrollment and wait-list data, see *2002–2003 SABIS International Charter School Annual Report* (Eden Prairie, Minn.: SABIS, 2003), 28–29.

94. Quoted in Cohen, "Large Classes, Discipline—and Profit."

95. Sarah Fishman, "Somerville School Tries Different Course," *Boston Globe,* January 4, 1998, 1.

96. Ed Hayward, "Charters Leave Their Roots: Schools Part Ways with For-Profits," *Boston Herald,* June 16, 2002, 8.

97. Rosalind Rossi, "Expectations and Rules Focus on the Traditional," *Chicago Sun-Times,* July 13, 1998.

98. Ibid.

99. Rosalind Rossi, "Charter School Ends Operator's Contract," *Chicago Sun-Times,* January 23, 1999, 10.

100. Quoted in the SABIS website, www.sabis.net, accessed February 6, 2003.

101. Daniel Golden, "Common Prayer: Old-Time Religion Gets a Boost at a Chain of Charter Schools—Many Christian Parents Opt for No-Cost Academies Run by J. C. Huizenga—Backlash from Evangelicals," *Wall Street Journal,* September 15, 1999, A1.

102. "ACLU Takes on Charter School for Church/State Violations," press release, American Civil Liberties Union, April 1, 1999, on www.aclumich.org, accessed October 6, 2003; Naomi Schaefer, "Vista Charter School (National Heritage Academies) Grand Rapids, Michigan," in Martin Morse Wooster, *Fourteen Model Schools.* Part 1: *Model Schools* (Washington, D.C.: American Enterprise Institute, 2001); "ACLU Declares Victory in Lawsuit over Promotion of Religion in Charter School," press release, American Civil Liberties Union, October 23, 2000, on www.seaverlink.com, accessed October 8, 2003.

103. Golden, "Common Prayer."

104. Roland Wilkerson, "Charter Captain J. C. Huizenga Runs Four Schools—Part One of His For-Profit Education Dream," *Grand Rapids (Mich.) Press,* April 6, 1997, E1.

105. J. C. Huizenga, interview with the author, July 10, 2003.

106. Quoted in Lynn Schnaiberg, "Entrepreneurs Hoping to Do Good, Make Money," *Education Week,* December 1, 1999, www.kqventures.com, accessed October 6, 2003.

107. Huizenga interview, July 10, 2003.

108. Wilkerson, "Charter Captain"; Roland Wilkerson, "Charter Firm to Add Twelve Schools, Three in Area," *Grand Rapids (Mich.) Press,* December 9, 1998; Huizenga quotation is in Beth Loechler, "Charter School Company to Expand Nationwide," *Grand Rapids (Mich.) Press,* April 23, 1998.

109. Quoted in Deanne Molinari, "Peter Ruppert: Inside Track," *Grand Rapids (Mich.) Business Journal* 15, no. 26 (June 1997): 5.

110. Ibid.

111. Quoted in Loechler, "Charter School Company to Expand."

112. "National Heritage Makes Money Running Charter Schools," *Associated Press State & Local Wire,* December 2, 2001.

113. Ruppert quoted in ibid.; *Inc.* ranking is from "Charter Company Skims 'Cheap' Students, Critics Say," *Associated Press,* January 9, 2003; NHA revenue claim is from Huizenga interview, July 10, 2003.

114. Huizenga quoted in Schnaiberg, "Entrepreneurs Hoping to Do Good"; DeHaan and Peter Huizenga quoted in Wilkerson, "Charter Captain."

115. Quoted in Schnaiberg, "Entrepreneurs Hoping to Do Good."

116. National Heritage Academies website, www.nationalheritageacademies. com, accessed July 30, 2004; Schaefer, "Vista Charter School."

117. Huizenga interview, July 10, 2003.

118. Mark DeHaan, interview with the author, July 10, 2003.

119. Peter Ruppert, interview with the author, July 10, 2003; "Secrets to Unbelievable Success: Why Top Urban Schools Are the Finest Schools in America," Grand Rapids, Mich., National Heritage Academies, undated, in author's possession.

120. Alex Molnar, Glen Wilson, and Daniel Allen, *Profiles of For-Profit Education Management Companies, Sixth Annual Report, 2003–2004,* Arizona State University, February 2004, p. 14.

121. "CDC Reports Record Fourth Quarter and Full Year 1994 Results," Children's Discovery Centers of America, Inc., press release, February 27, 1995, in author's possession.

122. Katie Wang, "Charter Schools Fight to Exist, But Do They Work?" *Allentown Morning Call,* March 12, 2000.

123. Gene Eidelman, interview with the author, December 2, 2003.

124. Both quotations by Eidelman are in Eleanor Chute, "School Firm Charts New Course," *Pittsburgh Post-Gazette,* November 29, 1997, A1; Mosaica Education website, www.mosaicaeducation.com, accessed July 15, 2004; on the "four R's," see Chute, "School Firm Charts New Course."

125. Ibid., accessed October 7, 2003.

126. Description of Mosaica Academy of Saginaw, Michigan, at www. charterschools.org, accessed August 16, 2002.

127. Ibid.; see also the Mosaica Education website, www.mosaicaeducation. com. On parental involvement, see Molly Rath, "Sizing Up the Companies Vying to Run Baltimore's Schools," *Baltimore City Paper: Education Inc.,* February 16–22, 2000.

128. Both quotations are from Chute, "School Firm Charts New Course."

129. Sara Barton, "Mixed Reviews for Company Pushing Charter School," *Lancaster (Pa.) New Era,* December 15, 1998, C24.

130. Torsten Ove and Joanna Pro, "Upper St. Clair Charter School Plans Halted as Rumors Swirl around Official," *Pittsburgh Post-Gazette,* December 10, 1997, B8.

131. "Gaston County Looking into Background of Charter School Promoter," *Associated Press Newswires,* December 2, 1997; Eidelman is quoted in Torsten Ove and Caroline Abels, "Executive with Charter School Firm Submits Resignation," *Pittsburgh Post-Gazette,* December 11, 1997.

132. Steve Farr, "Charter School Wins Key Battles on Funding and Busing," *Associated Press Newswires,* September 9, 1998.

133. For the parents' response, see Barton, "Mixed Reviews"; on Mosaica's growth plans, and for the quotation by Eidelman, see "Firm Promises More Charter Schools for Pennsylvania," *Associated Press,* October 19, 1998.

134. "Mosaica Education Names CEO and Plans Expansion with Venture Capital Partner," New York, Mosaica Education, press release, October 12, 1998; David Carey, "Rich Man's Game (Venture Capitalism)," *Financial World* 34 (March 8, 1988).

135. "Mosaica Charter School Students Show Exceptional Growth," New York, Mosaica Education, press release, September 6, 2000.

136. "Mosaica Contract Dissolved in Bucks," *Philadelphia Inquirer,* April 19, 2001; Alicia A. Caldwell, "PA: Audit of School Incomplete," *Philadelphia Inquirer,* November 7, 2001, B3.

137. For the Harr quotation, see Alex Molnar, "Calculating the Benefits and

Costs of For-Profit Education," *Education Policy Analysis Archives* (April 2001); on Mosaica's suit, see Alicia A. Caldwell, "Formerly Mosaica, School Starts Afresh," *Philadelphia Inquirer,* September 16, 2001.

138. Mosaica Education, "Mosaica Education, Inc. to Acquire Advantage Schools Inc.," New York, Mosaica Education, press release, July 2, 2001.

139. Stig Leschly, "KIPP National, 1999 (A): Designing a School Network," case study, Harvard Business School, March 21, 2003. Much of the material in this section was drawn from the case study.

140. The quotation and credo are in ibid.

141. KIPP website, www.kipp.org, accessed August 12, 2002.

142. Leschly, "KIPP National, 1999 (A)," 5.

143. Interview with Michael Feinberg, *Doyle Report,* October 13, 2003, www.thedoylereport.com. Emphasis added.

144. Leschly, "KIPP National, 1999 (A)," 11–12.

145. Ibid., 13.

146. Ibid., 14.

147. Ibid., 13.

148. KIPP website, www.kipp.org, accessed August 12, 2002.

149. Ibid.; quotation from Feinberg is from Michael Feinberg interview, *Doyle Report.*

150. KIPP website, www.kipp.org, accessed April 25, 2005.

151. Stig Leschly, "KIPP National, 2002 (B): Managing a School Network," Harvard Business School, case study, N9–803–125, February 23, 2003, 3; KIPP website, www.kipp.org, accessed October 27, 2003.

152. Ibid., accessed January 8, 2003.

153. John Dolan left the company early in its history.

154. Steven Wilson, *Reinventing the Schools: A Radical Plan for Boston* (Boston: Pioneer Institute for Public Policy Research, 1992).

155. Ibid.

156. Lois Harrison-Jones was superintendent of Boston public schools from 1991 to 1995.

157. Advantage Schools, Inc., 1997 Business Plan, in author's possession.

158. Advantage Schools, Inc., *Annual Report on School Performance: 1999–2000 School Year,* Boston, March 2001, p. 2; Edison Schools, Inc., *Third Annual Report on School Performance,* New York, 2000, p. 2.

159. Quoted in Symonds et al., "For-Profit Schools."

2. Business Models

1. Joan Magretta, "Why Business Models Matter," *Harvard Business Review* (May 2002).

2. Eric A. Hanushek, "Assessing the Effects of School Resources on Student Performance: An Update," *Educational Evaluation and Policy Analysis* (Summer 1997): 141–164.

3. Eric A. Hanushek, "Spending on Schools," in Terry Moe, ed., *A Primer on America's Schools* (Stanford, Calif.: Hoover Institution Press, 2001), 69.

4. Alan B. Krueger, "Economic Considerations and Class Size," NBER Working Paper 8875, Cambridge, Mass., National Bureau of Economic Research, 2002.

5. Rob Greenwald, Larry V. Hedges, and Richard D. Laine, "The Effect of School Resources on Student Achievement," *Review of Educational Research* 66, no. 3 (Fall 1996): 361–396.

6. See the KIPP New York website, www.kippny.org, "Highlights of the KIPP Academy," accessed April 14, 2005. The school ranked the highest of public middle schools in the Bronx in math scores, reading scores, and attendance. Fifth-graders enrolled by lottery and without regard to prior achievement.

7. KIPP student, interview with the author, March 24, 2003.

8. "SABIS Edge Program Description," Eden Prairie, Minn., SABIS Educational Systems, Inc., 1999, 3.

9. Eric Hanushek et al., *Making Schools Work: Improving Performance and Controlling Costs* (Washington, D.C.: Brookings Institution, 1994), xv–xvi.

10. For more information, see the Arizona Department of Education website at www.ade.state.az.us/charterschools/info/. Expenditure data are from National Center for Education Statistics, Nation's Report Card, State Profiles, www.nces.ed.gov.

11. Salary data are from National Center for Education Statistics, *Digest of Education Statistics, 2002,* table 78, www.nces.ed.gov.

12. Boston Municipal Research Bureau, "Fiscal 2004 Budget Scaled Back," Special Report, April 30, 2003, www.bmrb.org.

13. See National Center for Education Statistics, Nation's Report Card, State Profiles, www.nces.ed.gov.

14. "SABIS Edge Program Description."

15. Sol Stern, *Breaking Free: Public School Lessons and the Imperative of School Choice* (San Francisco: Encounter Books, 2003), 177–180.

16. In 2002, the New York City schools reportedly employed half as many people as in 1993. See "A Slimmed-Down Education Department," *New York Times,* December 4, 2002.

17. Diane Ravitch and Joseph P. Viteritti, *New Schools for a New Century: The Redesign of Urban Education* (New Haven, Conn.: Yale University Press, 1997), chapter 1.

18. For a recent examination of corruption and waste in large urban school systems, see Lydia Segal, *Battling Corruption in America's Public Schools* (Cambridge, Mass.: Harvard University Press, 2003).

19. Hanushek et al., *Making Schools Work,* 37.

20. "Over Ruled: The Burden of Law on America's Public Schools," *Common Good,* 2004, www.cgood.org/burden-of-law.html.

21. William Tucker, "Foot in the Door," *Forbes,* February 3, 1992, p. 50.

22. "CFNN Federal Policy Update," St. Paul, Minn., Charter Friends National Network, bulletin, September 13, 2002.

23. Whittle and Moe quoted in William C. Symonds et al., "For-Profit Schools," *Business Week,* February 7, 2000.

24. "Edison Schools, Preliminary Prospectus," New York, Edison Schools, October 19, 1999.

25. Contract, SABIS and Schenectady, New York, school; Contract, SABIS and Springfield, Massachusetts, school; both in author's possession.

26. William Celis, "Clinton Hails Annenberg's $500 million Education Gift," *New York Times,* December 17, 1993; "A Progress Report," The Annenberg Challenge website, www.annenbergchallenge.org, accessed October 15, 2003.

27. John O'Leary, "Education by Gap," *The Times (London),* October 5, 2000.

28. Ibid.

29. Aspire website, www.aspirepublicschools.org, accessed April 19, 2004.

30. Bill and Melinda Gates Foundation, "Investment to Build Effective Charter Schools in Los Angeles: $5.7 Million Grant to Create Six New Schools, Bolster Management Organization," press release, May 28, 2003, www.gatesfoundation.org, accessed October 15, 2003.

31. Green Dot website, www.greendotpublicschools.org, accessed April 19, 2004.

32. John Alford, interview with the author, July 6, 2004.

33. James Q. Wilson, *Bureaucracy: What Government Agencies Do and Why They Do It* (New York: Basic Books, 1989), 91.

34. Paul T. Hill, Gail E. Foster, and Tamar Gendler, *High Schools with Character* (Santa Monica, Calif.: RAND Corporation, 1990).

35. National Center for Education Statistics, "Statistics in Brief: Revenues and Expenditures for Public Elementary and Secondary Education, School Year 2000–2001" (Washington, D.C.: NCES, May 2003).

36. Brian O'Reilly, "Why Edison Doesn't Work," *Fortune,* December 9, 2002.

37. Edison Schools, Inc., *Seventh Annual Report on School Performance, 2003–2004* (New York: Edison Schools, 2005), 26.

38. Edison Schools, Inc., *2002 Annual Report* (New York: Edison Schools, 2003), 13–15.

39. Chancellor Beacon website, www.chancellorbeacon.com.

40. Beacon Education Management website, www.beaconedu.com/history.stm, accessed August 22, 2002.

41. Beacon Education Management, Inc. S-1. Filing date: July 17, 2001, downloadable at www.hoovers.com.

42. Michael Ronan, interview with the author, November 26, 2002.

43. "SABIS Edge Program Description," 3.

44. Agreement between the Board of Education of the Academy 20 School Districts and the Edison Project, April 3, 1997, in author's possession.

45. Peter Ruppert, interview with the author, July 13, 2004. Examples of Edison's surplus contracts are Stepping Stone Academy Charter School and New Covenant Charter School.

46. Edison Schools, *2003 Annual Report* (New York: Edison Schools, 2003), 35. Examples include Edison's contracts with Stepping Stone Academy Charter School and New Covenant Charter School and Beacon's contract with Central New York Charter School for Math and Science.

47. Edison Schools, *2002 Annual Report.*

48. "Agreement between the Stepping Stone Academy Charter School and Edison Schools, Inc.," New York, Edison Schools, July 10, 2001.

49. "Trademark License Agreement between KIPP Foundation and KIPP STAR College Preparatory Charter School, Inc.," San Francisco, KIPP, November 13, 2003, pp. 4–9.

50. Ibid.

3. School Designs

1. Edison Schools website, www.edisonschools.com, accessed May 2, 2005; KIPP website, www.kipp.org, accessed February 6, 2003; Advantage Schools,

Annual Report on Student Performance, 1999–2000 School Year (Boston: Advantage, 2001).

2. NAEP scores (Washington, D.C.: National Center for Education Statistics, U.S. Department of Education, Office of Education Research and Improvement, 2003). "Central cities" of all standard metropolitan statistical areas are defined by the Office of the Management and Budget. Students perform at four levels: below basic, basic, proficient, and advanced. The 2001 *Report Card* explains that fourth-grade students who read at the below-basic level are unable to demonstrate an understanding of the overall meaning of what they read and cannot make relatively obvious connections between the test and their own experiences. Fourth-graders who perform at the advanced level, by contrast, can generalize about topics in the reading selection and demonstrate an awareness of how authors compose and use literary devices; when reading text appropriate to their grades, they can judge text critically and give thorough answers that indicate careful thought. See "The Nation's Report Card: Fourth Grade Reading 2000," April 2001, p. 14, www.nces.ed.gov.

3. A 2002 study by the American Federation of Teachers concluded that "charter schools do not cream middle-class and bright students." In hindsight, it is not surprising that new schools would attract parents whose children have not fared well in their previous public schools. See American Federation of Teachers, *Do Charter Schools Measure Up? The Charter School Experiment after Ten Years,* 2002, p. 17, www.aft.org.

4. Organization for Economic Cooperation and Development (OECD), *Education at a Glance, 2003* (Paris: OECD, September 2003), tables B1.1, A6.1, and A6.2; Eric A. Hanushek, "Spending on Schools," in Terry Moe, ed., *A Primer on America's Schools* (Stanford, Calif.: Hoover Institution Press, 2001); Caroline M. Hoxby, "What Has Changed and What Has Not," in Paul E. Peterson, ed., *Our Schools and Our Future . . . Are We Still at Risk?* (Stanford, Calif.: Hoover Institution Press, 2003); and *Digest of Education Statistics 2002,* www.nces.ed.gov.

5. J. C. Huizenga, interview with the author, July 10, 2003.

6. Enrollment figures from *SABIS International Charter School Annual Report, 2002–2003* (Eden Prairie, Minn.: SABIS, 2003).

7. "Small high schools (ideally 400 students or fewer) can provide a personalized learning environment where every student has an adult advocate. Students in small schools feel less alienated and tend to be more actively engaged in school activities." Gates Foundation, www.gatesfoundation.org, accessed April 17, 2005.

8. National Education Association website, www.nea.org/classsize/; American Federation of Teachers website, www.aft.org/issues/class_size.html. The AFT website text continues: "Reducing class size is a significant means of improving student achievement, but it is not the only piece. High academic standards and a challenging curriculum, safe and orderly classrooms, and qualified teachers are also necessary. When smaller classes are joined with these other reforms, the potential impact on student achievement will likely be far greater."

9. Gary Hopkins, "The Debate over Class Size, Part 2: The Critics Have Their Say," *Education World,* February 23, 1998.

10. The results of the 1994 NAEP were released in 1995. See also California Senate Bill 1777, passed in 1996, Class Size Reduction (CSR) Program.

11. CSR Research Consortium, "What Have We Learned about Class Size Reduction in California?" September 2002, www.classize.org, 7.

12. Ibid., 5, 35, 37.

13. Ibid., 49.

14. Caroline M. Hoxby, "The Effects of Class Size on Student Achievement: New Evidence from Population Variation," *Quarterly Journal of Economics* 115, no. 4 (2000): 1239–1285.

15. Ludger Wössmann and Martin West, "Class-Size Effects in School Systems around the World: Evidence from Between-Grade Variation in TIMSS," Harvard University, Program on Education Policy and Governance, working paper no. PEPG/02–02, 2002, pp. 31–32.

16. Quoted in Abigail Thernstrom and Stephen Thernstrom, *No Excuses* (New York: Simon & Schuster, 2003), 57.

17. The defining features of the SABIS education system, including class size, are outlined on the company website, www.sabis.net, accessed April 18, 2005.

18. Ralph Bistany, interview with the author, July 21, 2004.

19. Ibid.

20. Wayne C. Frederick and Herbert J. Walberg, "Learning as a Function of Time," *Journal of Educational Research* 73 (1980): 183–194.

21. National Commission on Time and Learning, *Prisoners of Time* (Washington, D.C.: Government Printing Office, 1994), transmittal letter to Congress.

22. Ibid. Emphasis in the original.

23. Edison Schools, *Prospectus* (New York: Edison Schools, October 19, 1999), 44.

24. Ibid., 45.

25. KIPP website, www.kipp.org, accessed November 11, 2003.

26. National Commission on Time and Learning, *Prisoners of Time.*

27. Alan Olkes, interview with the author, February 12, 2003.

28. Napa Edison School, Napa, California, faculty and staff interview with the author, March 3, 2003.

29. As summarized by John E. Chubb, "Real Choice," in Paul E. Peterson, ed., *Our Schools and Our Future: Are We Still at Risk?* (Stanford, Calif.: Hoover Institution Press, 2003).

30. Ibid., 333–334.

31. National Heritage Academies website, www.heritageacademies.com, accessed August 13, 2004.

32. Teachers and parents of Paramount Academy, Kalamazoo, Michigan, interview with the author, December 17, 2002.

33. KIPP website, www.kipp.org, accessed November 11, 2003.

34. Edison Schools, Inc., *Fifth Annual Report on School Performance, 2001–2002* (New York: Edison Schools, 2003), 27.

35. Edison Schools, Inc., *Seventh Annual Report on School Performance, 2003–2004* (New York: Edison Schools, 2005), 30.

36. Advantage Schools, *Annual Report on School Performance, 1999–2000 School Year* (Boston: Advantage Schools, 2001), 3.

37. National Heritage Academies website, www.heritageacademies.com, accessed August 13, 2004.

38. Chester E. Finn Jr., Bruno V. Manno, and Gregg Vanourek, *Charter Schools in Action: Renewing Public Education* (Princeton, N.J.: Princeton University Press, 2000), 85.

39. KIPP website, www.kipp.org, accessed April 18, 2005.

40. "Phillips-Edison Teacher Expectations and Beliefs," Phillips-Edison Partnership School, Napa, Calif., undated, in author's possession.

41. Terry M. Moe, "Teachers Unions and the Public Schools," in Moe, *A Primer on America's Schools,* 163–164.

42. Reg Weaver, "Solution Isn't That Simple," *USA Today,* June 28, 2004.

43. Advantage Schools Instructional Performance Appraisal Form, in author's possession; Steve Mancini, interview with the author, July 16, 2004.

44. Steven F. Wilson, *Reinventing the Schools: A Radical Plan for Boston* (Boston: Pioneer Institute for Public Policy Research, 1992), 285, 295.

45. Weaver, "Solution Isn't That Simple."

46. Olkes interview, February 12, 2003.

47. Focus group held by the author, Chancellor Weston Charter School, February 11, 2003.

48. Edison Schools, *2002 Annual Report,* 20. Based on spending for the 1999–2000 school year.

49. Ibid., 9.

50. Christopher D. Cerf, president and chief operating officer, interview with the author, August 12, 2003.

51. Matt Bach, "Flint Schools May Not Stay Open for All of Next Year, Chow Warns Board," *Flint Journal,* November 6, 2003.

52. Edison staff members, interviews with author, 2003.

53. Stig Leschly, "KIPP National, 1999 (A): Designing a School Network," case study, Harvard Business School, March 21, 2003, 7.

54. John Chubb, interview with the author, August 12, 2003.

55. Charles Abelmann and Richard F. Elmore, *When Accountability Knocks, Will Anyone Answer?* Consortium for Policy Research in Education and University of Pennsylvania Graduate School of Education, Philadelphia, 1999, p. 39, www.cpre.org.

56. Susan Ohanian, *One Size Fits Few: The Folly of Educational Standards* (Portsmouth N.H.: Heinemann, 1999), 140, 147. Emphasis in the original.

57. Christopher Barnes, "What Do Teachers Teach? A Survey of America's Fourth and Eighth Grade Teachers," Manhattan Institute, Center for Civic Innovation, civic report no. 28, September 2002, www.manhattan-institute.org. Survey conducted by The Center for Survey Research and Analysis, University of Connecticut.

58. Abelmann and Elmore, *When Accountability Knocks,* 41.

59. Wade Dyke, interview with the author, February 12, 2003; Focus group with the author, February 11, 2003.

60. E. D. Hirsch Jr., "Curriculum and Competence," in Moe, *Primer on America's Schools,* 188.

61. E. D. Hirsch Jr., *The Schools We Need and Why We Don't Have Them* (New York: Doubleday, 1996), 239–271.

62. Ibid., 7.

63. Hirsch, "Curriculum and Competence," 191.

64. Doug Carnine, *Why Education Experts Resist Effective Practices (and What It Would Take to Make Education More Like Medicine)* (Washington, D.C.: Fordham Foundation, 2002), 9.

65. "Focus: What Was That Project Follow Through?" *Effective School Practices* 15, no. 1 (Winter 1995–1996).

66. "Excerpts from the Abt Reports: Descriptions of the Models and Summary of Results," *Effective School Practices* 15, no. 1 (Winter 1995–1996). The article is made up of excerpts from the article by Geoffrey Bock, Linda Stebbins, and Elizabeth C. Proper, "Education as Experimentation: A Planned Variation Model, an Evaluation of Follow Through IV, B" (Cambridge, Mass.: Abt Associates, April 1977).

67. Bonnie Grossen, "Overview: The Story behind Project Follow Through," *Effective School Practices* 15, no. 1 (Winter 1995–1996).

68. Carnine, "Why Education Experts Resist Effective Practices," 8.

69. "Excerpts from the Abt Reports."

70. Bock, Stebbins, and Proper, "Education as Experimentation," 73.

71. Grossen, "Overview."

72. E. House, G. Glass, L. McLean, and D. Walker, "No Simple Answer: Critique of the FT Evaluation," *Harvard Educational Review* 48, no. 2 (1978): 128–160.

73. Gene V. Glass and Gregory A. Camilli, "'Follow Through' Evaluation" (Washington, D.C.: National Institute of Education, February 1, 1981), 1, 9, 14, 19.

74. Ibid., 3–4.

75. For "exemplary and effective," see Cathy L. Watkins, "Follow Through: Why Didn't We?" *Effective School Practices* 15, no.1 (Winter 1995–1996): 5.

76. Educational Research Service, "An Educators' Guide to Schoolwide Reform," 1999, www.aasa.org. Prepared by the American Institutes for Research under contract to the American Association of School Administrators, American Federation of Teachers, National Association of Elementary School Principals, National Association of Secondary School Principals, and the National Education Association.

77. American Federation of Teachers, "Building on the Best, Learning from What Works: Seven Promising Reading and English Language Arts Programs," 1999, p. 9, www.aft.org.

78. Diane Ravitch, *Left Back: A Century of Failed School Reforms* (New York: Simon and Schuster, 2000), 439. Morris Kline, *Why Johnny Can't Add: The Failure of the New Math* (New York: St. Martin's Press, 1973).

79. National Council of Teachers of Mathematics, www.standards.nctm.org, accessed April 18, 2005.

80. Lawrence S. Braden and Ralph A. Raimi, *State Math Standards* (Washington, D.C.: Fordham Foundation, 1998), viii.

81. "The Mathematics Program Advisory of 1996," Mathematically Correct, September 1996, www.mathematicallycorrect.com.

82. California Department of Education, "Mathematics Content Standards for California Public Schools: Kindergarten through Grade Twelve, 1999," www.cde.ca.gov.

83. National Council of Teachers of Mathematics, *Principles and Standards for School Mathematics* (Reston, Va.: NCTM, 2000).

84. Glass and Camilli, " 'Follow Through' Evaluation," 14.

85. Daniel Radosh, "The Pet Goat Approach," *New Yorker,* July 26, 2004.

86. Success for All website, www.successforall.net, accessed April 18, 2005.

87. Ibid.

88. See www.letterland.com for more on how the program is designed to help children learn to read.

89. *SABIS International Charter School 2002 Annual Report.*

90. Charter Schools Institute, State University of New York, "Report to the Board of Trustees: Findings and Recommendations of the Charter Schools Institute as to the Application for Charter Renewal of the Central New York Charter School for Math and Science," Albany, N.Y., February 17, 2005.

91. Matthew Clavel, "How Not to Teach Math: New York's Chancellor Klein's Plan Doesn't Compute," *City Journal,* March 7, 2003.

92. Observed by author at Phillips-Edison Charter School, March 4, 2003. Instruction in computation, including "fact drills," was added to later versions of Everyday Math; see everydaymath.uchicago.edu, accessed May 16, 2005.

93. Edison Schools, Inc., *Seventh Annual Report on School Performance, 2003–2004* (New York: Edison Schools, 2005).

94. See www.saxonpublishers.com/history/index.jsp.

95. SRA website, www.sraonline.com, accessed April 18, 2005.

96. The Edison Project, "Partnership School Design," 1994, p. 3.

97. John E. Chubb, "Lessons in School Reform from the Edison Project," in Diane Ravitch and Joseph Viteritti, eds., *New Schools for a New Century: The Redesign of Urban Education* (New Haven, Conn.: Yale University Press, 1997).

98. Mark Walsh, "Edison Schools Joins with IBM in Technology Alliance," *Education Week,* June 21, 2000.

99. Quoted in Brian O'Reilly, "Why Edison Doesn't Work," *Fortune,* December 9, 2002.

100. Census 2000 data confirmed that white, non-Hispanic children

were more likely to have computers in their homes and Internet access than were black or Hispanic children. See "Home Computers and Internet Use in the United States: August 2000," U.S. Census Bureau, September 2001, www.census.gov.

101. Austan D. Goolsbee and Jonathan Guryan, "The Impact of Internet Subsidies in Public Schools," National Bureau of Economic Research, Cambridge, Mass., working paper no. 9090, August 2002, p. 1.

102. Ibid., 16.

103. Lawrence W. Cheek, "Pretty Cool for a School," *Architecture,* February 2, 2001, p. 42.

104. John Chubb, interview with the author, December 8, 2003.

105. Chris Malmgren, technology director, interview with research assistant Lisa Cohen, March 4, 2003.

106. Richard F. Elmore, *Building a New Structure for School Leadership* (Washington, D.C.: Albert Shanker Institute, 2000), 6, www.ashankerinst.org.

107. Ibid., 7.

108. Thomas E. Glass, "Superintendent Leaders Look at the Superintendency, School Boards, and Reform," Education Commission of the States, July 2001, www.ecs.org.

109. Frederick M. Hess, *Spinning Wheels: The Politics of Urban School Reform* (Washington, D.C.: Brookings Institution Press, 1999), 39.

110. Henry M. Levin, "Thoughts on For-Profit Schools," National Center for the Study of Privatization in Education, Teachers College, Columbia University, February 2001, pp. 8–9.

111. The Edison Project, "Partnership School Design," 1994, p. 82, in author's possession.

112. Teacher at Montebello Elementary School, interview with the author, November 7, 2002.

113. For the quotation, see David K. Cohen and Deborah Loewenberg Ball, "Instruction, Capacity, and Improvement," CPRE research report no. RR-43, Consortium for Policy Research in Education, University of Pennsylvania, June 1999, 11–12.

114. Katrina Bulkley and Jennifer Hicks, "Educational Management Organizations and the Development of Professional Community in Charter Schools," National Center for the Study of Privatization in Education, Teachers College, Columbia University, undated, www.ncspe.org.

115. Ibid., 37. Emphasis in the original.

116. Focus group with Phillips Edison Charter School teachers, convened by the author, March 3, 2003.

4. School Culture

1. Anti-intellectualism infects schools in every community, but for an examination of its role in black underachievement, see John McWhorter, *Losing the Race: Self-Sabotage in Black America* (New York: Perennial, 2001).

2. See Richard Arum, *Judging School Discipline: The Crisis of Moral Authority* (Cambridge, Mass.: Harvard University Press, 2003).

3. Paul T. Hill, Gail E. Foster, and Tamar Gendler, *High Schools with Character* (Santa Monica, Calif.: RAND Corporation, 1990).

4. Sharon L. Foster, Patricia Brennan, Anthony Biglan, Linna Wang, and Saud al-Ghaith, "Preventing Behavior Problems: What Works," International Bureau of Education, Geneva, pamphlet, 2002, p. 13.

5. Visit by the author to Learning Leadership Charter Public School, January 14, 2003.

6. Frances Barr, interview with the author, November 7, 2002.

7. Visit by the author to Rochester Leadership Charter Public School, November 7, 2002.

8. Ibid.

9. Randall Sprick, Mickey Garrison, and Lisa M. Howard, *CHAMPS: A Proactive and Positive Approach to Classroom Management* (Longmont, Colo.: Sopris West Educational Services, December 1998); Advantage Schools, Inc., *Contract Schools Proposal: Kansas City, Missouri* (Boston: Advantage, 2000).

10. The Code is described in Advantage Schools, *Annual Report on School Performance, 1999–2000, Technical Report* (Boston: Advantage, 2000), 14.

11. Advantage Schools, *Contract Schools Proposal: Kansas City*, 49–50.

12. Advantage's chief education officer, Theodor Rebarber, had served as associate director for curriculum and assessment at Edison during its first years.

13. Advantage Schools, Inc., *Code of Civility: A Blueprint for Living and Learning* (Boston: Advantage Schools, 1999), 5.

14. *SABIS International Charter School Annual Report, 2002–2003* (Eden Prairie, Minn.: SABIS, n.d.).

15. Visits by the author to SABIS International Charter School, Springfield, Mass., 2003.

16. Memorandum, "SABIS Edge Program Description," Eden Prairie, Minn., SABIS, 1999.

17. Visit by the author to SABIS International Charter School of Schenectady, New York, April 7, 2003.

18. Visit by the author to KIPP school in the South Bronx, May 13, 2002.

19. Interview with research assistant Lisa Cohen, April 24, 2003. The names of the students have been changed.

20. Ibid.

21. KIPP New York website, www.kippny.org.

22. "KIPP's Success in Reading and Math," New York, KIPP company document, 2004.

23. "KIPP Academy New York Stanford 10 Results," New York, KIPP New York school document, 2004.

24. Richard Rothstein, "Must Schools Fail?" *New York Review of Books,* December 2, 2004.

25. Abigail Thernstrom and Stephan Thernstrom, *No Excuses: Closing the Racial Gap in Learning* (New York: Simon & Schuster, 2003), 67–70. The Thernstroms attribute their analysis of culture to George Farkas.

26. Ibid., 70.

27. Ibid., 67.

28. Ibid., 74–75.

29. Visit by research assistant Lisa Cohen to KIPP Ujima Village school, November 6, 2002.

30. Thernstrom and Thernstrom, *No Excuses,* 73.

31. Ibid., 75.

32. Quoted in Ellen R. Delisio and Diane Weaver Dunne, "More than Reading Scores and Stereotypes: The Voices of City Teachers and Students," *Education World,* 2001, www.education-world.com, accessed May 2, 2005.

33. As quoted in Sybil Fix, "Results Validate No-Nonsense Learning," in "Building on Common Ground," special report, *Charleston Post and Courier,* November 26, 2000.

34. Visit by author to KIPP school in the South Bronx, May 13, 2002.

35. "The KIPP String and Rhythm Orchestra," San Francisco, KIPP company pamphlet, undated, in author's possession.

5. Execution

1. Peter Ruppert, president of NHA, interview with the author, July 10, 2003.

2. "Theglobe.com falls off the edge of the world," June 9, 1999, archived at www.redherring.com.

3. William C. Symonds et al., "For-Profit Schools," *Business Week,* February 7, 2000.

4. National Center for Education Statistics, "Statistics in Brief: Revenues and Expenditures for Public Elementary and Secondary Education: School Year 2000–2001," May 2003, www.nces.ed.gov.

5. Symonds et al., "For-Profit Schools."

6. Michael Moe, as quoted in ibid.

7. Mark Walsh, "Lack of Profitability Spurs School-Management Shake-out," *Education Week,* September 12, 2001, www.edweek.org. See also Walsh, "School Managers Chancellor and Beacon Merge," *Education Week,* January 16, 2002.

8. Senior Edison official, interview with the author, August 2003.

9. Quoted in Brian O'Reilly, "Why Edison Doesn't Work," *Fortune,* December 9, 2002.

10. *Frontline,* interviews with Chris Whittle, October and December 2002, www.pbs.org.

11. Ibid.

12. Quoted in Larry Fish and Martha Woodall, "Edison Gets Funding to Open Schools," *Philadelphia Inquirer,* August 2, 2002.

13. Chris Scarlata, Q4 2002 Investor Call, September 6, 2002, transcribed portions in author's possession.

14. Center for Education Reform, *Charter School Laws across the States: Ranking Scorecard and Legislative Profiles* (Washington, D.C.: Center for Education Reform, 2003). Every year, the Center for Education Reform tracks change to the states' charter laws, and awards them a letter grade.

15. All quotations in this paragraph are from Chancellor Beacon management team, interview with the author, February 12, 2003.

16. Scott Hamilton, interview with the author, May 7, 2004.

17. Ibid.

18. Public school revenue per student in fall enrollment, 2001–2002, in National Education Association, *Rankings and Estimates: Rankings of the States 2003 and Estimates of School Statistics 2004* (Washington, D.C.: NEA, May 2004), 39.

19. Michael Connelly, interview with the author, December 2, 2003.

20. All quotations from Connelly in this paragraph are from ibid.

21. Ralph Bistany, interview with the author, July 21, 2004.

22. George Saad, interview with the author, October 23, 2003.

23. Joe Keeney, president, charter development, Edison Schools, interview with the author, September 8, 2003.

24. Connelly interview, December 2, 2003.

25. National Association of Homebuilders, "Building for Tomorrow: Innovative Infrastructure Solutions," Washington, D.C., 2003, www.nahb.org, accessed May 2, 2005.

26. Data on the California initiatives, as well as the quotation from Robitaille, are given in Doug Lemov, "Aspire Public Schools Case Study," Harvard Business School, in press.

27. Hubert H. Humphrey Institute, Center for School Change, New Twin Cities Charter School Project, *Charter School Handbook* (Minneapolis: Regents of the University of Minnesota, 2000), www.hhh.umn.edu/centers/school-change/handbook/finance.htm, accessed May 10, 2005.

28. Michael Connelly and Gene Eidelman, interview with the author, December 2, 2003.

29. Jeff Poole, interview with the author, July 10, 2003.

30. Wade Dyke, interview with the author, February 12, 2003.

31. George Saad, interview with the author, October 23, 2003.

32. Jordana Hart, "U.S. Calls Charter School Biased against Special-Needs Student," *Boston Globe,* September 11, 1997.

33. Ibid.

34. Quoted in Symonds et al., "For-Profit Schools."

35. Senior Edison official interview, August 2003.

36. Chancellor Beacon senior management team, interview with the author, February 12, 2003.

37. "Edison Schools Settles SEC Enforcement Action," press release, U.S. Securities and Exchange Commission, May 14, 2002, www.sec.gov, accessed May 2, 2005. See also U.S. Securities and Exchange Commission, "In the Matter of Edison Schools, Inc., Respondent: Order Instituting Cease-and-Desist Proceedings Pursuant to Section 21C, Making Findings, and Imposing a Cease-and-Desist Order," May 14, 2002, www.sec.gov, accessed May 2, 2005.

38. "Edison Schools Settles SEC Enforcement Action."

39. Ibid.

40. "Edison Schools Concludes and Resolves Informal SEC Inquiry," New York, Edison Schools, press release, May 14, 2002.

41. "Edison Schools Settles SEC Enforcement Action."

42. Gene Eidelman, interview with the author, December 2, 2003.

43. Mosaica Education website, www.mosaicaeducation.com, accessed January 24, 2003.

44. Connelly interview, December 2, 2003.

45. Ibid.

46. Chancellor Beacon website, www.chancelloracademies.com, accessed January 24, 2003.

47. Contract, Chancellor Beacon and Oakland, Florida, school, December 10, 2002, Coconut Grove, Fla., Chancellor Beacon Academies, 2002.

48. Contract, Edison Schools' and New Covenant Charter School, July 1, 2000, New York, Edison Schools, 2000.

49. Octavio Visiedo, interview with the author, February 12, 2003.

50. David B. Caruso, "Philadelphia Fires One Private Group Managing Public Schools," *Associated Press,* April 17, 2003.

51. Ibid.

52. Gary Miron and Brooks Applegate, *Evaluation of Edison Schools, Inc.,* p. 5, Western Michigan Evaluation Center, www.wmich.edu/evalctr/.

53. Josh Funk, "Officials: Edison Did Not Deliver," *Wichita (Kans.) Eagle,* December 1, 2002.

54. Ibid.

55. Ibid.

56. Nelson Smith, "Catching the Wave: Lessons from California's Charter Schools," Progressive Policy Institute, Washington, D.C., July 9, 2003.

57. Michael Winerip, "Schools for Sale," *New York Times Magazine,* June 14, 1998.

58. Steven Wilson, letter to *New York Times,* June 22, 1998.

59. "Rocky Mount Advantage School: Summary of ITBS Pretests and Posttests, October 1998," Boston, Advantage Schools, 1998.

60. Anny Kuo, "Albany Charter School on New Test: Ninety-one Percent Fail," *Associated Press,* June 2, 2000.

61. Elizabeth Benjamin, "Charter's Scores Renew Criticisms," *(Albany) Times Union,* June 2, 2000.

62. Ibid.

63. Chris Whittle, interview with the author, September 8, 2003.

64. John Chubb, interview with the author, August 12, 2003.

65. The Edison Project, "Partnership School Design," 1994.

66. Ibid.

67. Chester E. Finn and Michael J. Petrilli, eds., "The State of State Standards, 2000," Thomas B. Fordham Foundation, January 2000, p. 5, www.edexcellence.net.

68. Ibid.

69. Chubb interview, August 12, 2003.

70. Ed Hayward, "Boston Renaissance to Dump Edison Schools Inc., Chart Own Course," *Boston Herald,* May 17, 2002.

71. Ed Hayward, "Charters Leave Their Roots; Schools Part Ways with For-Profits," *Boston Herald,* June 16, 2002.

72. Jay Lindsay, "Boston Charter School Severs Ties with Edison Schools Inc.," *Associated Press State and Local Wire,* May 16, 2002.

73. Ibid.

74. Ford Fessenden, "How to Measure Student Proficiency? States Disagree on Tests," *New York Times,* December 31, 2003.

75. For instance, Contract, Advantage Schools, Inc. and Community Development Foundation of Rocky Mount, April 30, 1997, p. 5, Boston, Advantage Schools.

76. Ibid.

77. Kelly Gollobin, "Charter School Appeal Filed," *Rocky Mount Telegram,* May 9, 1997; Gollobin, "Nash-RM School Board Drops Charter School Appeal," *Rocky Mount (N.C.) Telegram,* July 16, 1997.

78. Principal Robert Bone of Syracuse, New York, Beacon Management school, interview with the author, November 6, 2002.

79. Ibid.

80. EMO executive, interview with the author, August 2003.

81. Senior SABIS officials, interview with the author, August 2003.

82. Ohio State Board of Education et al. v. Learning Opportunities of Greater Cincinnati et al., Complaint for Temporary Restraining Order and/or Preliminary Injunction and Recovery of State Funds, October 11, 2002. "Secret location" is from ibid.

83. KPMG document in author's possession.

84. Connelly interview, December 2, 2003.

85. Senior Edison official, interview with the author, August 2003.

86. Letter from Edison to school board president, in author's possession.

87. Ibid.

88. Ibid.

89. Udo Schulz and Carl Bistany, interview with the author, August 18, 2003.

90. Despite a very rocky opening, students in grades K–3 made gains in their first months at the new school on the Iowa Test of Basic Skills: Kindergartners improved from the 13th to the 31st percentile, first-graders from the 4th to the 8th percentile, second-graders from the 10th to the 23rd percentile, and third-graders from the 10th to the 13th percentile. Students in the upper grades, however, showed slight declines, with fourth-graders declining from the 15th to 12th percentile, fifth-graders from the 18th to 15th percentile, and sixth-graders from the 17th to 14th percentile. Results the following fall would have offered a more accurate assessment of students' progress in their first year.

91. David Evans, "Trouble Looms for Edison Schools Founder," *Philadelphia Inquirer,* August 9, 2002.

92. Ibid.

93. Deborah McGriff, presentation at Authorizer's Conference in San Antonio, October 21, 2002.

94. Whittle interview, September 8, 2003.

95. Contract Agreement, Dallas Independent School District and Edison Schools, Inc., November 19, 1999, New York, Edison Schools, 1999; Tawnell D. Hobbs, "Dallas School Superintendent Plans to End Privatization Experiment," *Dallas Morning News,* August 17, 2002.

96. Tawnell D. Hobbs, "Dallas School Trustees End Relationship with For-Profit Edison Schools," *Dallas Morning News,* August 23, 2002.

97. Quoted in Tawnell D. Hobbs, "Dallas Independent School District May End Edison Contract," *Dallas Morning News,* August 16, 2002.

98. SABIS also operates a private school in Minnesota and a charter school in Phoenix, Arizona, where the law permits the company to control the board.

99. Connelly interview, December 2, 2003.

100. Ralph Bistany, interview with the author, March 28, 2002.

101. Senior Edison official, interview with the author, August 2003.

6. School Leaders

1. Joan Lipsitz, *Successful Schools for Young Adolescents* (New Brunswick, N.J.: Transaction Books, 1984). The characteristics associated with successful

schools identified by Lipsitz, Sara Lawrence Lightfoot, and others are summarized in Thomas B. Corcoran, "Effective Secondary Schools," in Regina M. J. Kyle, ed., *Reaching for Excellence: An Effective Schools Sourcebook* (Washington, D.C.: U.S. Department of Education, 1985).

2. Lipsitz, *Successful Schools,* 171–174. Emphasis in original.

3. Broad Foundation and Thomas B. Fordham Institute, *Better Leaders for America's Schools: A Manifesto,* May 2003; New Leaders for New Schools website, www.nlns.org, accessed August 23, 2003.

4. KIPP website, www.kipp.org, accessed October 27, 2003.

5. John Chubb, chief education officer, Edison Schools, interview with the author, August 12, 2003.

6. Gene Eidelman and Michael Connelly, interview with the author, December 2, 2003.

7. Octavio Visiedo, interview with the author, February 12, 2003.

8. Clarence Dixon, principal, Options Public Charter School, interview with the author, October 16, 2002.

9. Jabeen Bhatti, "Charter School to Sever Ties with Firm: Management Hit for Hiring 'Fiasco,'" *Washington Times,* May 29, 2003.

10. Confidential interview with the author, July 2003.

11. Ralph Bistany, interview with the author, March 28, 2002.

12. Octavio Visiedo, chief executive officer, and Alan T. Oakes, senior vice president, human resources and school services, Chancellor Beacon Academies, interview with the author, February 12, 2003.

13. Peter Ruppert, interview with the author, July 10, 2003.

14. Connelly interview, December 2, 2003.

15. "An Invitation to Apply for the Position of School Director for Advantage Schools, Inc.," Boston, Advantage Schools, January 8, 2001, p. 1.

16. Ibid., 7–8.

17. Scott Hamilton, interview with the author, May 7, 2004.

18. Michael Ronan, interview with the author, November 26, 2002.

19. Bistany interview, March 28, 2002.

20. Confidential interview with the author, August 2003.

21. KIPP website, www.kipp.org, accessed October 27, 2003.

22. "Trademark License Agreement between KIPP Foundation and KIPP Star College Preparatory Charter School, Inc.," San Francisco, KIPP, July 1, 2003, pp. 6–7, 9.

23. KIPP website, www.kipp.org, accessed October 27, 2003.

24. In focus groups we held at EMO-run schools, staff were asked whether they identified themselves as school staff or employees of the management companies.

25. Teachers at Rochester Leadership Charter School, focus group and interview with the author, November 7, 2002.

26. Teacher, interview with Lisa Cohen, research assistant, Paramount Academy, Kalamazoo, Mich., December 17, 2002.

27. All of the quotations in the paragraph are from a senior NHA official, confidential interview with Doug Lemov, n.d.

28. Ibid.

29. "Priorities and Barriers in High School Leadership: A Survey of Principals," Reston, Va., National Association of Secondary School Principals, press release, November 13, 2001.

30. Confidential interview with Doug Lemov, summer 2003.

31. See Tom Loveless, "Charter Schools: Achievement, Accountability, and the Role of Expertise," in *2003 Brown Center Report on American Education: How Well Are American Students Learning?* (Washington, D.C.: Brookings Institution, 2003), 34.

32. Bistany interview, March 28, 2002.

33. Broad Foundation and Thomas B. Fordham Institute, *Better Leaders for America's Schools,* 32.

34. Confidential interview with the author, August 2003.

35. Stig Leschly, "KIPP National, 1999 (B)," Exhibits 6 and 7, "Average Years of Teaching among Thirty-two Fellows in Three Cohorts, 2001–03," case study, Harvard Business School, March 21, 2003.

36. Confidential interview with Doug Lemov, summer 2003.

37. Staff member of Central New York Charter School for Math and Science, Syracuse, New York, interview with the author, November 6, 2002.

38. Senior NHA official, confidential interview with Doug Lemov, n.d.

39. Kevin Hall, senior vice president, Chancellor Beacon, interview with the author, February 12, 2003.

40. Ibid.

41. Former Beacon manager, interview with the author, 2003.

42. Edison executive, interview with the author, August 2003.

43. Chubb interview, August 12, 2003.

44. Joe Keeney, president, Edison Charter Schools, interview with the author, September 8, 2003.

45. All quotations in the paragraph are from ibid.

46. John Alford, interview with the author, July 6, 2004.

7. Politics and Schools

1. Telephone surveys conducted by Gallup Organization of over 1,000 adults between 1973 to 2003. See Linda Lyons, "School Confidence Low after Decades of Reform," *Gallup Pool Tuesday Briefing*, July 1, 2003, pp. 81–82. The question asked about several institutions was, Tell me how much confidence you, yourself, have in each one—a great deal, quite a lot, or very little? By contrast, confidence in the military increased significantly over the period. As of 2002, Americans had less confidence in the public schools than all other polled public institutions (behind the Supreme Court, the presidency, police, and the military), with the exception of Congress and the justice system. See Frank Newport, "American's Confidence in Military, Presidency Up: Big Business, Organized Religion Drop," *Gallup Pool Tuesday Briefing*, June 28, 2002, pp. 98–100.

2. Telephone survey conducted by Gallup Organization of 1,019 adults by Gallup Organization on August 24–27, 2000, accessed September 22, 2003 from Public Agenda (www.publicagenda.com/issues). The question asked was, Overall, how satisfied are you with the quality of education students receive in grades kindergarten through grade twelve in the U.S. today—completely satisfied, somewhat satisfied, somewhat dissatisfied, or completely dissatisfied?

3. Gallup Organization poll, August 2000, accessed September 22, 2003 from Public Agenda (www.publicagenda.com/issues). The question was, How satisfied are you with the quality of education your oldest child is receiving?

4. Telephone survey conducted by Public Agenda of 251 employers and 252 professors between November 9 and December 9, 2001, from Public Agenda's website, www.publicagenda.com, accessed September 22, 2003.

5. Telephone survey conducted by Public Agenda between March 26 and April 17, 1998, from Public Agenda's website, www.publicagenda.com.

6. Terry M. Moe, *Schools, Vouchers, and the American Public* (Washington, D.C.: Brookings Institution, 2001), 87.

7. Charles Leslie Glenn Jr., *The Myth of the Common School* (Oakland, Calif.: Institute for Contemporary Studies Press, 2002), ix.

8. Moe, *Schools, Vouchers, and the American Public,* 88.

9. Telephone survey conducted April 3–9, 2000, by International Communications Research of 1,225 registered voters, sponsored by the *Washington Post,* the Kaiser Family Foundation, and Harvard University. Reproduced on Public Agenda's website, www.publicagenda.com, accessed September 22, 2003.

10. Alex Molnar, interview with Kathleen Burke, "The Commercial Assault on Children and on School Academic Standards," ASCD Annual Conference Online 2003, www.simulconference.com/ASCD/2003/ptc/molnara.shtml.

11. Jonathan Kozol, quoted in *Education Week,* June 3, 1992, cited in Myron Lieberman, *Public Education: An Autopsy* (Cambridge, Mass.: Harvard University Press, 1993), 321.

12. Chris Whittle, interview with the author, September 8, 2003.

13. John E. Chubb, "Lessons in School Reform from the Edison Project," in Diane Ravitch and Joseph Viteritti, eds., *New Schools for a New Century: The Redesign of Urban Education* (New Haven, Conn.: Yale University Press, 1997), 113.

14. San Francisco School Board member Jill Wynns, quoted in Julie Light, "A Local Battle Highlights the National Debate over EMOs," July 8, 1998, Corpwatch, www.corpwatch.org, accessed May 3, 2005.

15. Arbor Hill Neighborhood Plan, July 2003, www.albanyny.org.

16. Rick Karlin, "Lessons Taken from a Charter School," *(Albany) Times Union,* June 23, 1999.

17. Rick Karlin, "Three Charter Schools Get SUNY Licenses," *(Albany) Times Union,* July 14, 1999.

18. Ibid.

19. Rick Karlin, "Charter School at Center of Storm," *(Albany) Times Union,* August 4, 1999.

20. Rick Karlin, "Charter School Receives Nod," *(Albany) Times Union,* August 18, 1999.

21. Advantage Schools, *Annual Report on School Performance, 1999–2000 School Year,* Boston, Advantage Schools, March 2001, p. 53.

22. Elizabeth Benjamin, "Charter School Ponders Switch," *(Albany) Times Union,* January 15, 2000.

23. Rick Karlin, "Houston Educator Named New Covenant Director," *Times Union,* December 17, 1999.

24. Ibid.; Elizabeth Benjamin, "Updates Satisfy School Panel," *(Albany) Times Union,* January 28, 2000.

25. Anny Kuo, "Albany Charter School on New Test: Ninety-one Percent Fail," *Associated Press,* June 2, 2000.

26. Advantage Schools, *Annual Report on School Performance, 1999–2000 School Year,* 53.

27. Elizabeth Benjamin, "New Covenant Called Success," *(Albany) Times Union,* June 15, 2000.

28. Elizabeth Benjamin, "Dare Exits Board amid Critical State Report," *(Albany) Times Union,* August 3, 2000.

29. Advantage Schools to James R. Butterworth, Assistant Commissioner, The State Education Department/The University of the State of New York, August 16, 2000, in author's possession.

30. Rick Karlin, "Doors Open to New Home, Hope," *(Albany) Times Union,* September 6, 2001.

31. Elizabeth Benjamin, "Charter School Chief Resigning from Post," *(Albany) Times Union,* December 16, 2001.

32. Fred Lubrun, "Bartlett's Resignation Reverberates," *(Albany) Times Union,* December 21, 2001.

33. Brian Nearing, "New Covenant Claims Recent Upheaval Caused Poor Test Scores," *(Albany) Times Union,* April 20, 2003.

34. Mitchell quoted in Julian Guthrie, "Board Hands Public School to Private Firm," *San Francisco Examiner,* June 24, 1998; see also Nanette Asimov, "Board OKs Plan for Private Firm to Run S.F. School," *San Francisco Chronicle,* June 24, 1998.

35. Nanette Asimov, "Trying to Save S.F.'s Worst School," *San Francisco Chronicle,* September 21, 1997, review of Ken Romines, *A Principal's Story* (San Francisco: Study Center Press, 1997).

36. Romines, *A Principal's Story,* 14; Sally C. Pipes, "S.F. Education Reactionaries Strike Again," *San Francisco Examiner,* February 26, 2001.

37. Asimov, "Trying to Save S.F.'s Worst School."

38. Letter from Linda Gausman to *San Francisco Examiner,* May 15, 2002.

39. Mark MacNamara, "The Lesson of Bill Rojas," *San Francisco Magazine,* September 2001, p. 68.

40. California Department of Education, STAR Results website, www.star.cde.ca.gov, accessed January 3, 2004.

41. Joan Walsh, "The Shame of San Francisco," *www.salon.com*, March 29, 2001.

42. "Stand in Line!" *Economist*, January 26, 2001.

43. Michael Bazeley, "Foes of S.F. Charter School Seek Repeal Again," *San Jose Mercury News*, November 27, 2000.

44. "Stand in Line!"

45. Ben Wildavsky, "At the Crossroads of Invention for Edison," *U.S. News & World Report*, March 26, 2001.

46. Quoted in Pipes, "S.F. Education Reactionaries Strike Again."

47. Quoted in Walsh, "Shame of San Francisco."

48. Edward Wyatt, "Higher Scores Aren't Cure-All, School Run for Profit Learns," *New York Times*, March 13, 2001.

49. Ibid.

50. California Department of Education website, data1.cde.ca.gov/dataquest/, accessed January 3, 2004.

51. Arlene Ackerman, Superintendent of Schools, San Francisco Unified District, "Edison Charter Academy: Preliminary Report of Findings: Investigation into Complaints," March 26, 2001, p. 2, in author's possession.

52. Diallo Dphrepaulezz, "The Fight to Save the Edison Charter in San Francisco," San Francisco, Pacific Research Institute, June 2001.

53. Romines, *A Principal's Story*.

54. Dphrepaulezz, "The Fight," 10. See also San Francisco Unified School District, "Excellence for All: A Five-Year Comprehensive Plan to Achieve Educational Equity in San Francisco Unified School District for School Years 2001–02 and 2005–06," adopted April 4, 2001, www.sfusd.edu, accessed May 5, 2005.

55. Ackerman, "Edison Charter Academy: Preliminary Report," 8.

56. Dphrepaulezz, "The Fight," 12.

57. Ibid., 15.

58. Joanne Jacobs, "Threatened by Success," February 2002, accessed from www.reason.com; Kent Sims, "San Francisco Economy: Implications for Public Policy," report prepared for San Francisco Planning and Urban Research Organization, July 10, 2000, table 5B, www.spur.org, accessed May 3, 2005.

59. Dphrepaulezz, "The Fight," 13. See also California Department of Education, Educational Demographics Unit, www.cde.ca.gov, accessed May 2, 2005.

60. Ackerman, "Edison Charter Academy: Preliminary Report," 14.

61. Quoted in Kathy Dalle-Molle, "Local Parents Steer Clear of Edison Charter Academy," *Noe Valley Voice*, May 2001.

62. Ibid.

63. Ibid.

64. Quoted in Gary Larson, "How SF Parents Saved Edison School," *School Reform News,* September 2001.

65. The exchange is documented in MacNamara, "The Lesson of Bill Rojas," 154.

66. Larson, "How SF Parents Saved Edison School."

67. Ibid.

68. Laura Baker, telephone interview with research assistant Emily Potts, August 28, 2003.

69. Jill Wynns, interview with Emily Potts, August 11, 2003.

70. Edison Schools, "Edison School in San Francisco Posts Strong and Consistent Academic Gains: Teachers and Parents Are Overwhelmingly Satisfied," New York, Edison Schools, press release, September 3, 2002.

71. California Department of Education, California Standardized Testing and Reporting (STAR), Stanford-9 scores, 2000–2001 and 2001–2002, star.cde.ca.gov, accessed July 5, 2004.

72. Edison Schools, "All Edison Schools in California Post Strong and Consistent Gains; Eight Edison Schools Score Improvements on the California Standards Test," New York, Edison Schools, press release, September 30, 2003.

73. Larson, "How SF Parents Saved Edison School."

8. Academic Results

1. Every test embodies a set of implicit standards for what students should know and be able to do at each grade level. The United States has not established such standards.

2. Steven Wilson, Harvard University, to the CEOs of the six organizations, January 6, 2003; letter in author's possession.

3. *SABIS International Charter School, 2002 Annual Report.* The full report is available online at www.doe.mass.edu/charter/reports/2002/annual/0441.pdf.

4. Ibid., 9.

5. Ibid., 10.

6. Ibid., 6.

7. Chancellor Beacon Academies, Inc., *2001–2002 Annual Education Report* (Coconut Grove, Fla.: Chancellor Beacon Academies, n.d.).

8. Gary Wolfram, *Making the (Better) Grade: A Detailed Statistical Analysis of National Heritage Academies on Student MEAP Scores* (Hillsdale, Mich.: Hillsdale Policy Group, 2001). In September 2003, another study of NHA schools, by Frederick M. Hess, a researcher with the American Enterprise Institute, and David L. Leal of the University of Texas at Austin, was published. This work was released too late to be included in this review.

9. Wolfram, *Making the (Better) Grade,* 20.

10. Ibid., 1.

11. The 2003 Hess study found that NHA schools made an average gain of 2.74 NCE points over the 2002–2003 year. See Frederick M. Hess and David L. Leal, "An Evaluation of Student Performance in National Heritage Academies Charter Schools: 2002–2003," p. 6, www.nationalheritageacademies .com.

12. Harold C. Doran and Darrel W. Drury, *Evaluating Success: KIPP Education Program Evaluation,* Education Performance Network, New American Schools, October 2002. The report is available online at www. kipp.org/Results/KIPP.Program.Evaluation.10.02.Full.pdf.

13. Ibid., 7.

14. Ibid.

15. Ibid., 8.

16. Ibid., 27–28.

17. Advantage administered the Stanford Achievement Test—Ninth Edition (SAT-9), in grades K–2, and the Woodcock Reading Mastery Tests—Revised (WRMT-R). See Advantage Schools, *Annual Report on School Performance, 1999–2000 School Year* (Boston: Advantage, March 2001).

18. Edison Schools, Inc., *Fifth Annual Report on School Performance, 2001–2002* (New York: Edison Schools, 2003). The report is available online at www.edisonproject.com/fifthannualreportpart1.pdf.

19. Ibid., 16.

20. Ibid., 24.

21. Ibid., 40.

22. Ibid., 147–151.

23. See Edison Schools, *Fifth Annual Report,* exhibit 7, p. 21.

24. Ibid., 23.

25. Ibid., exhibit 3, p. 15.

26. Ibid., 14–15. Emphasis mine.

27. The Mislevy studies are available online at the American Federation of

Teachers website, www.aft.org. Edison commissioned Mislevy to perform the studies; they were not conducted under the auspices of the Educational Testing Service.

28. "Effect size" is an expression of both the magnitude of the differences and their statistical strength. Because effect sizes are independent of the unit of measure, they permit program effects from one study, with one set of conditions and sample of students, to be compared with others, even when different test data are used. A conventional way of calculating effect sizes is to divide the difference between program and control group means (or averages) by the standard deviation (or spread) of the control group. For designs that compare scores on tests given at the beginning and end of the period ("pre-post designs"), the gain may be divided by the pretest standard deviation. The underlying scores must be raw scores, normal curve equivalents (NCEs), or another equal interval expression.

29. Robert J. Mislevy, "Reading Achievement Test-Score Analysis: 1997/98, Dodge-Edison vs. Control Schools, Grades 2–4," Wichita Unified School District #259, 1998, p. 10, in author's possession.

30. Robert J. Mislevy, "Reading Achievement Test-Score Analysis: 1995/96 Washington-Edison School, Grades K–2," September 17, 1996, introduction, in author's possession.

31. James Harrison to Robert Mislevy, n.d., in author's possession. Quotation is from p. 1 of this letter.

32. See American Federation of Teachers website, www.aft.org, accessed April 1, 2004.

33. Ibid.

34. Jerry Horn and Gary Miron, *An Evaluation of the Michigan Charter School Initiative: Performance, Accountability, and Impact,* July 2000. The study is available online at the Western Michigan University Evaluation Center website, www.wmich.edu.

35. Ibid., 10.

36. Ibid., vi.

37. F. Howard Nelson and Nancy Van Meter, *Update on Student Achievement for Edison Schools, Inc.,* American Federation of Teachers, February 2003, www.aft.org.

38. Ibid., i–iii.

39. Ibid., 6.

40. Ibid., n.p.

41. "Edison's Response to the American Federation of Teachers Report: Update on Student Achievement for Edison Schools, Inc," February 26, 2003, in author's possession.

42. Nelson and Van Meter, *Update on Student Achievement for Edison Schools*, 7–8.

43. Ibid., 30.

44. "Edison's Response to the American Federation of Teachers Report."

45. Gary Miron and Brooks Applegate, *An Evaluation of Student Achievement in Edison Schools Opened in 1995 and 1996*, 2000, www.wmich.edu.

46. Ibid., 20.

47. Ibid., xxiv.

48. Ibid.

49. Ibid., 69–72.

50. Ibid., 19.

51. Ibid., 46.

52. Ibid., 38.

53. Ibid., 23.

54. New York, Edison Schools, press release, February 22, 2001.

55. "Rebuttal of Edison's Criticisms of the Evaluation Center," Western Michigan University, Kalamazoo, The Evaluation Center, undated.

56. Dallas Independent School District, *Achievement Performance Report: Dallas-Edison Partnership Schools, 2001–02*, August 2002, www.aft.org.

57. Ibid., 3.

58. Edison Schools, "Edison Schools Reports Second Successive Year of Large Test Score Gains in Dallas, 6 of 7 Edison Schools Up Significantly over Two Years," New York, Edison Schools, press release, May 20, 2002.

59. June 2002 report, quoted in Edison Schools, "Dallas Suit Brief Revised," New York, n.d.

60. Sally A. Shay and Joseph J. Gomez, "Privatization in Education: A Growth Curve Analysis of Achievement," Miami-Dade Public Schools, April 2002. The paper was presented to the American Educational Research Association at its meeting in New Orleans in April 2002.

61. Ibid., 32.

62. Ibid., 3, 28, 37.

63. John E. Chubb, Edison Schools, to Ms. Carol Cortes, Miami-Dade County Public Schools, Office of Evaluation and Research, April 5, 2001, in author's possession.

64. Edison Schools, *Fifth Annual Report, 2001–2002*.

65. Ibid.

66. Nelson and Van Meter, *Update on Student Achievement for Edison Schools*, 6.

9. Business Results

1. Stig Leschly, "KIPP National, 2002 (B): Managing a School Network," case study, Harvard Business School, February 23, 2003, p. 23.

2. Edison Schools, 10-K filing with the Securities and Exchange Commission, June 30, 2003, p. 72.

3. Chris Whittle, interview with the author, September 8, 2003.

4. Ibid.

5. Edison Schools, "Edison Schools Reports Fourth Quarter Net Income of $10.2 Million, Full-Year EBITDA of $23.2 Million," New York, Edison Schools, press release, September 12, 2003.

6. Edison quarterly investor conference call, September 12, 2003, partial transcript in author's possession.

7. Edison Schools SEC filing, "Proxy Statement Pursuant to Section 14 (a) of the Securities Exchange Act of 1934," August 22, 2003, p. 20.

8. Quoted in Diana B. Henriques, "Edison Stays Afloat by Altering Course," *New York Times,* July 3, 2003.

9. Ibid.

10. Trace A. Urdan, ThinkEquity Partners, "EDSN: Q3Results—Solid Progress Continues," May 16, 2003.

11. Alan Richard, "Edison Alliance Hired to Help Struggling S.C. District," *Education Week,* August 11, 2004.

12. Quoted in Henriques, "Edison Stays Afloat."

13. Peter Ruppert, interview with the author, July 13, 2004.

14. Frederick M. Hess and David L. Leal, "An Evaluation of Student Performance in National Heritage Academies Charter Schools: 2002–2003," p. 9, www.nationalheritageacademies.com. See also Edison Schools, *Fifth Annual Report on School Performance, 2001–2002* (New York: Edison Schools, 2003), 24.

15. National Heritage Academies, "Secrets to Unbelievable Success: Why Top Urban Schools Are the Finest Schools in America," Grand Rapids, Mich., National Heritage Academies, undated, in author's possession.

16. Hess and Leal, "Evaluation of Student Performance in National Heritage Academies Charter Schools," p. 8.

17. Leschly, "KIPP National, 2002 (B)," 22.

18. Ibid.

19. John Alford, interview with the author, July 6, 2004.

20. Scott Hamilton, interview with the author, May 8, 2004.

21. Leschly, "Kipp National, 2002 (B)," 4–5.

22. Ibid., 23.

23. Hamilton interview, May 8, 2004.

24. Quotations in this paragraph are from Carl Bistany and Udo Schulz, interview with the author, August 18, 2003.

25. Senior vice president Kevin Hall, interview with the author, February 12, 2003.

26. Michael Connelly, interview with the author, December 2, 2003.

27. Heidi Steffens and Peter W. Cookson Jr., "Limitations of the Market Model," *Education Week*, August 7, 2002.

28. Ibid.

29. Henry M. Levin, "Potential of For-Profit Schools for Educational Reform," occasional paper no. 47, National Center for the Study of Privatization, Teachers College, Columbia University, June 2002, 10.

Conclusion

1. The No Child Left Behind Act of 2001, signed into law by President Bush in January 2002, was the reauthorization of the Elementary and Secondary Education Act of 1965. On defects in the NCLB, see Paul A. Herdman, Nelson Smith, and Harold Doran, "Value-Added Analysis: A Critical Component of Determining Adequate Yearly Progress (AYP)," Charter Friends National Network Policy Brief, December 2002, www.charterfriends.org. On sixteen state officials, see Lynn Olson, "Critics Float 'No Child' Revisions," *Education Week*, August 11, 2004.

2. Tom Loveless, "Charter Schools: Achievement, Accountability, and the Role of Expertise," in *2003 Brown Center Report on American Education: How Well Are American Students Learning?* (Washington, D.C.: Brookings Institution, 2003), 34. Loveless's observation is consistent with Edison's report that the average beginning score for the schools it opened or began managing from 1995 to 2001 was at the 25th percentile on norm-referenced tests, whereas the

average score for all public schools in the district in which Edison schools are located was at the 37th percentile. See also Edison Schools, Inc., *Fifth Annual Report on School Performance, 2001–2002* (New York: Edison Schools, 2003), 14.

3. Loveless, "Charter Schools," 35.

4. Edison Schools, Inc., *Seventh Annual Report on School Performance: 2003–2004* (New York: Edison Schools, 2005), viewable at www.edisonschools.com.

5. Advantage is excluded here because of its sale to Mosaica.

6. Doug Lemov, "Aspire Public Schools Case Study," Harvard Business School, in press.

7. Jon Schroeder is coordinator of Education/Evolving, a joint venture of the Center for Policy Studies and Hamline University, both in St. Paul, Minnesota. He cofounded and was director of Charter Friends National Network (CFNN). See his "Minnesota Charters Breaking New Ground on Facilities," Charter Friends National Network, www.charterfriends.org, reprinted from *Citizens League Minnesota,* April 1, 1998.

8. Frederick M. Hess, *Spinning Wheels: The Politics of Urban School Reform* (Washington, D.C.: Brookings Institution Press, 1999).

9. Joetta L. Sack, "California Charter Failure Affects 10,000 Students," *Education Week,* September 1, 2004.

10. Ibid.

11. *Zelman v. Simmons-Harris,* U.S. Supreme Court, June 27, 2002.

12. Charles Lane, "A Case of Church and the States," *Washington Post,* December 1, 2003; Linda Greenhouse, "Supreme Court's Docket for Term Includes 48 New Cases," *New York Times,* October 6, 2003.

13. "A Contract on Schools: Why Handing Education over to Companies Can Make Sense," *Economist,* January 16, 1999.

14. "Tax-Supported K–12 Voucher Programs (Wisconsin, Ohio, and Florida): Summary of Key Provisions," www.friedmanfoundation.org/media/FactsNFigures.pdf.

15. "The Wrong Ruling on Vouchers," *New York Times,* editorial, June 28, 2002.

16. Alan Richard, "Wis. Officials Flex New Power over Milwaukee Vouchers," *Education Week,* September 1, 2004.

17. Advantage Schools, *Annual Report on School Performance: 1999–2000 School Year* (Boston: Advantage, March 2001).

18. Paul S. Grogan and Tony Proscio, *Comeback Cities* (Boulder, Colo.: Westview, 2000), 215.

Index